THE RISE AND FALL OF CHRISTIAN IRELAND

The Rise and Fall of Christian Ireland describes the emergence, long dominance, sudden division, and recent decline of Ireland's most important religion, as a way of telling the history of the island and its peoples.

Throughout its long history, Christianity in Ireland has lurched from crisis to crisis. Surviving the hostility of earlier religious cultures and the depredations of Vikings, evolving in the face of Gregorian reformation in the eleventh and twelfth centuries and more radical protestant renewal from the sixteenth century, Christianity has shaped in foundational ways how the Irish have understood themselves and their place in the world. And the Irish have shaped Christianity, too. Their churches have staffed some of the religion's most important institutions and developed some of its most popular ideas.

But the Irish church, like the island, is divided. After 1922, a border marked out two jurisdictions with competing religious politics. The southern state turned to the Catholic church to shape its social mores, until it emerged from an experience of sudden-onset secularization to become one of the most progressive nations in Europe. The northern state moved more slowly beyond the protestant culture of its principal institutions, but in a similar direction of travel.

In 2021, 1,500 years on from the birth of Saint Columba, Christian Ireland appears to be vanishing. But its critics need not relax any more than believers ought to despair. After the failure of several varieties of religious nationalism, what looks like irredeemable failure might actually be a second chance. In the ruins of the church, new Patricks and Columbas shape the rise of another Christian Ireland.

Crawford Gribben teaches at Queen's University Belfast, and is the author of several books on Irish, British and American religious history. He writes for newspapers and magazines including *The Wall Street Journal*, *The Irish Times*, and *History Today*.

THE RISE AND FALL OF CHRISTIAN IRELAND

CRAWFORD GRIBBEN

OXFORD
UNIVERSITY PRESS

OXFORD
UNIVERSITY PRESS

Great Clarendon Street, Oxford, OX2 6DP,
United Kingdom

Oxford University Press is a department of the University of Oxford.
It furthers the University's objective of excellence in research, scholarship,
and education by publishing worldwide. Oxford is a registered trade mark of
Oxford University Press in the UK and in certain other countries

First published 2021
First published in paperback 2024

Published in the United States of America by Oxford University Press
198 Madison Avenue, New York, NY 10016, United States of America

British Library Cataloguing in Publication Data
Data available

Library of Congress Cataloging in Publication Data
Data available

ISBN 978-0-19-886818-7 (Hbk.)
ISBN 978-0-19-886826-2 (Pbk.)

Paperback Printed and bound in the UK by
Clays Ltd, Elcograf S.p.A.

For Daniel, Honor, Finn, and Samuel

Preface and acknowledgements

Perhaps it is only now, after the collapse of Christian Ireland, that we can begin to recover its history. *The rise and fall of Christian Ireland* describes the slow emergence, long dominance, debilitating division and rapid decline of the communities of faith that for 1,500 years did most to shape and sustain the religious, social, and political life of this island and its people in their movements around the world. It shows how the beliefs and behaviours that sustained Christian Ireland went so long unquestioned and yet were so suddenly destroyed—and how, in the aftermath of this sudden-onset secularization, while many Irish Christians have quite comfortably adapted to the new cultural landscape, and have appropriated its mores, others represent themselves as members of an increasingly powerless counter-culture, even as, in their adaption to this changing world, they have begun to evidence new signs of life.

I have written this book neither as elegy nor as eulogy. Published in the year that is both the 1500th anniversary of the birth of the island's most famous missionary, St Columba, and the one hundredth anniversary of the island's partition, this book has been, in part, a labour of love for the religious world in which I was formed. Growing up in a county Antrim family with a long history of commitment to the so-called Plymouth Brethren, in which I heard stories about fairies and accounts of charming, I grew to understand the possibility that widely held folk traditions, particularly in country areas, might point to the existence of a religious culture that in some respects includes a 'non-Christian supernatural' and that in other respects transcends that faith's more recent divisions.[1] Finding within this supposedly apolitical community some surprisingly enduring sympathies for both Home Rule and the Ulster Covenant, I became aware of the diversity of social and political opinion on the so-called religious margins. And so, in the narrative that follows, I have tried to recognize both what binds together supposed enemies and what sometimes keeps friends apart.[2]

That might be an inauspicious way to begin to acknowledge my debts. This book draws upon almost three decades of conversations with friends and colleagues in literature, religion, and history at the University of Strathclyde, the University of Manchester, Trinity College Dublin, and Queen's University Belfast. Over the years, those who have done most to stimulate (and, more often than not, correct) my thinking on this subject include Donald Akenson, Michael Brown, Jenny Butler, Eamon Cahill, James Cassidy, Marie Coleman, Philip Coleman, Niall Coll, Sean Connolly, Scott Dixon, Anne Dolan, John Dunne, Elaine Farrell, Maurice Fitzpatrick, Gladys Ganiel, Raymond Gillespie, Peter Gray, D. G. Hart, Gerard Howlin, Stephen Kelly, Jarlath Killeen, David Livingstone, David McKay, John Morrill, Graeme Murdock, Mary O'Dowd, Mícheál Ó Mainnín, Micheál Ó Siochrú, Jane Ohlmeyer, Eve Patten, David Quinn, Ian Campbell Ross, Scott Spurlock, Timothy Stunt, Mark Sweetman, Mike Tardive, and Patrick Zuk. Sparky Booker, Matthew Brennan, Ian Campbell, Marie Coleman, and Elizabeth Dawson deserve special thanks—if not actual canonization— for reading and advising upon large parts of the text. I am enormously grateful to Salvador Ryan for his comments on the manuscript as a whole. And a very special thanks to Andrew Holmes, who on many happy occasions has challenged my methods, conclusions, evidence base, and almost everything else besides. The mistakes that continue to exist are entirely my own. For, as these friends will be only too aware, this book is too idiosyncratic in content; too fully organized; and too linear, perhaps even too teleological, in structure (though the title is a clue). As a short and necessarily selective survey, designed to be comprehensible rather than comprehensive, *The rise and fall of Christian Ireland* leaves many things unsaid.

Others have offered very practical assistance. I am extremely grateful to Matthew Cotton for commissioning this work, to the anonymous readers of the proposal, and to colleagues at Oxford University Press for guiding it through the process of production. Bill Hamilton of A.M. Heath has proved that the age of miracles has not ceased. Most of all I thank Pauline, who did more than anyone to make this project possible. I have written this book for our children, with love and in hope.

Crawford Gribben
Tulaigh na Mullán

Contents

List of illustrations

List of maps

Too long a sacrifice
Can make a stone of the heart
    W.B. Yeats

And I will give you a new heart, and a new spirit I will put within you. And I will remove the heart of stone from your flesh and give you a heart of flesh.
    Ezekiel 36:26[1]

Timeline

c. 8000 BC	Mesolithic Ireland: arrival of first humans
c. 4000 BC	Neolithic Ireland: beginning of agricultural activity
c. 3000 BC	Construction of major megalithic tombs
c. 2500 BC	Bronze Age: arrival of 'Beaker People' culture
c. 2000 BC	Deposition of Cashel Man
c. 300 BC	Iron Age: arrival of 'Celtic' culture and deposition of Clonycavan Man
c. 27–30	Ministry of Jesus Christ
312	Conversion of Constantine
313	Edict of Milan allows for the toleration of Christianity
380	Edict of Thessalonica identifies Christianity as the official religion of the Roman empire
381	Nicene-Constantinopolitan creed
407	Roman army begins its withdrawal from the province of Britain
410	Rome sacked by Visigoths
418	Synod of Carthage rejects Pelagianism
431	Arrival of Palladius, with Patrick following
521	Birth of Columba
c. 525–75	Foundation of major monastic institutions and networks
563	Foundation of monastery on Iona
764	Battle between the monks of Clonmacnoise and Durrow
795	Beginning of Viking raids
c. 830–70	Erection of major high crosses
841	Vikings establish Dublin as a trading centre
1014	Battle of Clontarf
1054	Great Schism
1111	Synod of Ráth Breasail
1142	Foundation of first Cistercian community in Ireland
1152	Synod of Kells
1155	Pope Adrian IV issues *Laudabiliter* decree
1169	Arrival of the Normans
1171–72	Henry II's invasion
1172	Synod of Cashel
1215	Fourth Lateran Council
1274	Second Council of Lyon
1315–18	Edward Bruce campaign
1366	Statutes of Kilkenny
1534–35	Kildare rebellion

1536	Henry VIII proclaimed supreme head of the Church of Ireland
1541	Henry VIII proclaimed king of Ireland
1556	Plantation projects in counties Laois and Offaly
1580–84	Desmond rebellion and plantations in Munster
1593–1603	Nine Years' War
1609	Plantation projects begin in Ulster
1641	Rebellion in Ulster
1642–49	Irish Catholic Confederation
1649–53	Cromwellian conquest
1654–57	Cromwellian land transfers
1660	Restoration of Charles II
1689–91	War between James II and William of Orange
1690	Battle of the Boyne
1692	Penal laws begin to undermine the Catholic landowning class
1704	Penal laws bar protestant dissenters from crown offices
1740–41	Famine
1756	Catholic Committee formed
1778	Penal laws begin to be repealed
1782	Irish parliament gains legislative independence
1791	United Irishmen formed
1798	United Irishmen rebellion
1801	Union of the Irish and British parliaments
1823	Catholic Association formed
1828	Election of Daniel O'Connell
1845–49	Famine
1867	Fenian rebellion
1869	Disestablishment of the Church of Ireland
1870	First Land Act
1879–82	Land war
1886	First Home Rule bill
1893	Second Home Rule bill
1912–14	Third Home Rule bill and the Ulster crisis
1916	Easter Rising
1919–21	War of independence
1921	Partition
1922–23	Irish civil war
1937	New constitution for the Irish Free State
1939–45	Second World War, known in Ireland as 'the emergency'
1949	The Irish Free State is declared a Republic
1956–62	IRA border campaign
1969	Troubles begin in Northern Ireland
1979	Pope John Paul II visits Ireland
1982	Decriminalization of same-sex sexual activity in Northern Ireland
1983	First abortion referendum in Ireland
1985	Anglo-Irish Agreement
1986	First divorce referendum in Ireland
1993	Decriminalization of same-sex sexual activity in Ireland

1994	Major paramilitary groups agree a ceasefire in Northern Ireland
1995	Second divorce referendum in Ireland
1998	Belfast ('Good Friday') Agreement
2005	Ferns report
2008	Financial crash
2009	Ryan and Murphy reports
2011	Cloyne report
2015	Same-sex marriage referendum in Ireland
2018	Abortion referendum in Ireland
2018	Pope Francis visits Ireland
2019	Liberalization of abortion law in Northern Ireland
2020	Legalization of same-sex marriage in Northern Ireland

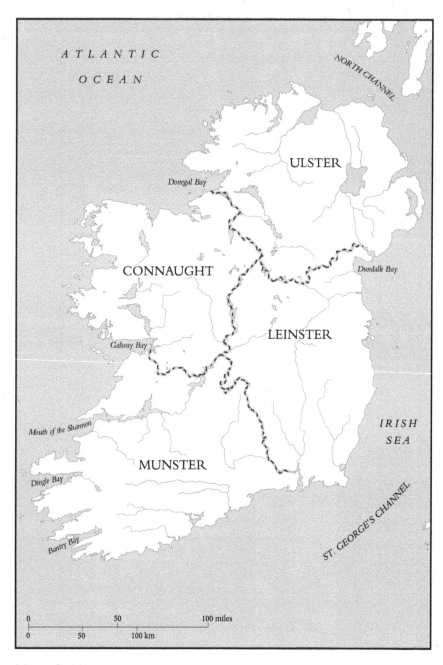

Map 1 Provinces

Map 2 Counties

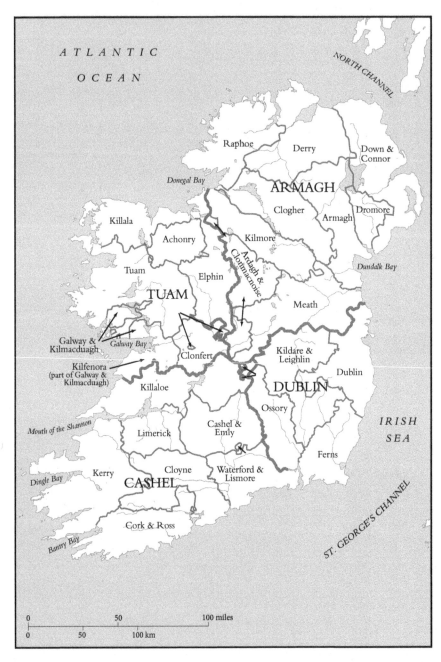

Map 3 Catholic dioceses

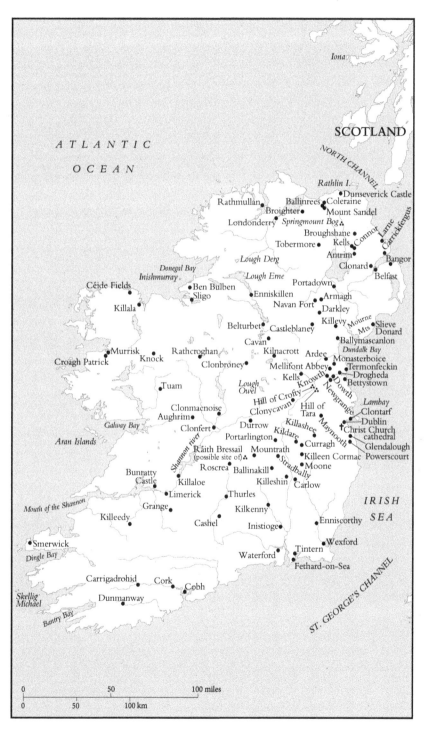

Map 4 Principal sites mentioned in this book

Introduction

In the beginning was the word. But no one knows where it came from. The beginning of Christianity in Ireland is now impossible to reconstruct. We do not know when, how, where, or with whom the new religion arrived. We know remarkably little about the cults and cultures that it eventually replaced. Perhaps the only thing we can be sure of is a date—the year of our Lord, 431.

It is in that year that the documentary history of Ireland begins. It is the earliest date that can be fixed upon in the island's past—the moment in which its culture begins to move from the myth and mirage of pre-history into an emerging documentary record.

For, by the early fifth century, a small group of Christians had gathered in Ireland. Just beyond the boundaries of the declining western Roman empire, they were just beyond the supervision of the European church. We don't know who these people were. They may have been local converts, travelling merchants, or slaves who had been transported from elsewhere, like some of their most important early leaders. They may have been Catholics, or members of one of the several new religious movements that had sprung up in Britain to revise central elements of the orthodox faith. They might have resisted control from elsewhere, or been anxious to benefit from external guidance and pastoral support. What we do know is that their situation changed in 431, when Pope Celestine sent Palladius, a high-ranking deacon from the church in Gaul, as the first bishop of 'the Irish believing in Christ'.[1] It is with a record of that decision, marking the organization of the Christian faith, that Ireland's historical record properly begins.

Since the arrival of Palladius, the 'land of saints and scholars' has had a long and complex relationship with its dominant religion.[2] Over the following fifteen centuries, the island of Ireland and the cultures of its peoples have been shaped and misshaped by their experience of Christian faith.

Ireland's social, political, and intellectual history has always been integrated with its experience of Christianity, for the religion that began to organize in 431 has shaped in powerful ways the island's cultures and languages, as well as its people's conceptions of what it means to be an individual, a family, a community, and a nation. Over one-and-a-half millennia, the Christian faith fashioned ideas about Irish-ness and Ireland, just as Irish missionaries, theologians, ideas, and experiences shaped Christianity as it expanded around the world.[3] In the fifth, sixth, and seventh centuries, after the collapse of the western empire, Irish missionaries began their extraordinary campaign to re-evangelize Europe and, along the way, to preserve the western intellectual heritage. And the contribution made by Irish Christians in the last few centuries may be just as significant. Irish priests powerfully influenced the expansion of the Catholic Church in North America and elsewhere: almost one-third of the 730 bishops who attended the First Vatican Council (1867–1870) were Irish or of Irish descent, and Catholics who had arrived from other parts of Europe noted the distinctively Irish flavour of large parts of the American church.[4] Irish protestants have made an impact, too: the apocalyptic beliefs that were developed in the early nineteenth century, in an evangelical movement that began in Wicklow, now dominate the North American religious mainstream and have influenced the foreign policy of every American president since Jimmy Carter.[5] Whatever else may be said of it, the contribution made by Irish Christians has been extraordinary, and it has always been international in scope.[6]

Nevertheless, the dominance of Christianity in Ireland was never complete and has never been uncontested. Despite the efforts of early missionaries to eradicate traces of pre-Christian ritual and cosmology, some of the older traditions never fully disappeared.[7] Some of these customs were sanctified by early Christians. The practice of erecting standing stones, long associated with the druids, found its counterpart in the construction of high crosses in the early Christian centuries.[8] To the present day, the devotional habits of many Irish Catholics include activities at rag trees and holy wells that have a very uncertain historical origin, while *Lúnasa*, the traditional festival that marked the beginning of harvest, was widely celebrated until the mid-twentieth century, and now survives in Christian pilgrimages such as the annual ascent of Croagh Patrick.[9] But, in an effort to project their dominance, and to disguise their competition with alternative or unofficial expressions of faith, the Irish churches have taken pains to emphasize their historicity, using monuments or architecture to present their practice as being authentic by virtue of being antique. The grottos in honour of the Blessed Virgin Mary that appear so frequently in many parts of the island are often not nearly as old as they have been designed to appear. Although Patrick's writings never mentioned the Blessed Virgin, she came to play a prominent role in medieval piety, during which period she was granted a distinct name in the Irish language (*Muire*), to set her apart from other biblical Marys. Her commemoration in wayside monuments came largely as a consequence of the revival of Marian piety that was encouraged in the 1950s.[10] These constructions were built as ruins, primarily to imitate the grotto at Lourdes, where the Blessed Virgin had appeared to a teenager in 1858, but they also reflected an Irish Catholic tendency to build monuments that appeared antique, perhaps symbolically to simplify, appropriate, and control a difficult and complicated past.[11]

But, as we now understand more clearly than ever before, the influence of Christian Ireland has always been difficult and complicated. In the early twenty-first century, reacting to several decades of devastating revelations of abuse, and compelling evidence of the complicity of high-ranking churchmen in the exploitation of the vulnerable and defenceless, cultures that were dominated by Christian influence for the entirety of their history seem anxious now to shrug it off. There are sinners, as well as saints and scholars, in the story of Ireland's faith, and believers, as well as unbelievers, are anxious to escape from its horror and pain. But there is no easy or obvious way out. In Ireland, to attempt to escape from Christianity is to attempt to escape from the shaping influence of the past.

But historians of Ireland sometimes find it difficult to engage with this kind of investigation.[12] Their most pressing problem may be to find the right kind of voice in which to describe or analyse ideas or activities that ought to provoke outrage and demands for redress. 'Religion's never mentioned here, of course', Seamus Heaney once complained, and modern readers may find his silence to be appropriate.[13] As the influence of the churches upon culture continues to decline, especially in the Republic, historians are moving away from studies of religion to investigate identity politics and other forms of collective belonging. This book may be unfashionable in its effort to put religion back at the centre of Irish history and to enquire about the meaning of Irish Christianity.[14] It does not provide a history of the Irish church, or of its theological achievements, but sets out to investigate the ways in which religious beliefs and behaviours have been lived out in the Irish experience of Christianity.[15] This book traces the emergence,

dominance, division, and decline of Ireland's most important religion, in the
construction and disintegration of competing varieties of religious nationalism. There have been many winners and many losers in the rise and fall of
Christian Ireland.

I

Located at the 'western end of the known world', the island that we know
as Ireland had been populated for many centuries, and by several different
cultures, before the arrival of its first Christian inhabitants.[16] The experiences of these early peoples can be reconstructed to some extent from
environmental, if not archaeological, remains. We know quite a lot about the
climactic conditions they experienced. Working from the evidence of surviving tree-rings, dendrochronologists have established a record of atmos-
pheric and environmental conditions that dates back to 5289 BC.[17] This
record allows for the remarkably precise dating of bowls, building materials,
and other surviving oak fragments. This record is not sufficient for the construction of an historical account of Ireland's earliest peoples, of course—so
much more needs to be known of any archaeological artefact than merely
the environmental context of its production. In addition, the available data
is often ambiguous and is certainly incomplete, and a great deal of evidence
has been lost, overlooked, misinterpreted or deliberately destroyed. Even
some of the interpretation of this data has been mendacious. We are still
coming to terms with the fact that the team of Harvard archaeologists that
did so much in the 1930s to uncover and describe Irish pre-history was
managed by Earnest A. Hooton, an anthropologist who specialized in 'racial
science', and advised by Adolf Mahr, a member of the Nazi party and director of Dublin's National Museum, so that its conclusions were informed
by highly questionable cultural and scientific assumptions.[18] Nor did our
knowledge of Ireland's 'deep history' suddenly improve after mid-century.
Even in the 1960s, Estyn Evans, one of the most important mid-twentieth-
century pioneers of the study of Irish archaeology, railed against the continuing 'wholesale wanton destruction' of ancient remains, many of which
remained unmarked and unprotected.[19] In the mid-1990s, the historian
Dáibhí Ó Cróinín had cause to complain that around 80,000 medieval
settlement sites had still to be investigated.[20] The boom in archaeology that
followed his comments may have owed more to the building bonanza of the

Celtic Tiger economy, during which developers were required to complete archaeological surveys, than to positive intellectual agendas. But the archaeological data that has been gathered must be very carefully interpreted. Evidence from excavations is very unevenly distributed, even in the early Christian period, and the fact that most artefacts have been discovered in Leinster and Ulster makes it extremely difficult to describe conditions elsewhere.[21] While the study of archaeology in Ireland is changing rapidly, and while many well-established conclusions have been radically revised, not least through recent advances in genetics and the study of language transmission, this work has not always kept pace with the work of the historians who depend upon it to understand the history of Ireland before the arrival of Christianity.[22]

Nevertheless, some parts of the story are clear. Ireland was 'one of the last places in western Europe to be inhabited'.[23] We can be fairly sure that the first humans arrived in Ireland around 8000 BC, though some recent work has suggested that this date could be pushed back to 10500 BC.[24] This migration was made possible by a cooling climate, and these people travelled to Ireland either over one of several frozen land-bridges with Britain, or by floating across one of the narrower passages over the Irish Sea.[25] In their new environment, these settlers encountered a heavily wooded landscape that sustained a population of bears, foxes, wolves, hares, and massive Irish elks. But this environment was changing. As temperatures rose and the ice began to melt, around 7000 BC, the island's landmass began to tilt, so that some parts of the north-east were raised by around 8 metres, while some parts of the southern coast were submerged to a similar extent. As the ice receded, the landscape became densely wooded with hazel and smaller numbers of ash, birch, oak, and elm trees. In these forests lived deer, wild pigs, and wolves, and in the rivers and estuaries were abundant supplies of fish. Early peoples settled first in the north-east of the island, where excavations at Mount Sandel, near Coleraine, discovered three more-or-less circular huts, built around hearths, with evidence of the year-round consumption of pigs, hares, birds, and very large quantities of salmon and eel. The settlers gradually moved south, wherever food supplies could be discovered, taking with them the flints that they had manufactured in extraordinary numbers in the workshops that developed around modern-day Larne, where an excavation of a 5-metre square in the 1930s discovered over 15,000 manufactured flints.[26] Despite the amazing density of this production, as so often with pre-history, we know virtually nothing about the lives, languages, or

beliefs of these hunter-gatherers, or whether it is appropriate to describe
them as members of one community or language group, or of several. But
their communities would not have been large, and they appear to have been
entirely isolated from comparable groups in Britain or on the continent.[27]
Over several thousand years, their population may never have much
exceeded a total of 3,000 individuals.[28]

As waves of new immigrants arrived, and as the several population groups
began to mingle, these Mesolithic hunter-gatherers would have co-existed
with Neolithic farmers. These communities began to adopt agricultural
methods around 4000 BC, when temperatures that were around 2 degrees
warmer than at present allowed for the development of farming and year-
round production.[29] Some of this agricultural work was intensive. As the
need for land increased, settlers in north-west Mayo, and likely elsewhere,
cleared hundreds of acres of forest. This kind of clearing was made possible
by the development of factories, especially in north Antrim, around 3000 BC,
which produced high-quality porcellanitic axes that were exported across
the island and throughout Britain. A settlement in Mayo, the Céide fields, is
now widely recognized as the world's oldest known field system, and suggests that these farmers were preparing to live permanently on their land.[30]
The new pasturelands that they created allowed for the production of cereal
crops and the rearing of cattle and sheep, innovative farming practices that
were introduced to Ireland by new settlers and which could support a larger
population than scholars of 'deep history' once imagined. Their achievements were enduring: some of the techniques that these farmers developed
have continued almost to the present day. Some of their religious beliefs
may have had similar longevity. Along with innovative field systems, these
settlers began to develop a cult of the dead, a ritual system that shared the
designs of its monuments with other peoples across western Europe. Of the
huge number of wooden buildings that these famers must have constructed
there remains little trace: 'millennia of Irish wind and rain pretty well
accounted for the disappearance of anything which was not stone'.[31] But,
from around 3000 BC, continuing over a period of perhaps 500 years, this
small population of farmers, mostly likely living in tents or other forms of
impermanent construction, built at least 1,400 megalithic tombs, with four
distinct regional designs, several of which were shared with related groups
elsewhere on the Atlantic seaboard.[32] And with the erection of these tombs
there may have emerged the earliest traces of Irish ritual practice.[33]

The most impressive of these tombs have been found in the Boyne valley. The constructions at Knowth and Dowth are relatively simple monuments, although the burial chamber at the former site, which contains the longest passage tomb in western Europe, contains the oldest map of the moon that has ever been discovered.[34] But the passage tomb at Newgrange, which, the historian Thomas Bartlett has observed, is 'the oldest known astronomically designed structure in the word', represents something else entirely: a respect for the dead that was connected to a determined effort at the calculation of time and an appreciation of the power of the sun.[35] The Newgrange construction is massive in size and sophisticated in design: 76 metres in diameter, up to 12 metres in height, over one acre in area, and surrounded by a circle of standing stones, which may have been a later erection. Many of these stones feature Neolithic art forms that are difficult to interpret—carvings of spirals, circles, radials that vary in depth and quality. What is much easier to understand is the scale of the enterprise. The construction required over 200,000 tons of stone, some of which had to be carried a considerable distance: the builders sourced their quartz from fifty kilometres south, in the Wicklow mountains, and their granodiorite from the mountains of Mourne, fifty kilometres to the north. Whatever their philosophical beliefs, the leaders or patrons of this ritualized cosmology could command significant material resources. Given the close connections between DNA samples discovered in megalithic tombs across Ireland, it is possible that this society was governed by a tiny elite, which likely projected its power by drawing upon cosmological beliefs.[36] However they were persuaded to do so, farmers living in tiny wooden huts built one of the most impressive stone structures in the prehistoric world—and they built it to last.[37]

The burial chamber at Newgrange was almost certainly built with ritual purpose. The design of the site, and its orientation to the sun, suggest what this purpose might have been. Each year, at dawn on the winter solstice, a shaft of light stretches to the far end of its low, narrow 19-metre central tunnel, to illuminate for over 15 minutes the elaborate but mysterious carvings on the back wall. This was clearly a space for performance—though not a space in which that performance could be easily observed. The chamber at the end of the tunnel provides access to three smaller rooms, in each of which stone basins were placed, perhaps as funerary receptacles. Archaeologists have found evidence of human remains within the passage, and have suggested that it was used to deposit corpses, some of which had been cremated. These remains include those of an adult male, who has been identified as the son of a first-degree union—an incestuous relationship that is entirely atypical of this population insofar as its sexual behaviour can be reconstructed from DNA samples recovered from other ritual sites, but which is similar in many respects to the socially sanctioned incest that marks out elite groups of god-kings in other early cultures.[38] Many questions remained unanswered. We are still learning how many monuments were built in this confined location, and what they might have been built for. During the long, hot summer of 2018, archaeologists completing drone surveys were able to identify a large number of new structures on the site, leading to suggestions that its ritual significance would need to be reconsidered. There was much more to Newgrange than meets the modern eye.[39]

For, then as now, religious fashions change. By the late Neolithic period, the monument had fallen out of use, and by 2500 BC it may also have fallen into disrepair. During this period, the island's population markedly increased. Devotees may have stopped building new stone monuments, but they did not stop attending traditional ritual sites. Newgrange retained its symbolic importance while changing in its liturgical function. These later inhabitants erected several wooden henges on different sides of the tomb, which were used, among other purposes, for the burning of animals in pits. This turn towards a practice that may have been understood as sacrifice could have represented a change in ritual behaviour and perhaps a development in cosmology. In the middle Neolithic, devotees were less interested in looking at the stars, and more interested in looking at the earth. They sunk high-value artefacts in water, including the bodies of high-status ritual victims. The mummified corpses of these victims still display manicured hands, distinctive hairstyles, and sometimes the use of cosmetics. Seventeen of these bog bodies have been discovered in Ireland. The oldest of these, Cashel Man, whose body was discovered in county Laois in 2011, was almost certainly killed around 2000 BC, in an action that may have been designed as a fertility ritual—a young king dying to secure a good harvest for his hungry people. Newgrange continued to be a site for other forms of ritual practice for a further 1,000 years, and continued to be visited thereafter, as discoveries of Roman jewellery suggest.[40] The technological revolution that marked the end of the age of stone may have involved what some devotees considered to be the end of a long-standing ritual tradition. For Newgrange fell into disuse as a ritual site at the beginning of the Bronze Age, when burial arrangements were simplified, and corpses were deposited in small stone boxes or pits, and as burial gave way to cremation. There were some very significant religious changes in pre-Christian Ireland.[41]

This quite striking moment of religious change may have been linked to the emergence of a new kind of culture, that of the 'Beaker People', who arrived in Ireland around 2500 BC and were among Ireland's earliest adopters of metal technologies.[42] These settlers represented a culture that stretched across Europe and into the north-east of the island, and seem to have taken full advantage of their trading connections. By 1750 BC, more or less, these emerging metallurgists were adding tin to copper, and importing raw materials from Cornwall and Spain. The quality of their products was extraordinary, and they established an international market for their work. These weapons, tools, and ornaments, produced in bronze and gold, were valued across Europe. But, whatever the cosmology, ritual practices, or social structures of these peoples, and however those beliefs and structures interacted, they were continuing to change. There is not much evidence that Beaker People in Ireland participated in the solar cult that engaged Beaker People elsewhere.[43] What is more obvious is that Beaker People seem to have preferred simple burials in wedge tombs to massive megalithic constructions.[44] The data that may be gathered from their burials indicate that these peoples were low in stature, with women typically less than 1.5 metres and men less than 1.7 metres tall, and short in lifespan, with very few adults being buried after the age of thirty. Their inhumation may also have been ritualized. But Beaker People were also interested in henges made from stone—with some of their standing stones, like that at Grange, near Lough Gur in Limerick, weighing in the region of 50 tonnes—and the conservatism of their culture ensured that it varied very little in the following 1,000 years. Over those centuries, stone henges remained concentrated in the far north-west and the far south-west, perhaps suggesting that new cosmologies, or at least new ritual practices, were developing in these areas. A major gap in the archaeological record means that we cannot reconstruct the lives or ritual habits of these peoples or accurately compare them to others on the island. But when that record resumes, several centuries later, the situation is altogether different.[45] Social customs were changing alongside ritual practices in the island to which these early peoples gave the enduring name of Ériu—Ireland.[46]

II

The most significant social change in prehistoric Ireland came with the arrival of a new culture, somewhere around 300 BC. In its patchwork of tribes and peoples, this turbulent and flamboyant culture had grown from uncertain origins in central Europe to stretch from the Atlantic seaboard to the Ukraine in the east and Greece in the south (where its peoples were known as 'Galatians'). The migrations of the Celtic peoples can be traced through their shared material culture and their related religious practices and languages. Some of these languages have been forgotten, like Lepontic and Gallic, which probably died out under Roman rule, and Pictish and Brithonic, which eventually disappeared during the expansion of Scottish Gaelic culture in the ninth century AD. Others of these languages have evolved into modern Irish, Scots Gaelic, Welsh, Cornish, Manx, and Breton. In the early twenty-first century, Celtic languages may be among the most vulnerable in Europe, but around 300 BC they represented what was 'probably the most widespread language group' on the continent.[47] This culture was first described by Greek writers, when they identified the population group that lived north of modern-day Marseille as the *keltoi*. While there is

Figure 1. The Boa island statues

some evidence that these peoples appropriated this term to describe themselves, as Julius Caesar observed around 50 BC, in his account of the *Gallic war*, the Irish were not likely among those to do so.[48] (In fact, before the seventeenth century, no one claimed that the Irish were 'Celts'.) And there is some merit in this hesitation about the suitability of the Celtic descriptor. Across Europe, Celtic culture was evolving as its influence was expanding. The Celtic culture that eventually made its way to Ireland may not have been typical of other European contexts. Yet it was in Ireland that Celtic language and culture would be best preserved.[49]

In the mid-fifth century BC, Celts developed a new artistic style, linked to new forms of political organization and ambition, which has become identified, after the location of one of its most important excavations, as 'La Tène'. Across Europe, the La Tène peoples were organized, determined, and, increasingly, dangerous. Around 400 BC, they mounted a series of increasingly ambitious incursions into the Mediterranean world. In 390 BC, one of their tribes defeated the Roman Republic and sacked its capital. After the death of Alexander, with whom they had made a treaty, these tribes drove into Macedonia, where, in 281 BC, they killed Ptolemy Ceraunus, its king. Later in the third century, a Greek sculptor marked the defeat of the Galatians in bronze: *The dying Gaul*, copied by a Roman sculptor and now housed in the Musei Capitolini, is wearing nothing but a torc (a stiff ring) around his neck, and holding himself with what dignity he can summon while the wound in his chest continues to bleed. However accurately the statue captures the world of these extraordinary warriors—a world that their Greek and Roman enemies must have found utterly alien—his death appears to represent on a grand scale the wishful thinking of his enemies. For, as well as noting their love of arts and crafts, their relentless pursuit of honour, and the combustibility of their religious fervour, the earliest descriptions of Celts emphasized their extraordinary capacity for violence. No doubt Julius Caesar, like other of these ancient writers, had reason to exaggerate in his descriptions of his victories the worthiness of his enemies and the threat they might pose to Roman civilization.[50] But these stereotypes were not far off the mark. The La Tène peoples really were a dangerous and unpredictable people, and the Romans worked hard to push them out of central Europe and beyond the borders of their expanding empire. The peoples of Ireland—at least the peoples of the northern two-thirds of the island, where most La Tène artefacts have been discovered—could not hope to withstand the arrival of this restless, violent, and technologically advanced culture.[51]

Although we are not clear exactly when, where, how, or how quickly this new culture arrived on the island, after a long discussion of the possibility, there is now widespread agreement among archaeologists and historians that it arrived as a consequence of migration. A small number of Celts seem to have established a presence in Ireland, where they assimilated well with the existing population, over whom they came to exercise power as a 'dominant minority'.[52] But, just as their arrival did not constitute an invasion, so the La Tène peoples did not displace the island's existing inhabitants. Instead, inadvertently, their culture may have brought the peoples of Ireland together. The new language that developed during this long assimilation combined a Celtic dialect with some words and a small number of place-names from the island's several existing languages, almost completely obliterating the vast majority of place-names that had been established by that point. This hybrid language was widely adopted, uniting the existing population groups and making possible the development of a common culture, although, as the historian T. M. Charles-Edwards noted, 'no one has yet found evidence that would determine when and how this change occurred'.[53] The hybrid language and culture that was created by this combination of peoples has become known as 'Gaelic'.

Perhaps unexpectedly, the strongest evidence for the arrival of the new culture is, again, in the north-east, in the bog-land around the river Bann, and especially around Broughshane, county Antrim, where in the late nineteenth century there was discovered the 'most important assemblage of La Tène artefacts from Ireland'. The excavation of a significant amount of weaponry, with decorations that found no parallel in Britain but distinct parallels in Gaul, Switzerland, and Hungary, has been considered as evidence of an 'accomplished armoury' that might have been created by 'a handful of fighting men with their followers and their craftsmen' who had travelled from central Europe.[54] It may be significant that the most important discovery of La Tène artefacts is associated with conflict.[55] For it is with the arrival of La Tène culture, the introduction of horses, and the full development of Iron Age technology that we enter the world of the great Irish epics.

These epic stories might provide us with some insights into the Irish experience of La Tène culture.[56] While these stories were recorded at a much later stage, and bear the literary and cultural accretions of later ages, as well as editorial interventions that represent an entirely different cosmology, they suggest something of the honour, strength, malevolence, and chaos of Ireland in the Iron Age. The values of the heroes of the stories are those of the epics of Greece—hospitality, adventure, loyalty, courage, and relentlessly bloody acquisition. These epics certainly show us how pre-Christian Ireland was remembered by its earliest historians. While it is impossible to take these stories at face value, they do contain elements of historical truth—evidence that confirms Caesar's point that Celts were mad, bad, and extremely dangerous to know.[57] The most famous of these stories is, of course, *The Táin*—Ireland's greatest epic, a long account of the conflict between Ulster and the rest of the island that is centred around the theft of a prize bull. For all its fantastic elements, the principal narrative assumptions of *The Táin* have been borne out by archaeological investigation: the political difficulties between the peoples of Ulster and the rest of the island really were serious enough to warrant the construction of a border wall, almost three miles in length, made of oak around 100 BC—exactly the period in which the narrative is set (though the narrative itself may have been pulled together many hundreds of years later).[58] The bravado and violence of Celtic culture suggests why it so completely replaced what came before it. If Estyn Evans was correct to believe that the cultures facing the intrusion of the La Tène peoples 'were already attenuated and archaic by the time they reached Ireland', their resistance may have been futile.[59] La Tène migrants brought their culture to Ireland, and it stayed.

Yet, for all that this La Tène culture delighted in violence, it also delighted in the arts. Some of the artefacts that date from this period are, by any measure, beautiful, and evidence of the power of religious belief.[60] These objects show how their makers loved display. Discoveries have included mirrors, combs, and torcs, as well as the model boat that was found in Broighter, county Londonderry, which was made from 85g of gold. Buried with other high-value items, including items that had been imported from elsewhere, this hoard may have been intended as a votive offering to the Irish sea-god, Manannán mac Lir. The model, which dates from the first century BC, is one of the earliest representations of an Irish sea-going vessel, with space for eighteen rowers around the hold, and evidence for what we might now describe as international trade. If this were part of a votive offering—perhaps made by a merchant who depended upon sea traffic for his trade in high-value items—it suggests something of the wealth that could be accumulated in maritime activity as well as the value of the sacrifices that could be made to the gods who sustained it.

For all that Ireland in the La Tène period continued to be deeply religious, it is now virtually impossible to reconstruct in any detail the

Figure 2. The Broighter boat

cosmology that these peoples may have shared.[61] Some objects remain without any documentary interpretation—such as the statue (idol?) that is preserved on Boa Island, Lough Erne, county Fermanagh—an island named after a goddess of war. But, with only the evidence of material artefacts, and without any exposition of the philosophy or worldview that these artefacts might represent, historians are left to sift for clues through the stories that were recorded after the organization of the Christian church, when clerics began to gather—and edit—traditional lore. This is no easy task. The best evidence for what remains of the older cultures must be teased out of the early lives of saints, but these are extremely unreliable accounts, written with polemical intent as well as fantastical content, and which were often, but not always, intended to present the older cultures in their worst possible light. What evidence they offer suggests that religion of the Celtic peoples varied across time and place.

But some conclusions are in order. Across Europe, Celtic religion was certainly polytheistic. It is possible to identify more than 200 deities in the pantheon, some of whom were worshipped in many parts of the continent, while others were worshipped in specific localities, where they were often linked to particular features in the landscape. Roman writers were the first to evaluate the religion of the Celts. They acknowledged that the gods of the Celts were very much like their own deities, and they interpreted them in that light. This habit of *interpretatio romana*—the Roman habit of interpreting foreign cultures as ciphers of their own—explains why Caesar understood the Gallic tribes to be worshippers of Mercury.[62] Similarly, in southern England, at the hot springs in Bath, Romans accepted the local goddess Sulis as their own Minerva, and fashioned their cult accordingly. At other times, they recognized differences between their deities and the gods of the Celts. Romans accepted some Celtic gods into their own pantheon, as in the recognition they gave to Epona, a fertility goddess associated with horses, who became the only Celtic deity to have worshippers in the imperial capital.[63]

Roman writers noticed that Celtic religion was led by a distinctive caste. Julius Caesar, writing his account of the Gallic war around 50 BC, may have been the first to describe their habits and beliefs—though it is possible that his account was shaped by his need to fashion a worthy foe.[64] The druids that he described were trained in Britain, in a course of study that lasted twenty years. They were literate, he claimed, and in this later period were using Greek characters, but made it an article of faith not to commit their knowledge to writing. Druids, who were both male and female, engaged in 'divine worship, the due performance of sacrifices, public and private, and the interpretation of ritual questions…It is they who decide in almost all disputes, public and private', including in cases of theft of property, disputed inheritance, and murder. Even at the time of writing, he believed, those who wished to advance in druidism travelled to Britain to study in order to do so.[65] Enjoying this privileged role in worship, politics, and law, as well as in medicine, it is hardly surprising that druids, as described by Caesar, would have been the one of the social groups that would be most threatened by the arrival of Christianity, and among those that, the early lives of Patrick suggest, most fiercely resisted it—even if, as seems to be the case, the 'druids' that crop up in Irish writing are quite different from those whom Caesar described.[66]

Roman writers also sought to explain the theology of the Celts as they encountered it in Gaul. Lucan believed that there were three principal gods in the pantheon, each of whom was placated by human sacrifice: Esus by a victim's hanging, Teutates by a victim's drowning, Taranis by a victim's burning.[67] Roman writers found the latter method of sacrifice especially horrific. According to Caesar and Strabo, Celts constructed combustible wicker statues, 'figures of immense size, whose limbs, woven out of twigs, they fill with living men and set on fire, and the men perish in a sheet of flame'.[68] Pliny linked this practice of human sacrifice to the gathering of mistletoe, and Tacitus recorded how the Roman invasion of Anglesey resulted in the obliteration of its horrific ritual centre, where the altars of the druids dripped in human gore.[69] Romans were not easily shocked. But they discovered that the violence of the Celts could be a very useful resource: Tacitus recorded that an Irish king threw his weight behind Agricola's military efforts in Britain.[70]

. For all that Roman writers were fascinated and repelled by the Celtic religion that they discovered in western Europe, they did not describe the cosmology or ritual practice that had developed among the La Tène peoples of Ireland. For the belief structure and ritual practice of the peoples of Ireland were distinctive. While, like some other cultures, they venerated as their common ancestor the god of the dead, ritual practice was centred upon a different pantheon from that of Celts elsewhere.[71] At its centre were the Dagda and his consort, the Morrigan, who was often represented in the myths as a crow flying near a battle. Irish ritual made some distinctive sacrificial demands. Deeply conservative, it combined with the Celtic admiration of death by fire the traditional commitment to burials in bogs and the deposition of valuable objects in water.[72] Clonycavan Man, whose preserved body was discovered in a bog in county Meath, was a victim of this kind of ritual slaughter in the third or fourth century BC, as La Tène culture was sweeping across the island. Buried while still in his twenties, and standing less than 1.6m tall, Clonycavan Man was wearing a form of hair gel that had been imported from Iberia, perhaps as a mark of his status (and important evidence that even in this period Ireland was not as isolated from the mainstream of European culture as both nativist nationalists and colonial critics would later, and for opposite reasons, claim). For unknown reasons, Clonycavan Man was killed by an axe blow and buried in a bog.[73] Other burials from the same period indicate that individuals left this life with their finest accoutrements, which may suggest that the afterlife they expected would be very similar to this, or would at least value similar kinds of things. This practice must have been pervasive. For Ireland gained an international reputation for its holy mysteries. In the sixth century BC, a Greek maritime manual described Ireland as a 'sacred island' that was populated by the 'race of the Érainn'.[74] Irish ritual practice kept on changing, but it never ceased to be important to the peoples whose lives it shaped. Developing over many thousands of years, the ritual that had been practised at megalithic burial sites, fire pits, and bogs had a longer history than the religion to which it would give way. For that ancient practice—whatever it meant to its adherents, and however it had developed over time—was about to be displaced.

III

The new religious movement that became known as Christianity had been three centuries in the making before it arrived in Ireland. Expanding from their base in and around Jerusalem, in the years after 30 AD, devotees of Jesus spread around the Mediterranean basin. These followers of 'the Way' recognized that the preaching carpenter from Nazareth was the promised messiah, the Word made flesh, the Son of God, who had come to be the saviour of the world. Under the leadership of individuals such as Paul of Tarsus, new communities of Christians evolved out of the Judaism that had been constructed around the expectations of an ethnically distinctive 'chosen people'. Paul's missionary activities and his letters provided the messianic community that emerged within Judaism with a rationale for their incorporation of Gentiles—and, as in the churches of Galatia, with whom Paul corresponded, for their inclusion of Celts.[75] Paul's arguments about how his followers should regard the Jewish law became so successful that the new faith soon took on an identity of its own.[76] By the end of the first century, the assemblies that had been planted throughout the Roman world had become dominated by Gentiles from a variety of ethnic backgrounds and were being recognized as part of an entirely new religion, which became known as 'Christianity'.

Paul's dealings with the congregations that he planted in Galatia and other parts of the Roman province of Asia Minor reflected his concern to create an orthodox centre for the Christian movement—a set of beliefs and practices that each of its members would be required to share. But the challenges facing this project were evident even within the writings that were eventually gathered together in the canon of the New Testament. Leaders of the 'Jesus movement' fell out over issues that some of their number regarded as foundational—as Paul admitted in his letter to the Galatian churches—while others whom they regarded as false teachers did their utmost to challenge apostolic influence and power. Those whom the authors of the New Testament regarded as false teachers and divisive leaders competed for the loyalty of Christian believers, and the orthodoxy that Paul and his followers had created was immediately challenged.

It was in the second century that Christian theologians began to work out in detail the leadership of churches, the connections that ought to exist between them, and the kinds of theological claims these churches should make.[77] The fathers created a rich and varied literature in which they debated central doctrinal claims and matters of organization. The question of leadership was critical for the movement as it passed into its third generation. Over time, the Christian community came to recognize the ministries of bishops, presbyters, and deacons. In the early second century, Ignatius argued that a bishop should provide leadership within a single congregation, with the support of a group of presbyters and deacons. Later in that century, the role of the bishop was revised to become territorial, rather than congregational, with the incumbent exercising pastoral authority over a much wider geographical area and over a corresponding number of churches. The doctrine of apostolic succession was used to control episcopal appointments, as its defenders elevated the office of bishop in order to claim continuity in leadership from the first disciples.

Simultaneously, Christian leaders began to refine the teaching of the church. The first major series of debates established the humanity and divinity of Jesus Christ, and allowed theologians to begin to think about how these human and divine natures came together in one person. Later in the second century, Christian theologians debated the claims of a bewildering array of Gnostics and Montanists. The response of the Catholics was to create short statements of the orthodox faith, some of which circulated widely, and one of which, emanating from the church in Rome, has come down to posterity as the Apostles' Creed. It was through the circulation and widespread acceptance of this creed, and others like it, that the Christian movement arrived at its claim to be truly catholic.

The worship of the Jesus movement was at first quite simple. Evidence from the second century suggests that Christians gathered on the first day of the week—Sunday—and that their meetings focused upon the reading and explaining of the Hebrew Bible and apostolic writings, congregational prayer, and the celebration of the eucharist. The worship service was divided into two parts. The first part, which anyone was welcome to attend, included the reading and preaching of Scripture, and was led by the local bishop. Only baptized Christians were allowed to stay for the second part of the service, which included prayer and the Lord's Supper. Descriptions of second-century meetings, such as that provided by Justin Martyr, emphasized teaching, fellowship, prayer, and the eucharist, perhaps to reflect the idealized description of the first church in Acts 2.[78]

It is not clear how well the different groups of Christians were connected to each other. Even in the first half of the second century, Justin Martyr, who taught a group of Christians above a bath house in Rome, knew that other meetings were taking place within the imperial capital, but he did not know where they were located.[79] This lack of connectedness may explain why historians are so uncertain as to when the new faith reached the Roman province of Britain. In or around the 190s, Tertullian noted that parts of the island that were 'inaccessible to the Romans' were now 'subjugated to Christ'.[80] These claims for the expansion of Christianity beyond the Antonine wall cannot be confirmed by archaeological evidence. It is possible that Tertullian was misinformed, or that these claims represent how he and other leaders of the new religious movement wanted their community to be perceived, and therefore that they should not be taken at face value. But these claims do illustrate the close connection between the spread of Christianity and the expanding borders of Rome.

Undoubtedly, the expansion of Christianity into Britain was helped by the conversion of the emperor, Constantine, in 312, and by the Edict of Milan in the following year, which granted the religion official tolerance.[81] After the Edict of Thessalonica, in 380, which identified Christianity as the empire's state religion, the British church accepted the Nicene-Constantinopolitan Creed (381).[82] The religion that had grown through the empire now had an agreed form and content. Converts to the new faith now made a very full confession of its propositional content:

> We believe in one God the Father of All—sovereign, maker of heaven and earth, and of all things visible and invisible; And in one Lord Jesus Christ, the only-begotten Son of God, Begotten of the Father before all the ages, Light of Light, true God of true God, begotten not made, of one substance with the Father, through whom all things were made; who for us men and for our salvation came down from the heavens, and was made flesh of the Holy Spirit and the Virgin Mary, and became man, and was crucified for us under Pontius Pilate, and suffered and was buried, and rose again on the third day according to the Scriptures, and ascended into the heavens, and sitteth on the right hand

of the Father, and cometh again with glory to judge both living and dead, of whose kingdom there shall be no end: And in the Holy Spirit, the Lord and the Life-giver, that proceedeth from the Father, who with Father and Son together is worshipped together and glorified together, who spake by the prophets: In one holy Catholic and Apostolic Church: We acknowledge one baptism unto remission of sins. We look for the resurrection of the dead, and the life of the age to come.[83]

This confession contrasted in every respect with the beliefs of the Celts. On an island beyond the edge of the empire, in the early fifth century, adherents of this new religious movement were compelled to recognize their own otherness, when 'the Christian faith found itself face to face with a prehistoric culture'.[84] But that culture, as it anticipated 'a period of radical social, technological and religious change', was primed for transformation, and would benefit from it.[85] For the good news that came 'for us men, and for our salvation' was the message that created Christian Ireland.

I

Conversions

Christianity arrived in Ireland at the end of the world. The earliest members of the 'first recognized Christian community beyond the western Imperial frontiers' were convinced that they were living in history's final days.[1] The apocalyptic mood of their leaders—some of whom had British backgrounds—reflected the very significant social and political changes that followed the slow contraction of Roman power on the western edge of the world.[2] These changes accelerated after 407 when, after being weakened by internal struggles, the army withdrew from the province of Britain in an attempt to repair the unravelling fabric of the western empire. Its soldiers never returned. Suddenly abandoned by the army by which they had been defended, Romano-Britons rushed to preserve what was left of Latin culture and Roman civilization. Their situation became weaker and ever more precarious.[3] Existing on a frontier, but now without military protection, and depending upon links to the empire that seemed continually to be unravelling, their vulnerability became especially obvious after 410, when the Visigoths sacked Rome, and brought to its knees the civilization that had been shaped by the new faith over several centuries. This attack on the centre of Christian culture, the historic seat of imperial power, sent shockwaves across the continent. The western Roman empire never recovered its influence upon the Atlantic seaboard.

After the destruction of Rome, British Christians felt the consequences of their isolation. Despite the fact that their religion had been present in Britain for several hundred years, these believers had not successfully exported their faith to the other side of the Irish Sea.[4] The Christian religion may not have been practised in the small number of Roman communities that may have been established in Ireland in this period.[5] Neither, despite Tertullian's claims, had the British exported their faith much beyond Hadrian's wall, other than in the colony of Romano-Britons that was centred on Dumbarton Rock, at the western end of the long-abandoned Antonine wall.⁶ In its Latin language, Roman culture, and Christian religion—as well as in its relative wealth—the kingdom of Alt Clud was in every respect foreign to the cultures by which it was surrounded.⁷ But its strengths now made it vulnerable. After the withdrawal of the army, the colony found itself at the mercy of Picts from the north and pirates from the west.⁸ As the Roman army withdrew, Irish brigands took full advantage of the vacuum in military power to plunder movable property and slaves, making substantial gains: it was in this period, around 425, that a hoard of 1,500 Roman coins, 200 ounces of silver and other articles of value was buried at Ballinrees, county Londonderry.⁹ As these pirate attacks continued, the security of Alt Clud continued to deteriorate, until it was finally cut off from British communities on the other side of Hadrian's wall, and from its easiest point of access to the continent. It became more isolated as the security of the province of Britain continued to decline. In the later part of the century, and with the absence of any credible military defence, a large region of south-east Britain was overwhelmed by invasions of Angles, Saxons, and Jutes.¹⁰ These German tribes had little time for Christianity, and, as their power consolidated, the British church was weakened by widespread decline. One early historian—who might have had an axe to grind—complained that some believers abandoned the faith while others turned to new communities such as that of the Arians, who rejected the doctrine of the Trinity and argued that Jesus Christ was a creature begotten by the Father in time.¹¹ These new views were incredibly popular. In fact, orthodox Christianity almost entirely disappeared from Britain in the middle of the fifth century.¹² The invasion subjected the British church to extraordinary pressure. One early historian described the desperation of those whom the empire had abandoned. Many British Christians 'were compelled to surrender to the invaders', Bede recollected. 'Others, trusting in God's help where no human hand could save them', retreated to 'mountains, caves, and forests', from which locations they 'continued their resistance' and began to 'inflict severe losses on the enemy who had plundered their country for so many years'. But the beginnings of effective resistance served only to expose the ruin of the British church, for 'the Lord's flock and their pastors' had given themselves up to 'drunkenness, hatred, quarrels, and violence'.¹³ Bede might have been exaggerating, but the experience of Patrick, who did not accept the faith of his father and grandfather, reveals how far intergenerational religious commitments had broken down. Under pressure in the north and west, and struggling to cope with invasion in the south and east, what was left of the Roman province was on its knees—but not all of its Christian people were praying.

For Christians, across the empire, the sack of Rome raised some searching and troubling theological questions. Although the numbers of believers had grown over the previous centuries, Christians still represented no more than 10 per cent of the empire's population. Nevertheless, these believers strongly identified with Roman culture. While Rome was no longer the western empire's capital city, that honour having passed to Ravenna, it remained symbolic as the most important episcopal see. Its destruction was therefore widely regarded as a catastrophic providence, which was understood by many Christians to be a sign of the last days. For the church had increasingly come to depend upon the structures and power of the empire. Roman civilization had, in the minds of many believers, become a vehicle for the salvation of the world. It is not hard to understand why so many Christians had arrived at this conclusion. After all, in the previous two centuries, believers had moved from being a small and persecuted minority to become a numerically significant community with an outsized influence upon Roman culture. The conversion of the emperor Constantine (312), the toleration of Christianity that was made possible by the Edict of Milan (313), and the identification of Christianity as the official religion of the empire by the Edict of Thessalonica (380) had encouraged believers to identify the empire as the earthly manifestation of the kingdom of God, as the necessary infrastructure for the expansion of the new religion throughout the world. The sudden end of the political system that had supported the mission of the church was, for many believers, shattering—and they understood the violence and chaos of the destruction of the old imperial capital in 410 as proof that the end was nigh.[14]

The sack of Rome called for a radical re-thinking of Christian hope. The most courageous theologians took time to consider the implications of the church's dependence upon political power. One of the most significant of these contributions, and certainly the most enduring, was Augustine's *City of God* (425). Augustine's argument was, in essence, simple: he counselled Christians to avoid the trap of identifying any earthly political power with God's kingdom. His measured and careful reflections on Scripture, philosophy, and history exercised enormous influence in the fifth century and beyond—and especially on a small island lying beyond the frontier of Christian civilization, beyond the old boundaries of the empire, on the western edge of the world.

At the beginning of the fifth century, Ireland was increasingly connected to this wider European civilization.[15] Its peoples were experiencing debilitating environmental and social change. Some of these changes are difficult to trace. The previous several centuries have been described as an archaeological 'dark age'. Pollen data suggests that between 200 BC and 300 AD the population of the island had steadily declined, and that farming and manufacturing might both have contracted.[16] As this contraction intensified, so too did the struggle for resources, which might explain the construction in the fourth century of a huge number of ringforts, or *raths*, some 40,000 of which remain to the present day, although scholars now dispute that the erection of such a large number of defensive fortifications suggests that Irish society was becoming more violent.[17] Nevertheless, its religious commitments were certainly changing, as the old centres for religious practice fell out of use. In the first century BC, for example, the ancient ritual site at Emain Macha, the extraordinarily impressive 40-metre diameter wooden building that is known today as Navan Fort, county Armagh, was abandoned, then carefully buried, and over the following centuries gradually decayed.[18] We have yet to find a compelling explanation for the discovery on the site of the partial skeleton of a Barbary ape—which may have been kept as a pet, as a royal gift, or which may have been used as a skeleton for some kind of ritual purpose.[19] It is not clear what these changes in ritual practice represented, but it is apparent that, on the eve of the new faith's arrival, Irish society was enduring environmental challenges and dealing with pressure for serious structural change.

These were the circumstances of Ireland as its people established closer contacts with the Roman empire and, later, its most significant new religious movement. The empire's contacts with Ireland were long-standing: Tacticus, an early historian, recorded Roman merchants visiting Irish ports in the first century, most likely looking for slaves.[20] The small number of *entrepôts* that these merchants visited were mostly located on the east and perhaps also on the north coast, and most likely provided the first converts, whether slaves or merchants, to the faith that was expanding through the empire. And it is possible that migrants established a small number of Roman communities on the island (among whom Roy Flechner, in his stimulating recent biography, suggests Patrick should be numbered, as a migrant fleeing some sort of civic responsibility).[21] But the soft power of Roman culture did not exist outside these scattered enclaves. Throughout the rest of the island, the population shared a common language and enjoyed good links with other Celtic cultures, from Brittany and Cornwall to the Hebrides. The island was divided into over 150 separate kingdoms, which existed in a hierarchy of power and responsibility, from which by the seventh century a small number of more powerful regional kingdoms and a much smaller number of over-kingdoms seem to have emerged.[22] This centralization of royal power was driven by the rise of a new dynasty, the Uí Néill, members of which would come to dominate the island's politics through much of the early medieval period.[23] These political changes had implications for the organization of the church: the interests of the Uí Néill in centralizing political power were to develop alongside efforts by ecclesiastical leaders to centralize power in the church.

This centralization was made possible by the fact that these kingdoms shared a common culture, with major ritual centres like those in Tara and Rathcroghan—a culture that was flamboyant, brutal, and led by kings and warriors whose extraordinary achievements warranted their being remembered as gods. These heroes were literary constructs, but stories of their 'high deeds' found audiences long after the arrival of the new faith. It is just possible, as we have already seen, that, underneath complex layers of mythology and the politics and anachronisms of textual transmission, stories that survive from the Irish Iron Age contain traces of historical truth. These stories were certainly widely circulated. Sharing a common culture and related languages, the peoples of Ireland and their Celtic neighbours were largely able to resist the influence of the Roman world—even if, as an enterprising missionary might have noted, their linguistic and cultural homogeneity might have created conditions that were ideal for the spread of new ideas.

Of course, the Christian movement was going to face some serious challenges in its gradual expansion into Ireland. One of the most basic problems faced by early missionaries was knowing how to communicate their good news. The Irish vernacular had never been written down, other than in an alphabet of twenty characters that were made of strokes cut across a continuous line. These *ogham* inscriptions represent the earliest writing in the Irish language, and might have emerged as early as the second century, though this claim is disputed. It is more likely that *ogham* script emerged in the fourth century, and that it was intended to provide the Irish language with a 'status on stone equivalent to that of Latin'.[24] While the burial site at Killeen Cormac, county Kildare, included an inscription that commemorated 'four true druids', it also contains Christian standing stones, perhaps showing how one religious community embraced the new faith without forgetting what it replaced. *Ogham* inscriptions have been discovered throughout Ireland, and from Cornwall to Shetland, offering some important evidence for the geographical range of Irish influence in the early Christian period. But *ogham* script had limited potential, and had not been used to express complex religious or theological ideas. On the other hand, not many Irish people understood Latin, the administrative and theological language of the church. The nearest Romano-British cultures used a vernacular similar to modern Welsh. Furthermore, from the days of the apostles, the Christian faith had advanced around written texts. In fact, these texts had become so central to the new faith that its adherents had developed the form of the book that, almost two millennia later, we continue to take for granted. The scrolls that were so familiar in the ancient world were much too unwieldy for use in a religion whose credibility depended upon the exegesis of critical proof texts. So, around the second century, Christians had developed a new form of the book—the codex—which allowed easier and more rapid access to crucial passages. The form of the book that you are holding in your hand—with pages joined down a bonded spine—was one of the unintended consequences of early Christian mission.[25] But, in Ireland, where the vernacular had never been reduced to writing, these bibliographical innovations meant nothing. In other words, the new religion was arriving in Ireland without the tools of literacy that had enabled its success elsewhere, as the infrastructure of the church crumbled, and as, thirty years after the new faith had been recognized as its official religion, the western Roman empire failed. The new faith was arriving in Ireland without much evidence of its ever having been any kind of success.

And so Ireland's first evangelists faced some very significant challenges. In Ireland, Christian missionaries faced for the first time the difficulties of working beyond the imperial frontier. The Irish had never been 'civilized', as the Romans liked to put it, and their political and social cultures would have seemed to be brutal and chaotic in comparison with imperial norms. Irish society represented a striking contrast to the structures of power that stretched across the empire, and which had enabled the development of a common Roman identity around shared experiences in education, business, politics, and military life. And so we should not suppose that the Irish quickly or universally welcomed the new faith. An early poem of uncertain provenance records the fear of those who wanted to resist the new religious movement, the preachers of which would 'chant false religion / at a bench facing East / and his people will answer / "Amen, amen"'.[26] Memories of native tradition would endure for hundreds of years—and, as we will see, might continue today in some elements of traditional religious practice. After all, there was nothing to make religious change compelling. The beliefs and behaviours that were part of the Irish religion had evolved over millennia to reflect the aspirations, expectations and uncertainties of life on the edge of the world. The old beliefs were venerable precisely because they made sense of the Irish situation. What had their adherents to fear from these new stories, promoted by men who, as far as they could see, represented a crumbling empire, and a religion that could not sustain it?

The challenges to Christian mission were real, but they were not insurmountable. For, despite widespread fears, the sack of Rome did not herald the end of Christianity. Instead, it encouraged its expansion. Missionaries in Ireland worked to ensure that an island with an unfamiliar language and culture beyond the edge of the western empire would accept Christianity more than 100 years before the Anglo-Saxons, and centuries before other northern European peoples. For the fall of Rome and the crisis of imperial Christianity were contexts for the emergence in Ireland, and elsewhere, of a new kind of faith. From the early fifth century, and over several hundred years, the Irish converted to Christianity, shaping their new faith, exporting their theological and missionary cultures, and working for the conversion of the Picts, the Northumbrians and Anglo-Saxons, as their Christian culture expanded throughout Europe, saving souls, if not 'saving civilization', at the end of the Roman world.[27] The arrival of the new faith initiated Ireland's documentary record—and destroyed almost every memory of what it came to replace. On the edge of a crumbling empire, the city of God confronted the city of man, and, in Ireland's year zero, the Christian mission began.

I

We may never be able fully to recover exactly how and when the new religion arrived in Ireland, but we can identify a few key moments in its early and very gradual expansion.[28] Followers of the new faith were certainly to be found in Ireland in the early fifth century. We know nothing of the number, social status, leadership, or convictions of these Christians, or whether they were able to meet together for worship or to participate in any other form of communal life. We also know nothing about their ethnicity, leaving untested Dáibhí Ó Cróinín's suggestion that 'the first Christians in Ireland were in fact Britons', who had arrived on the island by means of the cross-channel slave trade or as prisoners of war, perhaps like the individual from north Africa or southern Portugal who arrived in Ireland during the early Christian period, whose skeleton was discovered at Bettystown, county Meath.[29] But we can make some educated guesses as to where these believers were located. While the earliest literary sources are biased towards the north, so that the documentary record is very likely incomplete, we can be almost certain that the earliest Christians were to be found in the southeast, where links to Britain and the continent were strongest, and in Leinster, where the island's population and episcopal oversight appears initially to have been concentrated.[30] The history of this Christian community begins within a few years of the withdrawal of the army from Britain (407), the sack of Rome (410) and the publication of Augustine's *City of God* (425), with the beginning of the Irish Christian mission and the Irish documentary record. For, according to Prosper of Aquitane's *Chronicle*, it was in 431— 'the first reliable date in Irish history'—that Pope Celestine sent Palladius to become the first bishop of 'the Irish believing in Christ'.[31]

We know next to nothing about Palladius, nor about the challenges and achievements of his mission to provide pastoral support to the earliest Irish Christians. Palladius may have been born into a prominent family in Gaul, where he must have gained a reputation as a capable defender of orthodoxy and an experienced polemicist, for, in the late 420s, he became involved in attempts to combat the most serious heresy to have arisen within the British church.[32] This new theology was named after its best-known exponent. Pelagius, a prominent English theologian, was believed to have argued that humans could make a decisive contribution to their own salvation, using free will to decide whether or not to believe the gospel and so be saved.[33] Rival groups of theologians rejected these claims as seriously under-estimating the effect of sin on human nature and the absolute necessity of divine intervention—and no wonder. As one early historian put it, the 'blasphemous' claims of the Pelagians suggested that humanity had the capacity to save itself.[34] Pelagianism was condemned as heretical at the Synod of Carthage in 418. These ideas were as popular as they were controversial, and the Pelagian heresy 'seriously infected' the British church. But the efforts to contain it were successful. Palladius encouraged the pope to dispatch the bishop of Auxerre to support those defenders of orthodoxy who preached in defence of Catholic truth, Bede reported, 'not only in the churches, but in streets and fields'.[35] These preachers would have argued that the human will was bound, debilitated entirely by the effects of sin, so that salvation could only come as a consequence of divine intrusion. When these arguments were validated by miracles, the peoples of Britain were convinced of the catholic faith, and the Pelagian heretics were exiled.[36] Palladius's efforts to preserve the orthodox faith of the British church had been successful.

Several years later, Palladius's mission to Ireland may have come as a consequence of this work, and possibly as a recognition that this new and vulnerable Christian community might benefit from similar kinds of doctrinal guidance.[37] This was the view of some early important sources. In the 430s, Prosper's *Contra Collatorem* recorded that Pope Celestine had cured the British church of Pelagianism by 'ordaining a bishop for the Irish', who, 'while he strove to keep the Roman island catholic…also made the barbarian island Christian'.[38] The pope's decision to send a Gallican bishop to provide pastoral oversight in Ireland suggests that, in the immediate aftermath of the Pelagian controversy, the British church was considered too weak or too doctrinally suspect to provide the necessary pastoral leadership. And so, in 431, Palladius travelled to Ireland. His commitment to orthodox theology indicates the kinds of convictions that would have informed his work. He would not have been calling upon his hearers merely to improve themselves or to make more of an effort to live a moral life. He would have been calling upon his listeners to abandon their gods, and those elements of culture that were inextricably linked with the religion of their ancestors, and to commit themselves to a deity whom they could not see, whose trinity could not easily be explained, whose character was entirely unlike the ferocity and competition of the deities in the Celtic pantheon, a god who was associated with a declining empire, and who had never before sent to the island any emissaries to warn about the eternal punishment of unbelievers that his followers now threatened. Conversion to the new faith was going to be a very big ask. A Pelagian missionary—that is, a missionary who would have been depending upon the ability of individuals to determine their own response to the gospel—might never have attempted it.[39] But for Palladius and his colleagues, with their convictions about the sovereignty of God, who could so radically intervene to save sinners, nothing was impossible. And in any case, of course, these men were being sent to an existing Christian community, and could use it as a base.

Palladius and his fellow-workers would have needed this kind of confidence. While existing documentary records contains few traces of their work, their spheres of influence are evident in surviving place-names. These suggest that the earliest missionaries began working on the eastern seaboard, taking advantage of existing trade connections with Britain, before moving inland to establish centres of Christian community within the territory encompassed by modern Leinster. Palladius's principal assistants, Auxilius (d. 459), Iserninus (d. 465/8), and Secundinus (d. c. 447), had British names, and their participation in the Irish mission hints that the British church did have personnel who were equipped for the task of cross-cultural evangelization, even if they could not be trusted to lead in that kind of work.[40] Palladius may have delegated to his associates responsibility for the evangelization of particular regions in the midlands and south-east. Some traces of their movements exist to the present day: Auxilius, for example, is often linked to Cell Ausaili, modern-day Killashee, county Kildare.[41] But, if this small group of missionaries did decide to work simultaneously in different locations, they may well have found formidable the ancient religious cultures in which they had to preach. The religious practice of the Irish centred on megalithic monuments that were already over 3,000 years old and which in many areas, such as the Boyne valley, continued to dominate the landscape. In other words, these missionaries were coming to challenge ideas and practices that may have been accepted for over ten times as long as the history of the church that they were working to promote.

Whatever his other achievements, Palladius may not have made much of an impact upon local culture, for he was quietly forgotten when, several centuries later, Irish Christians began to write their history. In these stories, his reputation was eclipsed by that of Patrick, the 'apostle of the Irish', whose arrival, perhaps as early as 432, as early writers claimed, in a bid to associate Patrick with Palladius, or perhaps as late as 450, and whose ministry, throughout the middle or later decades of the fifth century, came to dominate every account of the emergence of the new faith.[42] Even Palladius's colleagues, Auxilius, Iserninus and Secundinus, were more often associated with Patrick's later mission.[43] This drift towards associating key elements of the early Christian mission with Patrick, rather than with Palladius, is hardly surprising. For Patrick is compelling. His *Confessio*, which may have been written around 470, is among the most psychologically revealing of ancient texts, and, deliberate or not, contains rhetorical as well as theological echoes of Augustine's *Confession* (397–400). But Patrick's rather modest account of his own achievements was obscured in the rapidly proliferating mythology that described his conversion of the Irish, a mythology in which he was represented as a typical hero of Iron Age saga, performing extraordinary feats of strength, often with supernatural support, defying druids at Tara, and driving out of Ireland its reptiles and snakes. (Of course, this may be because these 'Iron Age sagas' did not date from the Iron Age, but were constructed from various sources in the early medieval period.[44]) As these stories accumulated around Patrick's biography, they came to obliterate the memory of earlier religious practice, and even of the mission of Palladius, whose achievements and associates were increasingly associated with his better-known colleague. The memory of Patrick became almost overwhelming.

Patrick gained this prominence by revealing so much about himself. He is the 'only ancient Briton whom we truly know', a rare example from the ancient world of 'an ex-slave speaking of his slavery'.[45] His writings provide a remarkably clear contemporary description of life on and beyond the contracting Roman frontier. These are the 'only existing Latin books of the time of the Roman Empire which were written outside the Imperial Roman frontier in one of the lands of the barbarians'.[46] His narrative omits details that modern readers would regard as foundational to any historical discussion. For example, 'not a single date can be given to any event in Patrick's life'.[47] Patrick's writing provides some of the most vivid and considered biographical writing from the ancient world, so that we can know him 'more deeply than almost anybody in Antiquity'.[48] But Patrick was writing with an agenda that was not concerned with the stuff of modern historical writing—including such details as dates and names of places. Readers who approach Patrick's writings from the perspective of his later celebrity are often surprised by his modesty and reserve. 'I am first of all a simple country person, a refugee, and unlearned', he confessed, identifying himself later in life more closely with the Irish converts whom he served than with the Romano-British Christians among whom he had grown up. His Christianity seems to be 'wholly conventional, low-brow, and commonplace except in two respects—its intense sincerity, and his determination to export Christianity beyond the Roman frontier'.[49] What is most remarkable about Patrick might be his very ordinariness.

Yet, for all his modesty, Patrick's background was privileged. Patrick described his childhood in Bannavem Taburniae, a town or small estate of now-unknown location, which was likely to be found in the old Romano-British kingdom of Alt Clud, with its capital at the western end of the Antonine wall.[50] His family seems to have been relatively wealthy, owning a number of slaves that was large enough to draw the attention of Irish pirates. Patrick's family may have been among the earliest adopters of the Christian religion. His grandfather, Potitus, had been a priest, and his father, Calpornius, was a deacon. But Patrick had grown up without any decided religious convictions of his own. Later in life, recalling his early teenage years, he confessed that 'we would not listen to our priests, who advised us about how we could be saved', and so, he continued, 'the Lord brought his strong anger upon us, and scattered us among many nations even to the ends of the earth'.[51] Like Bede, writing of the experience of the English church in the same period, Patrick assumed that the violence of pagans was the judgement of God on unfaithful British Christians.

Patrick's own providential judgement fell quite unexpectedly, just before his sixteenth birthday. On an unknown date in an unknown year, an Irish raiding party attacked Bannavem Taburniae, kidnapped Patrick and several of his slaves, and transported them to an island that lay beyond the horizon—an island beyond the boundaries of the empire, with an unfamiliar language and an unfamiliar script, an island at the edge of the world.

Patrick must have been shattered by this experience. On his own, in a strange country, in an unfamiliar culture, and possibly receiving orders in an unknown language, he found himself on the lowest rung of the social ladder, with a status no higher than that of the slaves that he once had owned. It is not certain where he was worked—whether in Mayo in the west or in Antrim in the north-east, where he was located by competing early traditions.[52] (It is worth noting that the only location mentioned in Patrick's text, the 'wood of Vocut', has been identified with Foghill, near Killala, county Mayo.[53]) Patrick's account is more interested in spiritual than in geographical precision. His account of his conversion emphasized divine intervention, rather than his own activity, which came in response to and was enabled by God's grace. 'In Ireland…God first opened my heart', he later recognized. 'He had compassion for me, young and foolish as I was. He cared for me before I even knew who he was…He protected me and loved me'. Tending sheep, day after day, Patrick

> prayed frequently… More and more the love of God increased, and my sense of awe before God. Faith grew, and my spirit was moved, so that in one day I would pray up to one hundred times, and at night perhaps the same. I even remained in the woods and on the mountain, and I would rise to pray before dawn in snow and ice and rain.

And so, suddenly cast upon his own resources, and realizing their total insufficiency, Patrick 'turned with all my heart to the Lord my God… in the land of my captivity'.[54]

Patrick would have realized how sharply the Christian faith differed from the religion of the Irish. Irish religion was polytheistic, but Patrick remembered the Christian claim that one god existed in three persons. Irish religion seems to have regarded the sun as a divine being, but Patrick became convinced that the true god had to be sharply distinguished from the world that he had made. Irish religious practice assumed that human beings could influence the gods through rituals, but Patrick came to understand that the true god, the 'one from whom all beginnings come', was sovereign and could not be manipulated.[55] But Patrick's conversion was more than his being convinced of a set of ideas. It was deeply, and unusually, experiential. As he grew in faith, God spoke to him in dreams, through which, after six years of looking after sheep, he was persuaded to try to escape.

Patrick's journey back to Bannavem Taburniae—which seems to have taken several years—is not easy to reconstruct. Patrick's *Confessio* records his travelling over 200 miles to find a suitable port, his bargaining with a crew to find a reliable passage, their turning up on an unfamiliar shoreline in an entirely deserted countryside, the possibility that his rescuers sold him into a second period of slavery, and his eventual arrival home. Now in his mid-to-late twenties, and, presumably, happily reunited with his family, Patrick was given the opportunity to catch up on his education and to gain the skills that were necessary for late entry into what might count as a successful career in the increasingly beleaguered kingdom of Alt Clud. He may have taken advantage of some of these opportunities, although he never lost his inferiority complex about his limited education (perhaps we should not take his modesty at face value).[56] But, after his extraordinary adventures, normality was not something into which he could easily settle. His unusual dreams continued. One night, in a vision, he saw a man called Victoricus—whose Roman name suggests that he might have been a kidnapped slave. It was a strange dream, with an unsettling message. Victoricus was

> coming as it were from Ireland with so many letters they could not be counted. He gave me one of these, and I read the beginning of the letter, the voice of the Irish people. While I was reading out the beginning of the letter, I thought I heard at that moment the voice of those who were beside the wood of Voclut, near the western sea. They called out as it were with one voice: 'We beg you, holy boy, to come and walk again among us.'[57]

Patrick listened, and obeyed.[58]

Patrick's family were dismayed by his decision to return to Ireland. They tried to stop him, and offered him presents to encourage him to remain in Bannavem Taburniae. But he found the visionary appeal from the slaves in the wood of Voclut too impressive to ignore. It was his responsibility, he believed, to preach 'the good news...to the very edge of the inhabited world' in 'these last days...before the end of the world'.[59] Well past the age when clerical training was ordinarily completed, he threw himself into preparation for what would become one of the most important missionary careers in the history of Christianity.

Patrick was probably in his mid-forties when his life's work began. He struggled to overcome his limited education and the hostility of clerical rivals as the Roman world continued to collapse around him. Without strong or influential backers—perhaps even without a formal commission to missionary work, as his repeated invocations of direct revelation suggest—he seems to have financed his missionary work from his own resources.[60] His preaching insisted on the orthodoxy that had been established at Nicea (381). Later in life, he offered a summary of his faith, which appeared to rewrite the Nicene creed, to explain the emphases of his preaching to the Irish:

> There is no other God, nor will there ever be, nor was there ever, except God the Father. He is the one who was not begotten, the one without a beginning, the one from whom all beginnings come, the one who holds all things in being—this is our teaching. And his son, Jesus Christ, whom we testify has always been, since before the beginning of this age, with the father in a spiritual way. He was begotten in an indescribable way before every beginning. Everything we can see, and everything beyond our sight, was made through him. He became a human being; and, having overcome death, was welcomed to the heavens to the Father. The Father gave him all power over every being, both heavenly and earthly and beneath the earth. Let every tongue confess that Jesus Christ, in whom we believe and whom we await to come back to us in the near future, is Lord and God. He is judge of the living and of the dead; he rewards every person according to their deeds. He has generously poured on us the Holy Spirit, the gift and promise of immortality, who makes believers and those who listen to be children of God and co-heirs with Christ. This is the one we acknowledge and adore—one God in a trinity of the sacred name.[61]

Patrick's statement set out his basic theological claims. His faith was centred on the incarnation, life, death, resurrection, and ascension of Jesus Christ, God's son. He understood that Jesus Christ would 'return very soon', and that the evidence for this was that the gospel had been preached at the very edge of the world. He insisted that while, at the return of Jesus Christ, everyone would declare that he is 'Lord and God', only those who had already become Christians would be saved. Patrick taught that these Christians had been united by the Holy Spirit in one family, which transcended national or cultural barriers, and that the symbol of entry into this community was baptism, while its shared life was centred on the eucharist and the ministry of the Word.[62] In Ireland, these were foreign and startling claims. But many people believed his message. Patrick claimed to have baptized 'many thousands' of the Irish, and to have set apart many of the 'sons and daughters of the leaders of the Irish' as 'monks and virgins of Christ'. Under Patrick's leadership—so he liked to claim—the Irish church was born.[63]

But the work was not easy. If, in the first half of the fifth century, the earliest missionaries had concentrated their work in Leinster, where the earliest Christian communities may have been based, and perhaps in order to take advantage of the region's proximity to Britain and the material support of the British church, in the later part of the century, Patrick and his associates worked in the west of the island, where the culture was still strongly pagan.[64] It was a hazardous undertaking. Patrick recorded his being repeatedly enslaved, and his experience of being 'rescued…at least a dozen times from the threat of death'. Still he continued in his work.

> Every day I keep expecting to be murdered, assaulted, sold back into slavery, or some such thing. But I am not afraid because I know Heaven waits for me. I throw myself on the mercy of God, who is in charge of everything.

And that was how Patrick understood his ministry's remarkable achievements. On his own strength, he had accomplished nothing. Each one of his remarkable successes was a 'gift of God'.[65]

But Patrick's success was not complete. This older ritual culture was very well established, and the missionaries co-opted some of its central elements as their communities grew. Early Christians both rejected and appropriated the Irish religious past. Some changes were very gradual. Over several centuries, Christians reformed burial practice, for example, and moved away from the traditional custom of deposing metalwork in graves.[66] Christians more rapidly co-opted the traditional learned orders. During the new faith's first century, sages that were still identified as druids had roles in the courts of Christian kings, and their pagan predecessors were represented in written texts as prophets of the birth, life and achievements of Jesus Christ and the early saints.[67] Christians co-opted traditional legends: 'fragments [of pagan lore] floated down the stream of time, and recombined in fantastic shapes around the persons of pagan heroes and Christian saints', as Charles Plummer put it.[68] Christians took over the traditional religious calendar. They sanctified festivals that were already associated with the cycle of the agricultural year, so that, for example, the festival that was associated with the beginning of the lactation of ewes, on 1 February, became associated with Brigid, a 'euhemerized deity' whose reputation as a saint depended to a large extent upon the achievements of the Celtic goddess with whom she shared her name.[69] For Christians also co-opted traditional gods, perhaps even turning some deities into saints.[70] Armagh, which rose in the earliest centuries to become the leading site of Christian worship, continued to be known as 'the height of the goddess Macha'.[71] This strategy was deeply political, and it echoed broader patterns of conversion: after all, as some Christians were appropriating the reputation of the druids, others were appropriating their property.[72] But this adaptation to Irish cultural norms was so complete that it became difficult to know where the history of the Christian mission ended and where its homage to pagan heritage began.

The contextualization of Christianity was so complete that it comes as a surprise to see how hard some churchmen worked to establish critical distance between the new faith and the old ways. At the first synod of Patrick, sometime in the sixth century, church leaders marked out the strategies by which Christians could distinguish themselves in pagan society, encouraging the faithful not to take oaths before nor to accept charity from those outside the church.[73] For all that their church was adapting to—even adopting—important elements of traditional culture, believers were being told to maintain a critical distance from it. But this distance was not easy to sustain. In fact, as elements of the old and new religions were combined in a vigorous storytelling culture, Patrick and other early Christians became characters in the mythological world that they had contested.[74] The ferocity and glamour of the old stories never lost their appeal, as W. B. Yeats later noted:

> When Oisin is speaking with S[aint] Patrick of the friends and the life he has outlived, he can but cry out constantly against a religion that has no meaning for him ...'I will cry my fill, but not for God, but because Finn and the Fianna are not living.'[75]

Oisin was right: the genius and tragedy of the conversion of Ireland was that it remained so incomplete.

II

By the early sixth century, even though the west of Ireland may not have been fully evangelized in the Christian mission, it was evident that 'Irish paganism was a lost cause'.[76] The new faith was being supported by a growing number of local converts, who were now participating fully in efforts to extend the gospel throughout their own island, and, increasingly, overseas.[77] These believers established a basic ecclesiastical organization in their effort to consolidate the church.[78] Elsewhere in Europe, the governance of the church had come to reflect the location of major urban centres, so that the status of a bishop was often determined by the status of the city in which he happened to be based. But Ireland had no urban centres, and could not support this kind of organizational structure.[79] Instead, church authorities mapped their ecclesiastical jurisdictions onto existing political boundaries, so that dioceses reflected the boundaries of regional kingdoms, while over-kingdoms set the parameters for synods.[80] In Ireland, as elsewhere in Europe, bishops oversaw the work of priests as they consolidated religious gains among the people. Episcopal structures were not weak, but they were weaker than they were elsewhere.[81] The *Collectio Canonum Hibernensis* (716–725) referred to bishops and metropolitans, but not to archbishops, for example.[82] Nevertheless, as an effective governance structure continued to be developed, the Christian community became increasingly centralized, so that the 'Irish churches' became the 'Irish church': by the mid-sixth century church leaders were able to cooperate so effectively as to be able to issue sentences of excommunication, such as the sentence that was passed on Columba.[83] By around 700, the Irish church had developed the structures by which it would be managed until the twelfth century.[84]

Other arrangements made the Irish church distinct. For, alongside this hierarchy of bishops and synods, the Irish church developed networks of male and female monasteries.[85] These institutions were established in many of the scores of independent kingdoms into which the island was divided, where they operated as centres for worship, education, and service. Patrick's emphasis upon the celibate life, and his claim to have set apart many of the 'sons and daughters of the leaders of the Irish' as 'monks and virgins of Christ', shows that monasteries for men and women had existed from the church's earliest days.[86] The institutions for women that were established at Kildare, Killeedy, Killevy, and Clonbroney became particularly important,

with the foundation at Kildare gaining prominence through its association
with Brigid.[87]

As the number of these institutions grew, so did their influence and
power, until ecclesiastical authority became as obviously located in abbots
and their monasteries as in bishops and their dioceses. Office-holders carefully guarded their power. In fact, the office of abbot was often hereditary,
and passed between fathers and sons.[88] Of course, it is possible to exaggerate
the competition between abbots and bishops. In some instances both offices
were combined in a single institution, so that some monasteries became
bishops' seats, although in every such case the 'bishop of a monastery was
subordinate to its abbot'.[89] In other instances, both offices were combined
in a single individual. These were clearly complicated cases, for while the
jurisdictions of bishops and synods were regional, the links between monasteries were not. Monasteries were drawn into loosely organized federations, known as *paruchiae*, that traced their origins to a common founder
and shared a common rule: a standardized monastic rule was only introduced during the twelfth-century Gregorian reform.[90] These networks
extended across Ireland, and, from the mid-sixth century onwards, into
Pictland, Britain, and, increasingly, far beyond.

These monastic federations drove the expansion of the Irish church.
Between 525 and 575 monasteries were founded at Iona, Bangor, Clonard,
and Clonmacnoise. Members of these institutions went on to establish other
foundations, and to organize these institutions in intricate and overlapping
networks.[91] These federations were complex institutions. As they came to
incorporate within the new religion many of the traditional features of Irish
society, including its learned orders and their artistic interests, these federations gave birth to a culture that fused biblical imagery with the aesthetic
values of Celtic, Pictish, British, and Roman visual cultures, to produce
some of the most iconic artefacts of the Christian tradition.[92] With this
extraordinary cultural breadth, these institutions were led by entrepreneurial individuals, who were remembered for their rugged piety and for their
ability to work miracles, to ward off enemies in both the spiritual and physical realms, and to extend the Christian faith in speculative and dangerous
overseas expeditions. The most famous of these missionaries were Columba,
who founded one of the most influential Irish monasteries on Iona, an
island in the Scottish Hebrides that formed part of Dál Riata, one of the
most important of the Irish over-kingdoms, and Columbanus, who trained
for ministry at Bangor, county Down, and established similar institutions at

Annegray and Luxeuil, in France, and at Bobbio, in Italy, where, in 615, he died. While the federation that was associated with Columba was headquartered at Iona, the federation associated with Patrick was led from Armagh, and the federation associated with Brigid was based in Kildare. These federations shared a common faith, but diverged on a number of key liturgical practices, including the dating of Easter, for there was no common Irish monastic rule. These federations published waves of propaganda, of which hagiography (biographies of saints, often with fantastic content) was a central part, to defend their claims to primacy, so that Iona's promotion of Columba competed with Kildare's promotion of Brigid and the promotion of Patrick at Armagh.

Some missionaries took part in speculative journeys. Unknown pioneers established monasteries on Faroe and Iceland, where they were remembered in sagas as the 'Papar', and, if the traditional stories are true, Brendan the Navigator might even have reached the coast of North America, as the explorer Tim Severin did when he attempted to replicate the journey in a leather boat in 1976–1977.[93] Irish monks made bold and ambitious efforts to spread the gospel—even as the soft power of their monasteries grew in influence across Europe, shaping 'an international cultural province…created by a shared religion', in which was produced the most iconic Christian artefacts.[94] Wielding very significant cultural and ecclesiastical power, Irish monasteries become incredibly powerful, so that by around 700 the power of abbots was comparable to that of bishops. Decision-making within the Irish church was increasingly located in synods that represented each of the stakeholders in this Christian society—institutions in which bishops sat alongside abbots and even clerically educated kings. There was, therefore, no single source of authority within the Irish church. Power flowed from the sanctity of episcopal orders, the prestige and power associated with the large monasteries, and the economic and political power that could be wielded by a king, together with the knowledge accumulated by scribes, and this power was managed in synods. The 'Irish church was less episcopal than was normal in the Church at large', and monasteries became the laboratories of an energetic and often daring Christian culture.[95]

The locations of the monasteries were determined by geographical as much as by political factors. Some monks prioritized isolation from the world. Hermits sought solitude—like Donard, who made his home on the highest mountain in the northern half of Ireland, on which pre-Christian mythology had identified a great cairn as a door into another world. For

similar reasons, some monasteries were established in locations that were
difficult to reach. Monks sought and found peace in institutions like that on
Inishmurray, 4 miles off the Sligo coast, and on Skellig Michael, a craggy
outcrop located 7 miles off the coast of county Kerry (better known today
as the last refuge of the Jedi, after being featured as the hideaway of Luke
Skywalker in *Star Wars: The Force Awakens*). But most monks did not want
isolation. They located their monasteries on obvious access routes, in order
to facilitate travel, communication, and influence. The foundation at
Clonmacnoise, for example, developed beside a bridge (constructed c. 804)
that crossed the Shannon.[96] These institutions were often founded on the
boundaries of kingdoms, perhaps deliberately to replace pagan institutions.[97]
If that is the case, it suggests that Christian missionaries were following the
advice of Pope Gregory the Great, who had encouraged missionaries to situ-
ate centres for Christian worship on sites with which pagans were already
familiar—advice that may have been followed by the hermit on Slieve
Donard, for example. Wherever they were located—and with hardly any
exceptions—the Irish monasteries evolved into primitive communal centres.

Ireland's monastic foundations were organized in similar ways. While
archaeologists and historians debate whether these institutions can be properly described as 'monastic towns', it is clear that they were organized and
that those who lived within their enclosures were rigorously demarcated.[98]
Reflecting the importance of Jewish habits of thought, these monastic sites,
like the Temple in Jerusalem, were centred upon a sanctuary, around which
were organized concentric circles of decreasing holiness. At the centre of
each settlement were located the community's principal ecclesiastical buildings and the homes of its monks, which were surrounded by a more or less
circular wall. Beyond this enclosure were located the dwellings of the families that served the monastery in such activities as farming and fabrication.
These families were headed by monks who had married and raised children.
The sons of these *manaig* were provided with a clerical education, so that
part of the community at least was self-perpetuating. Some of the *manaig*
were slaves.[99] These dwellings were surrounded by another circular wall,
outside which were located lands for grazing, horticulture, and the humbler
dwellings of the poor. This area was enclosed by a third wall, which formed
the outer perimeter of the monastery.

While almost all early monastic institutions were organized in concentric
circles, they varied in other ways. Monastic settlements differed, for example,
in size. In some locations, their circular enclosures measured 30 metres in

Figure 3. An Irish high cross

diameter, while in others their diameter measured over 200 metres. For over half a millennium, the buildings on these settlements were constructed out of wood. Stone was used occasionally before the end of the eleventh century, and only slowly took over as the most important material for construction. The Irish institutions were distinctive for their habit of wooden construction. Even in the thirteenth century, the decision by Malachy, one of the foremost medieval reformers, to use timber for the rebuilding of the abbey at Bangor was described by Bernard of Clairvaux as following the 'Irish fashion'. But whatever their fabric, these church buildings were generally very small. The cathedral at Glendalough might represent one of the largest of these building projects—and might have been one of the most impressive buildings on the island upon its erection. But most churches were tiny, sometimes no more than 2 or 3 metres in length and width.[100] These buildings were not designed for congregational worship, but for use by the small number of monks at the heart of each foundation.

Monastic settlements became known for features that made their built environment distinctive. Reflecting their tendency to appropriate rather than to eradicate traditional religious practice, early Christians sanctified the sites of standing stones. Adherents of the new faith vandalized these monuments, by inscribing Christian symbols upon them.[101] Some monasteries developed a Christian alternative to these standing stones, similar in design, scale, and purpose. Over 100 of these monumental 'high crosses' were erected in Ireland, while a small number of other examples appeared in northern and western parts of Britain.[102] With this limited distribution, high crosses were 'unique to these islands', and, as products of a 'confident, well-established church in command of rich patronage, a church which has evolved in its own art styles', they became a distinctive feature of what is now identified as the 'insular aesthetic'—an artistic style that is distinctive to Britain and Ireland.[103] Among the most impressive are those at Clonmacnoise and Durrow, county Offaly, and at Moone, county Kildare. The high cross at Monasterboice, county Louth, still stands at 7 metres tall. These examples suggest something of the power of these monuments in the early to mid-medieval period. They were likely designed as teaching tools, providing visual aids to remind believers of stories from the Old Testament or the gospels—and, perhaps, in some of the more mysterious markings, even of incidents in pre-Christian Irish lore.[104] Many of the high crosses are impossible to date. It is possible that most were constructed in the period 830–870, during the most severe depredations of the Vikings, when religious institutions sought methods of cultural production that were not easily stolen, burned, or otherwise destroyed, but some suggest a provenance in the twelfth century, when Scandinavian settlers had converted to Christianity and had begun to influence its visual styles.[105]

Monasteries began to erect high crosses around the same time as they began to build round towers (which are known in Irish as bell towers). These round towers were—almost—unique to Ireland.[106] Only two similar constructions can be found elsewhere. Their construction continued into the thirteenth century, when the Viking threat had long since disappeared. It is impossible to know how many round towers were constructed at the height of their popularity. One nineteenth-century survey located 120 surviving examples—many of which have disappeared.[107]

Monasteries were, of course, communities that were dedicated to the service of God. Their abbots had high expectations of the life of piety: Columbanus's penitential teaching pushed devotees to strict asceticism in order finally to enter into the 'most perfect and perpetual love of God'.[108] But the monks themselves could be a varied lot. Some men entered monastic life as an expression of penance, in sorrow and perhaps to atone for some grievous misdeed. Others sought order for their lives, as they retreated from circumstances that were unpredictable and sometimes chaotic: the devastating outbreaks of plague in the mid-sixth century seem to coincide with rapidly increasing membership of monastic houses, for example.[109] For some, life in a monastery was filled with simple delights, which they recorded in the marginalia of the books that they copied in scriptoria, in which scribes wrote of the pleasure of birdsong and even, most famously, the company of Pangur, the most celebrated cat in Irish history.[110] But not everyone who felt sorrow for sin found the monastic life to be especially fulfilling. Monks would have spent much of their day outdoors. This field-work was necessary, because monks needed physical as well as spiritual nourishment. This explains why monasteries were often established in proximity to good agricultural land and to good supplies of fish. Monks could live well. They drank water, milk, and beer; they dined on hens, sheep, cattle, and, where they were available, seals; they fed on eggs, butter, and cheese; and they enjoyed honey from their bee hives. It was not a bad life. But not every monk would have wanted this kind of abundance. The monks on Skellig Michael—presumably by choice—would not have dined so well. Hermits and ascetics, who sought a more sparing diet, would have been 'immediately recognizable by their much lighter weight'.[111] But, whatever their location, and their dietary preferences, these monks would have followed the same routine of prayer.[112] For monastic life was highly structured. The *opus dei*—as the 'hours' for set prayer were known—began at dawn with lauds, followed in mid-morning by terce, at midday by sext, in mid-afternoon by none, in the evening by vespers, and, around midnight, by nocturns. Other prayers may have been scheduled for prime and compline, which marked the monks' rising and returning to bed. It was—at least ideally—an ordered and fulfilling life of worship and of work.

Monks would have spent a great deal of time in scholarly pursuits. Clerical education began in early childhood with the memorization of psalms. Irish monks loved the Psalter, delighted in 'its poetry, and probably accepted its violence and vengeance as a norm'.[113] In fact, one of the earliest extant Irish manuscripts was an edition of the Psalms, which Columba was said to have transcribed, that was read on fields of battle before fighting began. This interest in Scripture was typical. Christians prized literacy—that is, instruction in the reading and writing of Latin—and written culture had been central to the movement's growth throughout the empire. In Ireland, this interest in literacy took on a distinctive form. In the first few Christian centuries, believers were taught to write on wooden tablets, like the seventh-century examples found in Springmount bog, county Antrim.[114] Until around the end of the seventh century, most written texts circulating in Ireland would have been in Latin script. From the beginning of the ninth century, we can trace a shift to vernacular writing, as monks took up interest in the Irish language and began to conserve its literary heritage. But, in order to do so, they had to reduce the language to writing and to think about the heritage they might want to preserve.

Irish monasteries gained a reputation for the high quality of their educational provision and spiritual formation. These institutions had a well-developed theological culture.[115] 'Scriptural scholarship…had an even more central position in the early Irish Church than in other Churches at the time', and Irish monks worked hard to preserve the writings of the church fathers.[116] Around 750, for example, some monks created an annotated Bible, which 'attempted to bring together commentaries on all the books of the Old and New Testaments in one volume'.[117] Legal scholarship was also unusually developed. The *Hibernensis* was the earliest known attempt to set out the parameters of an idealized Christian society, for example.[118] A student who completed his higher education in a monastery was well prepared for high levels of discussion, and could sit alongside bishops and abbots in the synods that governed the Irish church.[119]

Monks also took an interest in the Irish past. Some saw their task as essentially historical, de-mythologizing traditional lore in an attempt to establish an historical record for the island. Their work to preserve pre-Christian lore seems to have gone beyond a high-minded or virtuous interest in sanctifying 'good pagans'. Irish monks had a much more conciliatory attitude to the pagan past than did their counterparts in England. Early Anglo-Saxon texts, like *Beowulf*, described that lost world without invoking its abandoned gods. But Irish texts incorporated the old gods whenever they could, sometimes in surprising ways. Monks wrote histories of Christian heroes in view of the pagan past they had ostensibly discarded, so that pagan myth and Christian hagiography began increasingly to intertwine. In Kildare, for example, the powerful cult of Brigid appears to have been the result of a 'carefully managed takeover of the cult of a pagan goddess' who shared the saint's name and who was venerated outside Ireland. This connection with pre-Christian cosmology might explain why Brigid was described as hanging her cloak on a sunbeam, amidst other wonders.[120] And some Irish monks may simply have enjoyed the mythology of the Iron Age, with its extraordinary range of emotion and violence, entirely for its own sake. A literary education may not have gone much further than this: the only non-Christian author known to Columbanus may have been Virgil.[121] Irish monasteries provided a grounding in literature that focused on Scripture, patristics, and the Irish past.

As the Irish church developed a reputation for saintliness and scholarship, its institutions attracted large numbers of international students. In the early seventh century, many members of Northumbrian noble families 'lived in exile among the Irish' and 'were instructed in the teachings of the Irish Church and received the grace of Baptism'.[122] One English abbot wrote in 675 of 'boatloads of Englishmen going to Ireland to study'.[123] Bede recorded English students travelling to Ireland for advanced training in exegesis.[124] Even bishops from Gaul were trained in Irish monasteries.[125] The educational institutions that had so effectively served the island's most famous missionaries were now training a more diverse student body, and were impacting upon the faith of the western European church.

Of course, as these links suggest, Irish monasteries found themselves influencing and being influenced by international cultural connections. This was particularly evident in the distinctive visual culture in which these monks participated. Irish monasteries participated in the formation of a distinctive 'insular aesthetic', which is regarded now as peculiarly Irish but which drew upon such a wide range of foreign cultures that it might better be regarded as European. The illustrated books produced in Irish scriptoria combined biblical texts with artistic motifs from Irish, Pictish, British, German, Byzantine, and Roman traditions—with sometimes stunning effect. The most famous of these illustrated books include smaller items such as the Book of Mulling or the Book of Dimma (both eighth century), the size of which suggests that they may have been designed for personal use and portability, and the Book of Durrow (c. 650–700) and the Book of Kells (c. 800), two extraordinary productions that must have possessed high-status liturgical significance.[126] In this extraordinary literary culture, the Book of Kells was thought to be spectacular. It quickly developed a

Figure 4. The Book of Kells

mythology of its own. Gerald of Wales saw the book during his visit to Ireland (1183–1185):

> Among all the miracles of Kildare nothing seems to me more miraculous than the wonderful book which they say was written at the dictation of an angel during the lifetime of the virgin...you will notice such intricacies, so delicate and subtle, so close together and well-knitted, so involved and bound together, and so fresh still in their colourings that you will not hesitate to declare that all these things must have been the result of the work, not of men, but of angels.

Gerald reported that the scribe who put the book together was visited by an angel, which inspired the monk's work by encouraging him to replicate heavenly illustrations:

By the help of the divine grace, the scribe, taking particular notice of them all, and faithfully committing them to his memory, was able to reproduce them exactly...And so with the angel indicating the designs, Brigid praying, and the scribe imitating, the book was composed.[127]

Of course, reality was more mundane. The book of angels was actually fabricated of vellum from the skins of around 185 calves.[128] Given the contexts of its production, the Book of Kells was a remarkable achievement. Drawing from across the visual cultures of Europe, if not of heaven itself, the monasteries were developing a visual culture that was not distinctively Irish—but was distinctively Christian.

As these international influences suggest, while the Irish church invested heavily in luxury items, it also invested heavily in mission. Its most famous missionary was born in 521. Columba is a dominating figure in the early history of the Irish church. We know more about his life and achievements than about those of any of his contemporaries. There are two important sources for his life. *Amra Coluim Chille*, a eulogy for Columba apparently composed soon after his death, provides an early and remarkably non-miraculous biographical account, emphasizing how much he was able to achieve without the extraordinary gifts with which he was credited by later hagiographers. Its author, Dallán Forgaill, may have provided the earliest impression of Columba's life and works, an admiring account that spoke highly of Columba's piety, and emphasized that 'none left this world with thoughts / more totally fixed on the Cross'.[129] As well as being a landmark text in the history of the Irish church, *Amra Coluim Chille*, which was composed in 597, remains the earliest datable Irish poem—and therefore marks the beginning of a literary tradition that has become world-renowned.[130] The other most important early source for Columba's biography was written by his relative and successor as abbot of Iona. Adomnán's admiring account of the *Vita Sancti Columbae* was the result of an oral history project, in which he combined monks' recollections of the monastery's early days with material from earlier manuscript sources.[131] The *Vita* must be read in terms of its genre, which delighted in stories of the extraordinary, as well as in term of its political purpose, which was to establish Iona as a principal centre of Irish Christianity, and the mother house of an expanding and powerful network of monastic institutions.[132] The genre and the political purpose of the text warranted its author's elaboration of its subject, and particularly its attribution to Columba of wonder-working powers. As the Iona federation promoted the reputation of its founder, these celebrations of his life were carefully preserved, and widely disseminated.[133] Artefacts that were associated with Columba and his immediate circle were highly prized: the copy of the *Vita* that is held in the public library at Schaffhausen, Switzerland, for example, may have been 'perused and handled by Adomnán himself'.[134]

Thanks to these early biographical efforts, we can reconstruct the key events of Columba's life. Columba was born in Donegal in 521 and died in Iona in 597. His family background was prestigious. His parents, Fedilmid mac Fergusa and Eithne, enjoyed the status of royalty within the Cenél Conaill and Uí Néill familial line. They called their son Crimthann, or 'Fox', and they fostered him out, following the practice of other Gaelic aristocrats in a child-rearing custom that promoted amity between family groups as well as the sharing of knowledge and expertise, and which found its counterpart within the institutions of the church.[135] Crimthann was fostered to an elderly churchman, Cruithnechan, who may have looked after a church near Tobermore, county Londonderry. Cruithnechan baptized the boy, and gave him the name by which he has been remembered—Colum, 'dove', which in Latin became 'Columba'. But Colum soon gained a nickname among the local children—Colum Cille, 'Colum of the church', an appropriate descriptor for a boy who threw himself into the memorization of psalms. Brought up in the nurture and admonition of the Lord, Columba pursued an ecclesiastical career, until his sudden emigration, in 563—a consequence, some early sources suggest, of his excommunication.

Columba's excommunication is a startling and unexpected event in what until that time had been a conventional if often rather privileged life. The sentence of excommunication was handed down only for the most serious offences, and may have been a consequence of Columba's having become involved in a political and subsequently military dispute between his family and their political rivals—a dispute that resulted in serious violence on the plain below Ben Bulben, in Sligo.[136] In the aftermath of this regional conflict, and following his formal exclusion from the church, Columba may have volunteered to travel in order to redeem himself, or he may have been forced into emigration by a synodical decree. Either way, in 563, together with a small group of colleagues, he set out for the Hebrides.

Columba's destination was a tiny island off the coast of Mull. Iona, the 'island of the yew trees', was a good location for a new monastic community. Its fertile land could certainly support the small foundation of monks. Indeed, the island had been inhabited for many hundreds of years, and the missionary party would have had to reckon with the built heritage of these earlier occupants, whose traces remained in the substantial hillfort at Dun Cul Bhuirg and elsewhere. This hillfort, or 'broch', bore witness both to the skills in stone construction of these earlier peoples as well as to their need for defensive structures. Elsewhere in the Hebrides, as at Dun Carloway in Lewis, these brochs could take on a commanding appearance, dominating strategic locations with their immense physical size. The best preserved, on Mousa, Shetland, is not the largest in diameter, but it reaches over 13 metres in height and provides stairs to a viewing platform on the top floor. These constructions were powerful symbols of the antiquity, longevity, and violence of the cultures that the monks had come to challenge—and a striking contrast to the wooden buildings that they would construct as their new home. For it is telling that very few archaeological remains from this period have been discovered on Iona. The small community of twelve monks would not have needed substantial buildings, even as its numbers began slowly to expand. Their accommodation needs were basic. Adomnán described Columba as living in a small hut, using a stone for a pillow.[137] None of his followers could reasonably have requested anything more comfortable.

Columba's monks would not have been surprised by these conditions. They were operating within a very familiar environment. After all, Iona was part of Dál Riata, the over-kingdom that encompassed territories in the north-east of Ireland and in the west and south-west of Scotland, the head-quarters of which were located in county Antrim, on the promontory where Dunseverick Castle now stands. For all that Iona looks remote by modern standards, it was centrally located on the sea lanes that connected Ireland to the west coast of Scotland and the Hebridean islands, and offered proximity to the Great Glen through which Irish missionaries would travel deep into the lands of the Picts. In 563, Iona was governed by Conall mac Comgaill, a Gaelic chieftain who offered the island to Columba and his party as a suitable base for their mission. The gift was appropriate, for, after all, the leader of the party was a prince of the increasingly powerful family of the northern Uí Néill, with whom Conall mac Comgaill would want to remain on good terms. The gift of a small island was, from this perspective, the proper response to the arrival in western Dál Riata of a well-connected and well-educated religious nobleman. And Columba, who took his social position in Gaelic society extremely seriously, seems to have won the respect of his new neighbours. For, when Conall mac Comgaill died, in 576, and while pagan priests continued to exercise enormous influence in power politics elsewhere, Columba was called upon to anoint his successor in what must have been one of the earliest Christian coronations in these islands.[138]

The foundation on Iona was, in many respects, a typical Irish monastery. On a daily basis, Columba's monks would have followed the 'hours' of the *opus dei*. They would have dressed in white to celebrate the eucharist at noon on Sundays and on other major feasts, while fasting on each Wednesday and Friday. Like their *confrères* in institutions elsewhere, they would have aimed to be self-sufficient, harvesting barley from fields surrounding the monastery, while raising cattle, sheep, and pigs, and dining on fish and baby seals. They maintained a vigorously intellectual culture, building a scriptorium for copying books brought by visitors, by means of which their library continued to expand, while also preparing fresh compositions, including the two hymns that have been attributed to Columba, 'Altus Prosator' and 'Adiutor Laborantium'. The foundation attracted many visitors, including some in search of medical assistance and others looking for various kinds of pastoral help, and gradually its influence expanded.

The monks on Iona carefully cultivated this growing influence. Taking advantage of their location, and its proximity to major sea lanes, the monks began to plant monastic foundations elsewhere in the islands, and then to develop these foundations into a formal federation. The most important of the early daughter foundations was located on Hinba, an island in the Hebrides that after the widespread adoption of Viking place-names can no longer be identified. Another foundation was established on Tiree, an island known as the 'land of corn', which may have been founded in order to help with food supply for the mother house on Iona, or which may have been used by monks seeking temporary isolation.[139] As the influence of Iona grew, and expanded back into Ireland, other federations began to reach into the Hebrides. Columba's was not the only Irish mission in the western isles, but it was the most successful.

Of course, for all that Columba's monastery was located in western Dál Riata, it was still part of the Irish world. And, as he repaired his reputation with the Irish bishops, Columba returned to the mainland on several important occasions. Sometime after 585, more than twenty years after the foundation of Iona, Columba established another monastery at Durrow, county Offaly, and in 590 (or perhaps in 575) he took part in a political conference that sought to improve relations between Dál Riata and the other Irish kingdoms.[140] The foundation of the monastery at Durrow provided Columba and his brethren with a strategic base in the Irish midlands. It became an important centre for cultural production, including the Book of Durrow. This monastery became the most significant node in the Columban network as it expanded through the north of the island, with the foundation at Derry running close behind. Despite his important political connections, and his success in building up an effective monastic federation on the Irish mainland, however, Columba is best remembered for his mission to the Picts.[141]

Columba was more of an 'occasional visitor to the northern Picts' than their most successful evangelist.[142] But his work among the Picts was enormously important nonetheless. In the sixth century, according to Columba's early biographers, Scotland was divided between Christian Gaels, living on the western seaboard, on one side of the Grampian mountains, and the Picts on the eastern plains. Their mysterious and almost entirely pre-literate culture is now understood largely by means of elaborately and obscurely decorated stone monuments and other uncontextualized archaeological remains. With the two populations being divided by this substantial range of mountains, the culture of the Picts was entirely different to that of the Gaels. Their culture was British, and their language a relative of Welsh, until in the ninth century they were absorbed into the expanding kingdom of Scotland, as a consequence of which they adopted the Gaelic language and eventually lost their cultural distinctiveness. But the distinction between these cultures was very real when Columba set out from Iona into Pictland, rowing up the lochs of the Great Glen. In his efforts to introduce the Picts to Christianity, Columba worked through an interpreter.[143] In this new world, some conversions came easy. Somewhere around Glen Urquhart, for example, Columba baptized Emchath and his household, whose faith appears to have endured. But other conversions were more difficult. One un-named family group were baptized, only to experience, a few days later, the death of their son. Pictish leaders condemned the family for abandoning the old gods in favour of a deity who could not keep them alive—until Columba, undeterred, raised the boy to life. In Adomnán's narrative, the account of the miracle made two important points.[144] The first point was to identify Pictland as a place of dangers and strange wonders. The most famous of these wonders involved Columba's encounter with a monster that lived in Loch Ness. When, in the course of their travels, the wandering missionary band stumbled upon the burial of a man who had just been attacked by the monster, Columba ordered one of his entourage, Luigne moccu Min, to swim across the loch, to fetch a boat that was moored on the other side. As Luigne moccu Min crossed the loch, the monster appeared, and made to chase him, until it was stopped by Columba's command that it should 'go no further'. The miracle impressed the watching Picts. The second reason why Adomnán recounted these miracle stories was that he wanted to associate Columba—and, by extension, his monastic federation—with unusual spiritual power. It was, after all, politically and financially beneficial to advertise the founder of your monastic federation as a worker of wonders— especially in a cultural context in which water monsters were feared.[145] Columba did succeed in setting up some monasteries among the Picts, as at Portmahomack, in Easter Ross, where archaeologists have discovered the remains of an ecclesiastical settlement that may date from the late sixth century, and which became an important fulcrum for the combination of Christian themes and Pictish art. But these early accounts suggest that Columba's mission resulted in only a small number of conversions.[146] Columba may not have engaged with the remnants of native tradition among the Irish—but he certainly met plenty of pagans among the Picts. Columba enjoyed his last days on Iona, an old man surrounded by his friends and fellow workers, where he died in June 597.

Columba's efforts to promote the Christian faith among the Picts may have encouraged others to travel further still. In 590–591, Columbanus, a Leinster man who had been educated at Bangor, county Down, set out on a peregrination in which he became the 'pre-eminent holy man of the Merovingian kings and their aristocracy'.[147] Like other missionaries and scholars, he set out with high hopes of doing good, which were expressed in the boat song that has become known as one of the earliest items in the Irish literary canon.[148] But Columbanus was appalled by the doctrinal chaos of this part of Europe, which he contrasted with the orthodoxy and simplicity of the Irish church. His almost mystical exhortation to his followers to 'live in Christ, that Christ may live in you' reflected his deep piety.[149] Columbanus was remembered as a holy man, rather than as a worker of wonders, and was never commemorated in the culture of relics, in which, in any case, the Irish church lagged somewhat behind European norms, in adopting a practice that was only normalized in the ninth century.[150] But even he fell under a shadow. His colleagues among the Franks in Gaul deemed the monastic rule that he promoted too strict. But the reason why he was attacked as being heretical was his tenacious defence of the Irish church's dating of Easter.[151] This dispute grew to become one of the great crises of the Irish and British churches, which marked the beginning of the end of the Irish religious influence in Britain and, increasingly, overseas—as well as the end of the partial independence of the Irish church.[152]

The dispute centred upon whether the date of Easter should be calculated with reference to the Jewish Passover (as the Irish church argued) or by using complex tables (as other national churches argued), for these alternative methods frequently resulted in alternative dates.[153] (This dispute continues to separate the eastern and western churches.) The diversity of practice became increasingly problematic as the Catholic Church pushed to establish international liturgical norms. Columbanus's disagreements with the bishops in Gaul reached a height around 602. Feelings were running high. Around 605, Dagán, an Irish bishop, paid an unhappy visit to Laurence, the archbishop of Canterbury. Dagán felt so strongly about the differences between the Irish and English churches that he refused to eat with his astonished hosts. After the visit, Laurence wrote to the Irish bishops to exhort them to maintain the 'unity, peace, and Catholic customs of the Christian Church established throughout the world'.[154] But the appeal fell on deaf ears, and tensions continued to mount. The debate was taken up in Ireland, when in 628 a synod accepted what it believed to be Catholic practice. A large number of the Irish churches fell into line with the synod's decrees—but other institutions, including the monasteries of Columba's federation, did not. As decentralized governance allowed debate to continue, the Irish church could not agree whether to maintain its traditional commitments or whether to adopt the new, Catholic, norms. Some authorities were clearly frustrated. In 634, Pope Honorius wrote to the 'little community' of Irish Christians, 'isolated at the uttermost ends of the earth', reminding them that their wisdom did not exceed that of 'all churches ancient and modern throughout the world', and encouraging them to fall into line with the more common dating of Easter.[155] But they did not. As the Irish church continued to resist Catholic norms, other problems may have resurfaced. In 640, Pope John warned the Irish church against the Pelagian heresy, which, he feared, was 'reviving among them'.[156] He begged the Irish Christians 'not to take up the ashes of controversies long since burned out. For who can do other than condemn the insolent and impious assertion that man can live without sin of his own free will and not of God's grace?'[157] These were serious charges—though the accusation about Pelagianism may simply have been a warning about the effects of liturgical independence—for it was the dispute about Easter that would do most to

cause problems in the Irish church and for its missionaries overseas. Then
the division of the Irish church spilled over into England. The English
churches that maintained links with Iona, and shared their practice of dating
Easter, were confronted at the Synod of Whitby (664). After the synod had
ruled on the matter, Irish missionaries could no longer promote their dating
of Easter on the continent. But that did not resolve the issue. Like their Irish
brethren, the English church divided, torn between competing loyalties to
Rome and to the tradition of Columba. After the Whitby synod, one group
of English churches entirely rejected the Irish calculation of Easter and fell
into line with Catholic norms. Another group accepted the Roman calculation but was reluctant to censure the Irish. Others were entirely unpersuaded by Roman arguments. Some Northumbrians threw in their lot with
the Irish church, and between 669 and 676 set up a community in Mayo.[158]
But the trend towards normalization continued. Sometime in the 680s, the
federation associated with Patrick adopted the Roman calculation for Easter.
The federation associated with Columba maintained the traditional Irish
dating for another generation, but, in 716, even it accepted the new liturgical norms.[159] The crisis had revealed the structural weakness of the Irish
church's decentralized governance. For all that the church had developed
consolidated structures of authority, its monastic federations continued to
make independent decisions about important liturgical debates, and maintained critical distance from the authority of the pope. But, by the early
eighth century, the international norms had prevailed. Ireland was becoming Catholic.

III

Two hundred years after its arrival in Ireland, the church that was founded
by Patrick had established strong if also idiosyncratic roots in its new environment. The conversion of Ireland was a process that continued over hundreds of years. Older ways of life were not rapidly destroyed. Memories of
the old cosmology were woven into the fabric of everyday life. Ireland's
very topography was sacred. Place-names provided constant reminders of
the old gods and of entry-points into their world.[160] In the sixth century,
burials in sites of pre-Christian ritual significance were still following pre-
Christian ritual forms.[161] Nevertheless, by the end of that century, it was
clear that the work of Christian missionaries had passed a tipping point.

The Irish had, mostly, embraced the new faith, and were driving its expansion throughout the Gaelic world, on either side of the Irish Sea. In the seventh century, while many Christians regarded druids as 'laughable fables', monks prepared written texts that combined elements of Catholic theology with positive references to the cosmology that it was supposed to have replaced. The social status of the old beliefs and behaviours was changing. By the eighth century, Christian documents could refer to the activities of druids without regarding them as a significant 'social problem'.[162] Christians had become so confident of their standing that they began to preserve—or, perhaps, invent—tradition. Beginning in the seventh century, monks began to collect—or create—stories of the Irish past.[163] In the same period, monks constructed long genealogies that linked contemporary kings to mythical heroes—a practice that continued until the eleventh century.[164] Whether their activity was carefully historical or more freely creative, it is remarkable that the 'clerically trained literate elite of a Christian society should have been so imaginatively preoccupied with their pagan antecedents'.[165] Scholars are not always sure what is represented by this historical interest in the pre-Christian past. Whatever its significance, by the ninth century, the movement away from *ogham* script was complete, and monks were writing in Old Irish, as well as in Latin. These authors 'had a keen sense of the value of their own language from an early date'. The effort by Christian historians to preserve traces of the pagan past represented the 'first evidence of a vernacular language...being taken as an object of scholarly study'.[166] For the scribes were preserving native tradition as culture, not as cult—and, almost, inventing literary studies as they did so.

The successful expansion of Christianity, and the surprising role of monks in preserving the legacy of pre-Christian religion, was made possible by the distinctive institutions of the Irish church. Its unusual shape could be traced back to Patrick, a bishop who believed that the foundation of monastic communities was among his most important achievements.[167] In institutionalizing Patrick's emphasis upon the importance of monastic life, the leadership of the Irish church combined elements that were often kept separate elsewhere. But it was the foundations that the Irish church established that did the most significant work to spread the gospel and to build a distinctively Christian culture. Monasteries became the laboratories in which an Irish Christian culture was developed and from which it was disseminated. These institutions brought together influences from multiple European cultures to fashion a distinctive aesthetic, literary, and liturgical style. This hybrid style was exported back into Europe as Irish monks led the cross-cultural evangelism through which their church made an extraordinary and increasingly controversial impact across what was left of the Roman world.

Christianity had converted the Irish. But Christianity might also have created the Irish: Muirchú, a biographer of Patrick in the later seventh century, might have been the first to think of the Irish as a nation.[168] Ireland had become a model Christian culture, its apologists believed, and if its church had sought to preserve its autonomy, it had done so in order to preserve the orthodox faith. Writing to Pope Boniface, Columbanus insisted that

> we Irish, inhabitants of the world's edge, are disciples of Saints Peter and Paul and of all the disciples who, by the Holy Spirit, wrote the divine scripture, and we accept nothing outside the evangelical and apostolic teaching; not one has been a heretic, not one a Judaiser, not one a schismatic, but the Catholic Faith as it was given to us first by you, that is the successors of the holy apostles, is preserved intact.[169]

Less than 200 years after the arrival of the first missionaries, the Christian mission was complete. Defending his church, and speaking on behalf of the national community that it represented, Columbanus announced the birth of Christian Ireland.

2

Foundations

Columbanus's defence of the orthodoxy and resilience of his native church was borne out by its rapid growth in Ireland and throughout the Irish world. The Irish church was extremely well provided with buildings, for example, around 5,500 of which were erected in the early medieval period.[1] But they were enterprising missionaries too. As Roman civilization crumbled, Irish monks exported the Christian faith into the varied linguistic cultures of Britain, from Pictland to Northumbria and the Anglo-Saxon kingdoms in the south-east. Irish missionaries such as Áedán of Lindisfarne (d. 651) made an enormous contribution to the rebuilding of Christianity among the Northumbrians.[2] Other monks pushed beyond the Atlantic islands.[3] Those who ventured onto the continent included Kilian of Würzburg (640–689), who established important foundations on the continent as part of his evangelization of the Germans.[4] Carolingian rulers encouraged Irish theologians to take up teaching roles in their empire—not always to the satisfaction of local churchmen. Heiric of Auxerre (841–876), a French Benedictine, complained that 'almost the whole of Ireland, setting the obstacle of the sea at nought, is migrating to our shores with a herd of philosophers'.[5] One of this 'herd' was John Scotus Eriugena (c. 810–c. 870/880), a talented theologian, philosopher, and poet whose efforts to revise the Augustinian consensus on predestination was condemned by multiple synods as being worth no more than 'Irish porridge'.[6] An Irish bishop called John was the first missionary to the Slavic peoples known as the Wends, among whom he was martyred to their god of hospitality in 1066.[7] And this missionary work or *peregrinatio* (travel or pilgrimage for the sake of Jesus Christ) continued into the far north, as monks who were motivated by a desire to embrace traditional forms of asceticism or even martyrdom threw themselves on the mercy of providence and set out in tiny boats in the hope of making landfall somewhere—anywhere—in the

stormy Atlantic. It is impossible to know how many of these aspiring hermits or missionary-explorers were lost. But their improbable strategy of
random discovery must have worked. By the end of the seventh century,
Irish monks had established bases in locations as far away as Orkney, Shetland,
Faroe, in Iceland, and possibly even beyond.[8]

The Irish monasteries were crucial to this successful expansion. As their
numbers grew, these foundations worked together in strong and sometimes
competing federations, whose power was marked in part by the acquisition
of relics.[9] Gaining more prominence than they enjoyed elsewhere in Europe,
monastic federations reinforced the church's hierarchy, and proved to be
resilient through successive crises, providing leadership for the Irish church
while supporting its social and administrative infrastructure for the best part
of 1,000 years. Their importance quickly became evident. By the middle of
the eighth century, and by combining elements of European piety and
learning, Irish scholars had begun to produce literary and liturgical artefacts,
such as the Book of Kells and the Ardagh Chalice, that are among the greatest achievements of their religious tradition. These accomplishments demonstrated the connectedness as well as the self-confidence of Irish monastic
culture, which accepted the theological claims of the European church and
learned from its many visual styles while holding onto some important
aspects of its native artistic heritage and defending its distinctive liturgical
traditions. Between the seventh and ninth centuries Irish monasticism
enjoyed its so-called 'golden age'. Irish monks did not 'save civilization', as
one best-selling book has argued, but they certainly preserved many classical
texts. The achievements of the Irish church in the early Christian period
were extraordinary, so that those nativist nationalists who, many centuries
later, remembered this as a time when Ireland was the 'literary centre of
Christendom' were not far off the mark.[10] Irish monasteries did a great deal
to protect Roman traditions of learning, as Roman power contracted. And,
as a consequence, the Irish church grew in wealth and prestige, with Irish
preachers, theologians, and biblical scholars doing much to lead movements
of evangelism and reform throughout western and central Europe.

This work developed as the Irish church faced unprecedented threats.
Among the most serious of these threats was the competition between
monastic federations. As the federations grew in power, these powerful
coalitions of institutions began to contend for resources and influence. The
stakes were high. Rivalries between federations could result in violence and
sometimes even in death. Much of this competition between monasteries

was caused by their lining up to support the ambitions of rival kings. This was one reason why violence was endemic in Irish society long before the arrival of the earliest Scandinavian pirates. These raiders began their campaign of terror in 795, when they destroyed a church that had been founded by Columba on an island described in the *Annals of Ulster* as Rechru—an island that has been variously identified as Rathlin, off the coast of county Antrim, or Lambay, off the coast of county Dublin. The pirates spoke an unfamiliar language, and their campaign of looting and enslaving was marked by horrific ferocity. For several generations, the Irish church found itself at the mercy of an enemy it did not understand. These raids intensified in the middle ninth century, and wrought devastation around the coasts and far inland along navigable rivers, even as the raiders began to compete with each other and to enlist Irish fighters in their cause. But local rulers fought back. Within a few decades, Ireland's monastic settlements took on a new and more determined aspect as their leaders responded to the crisis by constructing the round towers (described in Irish as bell towers) and high crosses that continue to mark the Irish landscape. But these violent interventions could not be effectively resisted, and over the following three centuries the Scandinavian pirates established permanent bases, assimilated into the religious culture of their new home, and found important roles in the economic and political life of the island, even as they colonized those remote locations in the far north of the Atlantic in which Irish hermits had made their home.[11] For Northmen, too, became Christians, and made their influence felt throughout the Irish world. By the 830s, they had begun to settle in the Hebrides, where they adapted to, and later adopted, the Gaelic language and Christian religion. Within a few decades, others had settled down in the *entrepôts* that they established in locations such as Dublin and Waterford, where they converted to Christianity, built the island's first urban centres, and began to make a significant contribution to political centralization, to the growing diversity of Irish cultural life, and to the material fabric of the Irish church, though the cult of Thor would survive in Dublin for at least a further century.[12] 'Vikings' represented an extraordinary threat to the security of the Irish church, but, upon their conversion, made important contributions to its structures.

A second intervention by external forces, several centuries later, would present a more fundamental challenge to the autonomy, stability, and overseas influence of the Irish church. In the eleventh and twelfth centuries, the English invasion and partial conquest changed at a fundamental level the structure and identity of Irish society, and complicated its relationship to its closest island neighbour.[13] Pope Gregory VII (1073–1085) had developed a programme for reform that, he hoped, would improve the moral standards of clergy and centralize ecclesiastical power in the person of the pope. In Ireland, under Hiberno-Scandinavian leadership, this programme of reform had advanced in fits and starts, and, while the bishops were never able fully to enforce clerical celibacy, the church did adopt European norms in most other aspects of its religious life.[14] It was the slow pace and uncertain achievements of this reform that justified the English invasion. The papal bull that warranted the conquest, *Laudabiliter* (1155), might have been forged, but it certainly represented the Irish as beyond the boundaries of Christendom, and encouraged Henry II—never the most pious of monarchs—to attempt what he regarded as their reconversion.[15] The circumstances in which he did so were not auspicious: Henry II set out to raise the spiritual tone of the Irish church shortly after murdering Thomas Becket, the archbishop of Canterbury. But the leaders of the colony that extended from the 'four obedient shires' throughout Ulster, Connacht, and much of Munster brought with them a determined commitment to the programme of Gregorian reform. In the aftermath of the English conquest, the structures of the Irish church were remodelled according to European norms, so that the existing system of governance that balanced the power of bishops and monastic institutions was undermined, with authority being placed more effectively in the hands of bishops, by whom the more advanced stages of the papal programme would be most effectively rolled out. In the later part of the twelfth century, the conquest pushed forward an agenda for change that had already shaped the Irish church, in what might be regarded as its Catholic reformation.[16]

Deeper cultural changes were also afoot. For several centuries, the Irish church had either managed to turn the island's cultural diversity into an asset, as in its extraordinary artistic achievements, or at least to manage the problems of cultural diversity, as in the sometimes rancorous relationships from which an Hiberno-Scandinavian religious culture eventually emerged, though until the beginning of the fourteenth century the 'assimilation' of Vikings into Irish society was neither unilateral nor complete.[17] But the invasion destabilized this situation, and introduced additional ethnic and political complications into Ireland's multi-cultural church. Although English power never extended beyond two-thirds of the island, and despite its eventual contraction in the fifteenth century, it succeeded in dividing the population of Ireland along ethnic, linguistic, and cultural lines, so that structurally significant tensions emerged between those individuals who were more closely aligned with the colony and others whose loyalties lay with the Gaelic population. Straddling these competing cultures, and with administrative structures that were never determined by the constantly shifting boundaries of English power, the church facilitated their integration, not least through the large numbers of Irish clergy that were recruited to work in the 'four obedient shires' after the demographic collapse of the Black Death. While the English made a distinct contribution to the formation of Christian Ireland, and provided the church with some of its best-known architectural monuments, from the now iconic monastic settlement at Tintern, county Wexford, to St Patrick's Cathedral in Dublin, their contribution was structurally damaging.[18] Adapting its material culture to cope with invasions, and melding these foreign influences into a hybrid but distinctive cultural style, the Irish church was developing in wealth, prestige, and power as its members divided in a bitter and enduring struggle for ethnic, linguistic, and cultural dominance.

Faced with these kinds of tensions, it is hardly surprising that many Irish Christians began to worry that the church was losing its focus, and showing more concern for its material than for its spiritual success. The new mendicant orders that arrived in Ireland in the early thirteenth century encouraged those who wished to see the church to return to its simpler, less institutional, origins. But the witness of these orders was truncated. The mendicant orders split largely along ethnic lines, with English and European members tending to remain in close proximity to the colony, while Irish-speaking friars worked in those western and northern parts of the island that were beyond that power's effective range, although by the end of the period Franciscan Observants had come to prefer to work with Irish friars inside the colony. Ministering in different ways to different kinds of people, friars and the regular clergy worked, in complex, competing, and sometimes violent relationships, to create a community of the faithful that, on the eve of the protestant reformation, was content with the teaching and practice of the church, and contributing generously to its upkeep.[19]

Of course, just as the Christian culture that permeated the island contained elements from elsewhere in Europe, so too it continued to preserve the heritage of the cultures that pre-dated it. If the church was never absolutely able to eradicate pre-Christian customs—or the memory of an older cosmology—it did work hard to find a space for these patterns of belief and behaviour. The habit of Irish Christians to combine sometimes competing cultural and religious influences became evident as the church adapted its administration—and even, occasionally, its practice—to local circumstances and needs. Whatever the achievements of the first few Christian centuries, Irish religion in the later medieval period was characterized by a mixture of orthodox theology and traditional practice, especially in relation to marriage practices, which in their flexibility pitted Irish custom against the law of the church.[20] In Gaelic regions, Brehon law allowed for informal contracting, concubinage, divorce, and remarriage. These practices were forbidden in those areas where canon law was more strictly observed. The effect was, at times, theologically ambiguous—but it worked. The Irish church was held together by its differences. At the end of the fifteenth century, there was no sign of religious discontent. The reformation that began before the invasion and accelerated in its aftermath consolidated the cultures of Christian Ireland.

I

None of this success was obvious in the 790s, when Scandinavian pirates launched brutal and remorseless attacks on isolated and defenceless monasteries, shattering the confidence of the Irish church and plunging it into the most horrific crisis in its three-and-a-half centuries of history. The raids represented the first great disruption of the Irish church.[21] Not everybody was astonished by this turn of events: in 793, those who paid attention to portents knew that something dreadful was in the air. The Anglo-Saxon Chronicle reported 'dreadful forewarnings over the land of the Northumbrians, terrifying the people most woefully'—portents that included 'great sheets of light rushing through the air, and whirlwinds, and fiery dragons flying across the firmament'. And then, as if unleashed by the violence of this storm, from across the North Sea there descended upon the monastery that monks from Iona had established on Lindisfarne, on the coast of Northumbria, boatloads of 'heathen men, who made lamentable havoc … by rapine and slaughter'.[22] This raid destroyed far more than the confidence of the monks. It was followed by further attacks on the eastern coasts of Northumbria, and a campaign of terror that extended through Shetland, Orkney, and the Hebrides, a wave of destruction that came ever closer to the centres of the Irish Christian world. In 795, Scandinavian pirates trashed the foundation at Iona. Pirates returned to Iona in 802, when they burned the abbey, and in 806, when they killed sixty-eight monks. These attacks on the headquarters of Columba's federation—as upon other monastic institutions—brought a sudden halt to the expansion of Christian influence along the northern and western sea lanes. As travel by sea became increasingly dangerous—including travel to Iona and other major ecclesiastical settlements—Irish monks turned their attention to the continent to cultivate spiritual fruit elsewhere.[23]

To modern readers, these pirates are better known as 'Vikings'. That term was not used in the early medieval period, except occasionally as a personal name, and it does rather unhelpfully put all the Scandinavian pirates into a single descriptive and analytical category. In fact there were significant differences among the pirates—differences in strategies and goals, differences in the locations from which they had set sail, and differences in their attitudes to the culture and religion of the island upon which they had descended. There was no binary distinction between Vikings and Gaels, not least because there was no single Viking identity. Scandinavian pirates tended to be young men—mostly in their later teens and twenties—but there their similarities ceased.[24] The earliest pirates came from a very specific location in south-west Norway.[25] Their strategies developed over time. There were only a handful of Viking attacks before 820, according to the Annals of Ulster, and these early incursions were met with determined resistance by the rulers of Gaelic society.[26] But Viking activity stepped up after 833, when they began to make significant raids elsewhere. By 837, Viking ships had begun to sail up the major rivers to hit targets in the midlands.[27] They began to operate overland. Their strategy may have taken advantage of the major roads—the *slige Midluachra* that connected Tara to Navan fort, county Armagh; the *slige Cualann* that connected Tara to Dublin; the *slige Asail* that led to Lough Owel, county Westmeath; the *slige Dála* that headed into county Kilkenny; and the *silge Mór* that provided access to the regions beyond the Shannon.[28] By the mid-800s, the pirates had begun to settle down. Vikings developed settlements in such locations as Dublin (841), Limerick (845), and Waterford (860), which became centres for trading and raiding. Dublin, in particular, became a major slave-trading port, dealing in human lives until the twelfth century.[29] Of course, this move to establish land-based trading posts made the Viking colonial project vulnerable to organized resistance.[30] This may explain why Vikings based in Ireland began to raid elsewhere: in 844, for example, a Moorish embassy travelled to

Ireland to negotiate with a Norse court, after Dublin Vikings launched an attack on Seville.[31]

Viking ambitions were most effectively thwarted by other Vikings. In the mid-ninth century, a second wave of pirates sailed to Ireland from Denmark.[32] In 851, these Danish pirates attacked the Norwegian stronghold of Dublin, a victory that was replicated at sea in an extraordinary three-day naval battle in Carlingford Lough in 853.[33] As they responded to this heightened competition for resources and power, some Viking leaders made alliances with Irish kings.[34] This may explain why Viking warbands were joined, from time to time, by local recruits—though whether these Irishmen were volunteers or enslaved soldiers is now impossible to say.[35] *Quid pro quo*, some Irish kings adopted Viking technology, learning no doubt from the manufacture of warships like that discovered in Roskilde fjord, Denmark, which was constructed from Irish timber in the eleventh century.[36]

Whatever their differences, Vikings agreed that nothing in Ireland was sacred. In 825, for example, in yet another raid on Iona, pirates pressured the abbot, Blathmac, to lead them to the hidden shrine of Columba. When he would not, they slaughtered him on the altar.[37] In 832, pirates attacked the most important Christian centre in Ireland, Armagh, three times in a single month.[38] In 863, pirates looted the prehistoric passage tombs at Newgrange, Knowth, and Dowth.[39] It didn't matter where their booty came from, or what religious significance it might have represented—the pirates were searching for treasure.

Despite their reputation, the most central preoccupation of these marauding Northmen was, in fact, trade. For all of their notorious barbarity, the Scandinavians took part in a complex international economy, in which they exported such resources as furs and slaves in return for silver from the Islamic world, which they used to purchase wine and weapons from southern Europe. In the later eighth century, these trading networks were so badly affected by political and financial crises that the Scandinavian economy had to source replacement commodities elsewhere.[40] The British and Irish monasteries were an ideal target, for these foundations had become important, accessible, and largely undefended repositories of wealth. Before the arrival of the Vikings, there was no circulating coinage in Ireland. Wealth was reckoned by the ownership of cattle, or sometimes slaves: in this economy, female slaves came to represent a fixed unit of value.[41] But wealth was still bound up in high-value artefacts. Faced with the need for storage of these items, monasteries had expanded their mission to provide basic banking facilities, while maintaining stores of the liturgical artefacts that Vikings must have regarded as cumbersome but attractive and transportable luxury goods. Of course, these pirates were not collecting ecclesiastical artefacts for their own sake. They were interested in manufacturing coinage to resource their own habits of international trade. But large high-value items that they discovered in Irish monasteries were not useful for this purpose. The pirates needed smaller units of value, and so cut up these larger artefacts into smaller pieces, hundreds of which have been uncovered.[42] We have no idea how many of the treasures of the medieval church were clipped into rudimentary tokens. Even the scale of the loss cannot be recovered.

In destroying these items of piety and heritage, Scandinavian pirates were attacking the history of the Irish church while undermining its most important institutions. Faced with this unprecedented violence, monastic federations considered whether they might be depending upon vulnerable lines of supply. Some institutions began to return their most sacred relics and most precious artefacts to safer locations on the mainland, while continuing to staff those institutions where, their serving monks must have realized, future raids would almost certainly take place. So, while monks continued to serve on Iona, where they rebuilt the monastery in 807, their *confrères* in the Columban federation rebuilt the abbey at Kells, county Meath, constructing its principal buildings between 807 and 814, where later in the century they would store artefacts that had been returned from Iona for safekeeping, including perhaps the extraordinary illustrated manuscript that became known as the Book of Kells. But the staggering violence of the Viking raids could not so easily be escaped. The abbey at Kells was attacked repeatedly in the following century—although, when its most famous book went briefly missing, it was returned with the loss of only a handful of pages. Kells was raided by Vikings in 920, who returned to enslave several thousand people from the surrounding area in 951. And, in further raids on the abbey, in 969 and 970, Vikings were joined by Irish opportunists, for whom the abbey no longer represented any kind of inviolable sacred space.[43]

Not even Irish churchmen consistently observed the inviolability of sacred space. Throughout this period, tensions between monasteries could result in violence and destruction similar to that delivered by rapacious Scandinavians. In fact, as one historian has noticed, 'before, during, and after the Viking period, more churches were plundered and burned and more clerics were killed by the Irish than by the Norse'.[44] Sometimes the tensions

Figure 5. Clonmacnoise monastery

between monasteries were political, as when foundations lined up with individual kings in their struggles against their rivals. In 764, for example, the monks of Clonmacnoise took part in a battle against the monks of Durrow, in which 200 men from the latter foundation were killed. Sometimes the tensions between monasteries were theological. Fedelmid, for example, was king of Cashel, an abbot, and champion of a reform movement called the *Céli Dé*.[45] In 833, frustrated that the monks at Clonmacnoise had refused to adopt stricter rules about prayer, Sunday observance, and relations between the sexes, he torched the monastery, and executed its members. His attack came only two years before an attack by Vikings wrought similar destruction.[46] With these kinds of tensions between institutions, and under pressure from Viking raids, the Irish church convened fewer synods in the ninth and tenth centuries. There were, after all, as Fedelmid had discovered, more effective ways to enforce religious discipline.

As the violence between Irish monks continued, the Scandinavian pirates appeared to be settling down. Their centres for raiding and trading became a normalized component of Irish life, and evolved into medieval towns.[47]

The area around Dublin, for example, came to be known by the Irish as Fíne Gall, the 'kindred of the foreigners'—a descriptor retained today in the name of the local county council.[48] Scandinavian centres were established throughout (and beyond) the sphere of Irish influence, in the Hebrides, south-west Scotland, north-west England, the Isle of Man, and Wales.[49] As these economic links suggest, Norse became an important commercial language, which explains why those Vikings who settled in Ireland did not immediately discard it in favour of the local vernacular. But these trading centres allowed Vikings to assimilate into the Irish world. Vikings never made in Ireland the impact upon place-names that they made in western Scotland—with the exception of sites such as Dublin, hardly any place-names in Ireland survive from the period of Viking power.[50] And similar trends towards assimilation can be traced in the changing names of the leaders of Viking society. By the end of the tenth century, lists of Irish Viking rulers include Gaelic names alongside Norse, a cultural combination that created in some parts of the island a 'distinctive Hiberno-Norse identity', which suggests the extent to which a distinctive Scandinavian identity was being diluted.[51]

Of course, there was nothing inevitable about this process of social change, and the assimilation of the Vikings was never uncontested, for the Irish knew how to resist. In fact, in the early tenth century, as a result of unprecedented coordinated action on the part of native rulers, the Scandinavian pirates were very nearly driven out of Ireland. In 902, the rulers of Viking Dublin were expelled, and were compelled to re-group in England.[52] They reasserted their presence in 914, when around 100 long-boats and 4,000 soldiers landed in Waterford, representing the 'largest build-up of Viking military power in Ireland during the ninth and tenth centuries'.[53] This conflict had a devastating effect on Irish political and military power, and 'Viking warlords' re-conquered their former territories by 919.[54] Their presence became incontestable as the Dublin fleet became 'one of the most formidable war machines in the Irish Sea area', and 'Hiberno-Scandinavian power' reached its 'zenith'.[55]

But military dominance did not equate to cultural power. One consequence of their assimilation into local culture was that Vikings became more aware of the content and character of Irish religion. They were certainly aware of its obligations, which they could use to their own advantage. On 10 November 921, for example, a force of Dublin Vikings attacked Armagh, almost certainly in the knowledge that the monks would be busy preparing for the feast of St Martin on the following day.[56] But some Vikings found the Irish faith attractive. There is little evidence in Irish sources for Viking conversions, but these certainly took place.[57] This process of religious change was, of course, gradual. Some individuals appear to have honoured both Viking and Christian deities. In Dublin, individuals were buried with Christian symbols, such as a cross, as well as symbols of Scandinavian religion, such as a miniature Thor's hammer.[58] Similarly, Christian commitment could be marked in both cultural styles: a church in Killaloe, county Clare, preserves inscriptions commemorating the same individual in both runic and *ogham* forms.[59] But some conversions were obvious and unambiguous. In his old age, Amlaíb (Olaf) Cuarán, a Viking king of Dublin, retired to Iona, where, in 981, he died.[60]

This context of religious change helps us understand why Ireland's Viking age did not end at the Battle of Clontarf, in 1014, as historians have often assumed. In popular culture, this action is sometimes represented as the Irish equivalent of the Battle of Stamford Bridge, in which the age of the Vikings was brought to a symbolic end. But that is not what happened at Clontarf. On the one hand, this was not a battle between native and invading armies: Irishmen and descendants of the Scandinavian pirates fought on both sides of the conflict. The result is better understood as the defeat of the Uí Néill dynasty, with the end of their efforts to centralize royal power, and the victory of the Dál Cais, a rival dynasty from Munster, who became dominant under the leadership of Brian Bórama (better known as Brian Boru), who at Clontarf came close to achieving his aspirations to become the undisputed high king of Ireland.[61] Neither did Clontarf represent the end of Viking influence on the island: Scandinavian communities continued to inhabit such locations as Dublin and Waterford, where they continued to move towards Christian religion and native ways. Some even became ambassadors for the Irish faith. Viking traders may have promoted in England the distinctively Irish cult of St Brigid.[62] Viking kings may have gone on pilgrimage to Jerusalem.[63] But, like all conversions, this process took time. Sitriuc 'Silkbeard', who followed Amlaíb (Olaf) Cuarán as king of Dublin, represented these changing religious commitments.[64] In 969, while still a young man and likely still a pagan, he took part in a raid on the abbey at Kells. After his mid-life conversion to Christianity, and his successful defence of Dublin on Good Friday 1014, he went on a long pilgrimage to Rome, at the head of a substantial party of the leaders of Irish society, returning in 1028 with an understanding of the benefits of Gregorian reform, and an

ambition to establish his city as the centre of Christian piety by setting up a
diocese, appointing its first bishop, and providing for the building of an
extraordinary new building—Christ Church cathedral.[65] Sitriuc may have
done more than anyone to promote the idea of Dublin as the centre of
Christian culture.[66] But he was still capable of atrocity against his co-religionists. In 1031, he 'plundered the church of Ardbraccan in the kingdom of
Meath; 200 people were burned to death in the stone church; 200 more
were taken prisoner; and herds of cattle were driven off'.[67]

Nevertheless, the arrival of the Vikings, at the end of the eighth century,
drew Ireland into extensive international networks. Over the following 300
years, the distinction between Gaels and Scandinavian settlers broke down,
as competing factions came to realize their common objectives. Sitriuc led
the way in transforming the fabric and institutions of the Irish church and
Irish Christians became more aware of their past. In the twelfth century, as
part of a broader Gaelic resurgence, monks prepared a *Book of invasions*,
which set out a chronology of the island's pre-history, and sought to establish correspondence between events in Ireland and the biblical records,
together with a history of the peoples who had migrated to its shores.[68]
Gaels remained sure of themselves, and uncertain of all others, regarding the
Vikings as foreigners (*gaill*) until the twelfth century.[69] But the church that
they served grew in strength. More than 5,000 church buildings were constructed before the end of the twelfth century.[70] For all of their cultural
differences, the Irish and the descendants of the Vikings were being brought
together in the structures of a common faith. That is why, when the English
invaded, they encountered a society that was diverse in its cultures but
largely united in its religious ideals.[71] After 1169, the invasion would demonstrate that the real division in Irish culture was not between resentful
natives and rapacious Scandinavians, but between the hybrid culture of the
Irish and the political and religious aspirations of the English who were
determined to suppress it.

II

The invasion was the culmination of a long campaign to reorganize the
Irish church. This drive for reform took place in the immediate aftermath
of the Great Schism (1054), when, after several centuries of growing theological tensions, the churches of the Greek east and the Latin west broke

communion with each other, and divided the Christian world between them. Greek theologians contested the claim of the bishop of Rome to have jurisdiction over all churches, and argued against other elements of Roman theology, such as the proposition in Trinitarian theology that the Holy Spirit proceeded from both the Father and the Son. In the immediate aftermath of the division of Christendom, the Roman hierarchy set about enforcing its authority within those churches that, at least in theory, accepted its jurisdiction. And so, from the middle of the eleventh century, and especially under the leadership of Pope Gregory VII (1073–1085), the Roman hierarchy pushed for root-and-branch reforms that promoted the authority of the pope over secular rulers, that insisted upon changes in the government of the church, and introduced new regulations for priests, while heightening the demand for celibacy that enforced a sharper division between clergy and laity.[72] These reformers had no time for the traditional governance structures of the Irish church, in which bishops and abbots sat side-by-side with clerically educated kings in synods.[73] Instead, Gregorian reformers located authority more emphatically within the episcopacy.[74] The reforms encouraged improvements in the material fabric of church buildings, some of which were inscribed with the new ideas: sculpture that survives from this period emphasizes a higher view of episcopal authority than had previously been the norm, for example.[75] Of course, argued the advocates of reform, this effort was not an attempt to reshape the church according to new ideals, but to insist that older ideals finally be realized.[76] Although there is 'less material surviving for the Irish church from the twelfth century than from the seventh and eighth centuries', it is clear that this was a period of significant 'institutional restructuring and religious renewal associated with a reform movement that was a regional manifestation of a much wider European phenomenon'.[77] Those who led in this movement of reform were determined to pull the Irish church closer to European norms.

At least in the opinion of its advocates, if not always in the estimation of historians, reform was certainly badly needed.[78] The Irish church did not compare well with the Gregorian ideals. In 1074, Lanfranc (c. 1010–1089), archbishop of Canterbury, who claimed responsibility for the oversight of the Irish church, wrote to Tairdelbach Ua Briain (1009–1086), the high king of Ireland, to complain about religious norms and sexual mores in the Irish church:

> in your kingdom a man abandons at his own discretion and without any grounds in canon law the wife who is lawfully married to him...Bishops are

consecrated by a single bishop; many are ordained to villages or small towns; infants are baptized without the use of consecrated chrism; holy orders are conferred by bishops for money.[79]

Two years later, Gregory himself wrote to this 'illustrious king of Ireland', exhorting his subjects to 'keep and love the catholic peace of the church'— in other words, to fall into line with his agenda for reform.[80] Lanfranc's criticisms were reiterated by Anselm (1033–1109), his successor as archbishop of Canterbury, who worried that the Irish church had too many bishops, so that almost every church had a bishop of its own.[81] This situation had not always been perceived as a problem. The Irish practice was, of course, a good reflection of the organization of the primitive church, according to patristic sources, in which single bishops led individual congregations, though some distance from the situation described in the New Testament, in which multiple bishops ministered within a single congregation.[82] But the Gregorian ideals were clear. Reformers sought to streamline the Irish church's organization under the jurisdiction of the papacy, to standardize its life and work in conformity to European norms.

This programme for reform was rolled out at the synods that, after the disruption that had been caused by Viking raids, met with increasing frequency through the twelfth century. Increasingly aware of European norms, Irish reformers came to see the 'organisation of their own church as decadent and eccentric, and in the early twelfth century they proposed an orthodox diocesan structure with metropolitan bishops and a primate'.[83] The details of this reorganization were hammered out at the Synod of Ráith Bressail (1111), which reduced the number of bishops in the Irish church, established diocesan structures, and created two archdioceses, in Armagh and Cashel.[84] This structure of governance was expanded at the Synod of Kells (1152): the 9,000 individuals who attended this synod agreed to recognize two more archdioceses, in Dublin and Tuam.[85] In the first half of the twelfth century, this division of the Irish church into two and then four archdioceses reflected the political divisions that were emerging between two and then four major provincial kingships: this organizational structure showed how ecclesiology came downstream from politics, and suggests that church leaders were still playing an important part in validating the structures of secular leadership.[86] But the reformers were as interested in pastoral care in localities as they were in trends in high politics, for it was under their auspices that the church began to mark out the parish structure that endures to the present day. These 2,500 territorial divisions were established initially for purposes of collecting tithes, and soon gained broader functions.[87] The structure was familiar across much of Europe. Throughout the twelfth century, the decisions of these synods, and others like them, made Ireland more recognizably Catholic.

The vision for this programme of reform was largely developed by Malachy (1094–1148), archbishop of Armagh. Malachy was one of the most important medieval churchmen. He was a 'man of steely ambition and unquestioning self-confidence', who could 'dismiss the leadership of powerful churches, reject all forms of Irish monasticism, transfer enormous assets from one institution to another, reshape the whole of the Irish church, and if possible society at large'. He was 'charismatic, political, persuasive, conciliatory, coercive, manipulative, subtle and disingenuous', and was prepared to 'dissimulate, and if necessary bully'.[88] Concerned by state of the Irish church, Malachy set out to replace the traditional monastic orders with newer varieties from the continent.[89] Born in Armagh, where he began his clerical career, Máel-Máedóc Ua Morgair chose the Latin name Malachy in a gesture towards the last of the Old Testament prophets, who had offered similar kinds of censure to the priests of his day.[90] Becoming abbot of Bangor, Malachy rebuilt the monastery, which Vikings had destroyed. Becoming the bishop of Down and Connor, he embedded the decisions of the Synod of Ráith Bressail. Becoming archbishop of Armagh, in the early 1130s, he and those who supported his vision of reform promoted the use of the Roman liturgy, required priests to carry out baptisms by triple immersion, pushed for stricter observance of Sunday, debated whether women should cover their heads in worship, and emphasized the importance of confirmation and confession.[91] In his role as primate, Malachy retained some sympathy for the distinctive traditions of the Irish church: he supported the co-location of male and female foundations, as at Termonfeckin, county Louth, for example, a practice that soon fell into disfavour.[92] But he campaigned against other native traditions, including the hereditary succession of monastic titles, and the private ownership of church estate.[93] Malachy's insistence on the old ideal of clerical celibacy was not likely to have been enthusiastically adopted, not least because it would have disrupted the family lives of those priests who entered the priesthood later in life, though happily he did not suffer the fate of Abbot of Fleury (d. 1002), who was murdered by the Gascon monks whom he had hoped to convert to the practice.[94] Malachy also sought to reform marriage customs among the laity.[95] These reforms were

based upon the practices that he had witnessed in his travels on the continent. Malachy had completed a pilgrimage to Rome, during which journey
he had become a friend of Bernard of Clairvaux, who inspired his vision of
reform, and wrote Malachy's biography, the most detailed account of the life
of any medieval bishop.[96] It was through Malachy's contacts with Bernard
that the Cistercian order arrived in Ireland. The Irish primate was evidently
more impressed by the discipline of Bernard's *confrères* than he was by that
of the foundations he knew at home. And so, under Malachy's auspices, the
first Cistercian community was founded in Ireland in 1142, with the first
Cistercian monastery, Mellifont Abbey, being consecrated in 1157—a building of almost impossible scale, and possibly the largest church to be built in
Ireland to that date, the French style of which prompted complaints from
those who might have preferred a more traditional Irish construction.[97] In
Bernard's hagiography, Malachy's life was given over to the promotion of
reform, and the Irish church was identified as its ideal subject: in highlighting the desperate need for the reform project that he represented, this biography, which was read across Europe, 'made Malachy a saint but did his
country grave wrong'.[98] It is ironic that Malachy, who did most to identify
the Irish church as backward and compromised, would become the first of
its members to be canonized (1190).

Of course, conditions within the Irish foundations were not as backward
as the reformers wished to believe. Since their foundation, the Irish monasteries had sustained a vigorous intellectual culture, and continued to promote educational excellence. The trivium and quadrivium were being
taught at Glendalough, in a community that sustained broad economic as
well as pastoral functions, providing local scholars and those who travelled
to learn alongside them with the intellectual tools with which to engage
with theology, philosophy, classical literature, mathematics, science, and
much else besides.[99] The scholarship that this education supported could be
of very high quality. Monks worked hard to establish how best to read the
biblical text, while paying attention to progressive revelation in the history
of redemption: the brethren in Glendalough, county Wicklow, and Killeshin,
county Laois, divided the structure of history into six dispensations, and
read different parts of scripture in that light.[100] Alongside these developments in biblical theology, monks continued to preserve key texts from the
ancient world, so that Irish adaptations of classical myths were among
the earliest in Europe.[101] These adaptations could be artful and thoughtful:
one copy of Boethius's *Consolation of philosophy*, which survives in Irish

miniscule hand, includes 5,000 interpretive glosses, over two dozen of them in Irish.[102] Monks continued to preserve their native literary heritage. During the period of reform, monks at Clonmacnoise copied out *Lebor na hUidre* ('The book of the dun cow'), which is one of the earliest sources for the Iron Age stories that they represented as surviving the coming of Christianity, with one scribe wondering, in a gloss to the text, whether its content should be classified as history or as fable.[103] His question was a good one—modern scholarship tends to see these stories as medieval fictions, albeit drawing upon existing material, rather than as a survivals from the pre-Christian past, although there are some startling correlations between these reconstructed sagas and the ancient world they represent.[104] Irish monks delighted in stories of native saints, and experimented with diffuse styles that combined brief biographical narratives with sometimes heavily stylized miracle stories.[105] And Irish theologians were leading in some of the doctrinal innovations that would do so much to mark later medieval piety. In the twelfth century, the so-called 'birth of purgatory' and the increasing popularity of belief in this intermediate state was made possible by the discovery of an entrance into another world in county Donegal (where else could it be?)—much like those entrances to other worlds that had been features of pre-Christian cosmology.[106] What made this discovery of an entrance to purgatory so striking was that it came in advance of the church's official confirmation of purgatory's existence, a question that was proclaimed at the Second Council of Lyon (1272). However bleak and forbidding, the site at Lough Derg became internationally famous, attracting pilgrims from as far away as Hungary, who travelled to the north-west of Ireland as part of a grand tour of sacred sites that could take many years to complete.[107] Of course, the discovery of this entrance into purgatory appeared to answer questions that had been haunting Irish Christians since the island's conversion: could Christians become unfit for heaven, and, if so, could anything be done to help them win salvation? In the hands of the unscrupulous, the doctrine offered an opportunity to profit from the worries of the faithful. The problem of opportunism was real. Even high-ranking churchmen became concerned that the doctrine was being abused. In 1497, Pope Alexander VI shut down the Lough Derg pilgrimage centre, worried that the wonder was a trick.[108] But the site continued to draw crowds. By the early nineteenth century, it was being attended by up to 15,000 pilgrims each year.[109]

The Gregorian reformation of the Irish church transformed its organization, and brought it more closely into alignment with European norms.

Its achievements were, in many respects, impressive. By 1230, for example, the Irish church had established around 200 monastic foundations and around forty more foundations for nuns.[110] An impressive building programme was underway, showing the influence of the turn to Gothic style, which some Irish churchmen found controversial.[111] The new English administration rebuilt Christ Church in stone in the 1180s. In 1191, St Patrick's in Dublin was recognized as a collegiate church, and eventually became Dublin's second cathedral, being rebuilt in stone sometime in the thirteenth century.[112] With its construction, Dublin became a city with two cathedrals—a situation that was almost unique in Christendom and that would provoke some bitter personal rivalries in the decades that followed.[113] These building projects were international efforts. Construction workers were brought in from south-east England to contribute to the architectural reform.[114] Similar kinds of renewal went on in other institutions. The Irish church abandoned the eccentricities of its traditional monastic culture, and tightened up on rules around clerical celibacy. But not everyone was convinced by the speed or direction of travel.[115]

This kind of foreign intervention looked more likely after 1155, when Pope Adrian IV (c. 1100–1159) tasked Henry II with the reformation of the Irish church, and gave him authority over the island in order to do so. No original copy of the decree of *Laudabiliter* (1155) has survived—leading to some speculation that it might have been a fiction of the invasion's propaganda.[116] The invasion that it was used to justify determined the shape of the Irish church, writing off the island's Christian history and dismissing the orthodoxy and good morals of its church while fomenting ethnic divisions and complicating relationships with the English church and crown. The soldiers taking part in the 'English invasion' were, of course, from Wales, only one day sailing from the east coast of Ireland, and they arrived at the request of an Irish ruler, with the support of a Plantagenet king, the permission of the pope, and as the harbinger of a larger force that would be drawn from across the Angevin empire.[117]

The opportunity for Henry II to realize the ambition of *Laudabiliter* began in 1166, when Diarmait Mac Murchada, king of Leinster, was ejected from his throne during his long confrontation with the high king, Ruaidrí Ua Conchobair.[118] Diarmait Mac Murchada appealed for help to Henry II, the first Plantagenet ruler, whose 'Angevin empire' included all of England and Wales and almost all of France. In response to this call for help, in 1169, a party of Anglo-Norman lords from the Welsh marches landed on the coast of Wexford, to help Diarmait reclaim his former territories. In summer 1170, these mercenaries were joined by Richard FitzGilbert de Clare, earl of Pembroke, better known in Irish history as 'Strongbow'. He seized control of the Viking towns of Dublin, Wexford, and Waterford, successfully repelled Ruaidrí Ua Conchobair's efforts to resist his intrusions, and married Diarmait's daughter, Aoife, to became heir of the kingdom of Leinster and occupant of its throne after Diarmait's death in 1171.

Henry, of course, could not permit any of his subjects to become kings in their own right, and Strongbow's accession prompted him to travel to Ireland to require the loyalty of his nobles. In October 1171, he landed in Waterford, and spent several months on the island in an effort to bring some of his most powerful lords to heel. Henry was not interested in conquering Ireland, which was a distraction from his real territorial ambitions on the continent. Instead, his policy was to intervene in Ireland much as he had intervened in Wales, not to establish complete control, but to pacify and manage a culturally complex borderland. In this respect, the invasion of Ireland was more like the Norman invasion of Wales than the Norman invasion of England—it remained incomplete and provisional, benefiting from occasional opportunities for growth, but suffering from slow and almost inevitable decline.[119] Henry's warrant for invasion was a papal bull, of dubious provenance, that framed his intervention in terms of re-establishing the orthodoxy of the Irish church. Some fifteen years after the bull was issued, but only months after his murder of Thomas Becket, the archbishop of Canterbury, Henry accepted the responsibility of remodelling the Irish church. As conflict between the Irish and the English continued, church leaders convened at the Synod of Cashel (1172), where they pushed to advance the structural reform of the Irish church, in a new effort to achieve Gregorian ideals.[120] Their arguments were clearly articulated: a document prepared for discussion at synod illustrated the structures of the church as a pyramid, with power flowing down from the pope to priests in parishes and to abbots in monasteries.[121] In other words, synod delegates agreed, the structure of the church should correspond to that of Henry's complicated multiple kingdom. Adopting a parallel governmental structure, the Irish church was being incorporated into a spiritual empire.

This imperial vision was more successful in the church than in Irish society. While the reorganization of the church continued, so too did the social problems that it was supposed to address—or so the invasion propagandists claimed. Gerald of Wales visited Ireland from the 1180s. Like advocates of reform elsewhere in Europe, he may have exaggerated the poor condition of the Irish church: he condemned its 'filthy people, wallowing in vice', and suggested that the Irish were among those least instructed in the faith.[122] He was not an unbiased observer—he acted as chief apologist for the invasion, which he justified as an attempt to address the chaos and incivility of Irish life, and his *Expugnatio Hibernica* is the only early source for the *Laudabiliter* decree that warranted the invasion.[123] Gerald exaggerated the problems in the Irish church in an effort to authorize the English intervention. The new rulers certainly made an impact on Irish life. They built on its institutions, sometimes literally, as when English castles were constructed on top of existing ringforts.[124] But they also changed some of these institutions. They established Ireland as a 'lordship', a constitutional status that endured until the island became a kingdom under Henry VIII (1541). Those Gaelic rulers who had styled themselves as kings were forced to adopt a new identity as Anglo-Norman lords.[125] To bring Ireland closer to English habits of power, colonial administrators began the process of 'shiring' that introduced the county structures that endure to the present day. They set out to normalize English common law, doing what they could to undermine the Brehon system, which had warranted the marital flexibilities that the reformers considered to be irregularities, and proclaimed the Irish Magna Carta in 1217, without extending its provisions to local people.[126]

The effect of this ruling was that Ireland, under the English, became two nations.[127] The invasion effectively set up a system of 'apartheid'.[128] As the colony settled down, after the initial period of conquest, its administration distinguished between colonists, who were granted full legal rights; the Ostmen (as the Hiberno-Scandinavians were now described), who were given some legal rights, but whose urban centres in Dublin, Wexford, Waterford, Cork, and Limerick were effectively subjugated, and who were moved into designated areas such as Ostmantown, now known as Oxmantown, in which they seem to have gradually assimilated into local populations; and, outside the bounds of common law, and often outside the colony, the Irish.[129] Those 'areas of Ireland that were ethnically English remained politically and culturally quite separate from those that were ethnically Gaelic'.[130] English common law did not apply to the vast majority of Gaelic natives, who consequently lacked any ability to defend themselves or their rights in the English courts.[131] These discriminatory practices reflected the deep-seated paranoia of colonial authorities, for whom Irish culture was so weak that it could be ridiculed while being so strong that it had to be destroyed. Naturally, these authorities constantly worried about miscegenation. Much later, in 1366, the Statutes of Kilkenny were enacted in order to keep the two nations apart. English people were forbidden from mercantile or sexual alliances with the Irish and from learning the Irish language, while Irish ecclesiastics were kept out of clerical positions within the colony.[132] But the Statutes of Kilkenny failed. English and Irish individuals did marry one another. Settlers did adopt Irish language and culture, just as members of leading Irish families were Anglicized.[133] Some settlers took on Gaelic titles.[134] And this undermining of the law may have been enabled by leaders in the church, as the historian of medieval Ireland Donnchadh Ó Corráin suggested: 'the cultural gaelicisation of the English colonists…was the work of the traditional churchmen'.[135]

Unfortunately many aspects of the experience of the Irish under Anglo-Norman rule have yet to be uncovered.[136] While a great deal of work has reconstructed patterns of life and work in the colony, the experience of the Irish in the twelfth, thirteenth, and fourteenth centuries has been 'poorly served by scholarship'.[137] This is particularly unfortunate in that this period witnessed a powerful Gaelic resurgence.[138] After three centuries of growth, the territory of the lordship had begun to contract into the four obedient shires. By 1500, the domain of English power 'had shrunk to an area extending roughly 50 miles north and 30 miles inland from Dublin', within which was established the fortified redoubt that became known as the Pale.[139] But the structures of the church remained unchanged, and religious leaders had to exercise their ministry across changing political boundaries. The colony was under threat—and so too was the integrity of the reformation that it had been established to support.

III

The agenda for Gregorian reform was nothing if not determined. One of its most important elements was the introduction into Ireland of new monastic orders. The most controversial of these orders were, of course, those that were connected with the crusades.[140] While Irish involvement in the crusades was small, it was not insignificant.[141] The Knights Templar were set up in the aftermath of the first crusade (1096–1099), when, under the patronage of Bernard of Clairvaux, the biographer of Malachy who was also an advocate for Gregorian reform and Christian military intervention in the Levant, they were given the task of protecting pilgrims in their journeys through the middle east. As conflict in the region continued, the role of the Templars expanded to include the provision of cross-border banking facilities and military involvement. In the same period, the Knights Hospitaller were formed to provide basic healthcare for pilgrims, but quickly developed a military capacity that compared with that of the Templars. Both orders arrived in Ireland in the immediate aftermath of the invasion, when between 1180 and 1200 they acquired a large amount of property, mostly in the south-east, and remained closely connected with the crown.[142] The knights were not especially interested in serving within the Irish church, and mostly kept to themselves. Their intention in Ireland was to build up a property portfolio that they might use to finance their crusades.[143]

As might be expected, given their close connection to the crown, those Templars and Hospitallers that were recruited in Ireland were English rather than Irish.[144] Nevertheless, there is some evidence that the knights appreciated the distinctive traditions of the Irish church. By the middle of the thirteenth century, for example, a church in Acre, in the crusaders' kingdom of Jerusalem, had been dedicated to St Brigid.[145] But the knights lacked any appreciation of the finer qualities of Gaelic life, and occasionally took part in military action against the Irish, seeking to expand the power of the colony.[146] Of course, for reasons that historians and conspiracy theorists still dispute, in the early fourteenth century the Templars fell out of favour with secular and spiritual lords. As part of a wider European suppression of the order, the Irish Templars were arrested on heresy charges in 1308, and were finally suppressed in 1311, when Pope Clement passed their property to the Hospitallers, and when Edward II, king of England, took the opportunity to claim much of their wealth, just as Henry VIII would do with the remaining monasteries in the early years of protestant reform.[147] But the knights' opposition to the native Irish was continued by other parties. Some advocates of the crusades were inspired to attempt something similar in Ireland. In the late 1320s or early 1330s, authorities in Ireland wrote to Pope John XXII, complaining that the Gaelic population included some who 'claimed that Mary the Lord's Mother was a whore, denied the resurrection of the dead, denied the king of England's right to rule Ireland and criticized papal policy', and asked that he might authorize a crusade. He did not—but the Hospitallers continued to attack the Irish regardless.[148] Their violence satisfied crown strategy. In 1360, King Edward III observed that, in addition to their crusading activities in the middle east, the Hospitallers attacked 'our Irish enemies, who daily maintain war upon our liege people'.[149]

The mendicant orders, who arrived in 1224, made a more positive contribution to Irish life.[150] The friars, who lived among the people, and depended for their maintenance upon begging, brought about a 'revolution' in popular piety.[151] The development of the mendicant orders had been encouraged by the papacy as a strategic contribution to the agenda for renewal that was rolled out after the Fourth Lateran Council (1215).[152] For many centuries, Irish monasteries had encouraged the faithful to withdraw from the world, in order the better to serve it, and their arguments led to the foundation of over four hundred monasteries and convents.[153] The friars turned this logic on its head. They aimed to improve the world by evangelizing it, and so focused on preaching in the most established urban centres while exemplifying a more rugged and perhaps more authentic spirituality than that on offer within the other institutions of the church. The arrival of the first Dominicans was followed soon after by that of the first Franciscans.[154] These orders made very rapid early growth. This was a period of relative prosperity within the colony, and patrons of the new orders supplied the orders with resources that made possible the construction of religious houses. It was not difficult to patronize friars—after all, it did not cost much to subvent the expenses of those who intended to beg for a living. While large monastic institutions required considerable estates, friars could live fairly simply. But this commitment to simplicity, poverty, and begging for alms discouraged friars from going too far away from dependable sources of supply. For the first two centuries of their existence, friars proved reluctant to move into Gaelic regions, where small and scattered populations, and less stable financial resources, made their mendicant lifestyles more precarious. Only in the late fourteenth and fifteenth centuries did friars make any substantial inroads in the north and west of the island.[155]

Whatever their differences, the mendicant orders shared similar goals. In terms of education, they promoted a 'broad and healthy intellectual climate'.[156] Friars tended to be better educated than parish priests. Their training emphasized biblical studies and theological instruction, and aimed to create able preachers and confessors. The preaching of the friars emphasized individual devotion, communion with the saints, and the importance of the emotions in spirituality.[157] Their work was extremely effective. 'The pastoral zeal of the friars', their most recent historian has noted, 'led to a quickening of devotion among the laity, and all orders attracted a coterie of followers who wished to live more intense Christian lives inspired by mendicant ideals'.[158] These ideals inspired many women, especially women from aristocratic and wealthy merchant backgrounds, who were prominent among the patrons of mendicant houses. Sometimes their enthusiasm for the mendicant cause created difficulties, especially when those who had acted as patrons ended up living as pensioners within priories—sometimes for several decades—much to the disruption of discipline.[159]

For discipline was certainly desired. Mendicant friars were led by priors, who upheld and enforced disciplinary standards. Each convent exercised its ministry—and solicited alms—within an agreed territory. Groups of convents within a common order gathered together into administrative networks, and these 'provinces' were led by a provincial prior. The provincial prior was in turn subject to the superior general, who periodically visited convents to ensure that good discipline was being maintained.[160] This was an ordered life, with a centralized authority structure—at least in theory. But the mendicant orders became badly divided by the concerns about ethnicity that did much to destabilize the church in the later medieval period. There emerged serious cultural differences between those friars who had been recruited from the native Irish and those who had come from elsewhere. Sometime between 1283 and 1299, for example, Nicholas Cusack, the Franciscan bishop of Kildare, wrote to Edward I to complain that 'the peace of the land is frequently disturbed by the secret counsels and poisonous colloquies which certain religious of the Irish tongue, belonging to diverse orders, hold with the Irish and their rulers'.[161] The Irish language was continuing to make religious leaders suspicious. These ethnic and cultural tensions could erupt within as well as between orders. In Cork, in 1291, for example, a brawl between Irish and English Franciscans left 'many...killed and wounded to the scandal of the order until finally the English with the help of the town prevailed'.[162]

These tensions between the Irish and the English colony came to a head in 1315. Edward Bruce, the brother of the Scottish king Robert I, who had defeated Edward II at Bannockburn in the previous year, invaded Ireland at the head of an army of 6,000 soldiers, and was proclaimed as king of Ireland. His purpose was to unite the peoples of Scotland, Ireland, and Wales against their Norman overlords. He certainly forced the issue. His attacks on the colony required the leaders of Gaelic society to take sides in a war that they might never have wanted. The mendicant orders found themselves in the thick of it. Irish Franciscans were at the heart of Bruce's plans.[163] Bruce's forces were certainly aware of the subtleties of Irish ecclesiastical politics. They distinguished between those monastic and mendicant houses that did and did not support their aims. In 1315, Scottish soldiers attacked the Carmelite foundation at Ardee, where they burned a church that was full of men, women, and children.[164] These outrages against the church and its property were reported back to Rome, prompting Pope John XXII to write to the archbishops of Dublin and Cashel to express his outrage that friars were encouraging rebellion against the crown. An anonymous response to the pope complained that English laymen, priests, and friars 'make the heretical assertion that it is no more of a sin to kill an Irishman than a dog or any other brute creature'—and named a Franciscan from Drogheda as having made this regularly recycled claim in the presence of Edward Bruce himself.[165] As the organization of the Irish church grew more complicated, and its institutions transcended the constantly shifting borderlands between the Irish and English spheres, these cultural tensions became more difficult to resolve, and gradually escalated into crisis. The Scottish invasion came to an end in October 1318, shortly after the death of Edward Bruce, but it had highlighted the ethnic and cultural tensions that would continue to undermine the effectiveness of the Irish church, and that would lead to several decades of prosecutions for heresy and even occasionally for witchcraft.[166]

In the first half of the fourteenth century, the English colony experienced disaster upon disaster. The Bruce invasion was followed by three years of famine that marked the beginning of a long climactic down-turn, as well as a moral panic about witchcraft and heresy. The crisis began to unfold in 1317, when a witch was burned in Kilkenny.[167] This traumatic discovery of *maleficum* was followed by famine, unusually heavy falls of snow, and an epidemic among cattle between 1322 and 1325. As the disasters unfolded, in 1324, witchcraft cropped up again, when Alice Kyteler was put on trial in Kilkenny, the first of several victims prosecuted by Richard Ledrede, bishop of Ossory, an overzealous outsider whose efforts at reform were often resisted within the colony.[168] Some of the problems were administrative. In 1325, the archbishop of Dublin, Alexander de Bicknor, was discovered to have engaged in fraud on a massive scale, counterfeiting receipts for alms that were only partially paid.[169] Other problems related to theology (or at least that is how they were represented). Some clergy were revealed not to believe in the real presence of Christ in the eucharist.[170] In Dublin, in 1328, Adducc Dubh O'Toole, a priest, was executed for heresy.[171] In 1329, another priest, Arnold le Poer, died in prison while awaiting trial on similar charges.[172] The environmental disasters continued. Storms destroyed harvests in 1328. There was unseasonably late snow in 1335, and a harmful disease among sheep in 1338. And then the real problems began. In 1348, there began a devastating outbreak of plague. While the 'Black Death' made little impact outside the Pale, where populations were less dense, it carried off around 40 per cent of the population of Dublin.[173]

In the aftermath of these environmental and demographic disasters came major political changes. In the colony, administrators became increasingly concerned by the diminishing writ of English common law. Political tensions were figured in religious terms—but the crisis in the church was real enough. In 1353, after a bitter local conflict, two MacConmaras were executed for heresy at Bunratty Castle.[174] In 1355, according to a complaint made by Pope Innocent VI, eleven laymen had attacked the Augustinian priory at Inistioge, county Kilkenny, where they killed one canon and tore out the eyes and tongue of another, as part of a broader effort to transfer ownership of the foundation to the notoriously corrupt Franciscan bishop of Ossory.[175] In 1379, Augustinian leaders were convicted of concealing the death of a *confrère* and hiding his corpse, an action that 'indicates a high degree of tension and dysfunction within the Dublin community'.[176] As the Gaelic resurgence continued, and English territory continued to contract, colonists used heresy trials to suppress political dissent, and a vehicle by which to draw the attention of the papacy to what they wanted to represent as Ireland's urgent pastoral needs. They drew attention to the assumptions about Irish religion that were encoded in *Laudabiliter*—the view that English intervention would be necessary in order to save the Irish from themselves. Even though no serious doctrinal issue appears to have been at stake— whatever the claims of the prosecutors—the colony turned upon its Irish enemies and in the first fifty years of the fourteenth century instigated more trials for heresy than would be held throughout the rest of the medieval period. The political strategy to which this tactic contributed was made clear in the representations that colonists made to the English crown and the papacy: the need for heresy trials vindicated their appeal for intervention against the Irish.[177] It was not just that the Irish had to be saved from themselves—the English had to be saved from the Irish too. The obvious solution was to call for a crusade.

Yet, while colonists panicked about their political and environmental reversals, the cultural ground was shifting underneath them. Large numbers of the colony's clergy had died during the Black Death, so that in the later part of the fourteenth century increasing numbers of Irish clergy were recruited to work in parishes in the Pale.[178] While these appointments were technically illegal, as undermining the divisions between the 'two nations', they were made possible by the fact that the church's diocesan boundaries did not coincide with the constantly shifting political boundaries between Irish and English territories.[179] It is true that these newly recruited Irish clergy may have held the poorer livings within the colony, but they also facilitated a revival of Irish language and culture, perhaps by encouraging in-migration.[180] And so, while the church's administrative units bound Irish and colonial society together, the changing culture of these spheres pushed their people apart.

The Irish church divided as the European church fractured. During the Western Schism (1378–1417), the Latin church separated into two and later three competing communions, each with its own pope. While Scotland and most of the rest of Europe supported the claims of Clement VII and the communion that was centred on Avignon, the English parliament supported the claims of Urban VI and the communion that was centred in Rome. The Irish church divided down the middle. While a majority supported the claims of Urban, those areas that sided with Clement tended to be Gaelic.[181] Christians now had to choose to which structure of authority they wished to submit—and, again, religious differences were rooted in ethnicity.

Yet—somehow—the Irish church held together. Its continuity owed a great deal to the movements of reform that inspired many of the most enthusiastic laypeople. Of course there were serious problems. Drunkenness was one besetting sin. In 1451 the friary in Cavan was burned to the ground after one of its members consumed too much wine and mishandled a candle, while in Roscrea, in 1477, a serious riot led to looting from the friary of wine, mead, whiskey, and a huge quantity of beer.[182] Ethnic difficulties continued to debilitate the life of the church. The orders were slow to promote Gaelic friars, who only gained significant influence from the mid-fifteenth century, and then mostly in Gaelic areas.[183] Torn apart by cultural tensions, the Dominican and Franciscan orders split along ethnic lines, with at best · uneasy cooperation.[184] Gaelic churchmen maintained distinctive moral standards: in 1498, the Annals of Ulster described the recently deceased dean of Lough Erne as a 'gem of purity and a turtle dove of chastity'—even though Cathal Óg MacManus Maguire had been the father of more than twelve children.[185] But still the church held together. Lay piety was inspired by Observants, who participated in campaigns for renewal and reform that developed across Europe. Emphasizing a lifestyle of disciplined obedience, and calling for higher standards of piety and probity among the friars, including Sunday observance, Observants among each of the orders gained the trust of the common people.[186] Inspired by a distinctive tradition of penitential literature, laypeople participated in a 'Third Order'.[187] These communities of laymen and women grew rapidly, and sometimes attracted secular priests into their ranks, with around fifty houses being established between 1426 and 1539.[188] But the enthusiasm with which many laypeople embraced this stripped-down monasticism contrasted with the difficulties that the church faced in ministering in many parts of the island. The Augustinian foundation at Murrisk, county Mayo, which held relics of St Patrick and served the needs of pilgrims en route to Croagh Patrick, had been established to reach out to the 'inhabitants of those parts [who] have not hitherto been instructed in the faith'.[189] One thousand years after the beginning of the Christian mission, the religious situation of large parts of the Gaelic territories was still far from encouraging. But the church as a whole was being well supported. On the eve of the protestant reformation, its prospects were looking good.[190]

IV

One thousand years after the arrival of Patrick, 600 years after the earliest Viking raids, and three centuries after the English invasion, the Christian religion dominated Irish culture. The Irish church was shaped by its geographical and political contexts. If the descendants of the Vikings had more-or-less successfully assimilated into Irish life, Anglo-Normans and their descendants within the English colony remained more critical of it. Other migrations continued, and added to the cultural mix. In the fifteenth century, over 10,000 Hebridean Scots migrated to the Antrim glens.[191] And the political situation continued to develop, when, in 1485, the House of Tudor came to control the English throne, and when, in 1495, the Irish parliament was effectively subordinated to the English parliament by means of Poyning's law, which marked the beginning of the 'direct rule' of the English parliament over Ireland.[192] Despite the divisions in the church, the peoples of Ireland were held together not by a common culture, language, or ethnicity, but by a shared allegiance to the church.

It is easy to argue that the Irish church was facing a crisis.[193] But, even with its ministry debilitated by serious ethnic and cultural differences, which were themselves largely the consequence of an incomplete conquest, the church on the eve of the reformation was nevertheless in robust good health. There were certainly problems in its infrastructure, as well as suspicions among its clergy, and travellers were right to note the poor state of the fabric of many ecclesiastical buildings. But, in the same period, many churches and other institutions were being newly decorated, refurbished, or even expanded. In fact, in the late medieval period, there were more parish churches and chapels per head of population than there would be during the seventeenth or eighteenth centuries. The poor behaviour of some of those who served in the church did not take away from the fact that laypeople were supporting the work of the church with surprising generosity. There were fewer complaints about clerical incontinence in Ireland than there were in England, for example, perhaps because while canon law forbade clerical marriage the Irish church seems to have winked at its continuation. Irish clergy could have informal families, and a large number of clergy were clerical sons.[194] As these local factors suggest, the rhetoric of complaint from different kinds of later reformers should not be taken at face value. The traditional view that the late medieval church was experiencing a crisis no longer makes sense. In fact, the church was experiencing widespread renewal, sustaining a huge number of building projects, which were themselves the fruit of deep piety, even if many of these buildings were chantries, and were related to a growing fear of purgatory.[195] After long centuries of division, Christian religion might have been one of the few things that the population of Ireland shared.

At the end of the fifteenth century, there was nothing to indicate large-scale dissatisfaction with the institutions of the Irish church. If the church was not exactly 'vibrant', as one recent historian has claimed, its members were generally content with its offer.[196] By the early sixteenth century, the difference between the Irish and the English colonists was finally reduced to one of blood.[197] This is the context for the beginnings of what would become Irish nationalism: a distinctive cultural identity may have promoted ideas of national belonging under the Anglo-Normans and an ethnic and then religious collective identity under the Tudors and Stuarts.[198] And this may be part of the reason why the church was so successful on the eve of the reformation. It existed as a genuinely incorporating body that provided the two ethnic groups on the island with a common identity, and offered a cultural combination that would be reinforced as its institutions were threatened by a new wave of ecclesiastical reform. In shared institutions, if not in a common identity, the peoples of the island participated in a vigorously Christian Ireland.

3

Reformations

In the sixteenth and seventeenth centuries, the administrative unity of the Irish church was destroyed as the peoples of Ireland were drawn into a new set of competing agendas for ecclesiastical change.[1] Protestant and Catholic programmes for the reform of the church shattered the structures by means of which the Irish church, over many centuries, had held together a range of ideas and cultures.[2] Its institutions had managed a long history of division. Since its organization, church leaders had been balancing competing demands for loyalty—whether in the Easter controversy that pitted Rome against Iona and its daughter churches in the sixth and seventh centuries; in the sometimes violent confrontations between expanding monastic federations in the eighth and ninth centuries; in the efforts to integrate Viking dioceses into Irish episcopal structures in the tenth and eleventh centuries; in the suppression of Irish customs and monastic orders during the period of Gregorian reform; or in the ethnic, political, institutional and sometimes theological divisions that followed upon the English invasion and the arrival of the crusading and mendicant orders. By the late medieval period, the unity of the Irish church was not based upon common culture, but was ensured by recognized structures of governance. Over several centuries, churchmen had held together disparate communities and their sometimes competing goals by appealing to a shared hierarchy and by projecting a common Christian identity. In the late medieval period, groups with divergent languages and cultures were combined in a church that was both recognizably Catholic and obviously Irish.[3]

Irish Christians shared a distinctive sense of collective belonging. In early modernity, the shared identity of Irish Catholics may not have been, as one eminent historian has claimed, a 'precocious national consciousness', but it was on its way to providing an ethnic and then religious collective identity.[4] (Nationalism, as a political discourse, emerged only at the end of the

eighteenth century.[5]) While this sense of common belonging assumed that
the people of Ireland were Christians, it also assumed that they could be
distinguished from those of similar religious persuasion who happened to
come from elsewhere. These assumptions circulated widely in the period's
writing. Prose work from this period came to overlook ethnic divisions
between the descendants of Gaelic and Anglo-Norman families (who
became known as the 'Old English') in order to promote a common Irish-
ness on the basis of a common faith. David Rothe's *Analectio sacra et mira*
(1616), Thomas Messingham's *Florilegium* (1624) and Geoffrey Keating's
Foras feasa ar Éirinn (c. 1634) represented Irish history as that of an independent people who had been united in a common religion, while emphasizing the importance of their martyrs.[6] This sense of a common Irish-ness
appears to have been widely shared by Catholics in the middle of the seventeenth century, perhaps as much as one century before a similar phenomenon appeared among protestants.[7] This sense of Irish particularity was
paradoxical, of course, for it was enabled by an ecclesiastical structure that
found its authority in Rome. A shared sense of collective belonging to the
institution of the church broke down as its infrastructures were successfully
challenged but only partially replaced. Of course, in early modern Ireland,
protestants and Catholics shared a common cosmology, and participated in
forms of folk practice or ritual tradition that could transverse more formal
religious divisions.[8] But, by the end of the sixteenth century, denominational differences were more obviously shaping identities. Catholics and
protestants promoted different ways of being Christian and different ways of
being Irish.

The difficulties that pressed upon the Irish church began in Saxony, in
1517. The arguments of an Augustinian Observant friar called Martin Luther
became a focus for broader conversations that began by questioning some
recent trends in church finance and theology and that ended by dividing
western Christendom into multiple religious confessions supported by rival
political claims. Luther's emphasis upon justification by faith alone cut
across the infrastructure that the church had elaborated over centuries to
turn sacramental participation into merit. Some early protestant ideas did
circulate in Irish monasteries—particularly among the Augustinians, among
whom Richard Nangle accepted the royal supremacy, being appointed
bishop of Clonfert by Henry VIII, while continuing to function as the
order's vicar provincial.[9] By the later part of the century, the circulation of
protestant writing was such that priests were permitted to read this literature

with a view to refuting its claims.[10] The Irish church entered into a second phase of 'reformation' after 1536, when Henry VIII was formally recognized as the supreme head of the Church of Ireland, and 1541, when he was proclaimed as Ireland's king.[11] But Ireland's experience of reformation was very different from that of Henry's other realm. For decades after the supposed beginning of protestant reformation, key clergy remained theologically ambiguous. The last bishop recognized by both Rome and the crown, for example, died in 1603.[12] While the colonial government hesitated to push for radical action, the Catholic Church pursued a bold programme of counter-reformation and retained the allegiance of the vast majority of the population.[13] By the end of the sixteenth century, there were only 120 Irish-born protestants, among whom only four were receiving communion according to the reformed rite.[14] Many 'converts' reverted to Catholic religion—but even so, it is not clear why the number of communicants was so low.[15] Perhaps the success of the Catholic reformation can be linked to clerical provision. While a Jesuit mission was established by 1596, by the 1620s the Catholic community appears to have been flooded with new pastors.[16] Despite strenuous and sometimes bloody efforts to impose its ideals—and despite the success of protestant ideas in Gaelic cultures elsewhere—the protestant reformation in Ireland comprehensively failed.[17]

The failure of protestant reform complicated the already difficult relationship between Ireland and its neighbouring island. As the peoples of Scotland and England turned towards reformed religion, with greater or lesser degrees of enthusiasm, the Irish church lagged far behind. Its pace of reform was slow. The Irish church did not develop any equivalent to the Scots Confession (1560) or the Thirty-nine Articles of the Church of England (1563) until its convocation accepted the Irish Articles (1615), almost 100 years after the German reformation began. The Irish Articles were controversial, and pushed far beyond the consensus of the Church of England to embrace views that were elsewhere dismissed as 'puritan': the articles promoted a vigorously Calvinistic theology as part of a religious vision that also understood the Pope to be Antichrist. Of course, the fact that this church was also prepared to permit the ministry of Scottish preachers who rejected the authority of bishops might tell us more about its character. Nevertheless, as church and state advanced this effort at 'confessionalization'—a process of social and religious change in which church and state worked together to create a disciplined population—they combined religious reform with ambitions for social and cultural change that represented the most determined effort yet to promote Anglicization.[18] After the Act of Uniformity of 1560, the Irish were required by law to attend protestant worship, yet most protestant churchmen were wary of the Irish language as well as suspicious of the ecclesiastical use of Latin.[19] Wishing to see their listeners move from the use of Irish to the use of English, they made little effort to develop a vernacular translation of the Bible, and only sporadic efforts to provide preachers who could expound reformed doctrine in the language that the majority population could best understand. And so, while the Church of Ireland provided some distinguished leadership to the European movement of protestant reform, including James Ussher (1581–1656), archbishop of Armagh, whose remarkable learning was respected across the period's confessional and political divisions, the Irish people, apart from a statistically irrelevant minority, remained loyal to the Catholic Church.[20]

Historians have long debated the reasons for the comprehensive failure of the protestant reformation to convert the Irish people—perhaps forgetting that one of the best ways to answer the question might be to consider why Catholic resistance to the protestant reformation eventually succeeded. The Old English families in the Pale seem key to these developments, for they provided support structures for a great deal of the church's work, while providing the majority of Jesuit recruits in the early years of reformation.[21] Had these families been won to the new faith, just as some of the Ussher family had converted, the religious history of Ireland might have gone in a very different direction. So the protestant reformation failed to persuade the majority of Catholics—but it also failed to persuade a large minority of Irish protestants. These nonconformists—later described as 'dissenters'— organized communities outside that of the state church, often at considerable social, political and financial cost. By the end of the seventeenth century, the largest of the dissenting denominations, the Presbyterians, challenged Anglican claims to the status of church by law established, while outnumbering its members in the most protestant part of the island, in the northeastern counties of Ulster. Anglicans were in power and their position was secure, but their political ascendancy had been achieved at tremendous cost. Their efforts to convert the natives—which were never very ambitious— grew less and less convincing. After all, it was not until 1685, over 150 years after the Lutheran reformation began, that readers of Irish were provided with a complete Bible in their own language. By then, too much had happened to persuade the majority of the population of the beneficence of the

AN IRISH BANQUET.
Derrick, "Image of Ireland," 1581.

Figure 6. John Derrick's *Image of Ireland*

crown or of the religion it endorsed. The vast majority of Irish people
retained their Catholic faith, often at significant personal cost, and venerated
the memory of the more than 250 of their co-religionists who, in these
bloodiest of centuries, became recognized as martyrs.[22] Faced with such
determined opposition, there was little that the reformers of the state church
could do. Protestant efforts to win the hearts and minds of Ireland's Catholics
came too little and too late.

I

The Irish reformation began as a consequence of religious change in
England.[23] After several years of growing pressure, the Irish reformation
commenced in 1536, when Henry VIII was proclaimed as supreme head of
the established church. After the disasters of the early fourteenth century—
which was marked by Irish resistance to English colonial rule, the Bruce
campaign's demonstration of the weakness of colonial government, as well
as the environmental disasters that preceded the Black Death—efforts to
control the Gaelic lordships had markedly declined. But, as the Gaelic lords
reasserted themselves, and expanded in territory, ability, and confidence,

Tudor governments set out to curb their expanding power in a colonial project that the religious revolution in England did nothing to interrupt.[24] From the twelfth century to early modernity, and whether dominated by Catholic or protestant voices, English policy followed much the same script. From the mid-sixteenth century, politicians and merchants established plantations in the midlands and later in the south-west, in an attempt to extend the writ of English common law and to undermine Irish culture, with results that were illustrated in the depictions of chaos, violence, and death that were included in John Derrick's regime propaganda, *The image of Ireland* (1581).[25] Derrick's message was simple and entirely familiar: only determined English intervention could save the Irish from their own barbarity.

The programme of protestant reform was developed in a context of rapid and sometimes confusing demographic change. The population of Ireland was growing markedly through the early modern period. In 1600, the total population amounted to around 1 million people. This rose to around 1.5 million by 1641.[26] But this population was divided into different ethnic and cultural groups. The native Irish were the descendants of the island's indigenous inhabitants, Catholic in religion, and Gaelic-speaking, with significant centres of power outside the Pale, even when Gaelic lordships collapsed after the Nine Years' War, where sometimes idiosyncratic ritual practice remained largely undisturbed and where land was held in family groups according to Gaelic law.[27] The 'Old English' were the descendants of the Anglo-Norman settlers, Catholic in religion, with bilingual facility in English and Irish, despite the prohibitions of the Statutes of Kilkenny, but loyal to the crown and dominant within the Pale around Dublin and in the area around Kilkenny. From the mid-sixteenth century, 'New English' planters formed colonies in the midlands and in Munster, in which they promoted a vigorous protestantism, and a vigorous hostility to Irish language and culture.[28] Their views were epitomized by Edmund Spenser, best-known as the author of the epic poem, *The Faerie Queene* (1590, 1596), but also the author of *A view of the present state of Ireland* (1596), a political pamphlet that argued for the most stringent repression of Irish culture, and which defended the suggestion that the lives of the Irish were worth 'no more than dogges'—a claim, of course, that stretched back to the English invasion, and that was therefore less characteristic of specifically protestant attitudes than of English attitudes more generally.[29] Finally, the Ulster Scots, who were concentrated in the north-east after the 1610s, and spoke a language closely related to English, were Presbyterian, and never entirely persuaded of the claims of the Church of Ireland, within which many of their ministers nevertheless found temporary employment.[30]

Across these communities, there existed widespread recognition that the Irish church was in need of serious reformation. In the minds of many Catholic churchmen, the Gregorian reforms had never entirely succeeded, with the result that the church's situation continued to be a cause for concern, especially after the Council of Trent (1545–1563), which codified the Roman response to protestant reform while advertising how far the Irish church fell short of papal goals. Despite the building projects of the late medieval period, the quality of the church's fabric was often poor.[31] The church struggled to control traditional practices of which it did not approve. The Statutes of Kilkenny had not preserved the English culture of the Pale. By the late fifteenth century, many of the descendants of the English outside the Pale had, in the minds of their critics, become 'more Irish than the Irish themselves'. In Gaelic areas, the church had a distinct complexion, accepting married priests and traditional if often irregular elements of worship. In fact, by the early sixteenth century, 'English observers were shocked and disillusioned to discover the extent to which the Anglo-Irish and Gaelic Irish lineages shared many aspects of the same political culture'.[32]

But if in the view of Catholic theologians the Gregorian reform had not succeeded, in the minds of many protestant churchmen, it had obviously failed. The literature of complaint that developed to analyse these failures encouraged the revival of some older ambitions to distinguish the English from the Irish. These social and political concerns dominated in the early stages of protestant reform—a programme of renewal that was designed more obviously to undermine cultural structures than it was to contradict the claims of the Catholic Church.

In Ireland, the early stages of protestant reform did not herald any significant theological changes. Nevertheless, the project of reformation promoted significant opposition—even before it officially began. In 1534, for example, Thomas, Lord Offaly raised an army to defend his interests and those of his father, whom he believed to have been executed. In the confused and fast-moving religious politics of the early 1530s, 'Silken Thomas' sought to legitimate his rebellion as acting in defence of the Catholic Church. Advertising the revolt as a religious struggle, Thomas won the sympathy of the mendicant orders, but lost the support of large parts of the clergy when his followers murdered John Alen, archbishop of Dublin.[33] As a direct threat to the royal agenda, the Kildare rebellion was met with extraordinary violence, including the beheading by English forces of prisoners outside Maynooth castle, and ended when Thomas surrendered on the promise of clemency, only to be transported to the Tower of London, where he was put to death.[34] His efforts to resist Henry's religious revolution—and the project of Anglicization that it represented in Ireland—would not be the last attempt to forestall protestant reform on the battlefield.

In line with his title as 'Defender of the Faith', a title that had been awarded by the pope, Henry was not any kind of enthusiast for religious change. His agenda was pragmatic—to warrant his divorce and remarriage in pursuit of a male heir—and was only slowly transformed into a theological movement by its managers on the ground. In the earliest years of reform, there was little to indicate that the church by law established would be significantly renewed. Perhaps the most obvious changes were financial and organizational. As in England, the Irish reformation began with the dissolution of the monasteries, which, like the suppression of the Knights Templar 300 years before, was a financial coup that provided the crown and its most trusted supporters with a source of significant revenue.[35] While, in the early sixteenth century, a large part of the island's ecclesiastical fabric was in disrepair, the church was in fact extremely wealthy.[36] In 1530, there were just over 200 friaries in Ireland, around half of them belonging to Franciscans.[37] Unlike their *confrères* elsewhere in Europe, who had long been the subject of vitriolic attack, Irish friars were well-regarded and generously supported by laypeople. Their holdings were often in good shape. Unlike their European colleagues, the orders in Ireland were largely uninterested in the spread of evangelical ideas. Some Irish foundations may have owned copies of key protestant texts, and some members of Irish foundations expressed support for the evangelical message, but, with very few exceptions, Irish institutions showed little enthusiasm for fundamental change.[38] This may explain why the crown's assault on the monasteries was so relentless: between 1539 and 1541, almost every mendicant house in the Pale was dissolved.[39] In Dublin, religious establishments were turned into private homes, educational institutions, communal ovens, drinking dens, and a tennis court, and even provided a site for a new university.[40] The effect of the dissolution was to cement the divisions of the Irish church, and further to identify ethnic with religious loyalties: many of the friars who remained loyal to Catholic teaching moved beyond the Pale, where they worked to consolidate the links between Gaelic culture and traditional religion.[41] But

Henry's break with Rome presented a serious constitutional problem. His authority over Ireland rested on a papal bull—a source of authority that he now rejected. And so, in order to clarify his standing, the Dublin parliament passed an act for kingly title in 1541. Ireland was now a kingdom—albeit a kingdom that looked very much like a colony—and Henry was now its king.

After Henry's death, the reformation in Ireland followed the twists and turns of the religious politics of his children. Under Edward, whose rule began in 1547, an effort was made to provide the Irish church with a definitive statement of reformed faith—a project that made no progress.[42] The king and the English council directed Irish authorities to provide translations of church services into Irish—an effort at enculturation that seems not to have been attempted.[43] Clergy who had arrived in Ireland from elsewhere were among the most vigorous proponents of reform. In Dublin, protestant doctrines were energetically promoted by Walter Palatyne, for example, a Scottish minister who pushed for advanced reformation against the reluctance and indifference of local ecclesiastical leaders, whose response to royal directives was disorganized if not actually chaotic.[44] After his arrival from England, John Bale, a former Carmelite who became bishop of Ossory, was similarly surprised to discover how little effort his fellow churchmen put into advancing religious change. In Kilkenny, he set about communicating protestant ideas to local people through drama, until his ministry ended after threats on his life.[45] But the numbers of convinced protestants remained extremely small. Religious change under Edward was, as Henry Jefferies has put it, 'a Reformation without reformers'.[46] Even these small triumphs were shrugged off when Mary came to the throne in 1553. A convinced Catholic—after whom Queen's county, now county Laois, was named—Mary used her royal supremacy, which she later renounced in favour of the pope, to undo the little that Edward's reformation had achieved. Those clergy who had not married were reconciled to the Catholic Church, heretical books were burned, property was reclaimed, and ecclesiastical law was enforced with a determination that entirely transcended the haphazard and careless religious changes that her father had introduced. In fact, Mary's reforms were actually helped by her father's indifference: the reconciliation to Catholicism of the Church of Ireland was greatly assisted by the fact that so many chantries had survived the monasteries' dissolution, allowing priests to continue to say prayers for the dead. And, while Mary's reforms led to the deaths of more than 200 English protestants, including Thomas Cranmer, archbishop of Canterbury, there were no protestant martyrs in Ireland. It was not necessarily that Mary's Irish regime was more lenient of religious dissent—it was simply that Ireland's rather lukewarm protestants were much less convinced of religious change than were their brethren elsewhere.[47]

With Mary's death, Ireland's Catholic reformation was reversed. In 1560, an Act of Supremacy made Elizabeth the supreme governor of the Church of Ireland.[48] The same act required the use of the Book of Common Prayer and set out fines for those who did not attend protestant worship. It was in Elizabeth's reign that there came the final break with Rome. In 1570, Pope Pius V excommunicated the Irish queen, effectively releasing Catholics from any obligation to submit to her authority. Some of Elizabeth's subjects seized the opportunity to revolt. In 1569 and 1579, the first and second Desmond rebellions became the most serious challenges to English government in Ireland in the middle and later sixteenth century. These rebellions were styled by their leaders as religious wars, a claim convincing enough to encourage participation by Spanish and Italian soldiers, hundreds of whom were massacred by Lord Grey's troops at Smerwick, county Kerry, in 1580. The second Desmond rebellion was mercilessly crushed. English troops experimented with tactics of total war. In the aftermath of the conflict, the population of the island as a whole was reduced by almost 10 per cent, paving the way for plantation of Munster in the 1580s.[49] These policies of cultural intrusion and military intervention were deeply resented by the leaders of Gaelic society, who responded by making further plans for their own defence. In the north-east, in 1593, Hugh O'Neill of Tyrone and Hugh Roe O'Donnell of Tyrconnell took to arms, beginning the Nine Years' War that called forth the largest expeditionary force ever to leave England, with over 17,000 troops, which ended only after the introduction by the English army of scorched-earth tactics and induced famine that made the submission of the rebels inevitable.[50] The use of induced famine as a terror tactic was desperately effective, and in the early 1600s, the north-east was pacified in much the same way as the south-west had been twenty years before. In both situations, total war was the prelude to plantation—the experiment in social engineering that drove forward colonial power in the bitterly quixotic hope that the barbarous Irish might come to emulate the civility of their conquerors.[51] The terms by which Tyrone agreed to a cessation of arms required that he swear allegiance to the English crown, renounce his Gaelic title, replace Brehon with English law, and promote the use of English language, in return for which he could keep his territories and continue in his

Catholic faith. The last point was important, for the treaty that ended the
Nine Years' War represented defeat for both parties: on the one hand, it
signalled the end of the Gaelic lordships, and on the other, it showed that
even with significant military backing the protestant faith was never likely
to succeed. In 1603, the accession of James VI of Scotland to the English
throne did not signal any substantial change in government policy in Ireland,
however much he attempted to deal flexibly and sympathetically with the
Gaelic chieftains. The writing for Gaelic culture was on the wall. In 1607,
around 100 Gaelic leaders set sail from Rathmullan, county Donegal, in an
effort to gather support in Spain for an invasion in favour of their rights. On
the continent, they found sympathy without any commitment to military
intervention, and, eventually abandoning their efforts, they never returned
home. Almost 500 years after the English invasion, those leaders of Gaelic
society who remained in Ireland recognized that their world was coming to
an end.[52] They were right to make this estimation. The 'flight of the earls'
left their lands available for use by the crown, which made possible the
large-scale projects of colonization by Scots and English settlers that are
known as the plantation of Ulster.

Inside the Pale, the religious revolution continued. It became increasingly
obvious that the crisis in the Irish church was not caused by the differences
between protestants and Catholics so much as by the convictions that they
shared. After all, those who supported and those who resisted protestant
reform agreed the island should support only one religious confession.
Theologians from both sides worked on the assumption that the nation that
prayed together would stay together. In early modern Europe, this was not
a universally held truth. In Poland-Lithuania, for example, a policy of religious toleration secured by the Warsaw Confederation (1573) extended religious freedom to Catholics, Lutherans, Calvinists, Anabaptists, Bohemian
Brethren, Unitarians, and Jews.[53] But the idea of religious pluralism had no
currency in Ireland in the sixteenth and the first half of the seventeenth
centuries—and certainly not before the Cromwellian administration
adopted the toleration of a range of orthodox protestants as a central part of
its programme of religious reform. An element of toleration might have
offered Ireland's competing religious communities a way to avoid the horrific violence of the seventeenth-century wars. But neither Catholic nor
reformed leaders could identify this opportunity, while successive English
governments could not countenance it, and no one could be satisfied with
the status quo. When the government went one way, the population went

another. Ireland remained the only European country in which, despite strenuous efforts at coercion and persuasion, the policy of *cuius regio, eius religio* ('the leader determines the religion of the people') did not apply.

Neither side was happy with the result of this project of reform. No one in the sixteenth century thought the Irish church was in good shape. Visiting the island in the 1560s, the English Jesuit William Good observed ruined churches, and lamented the immorality and greed of the Catholic clergy: 'The Priests minde nothing but gathering of goods and getting of children.'[54] Over fifty years later, in 1613, another Catholic observer noted that

> the people in [Ireland] are in general Catholics, and almost all of them profess their Catholic faith quite openly ... Only in the cities, and mainly in those cities involved in commerce, are a part of the people infected by [protestant] heresy. But even in such cities heretics are greatly outnumbered by Catholics. Throughout the countryside the inhabitants are all Catholics, even if they are for the most part wrapped in a deep and blind ignorance of the faith they profess.[55]

Protestant observers agreed that the situation of the Irish church needed to be improved. Even among the ostensibly reformed, one observer complained,

> most ministers are stipendiary men, and few have £5 a year to live on ... In truth such they are as deserve not living or to live. For they will not be accounted ministers but Priests. They will have no wives [though] they will have Harlots ... And with long experience and some extraordinary trial of these fellows, I cannot find whether the most of them love lewd women, cards, dice or drink, best. And when they must of necessity go to church, they carry with them a book in Latin of the Common Prayer set forth and allowed by her Majesty. But they read little or nothing of it or can well read it, but they tell the people a Tale of our Lady or St. Patrick or some other saint, horrible to be spoken or heard, and intolerable to be suffered, and do all they may to dissuade and allure the people from God and their prince, and their due obedience to them both, and persuade them to the Devil the Pope.[56]

Advocates of protestant and Catholic agendas for reform found the pace of change to be unacceptably slow. Large numbers of people found no compelling reason to change their religious beliefs or behaviours. The small number of committedly protestant clergy were sometimes left with nothing to do. One Church of Ireland bishop complained in 1604 that in the previous eleven years not one of the christenings, marriages, or funerals that had taken place in his diocese had followed protestant norms.[57] And yet, if the protestant reformation was failing, Catholic attempts to improve the state of the Irish church were not faring much better. Throughout the first century of reformation, the state of the Irish church satisfied neither the advocates of protestant reform nor those of the Council of Trent.[58]

It was not that reformers did not make an effort. The protestant reformation took advantage of significant technological change. The first book to be printed in Dublin was the Book of Common Prayer (1551). This was in many respects a symbolic achievement. Just as in the fifth century the introduction of Christianity had been followed by the beginnings of literacy and innovations in the production of books, so in the sixteenth century the protestant reformation was marked by a technological break-through in the production of writing. Never well resourced, and in an economy that depended upon English imports, Irish publishing lagged far behind that of other European countries.[59] This print culture was overwhelmingly Anglophone. Sometime before 1567, Adam Loftus and Hugh Brady, respectively the archbishop of Armagh and bishop of Meath, obtained a grant for the manufacture of a font that would allow the printing of the New Testament in Irish. It took a further three decades for the translation work to begin, with the result that 500 copies of the New Testament were printed in 1602. But distribution was extremely slow. At least eighty unsold copies were still available in the 1650s.[60] Nor was the rest of the Bible rapidly translated. The convocation of the Church of Ireland permitted the translation of the Old Testament in 1634. This work appears to have been completed by 1640, but it was not published until 1685, again to a rather muted response.[61] During the same period, Catholics developed a similar project. In 1611, Irish Franciscans established a printing press in Antwerp, and began to circulate a small number of devotional texts in the vernacular, though their audience may have been limited to Irish speakers resident in Flanders.[62] After 1674, the Propaganda Fide press in Rome printed a number of Irish-language texts that were used by Franciscans returning to their homeland.[63] Of course, the slow provision of a facility for Irish-language printing meant different things to protestants and Catholics. The advocates of the state's agenda for religious reformation had privileged access to print production but struggled to provide the church with adequate Irish-speaking preachers, while for Catholics, access to print was simply less important, for religious activity was more often centred upon liturgical action than upon the use of books.[64] And literacy remained a problem—especially for speakers of Irish.[65] In 1639, Theobald Stapleton published a catechism in Irish, but worried that the language had already become '*chomh fueletheach, chomh mucht a sion, nach mór na deacha si as coimhne na nduinne*' (so abandoned and stifled, that it has nearly been forgotten by the people).[66] Irish Bibles and religious materials were slowly being printed, but they were not being widely read.

The cultural power that was represented by the beginning of print enabled protestant and Catholic efforts at confessionalization. Education became a critical battleground, if not for Irish hearts then certainly for Irish minds. Schools in Dublin attracted students from both sides of the religious divide. After all, the city's leading Old English families were often closely connected and some had mixed religious loyalties. James Ussher's family would have been typical of many others. One uncle, Henry Ussher (1550–1613), had served as a protestant archbishop of Armagh, while another uncle, Richard Stanihurst (1547–1618), became one of the period's most important Jesuit writers.[67] This combination of religious commitments continued even after the founding of Trinity College Dublin in 1592. Established on formerly monastic lands, and modelled on Emmanuel College, Cambridge, the university from which large numbers of its early faculty were drawn, Trinity College was intended to advance the Irish prot-estant cause. Yet its student body, in the first decades of its operation, was religiously mixed, and Catholic students remained unpersuaded by the arguments of their protestant professors. Nevertheless, the situation was obviously unsustainable for those families who wished to see their sons educated in the Catholic faith, and many families looked for alternative provision to those Irish colleges that were established in Salamanca (1592), Lisbon (1593), Douai (1594), Bordeaux (1603), Toulouse (1603), Paris (1605), Santiago de Compostella (1605), Lille (1610), and Rouen (1610). These sem-inaries offered training for mission work in Ireland as well as an education suitable for the secular careers of the sons of leading families. They trans-formed the character of the Irish Catholic Church. If protestant educational reforms were a failure, despite the foundation of Trinity College, Catholic institutions did effect a generational step-change, by producing an elite of well-educated and highly committed young men with seminary training.[68]

While the Irish church remained theologically ambiguous, Trinity College was staffed by vigorous protestants. In its earliest years, the fellows of Trinity included James Fullerton and James Hamilton, who had fled from the Church of Scotland, as well as Walter Travers and Humphrey Fenn, two dissidents from England, whose Presbyterian views did not allow them to accept the authority of bishops within the church. In fact, the strongly prot-estant commitments of Trinity's early teaching faculty has led some historians to wonder whether the institution should be understood as a puritan stronghold. Puritans certainly sought sanctuary in the Irish church. Henry Ainsworth, who condemned the Church of England as bearing the 'yoke of antichrist', relocated to Ireland in the early 1590s, before leading a separatist congregation in Amsterdam.[69] In the 1620s, John Winthrop attempted to set up a puritan colony near Mountrath, county Laois, before becoming a leader of the Massachusetts Bay Company.[70] In the same period, some puritan congregations moved to Ireland *en masse*, including two groups of uncertain provenance that settled in Antrim and Carrickfergus. The Church of Ireland was attractive to individuals and congregations that wanted to work in a more emphatically Calvinist context without making any definite ecclesiological commitments. This explains why so many dioceses in Ulster were dominated by Presbyterian clergy from Scotland. In 1622, ten of the eighteen clergy in the diocese of Down, and thirteen of twenty-one clergy in Connor, were Scots, as were sixteen of the twenty-six clergy in the diocese of Raphoe. This attempt at comprehension was initially successful. Between 1613 and 1635, around two-thirds of clerical appointees in Down and Connor may have come from Scotland.[71] The congregations that were led by these ministers may have included up to 1,500 individuals—the size of which offers an extraordinary contrast with reports of congregations of only five individuals at protestant services in Cork.[72] The bishop of Down, Robert Echlin, and the bishop of Raphoe, Andrew Knox, had been especially welcoming to Scottish ministers, permitting them to work within their jurisdictions without requiring that they sign up to any of the episcopal regulations with which they might have found some difficulty. In 1631, for example, Knox had ordained John Livingstone according to Presbyterian norms. Before the ordination, Knox invited Livingstone to cross out anything in the service book to which, as a Presbyterian, he might have wanted to object. But, Livingstone later remembered, 'it had been so marked by some others before that I needed not mark anything'.[73] Whatever its doctrinal latitude—and perhaps even because of its doctrinal latitude—the church in the north-east counties was well-attended, well-supported and recognizably puritan.[74]

The puritan character of the Church of Ireland was confirmed in the confession of faith that it adopted in 1615. After almost one century of theological muddle, the Irish church now possessed one of the most exacting statements of protestant belief. The Irish Articles included twenty-eight of the Church of England's Thirty-Nine Articles, together with all of the

Lambeth Articles (1595), an enormously controversial declaration of high predestinarian doctrine prepared by the archbishop of Canterbury for use in the English church until it was suppressed by Queen Elizabeth. In incorporating a confessional statement that had been too 'hot' for the English church, the leading historian of this period has argued, the Irish Articles represented a 'remarkable declaration of independence by the Church of Ireland'.[75]

The theological platform upon which the Irish church now advanced provided a foundation for the extraordinary accomplishments in history, theology, and book collecting of a cadre of intellectuals that was led by James Ussher as archbishop of Armagh. Ussher's work was historical at its core. He determined to demonstrate that the Church of Ireland was apostolic in origin, and that it was built upon foundations that had been laid by Patrick. His *Answer to a challenge made by a Jesuit in Ireland* (1625) argued that the Catholic Church had apostatized at the Council of Trent, when it formalized its rejection of the gospel as outlined in the New Testament. *A discourse of the religion anciently professed by the Irish and British* (1631) made the same kinds of arguments from historical sources, arguing that the beliefs and behaviours of the early Irish church corresponded more closely to those of the Church of Ireland than to its Catholic rival. Developing these kinds of arguments, Ussher's commitment to reformed protestantism and its authoritarian politics was unwavering, yet he cultivated friendships with Catholic scholars, with whom he exchanged rare manuscripts and other research materials in the emerging 'republic of letters'—a cross-confessional network that says much about the role that religious difference did not play in the making and maintaining of scholarly friendships.[76]

The theological ideas that Ussher defended in his scholarly work were preached to extraordinary effect in the north-east of the island. In 1625, Scottish Presbyterian ministers based in towns along the course of the Six Mile Water, a river in county Antrim, found that their preaching was generating some very unusual responses. The planters, to whom they had been preaching, did not have a reputation for piety. In fact, one contemporary observer noted, they represented the

> scum of both nations [Scotland and England], who, for debt, or breaking and fleeing from justice, or seeking shelter, came hither, hoping to be without fear of man's justice in a land where there was nothing, or but little, as yet of the fear of God.[77]

But, in the mid-1620s, congregations that were made up of such unpromising sinners witnessed dramatic instances of sudden conversion. 'I have seen them myself stricken, and swoon with the Word', one witness reported:

> yea, a dozen in one day carried out of doors as dead, so marvellous was the power of God smiting their hearts for sin, condemning and killing; and some of those were none of the weaker sex or spirit, but indeed some of the boldest spirits...The stubborn, who sinned and gloried in it, because they feared not man, are now patterns of sobriety, fearing to sin because they fear God; and this spread throughout the country to admiration, so that, in a manner, as many as came to hear the word of God, went away slain with the words of his mouth.[78]

The remarkable movement of religious revival swept into south-west Scotland, where it became known as the 'Stewarton sickness', after the name of the town where it made its strongest impression. The revival revitalized the planters as a distinctive religious community. The intense piety that these meetings promoted became institutionalized in orders of service that, when they were exported back to Scotland, were reckoned to be informal to the point of being charismatic. And the experience of revival provided this community with a confidence in their cause, an almost ecstatic understanding of their status as a distinctive people, and the hope that God would do it all again.

Presbyterians in the north-east were gaining confidence at precisely the moment that their loyalty was undermined by the government of the new king. Almost immediately upon his coming to power, in 1625, Charles negotiated with leading Irish Catholics an agreement in which their provision of £40,000 towards his court's expenses would come in exchange for limited toleration for Catholic practice. Catholics had good reason to be hopeful. If the protestant reformation was failing, even after the foundation of Trinity College and the publication of the Irish Articles, the Catholic reformation was going from strength to strength. In the century since protestant reformation began, the situation of the Catholic Church in Ireland had never been stronger: by 1629, the church had provided bishops for almost every Irish diocese.[79] The Graces promised to formalize the reality that Catholics were already, in large parts of the island, the only credible religious community, gathering in congregations of enormous size. But if Charles's offer of toleration outraged protestants, his failure to keep his promise outraged Catholics. Both communities understood that the support of their monarch and their privileges as his subjects could no longer be taken for granted.

For toleration was going out of fashion. As new religious styles were rolled out in the Church of England under the leadership of William Laud, the new archbishop of Canterbury, the doctrinal consensus of the Church of Ireland began to change. For several decades, the church had provided sanctuary for refugee Presbyterians from the English and Scottish establishments. But this toleration was brought to an end in 1632, when, under pressure from English authorities, Bishop Echlin ejected Livingstone and other Scottish ministers from their charges. Some within the church advocated on behalf of the Scottish clergy, including Ussher, along with some significant local landowners. But church authorities began to clamp down on nonconformity. An investigation discovered that less than one-third of the churches in the diocese of Down and Connor possessed a copy of the Book of Common Prayer, and that twenty-four of its ministers were nonconformists. John Bramhall, bishop of Derry, complained that these Presbyterians were 'absolute irregulars, the very ebullition of Scotland'.[80] In 1634, the convocation of the Church of Ireland decided to replace the Irish Articles with the Thirty-Nine Articles of the Church of England. For all that they retreated from the earlier statement's emphatic Calvinism, these moves reflected a more determined effort to achieve religious uniformity. For all that they divided Irish protestants, the efforts of Thomas Wentworth, the lord deputy and later lord lieutenant of Ireland, to impose uniformity might have represented the most determined effort yet at the combination of ecclesiastical and political power that is known as confessionalization.[81] For a while, these efforts seemed to be effective. As liturgical discipline was imposed, a large number of Scottish ministers lost their posts. Some looked for better opportunities in the new world. In 1636, in response to an invitation from John Winthrop, who had finally decided upon Massachusetts over Mountrath, Livingstone and other Presbyterians boarded a ship in an effort to migrate to New England. Setting out late in the season, they spent two months at sea, experiencing violent gales, before returning home. For some mysterious reason, they believed, God had turned them back. For better or worse, Presbyterians would have to make their future in Ireland.

Their decision to dissent would cause them problems. The bishops of the Church of Ireland continued to pressure the Presbyterians to conform. And Presbyterians continued to resist. One advocate of conformity complained that the Presbyterian laity 'will hear no prayer at all. While the divine Service is reading, they walk in the Church-yard, and when prayer is ended, they come rushing into the Church, as it were into a Play-house, to hear a

Sermon.'[82] This critical distance was not a sign of apathy. By summer 1638, Presbyterians on both sides of the Irish Sea had begun to organize themselves around a manifesto for religious change that became known as the National Covenant. Wentworth attempted to break this political movement by requiring every Scot in Ireland over the age of sixteen to swear to the 'Black Oath', abjuring the claims of the covenant and promising fidelity to the king.[83] His efforts were fruitless. The covenanting movement was held together by the heightened, immediate, and deeply emotional Calvinist spirituality that had blown up ten years earlier in the Six Mile Water revival. In 1638, and in similar scenes of religious ecstasy, Presbyterians across Scotland and the north-east of Ireland signed the National Covenant, creating the movement of grievance that would destabilize the three kingdoms and begin twelve years of civil war. After several decades of contented ministry within a theologically ambiguously establishment, Presbyterians had been radicalized.

Wentworth's attempts to impose uniformity on the Irish church and to stamp out any trace of dissent had achieved its goals while creating a powerful and energetic community of dissent—a community separated by only twelve miles of sea from the national church with which it most closely identified and that had united militarily around the same political programme.[84] By the 1630s, as S. J. Connolly observes, 'what was to be the enduring line of division between Protestant settler and Catholic native had clearly been drawn'—and dividing lines between different communities of protestants had also been established.[85] One hundred years after the beginning of reformation in Ireland, there were different ways of being Christian, different ways of being protestant, and different ways of being Irish. In failing to create a single nation with a single faith, the protestant reformation had failed, and its failure would be marked by violence and mass death.

II

These conflicts continued at the end of the decade, when, inspired by the achievements of the Scottish Covenanters, Old English leaders combined in an effort to recalibrate their relationship with the English crown and to secure, among other goals, the toleration for Catholic worship that Charles had already promised. After all, Scottish Presbyterians, who took up arms to defend their religion in 1638, during which they invaded England, occupied

Newcastle, and shut down the supply of coal to London, had demonstrated that limited military interventions could achieve significant political ends. At the end of the 1630s, there were striking similarities between the situation of the Scottish Presbyterians and that of the Irish Catholics. Both communities represented major populations within their home nations, and both had been badly affected by the attempts of the archbishop of Canterbury, William Laud, to promote greater uniformity between the established churches of the Stuart kingdoms. Crucially, both Scottish Presbyterians and Irish Catholics were loyal to the Stuart crown. They explained their military adventures in the language of loyalty, and insisted that they wished to adjust, rather than overturn, the established political order. The Scottish Covenanters and the Irish Catholics who emulated them were very conservative religious revolutionaries.

Nevertheless, this dangerous combination of ethnic, linguistic, economic, and religious complaint exploded in October 1641. A coordinated rising among the Ulster Irish led to thousands of deaths among protestant settlers. The harrowing events of the following weeks shook the Irish establishment and provided the protestant imagination with haunting demonstrations of Catholic perfidy and power. The violence was driven by long-standing grievances. The Ulster plantation had dispossessed many thousands of Catholics of their land. While some local Catholic landowners worked to facilitate schemes for plantation—including some of those who turned out to lead the rising—these schemes had contributed to the feelings of vulnerability that were consolidated in the region's bitter ethnic and religious rivalries.[86] The rising pointed to the failure of the plantation project and the religious reformation to which it was meant to contribute.[87] Inspired by recent developments in Scotland, the Catholic gentry of Ulster planned a rebellion, with limited aims that included taking possession of Dublin Castle, in an effort to achieve goals that included the official toleration of the Catholic Church. This was not—initially—a rebellion of the dispossessed. One of the leading conspirators, Sir Phelim O'Neill, came of Gaelic stock, but had been educated at Lincoln's Inn in London and had introduced protestant planters into his large estates.[88] Nor were the victims of violence always those who had done best out of the plantation. John Fortune, a resident of Ballinakill, county Laois, had travelled a long way from his birth-place in Patagonia, at the tip of south America, before being stripped of his possessions by rebels.[89] Nevertheless, as the rising's leaders lost control of events, their limited and political objectives became obscured as local militias settled scores with planters in a frenzy of sectarian brutality. Historians have disagreed as to the number of resulting deaths, and whether they should include in that tally those who died of disease and exposure as well as those who were shot, impaled, forcibly drowned, burned, and buried alive. In the immediate aftermath of the rising, lurid reporting in the new genre of newsbooks contained horrific images alongside estimates of up to 200,000 deaths.[90] Of course, the statistics of horror that so enflamed contemporary passions were grossly exaggerated. Historians now agree that 12,000 of the 40,000 or so planters should be included in the fatalities—but that is still over one-quarter of the settler population as a whole.[91]

Death tolls increased as rebels abandoned the objectives that the leaders of the conspiracy had identified as its strategic goals. The violence was sudden, brutal, almost unprecedented in its horror, and very widely described.[92] Early stages of the rising were confusing, and there is some evidence that Scottish planters assisted the Irish in their attacks on English settlements.[93] As the rising continued, and planters combined to resist it, codes of war were rapidly abandoned, even if stories of the war may have grown in the telling, and reflected the basic division between Catholics and protestants. One victim statement reported that 'it hath been a very Comon & ordinary thing for the Irish to murther devowre and eate the persons of such English as they could light vpon, and when they could light vpon none of them then to kill devowre and eate one another'.[94] These claims were deeply disturbing. Several witness statements recorded instances of haunting. At Portadown, at the site of a mass drowning, a large number of rebels were recorded as witnessing 'divers apparitions & visions', observing a

> vision or spiritt assumeing the shape of a woman waste highe vpright in the water naked with elevated & closed handes, her haire disheivelled very white, her eyes seeming to twinckle in her head, and her skinn as white as snowe which spiritt or vision seeming to stand straight vpright in the water divulged and often repeated the word Revenge Revenge Revenge.[95]

Similar scenes were witnessed in Belturbet, county Monaghan, at another site of mass drowning, where 'it was a Common report amongst the very Irish themselves thereabouts that none durst come vnto nor stay at the bridge of Belturbett, becawse some spiritt or ghost came often thither & cryed Reveng Reveng'.[96] Whatever the death toll, the symbolic importance of this episode cannot easily be quantified. The horrors of winter 1641 left an indelible impression in the minds of many protestants. Such horrors called for drastic action. Even the ghosts were crying out for justice.

This reporting of the rebellion contributed to the political and constitutional instability that evolved into the civil war that, in 1642, broke out between the English parliament and king—a conflict that was rapidly exported into Ireland. In the same year, an army of Scottish Presbyterians landed in Carrickfergus to confront the rebel movement that they had inadvertently inspired. They organized a basic Presbyterian structure that oversaw social life as well as congregational worship. The community that began to mobilize around this structure followed the discipline of the Church of Scotland, and so immediately challenged the claims of the Irish establishment. The new community seemed to be attractive—as any viable community would be in such unprecedented chaos. Some Catholics subscribed to the Covenant and joined the Scottish army.[97] Others joined Presbyterian congregations and subjected themselves to the moral discipline they imposed.[98] With these kinds of gains, the Presbyterian community turned out to have enormous structural significance. For a little more than one century, Irish protestants had existed within the structures of a single denomination. In that context, the emergence of a Presbyterian community was as much a signal of the failure of the government programme for reform as was the rebellion to which the Scottish invasion had responded.[99] And it reflected a broader ambition of religious reform, for Presbyterians were mobilizing across the three kingdoms. Promoting subscription to the Solemn League and Covenant (1643), a document of political and theological grievance that was formally adopted by the Scottish and English parliaments, and sworn by Presbyterians in Ireland, they promoted the achievements of the Westminster Assembly (1643–1652), the most important church assembly of the seventeenth century, which produced catechisms, a statement of theological ideas that continues to exist as a standard for Presbyterian churches, a psalter for congregational singing, and a great deal more besides.[100] After more than one century of theological ambiguity in the established church, they had clear ideas as to how a reformation should develop. As the Presbyterian movement grew, with an army's backing, so did the threat that it represented to the establishment. The Irish church was becoming a victim of its own hospitality. Having provided a home to these large communities of Scottish refugees, it discovered that they wanted to take over.

Presbyterianism was no sooner established than it began to diversify.[101] The new movement struggled to make much headway outside the north-east counties of Ireland, where social and cultural links with Scotland were strongest. In the 1650s, some Dublin churches combined to create a Presbyterian structure, which was replicated by another group of churches in Munster. But these distinct networks were never united. The Presbyterians in the north-east continued to look for guidance to the national church of Scotland, while their counterparts in the Pale and in the south-west look for guidance to puritans in England. Within a couple of decades of their being established, these Presbyterian communities displayed quite different attitudes to some important theological questions, particularly relating to the Trinity, which became a focus of anxious debate in the 1670s and 1680s. While the Scots remained much more committed to upholding the claims of the Covenant and Westminster Confession than their co-religionists in southern parts of Ireland, they were also more effective at communicating their ideas to Irish-speaking listeners. A small number of Presbyterian ministers were fluent in Gaelic, and engaged in cross-cultural evangelism. The established church included among its leadership some serious advocates of Irish-language evangelism, including William Bedell, the bishop of Kimore and Ardagh, who instituted Irish-language daily worship in his diocese, and who was honoured in his death in 1642 by a party of rebels, who escorted his coffin to the graveyard and fired a volley of shots.[102] In fact, through the seventeenth century, it was Scottish Presbyterians who did the most significant work in communicating protestant ideas to native audiences. As growth continued, during the 1640s, Ulster Presbyterians mounted an increasingly serious challenge to the monopoly of the established church. In the north-east, two rival denominations, backed by the Scottish or Irish state, claimed the loyalty of protestants.[103] But the situation was about to grow more complex—for the leaders of the Ulster rising were about to establish an independent polity of their own.

In December 1641, at the Hill of Crofty and Tara, Gaelic and Old English leaders formed the Catholic Confederation, an autonomous political community that understood itself to be governing Ireland in the name of the king but in opposition to the government in Dublin Castle.[104] The Confederation was built on an uneasy coalition of interests. Its purpose was to govern the large parts of Ireland that its members controlled, and to safeguard their interests from the intervention of the Scots in Ulster and the colonial administration in Dublin, while negotiating their demands for religious toleration with the king. The Confederation functioned well for six years, and its members developed an outlook that, the historian Micheál Ó Siochrú has suggested, might represent the 'genesis of modern Irish nationalism'.[105] But it gradually failed, its goals undermined by recurring ethnic rivalries and competing visions for what a Catholic polity should look like. Its unity was most seriously threatened by the efforts of the papal nuncio, Cardinal Giovanni Battista Rinuccini, who worked to transform the limited goals of the nobles' rebellion into a full-blown religious war. These crusading ambitions were encouraged by publications such as *Disputatio apologetica* (1645), by the Irish Franciscan Conor O'Mahony, which argued that the rising in 1641 had not gone far enough and advocated for the expulsion or execution of all surviving protestants and for the election of a native king.[106] Most significantly, the Confederacy's institutions struggled to retain the loyalty of the landless poor from Ulster, who wanted to dismantle the plantations, with that of the Irish and Old English social elite whose wealth depended upon the maintenance of the established order. The Confederation divided over religious and economic policy. While the large landowners hoped to gain through an accommodation with the king a limited form of religious toleration that would allow them access to government office and rights to private worship, the clerical party pushed for more aggressive goals, including full rights to public worship and possession of church buildings. While lay Confederates wanted to achieve a polity that recognized subjects of all Christian confessions, the clerical party pushed for the establishment of the Catholic Church, and, when it was required to decide between them, prioritized religious over political goals.[107]

The civil war that followed upon the Scottish invasion and the institution of the Confederacy was chaotic and confusing.[108] By the end of the decade, there were five armies in the field, each operating with independent leadership and in a bewildering succession of alliances, in which a militia made up of planters, an army of Scottish Presbyterians, the army of the English parliament, an army of Irish royalists, and the Confederate army fought against and occasionally alongside each other, and sometimes in trans-confessional alliances that qualify any claim that, whatever its reality elsewhere, the conflict in Ireland was a religious war. The Irish conflict was fought for political ideals that were only pragmatically overlaid with religious pride and prejudice.

The situation grew more difficult in August 1649.[109] The invasion of Oliver Cromwell and some 18,000 seasoned veterans of the English civil war transformed the military situation in Ireland and achieved some long-standing goals of English policy.[110] The Cromwellian invasion simplified a confusing military situation. When Cromwell arrived in Ireland, he faced an uneasy coalition of the army of the Confederate Catholics, civil war royalists, and Presbyterians, under the command of James Butler, the earl of Ormond. The New Model Army fought against anyone, protestant or Catholic, who supported the cause of the king. Many of the English soldiers, including many of the army leaders, were fuelled by sectarian hatred, which Cromwell sometimes stepped in to control.[111] There is no doubt about the military capacity of his troops. In a campaign that extended from autumn 1649 into spring 1650, and in mopping-up operations that continued until spring 1653, the Cromwellian forces achieved what no other English administration had ever achieved. But victory came at a cost. Just as in the experiments in total war that followed upon the Munster rebellion and the Nine Years' War, the Cromwellian conquest led to massive numbers of deaths: from 1649 to 1652, the island's population may have been reduced by up to 20 per cent.[112] Cromwell's invasion advanced as one long revenge upon anyone who might have been complicit in the horrors of 1641. Irish Catholics were among his victims—but so were Scottish Presbyterians and English royalists. After eight years of horrific violence, the island was under English control.

As the island was annexed by the English republican regime, attempts were made to promote in Ireland the Cromwellian ideal of religious toleration, which was extended to all orthodox protestants who did not accept the authority of bishops, but which did not extend to Catholics. The Cromwellian revolution in Ireland had undermined the status of the established church, and forbidden the use of its prayer book, without ever defining the religious body, or the set of religious ideas, by which it would be replaced. Many groups, including the new religious movements that arrived with the English army, took advantage of the opportunity presented by this ideal of toleration to establish their distinctive structures.[113] Congregationalists believed that organized groups of 'visible saints' (as they liked to refer to themselves) should be independent of any other; Baptists agreed with the Congregationalists but added that the members of these congregations should be baptized as believers; Quakers rejected the role of clergy and abandoned the two protestant sacraments of baptism and eucharist; while other believers made it a point of principle not to associate with any particular religious group. The members of these movements established new communities in garrison towns throughout Ireland. Scattered and isolated, they struggled to communicate with each other and to build a common denominational identity, especially with their counterparts in England. They made huge efforts to proselytize among the soldiers, and virtually no effort to reach out to anyone else.

For, while Cromwellians were reunited in their efforts to achieve military conquest, they did not agree what should replace the national church. In England, the administration did attempt to establish a religious centre. The Blasphemy Act (1650) was followed by several attempts to define religious 'fundamentals' (1652–1654), until *A new confession of faith* (1654) summarized the Westminster Confession in twenty brief propositions, which were never officially approved.[114] No similar project was attempted in Ireland, where the religion that was to be supported by the Cromwellian government was never defined. Some preachers worried about the imbalance, and feared that some of those who did not satisfy the English criteria for orthodoxy would make their way to Ireland, where their ministry would face no serious theological tests.[115]

This imprecision created a religious pluralism that some people found compelling. The narratives of conversion that began to be published in this period offer telling evidence not only of the troubled social circumstances of the 1650s but also of the restless spirituality that it seemed to promote. Life writing from the period shows how many individuals moved between religious communities, in pursuit of a more authentic religious experience, or of a more precise theology. While Presbyterian communities remained resilient, Congregationalists lost members to Baptists, who in turn lost members to Quakers, who were themselves always susceptible to the appeals of other, more radical, groups. For the differences between these communities could be very significant, and were not always mere points of doctrine. Those who became known as 'antinomians' believed that because they had been predestined to salvation irrespective of their actions they had no obligation to obey the moral law, much to the scandal of more proper fellow-travellers. Others looked beyond Scripture for spiritual guidance to 'light within' or to other kinds of revelation.[116] Some began to work miracles, like Valentine Greatrakes, a faith healer and exorcist who became well known after the Restoration as 'the Irish stroker'.[117] Others believed themselves 'to be God', one preacher complained, and announced their claim 'in the open streets with detestable pride, atheism, and folly'.[118] A tiny handful of individuals denied the existence of any divine being. As ecclesiastical structures broke down, there was little to replace them. At times, religious life seemed out of control. Some reported the effects of preaching by charismatic children.[119] And the consequences were unpredictable. One settler, building a library of radical writing in his home in Stradbally, county Laois, believed that he had discovered a cure for death. Many individuals within each of these communities laid claim to extraordinary spiritual experiences. Some had dealings with angels and demons. Others discovered themselves to be prophets. For some, like Walter Gostelo, the experience could be life-changing:

> one Sunday morning...about day I did see, sitting at my beds foot, behind the curtain, a Man sent of God: whilest He continued there sitting, there fell a Showre of Fire, thick, and in drops, like Rain, all about my beds foot.[120]

Gostelo's responsibility, the angel insisted, was to persuade the parties torn apart by civil war to combine in a military effort against European Catholicism—a task that he attempted in the book that recorded that revelation, *Charls Stuart and Oliver Cromwel united* (1655). Of course, this culture could be open to abuse—as when one group of soldiers persuaded their commander to believe that he was hearing the voice of God by speaking to him through a pipe that they had hidden under his bed.[121] But what this incident reveals is not so much the credulity of these believers as the credibility of the supernatural claims upon which they depended.

The Cromwellian administration was driven by its certainty of the dangerous and anti-Christian nature of all those movements that did not support its religious ideals. Its targets included Catholics. But, Cromwell insisted, this was not merely for sectarian reasons. In December 1649, Catholic bishops claimed that Cromwell had travelled to Ireland 'with the resolution of extirpating the Catholic religion, which is not to be effected without the massacring or banishment of the Catholic people'. Cromwell denied this claim. The celebration of the mass would certainly be prohibited, he insisted, but other forms of devotion could continue and, in marked contrast with sixteenth-century policy, he insisted that no Catholic would be compelled to attend protestant worship.[122] Cromwell was inviting Irish Catholics to privatize their faith, to strip it of its sacramental significance, and to operate like one of the period's protestant new religious movements. Of course, those who adopted this course of action would not be Catholics in any sense of the word. Nevertheless, some Catholics may have bought into this idea, like some of their co-religionists in England, who were prepared to abandon key elements of Catholic ecclesiology in order to benefit from toleration.[123] After all, the parliamentary army, like the Presbyterian army in Ulster, included within its ranks a number of local, and Catholic, recruits.[124] And in 1661, a group of 121 Catholics—including noblemen, gentry, and a bishop—pledged to obey Charles II in all civil and temporal matters, despite the papacy's rival claim to temporal power—a statement that the pope himself condemned.[125] But most Irish Catholics remained unmoved by Cromwell's invitation. Those Catholics who did not convert were deemed eligible to lose their land holdings, as a result of a policy that ostensibly targeted those who had participated in the 1641 rebellion. This project of land transfer—which has been recognized as an early attempt at ethnic cleansing—was extraordinarily effective. By the end of the decade, Catholic landholdings had declined from over 60 per cent to less than 20 per cent of the island. Catholic landowners were forcibly moved across the Shannon. And there many of them remained. Even in the 1830s, the descendants of some of those who had been transplanted to Mayo were still speaking Ulster Irish.[126] The dispossessed had very long memories.

After a century of effort to achieve religious uniformity, the introduction into Ireland of such an extraordinary range of religious opinion was a remarkable turn of events. For 100 years after the beginning of reformation, there had existed only one Irish protestant church. From 1642, the claim of the Church of Ireland to national jurisdiction had been challenged by the growing power of the Presbyterians. But in the 1650s, the world was turned upside down. The Cromwellians tolerated any community of protestants that did not deny the Trinity, did not use the book of common prayer, and did not insist upon its own hegemony. So now it was scrupulous conformists like Jeremy Taylor who found themselves pushed into dissent. This was a negative confession, of course, which turned on its head the old assumption that government should prescribe faith—now it merely proscribed it. This ambiguity was not satisfactory. Observers knew what the Cromwellian government would tolerate, but they did not know what the Cromwellian government believed.

Meanwhile wider society began to feel the effects of conflict. Several counties around the Pale became zones of total war. Those caught in the cross-fire could be subject to terrible cruelty. Boetius McEgan, the bishop of Ross, was captured by Cromwellian forces, for example, and taken to Carrigadrohid, county Cork, where Roger Boyle, Lord Broghill, insisted that the garrison of Irish soldiers should surrender or face execution. When

McEgan encouraged the garrison not to surrender, Cromwellian soldiers hung him on the spot.[127] As the violence continued, treasures were shipped to the capital for safe-keeping, including the Book of Kells, which Henry Cromwell, Oliver's son and the leader of the Irish administration, transported from county Meath to Trinity College.[128] As the army pursued total war against Irish royalists, of whatever religious persuasion, the situation in the capital grew increasingly difficult. Refugees streaming into Dublin found little solace. One English visitor reported seeing 'poor parentless children that lie begging, starving, rotting in the streets, and find no relief; yea, persons of quality ... seeking for bread, and finding none'.[129] As conflict bled into ethnic cleansing, the war in Ireland became almost apocalyptic in its intensity. Some Cromwellian ministers, like John Rogers, turned to biblical descriptions of the end of the world to understand the events that he was witnessing.[130] Gaelic-language poets did the same. Seán Ó Conaill described the war as 'an cogadh do chríochnaigh Éire' ('the war that finished Ireland').[131] But the Cromwellian regime was finished too. After the death in 1658 of its founder and figurehead, anti-government feeling grew. The Cromwellian invasion had illustrated both the military collapse of Irish Catholicism and the religious failure of protestant reform. By the end of the decade, it was obvious to some Cromwellian officers and administrators that the best way to stabilize the country—and to ensure the security of their landholdings—was to work for the return of the king.[132]

III

The royalist counter-revolution began with the restoration of Charles II as king of England, Scotland, and Ireland in May 1660. The government of Charles II was determined to revenge the wrongs of the civil wars—but, with hardly any exceptions, only the wrongs that had been suffered by his protestant subjects. In Ireland, to the astonishment and anger of the Catholic landowning class, who had sacrificed much for his cause, the land transfers of the previous decade were largely confirmed. As a consequence, the 42 per cent of land held by Catholics in 1641 was reduced to 17 per cent by 1670.[133] In the same year, Sir William Petty estimated, the Irish population included 800,000 Catholics, 200,000 English, and 100,000 Scots.[134] In other words, the community that represented 70 per cent of the island's population now owned 17 per cent of its land. And that proportion would continue to fall until, in the later eighteenth century, it reached its nadir at 5 per cent. Old English families looked on with horror as the king rewarded his enemies over his friends. This confirmation of the economic status quo created the 'protestant interest' that, in the later seventeenth and eighteenth centuries, would provide a rationale for the cooperation of Anglicans and protestant dissenters, who would benefit from the suppression of Catholics by penal laws that were irregularly enforced and that aimed at increasing economic inequality instead of promoting religious conversion.[135]

After 1660, elite members of the established church were restored to what they regarded as their rightful position as the natural leaders of Irish society. Their plans to remodel the capital and to invest in iconic buildings, such as the house for parliament on College Green, reflected their new confidence and power.[136] Despite the role that they had played in ensuring the return of the king, those Presbyterians and former Cromwellians who did not conform to the established church found themselves castigated as 'dissenters'.[137] They were pushed beyond the protection of the law, as liturgical difference was represented as political threat.[138] After the restoration, ministers of sixty-one of the seventy parishes in one Ulster diocese refused to conform, and were ejected from the established church.[139] The restored government balanced its policy of revenge against protestant republicans while addressing the threat posed by native Catholics, even though they were still, ostensibly, loyal to the king.[140] This policy was rooted in demographic realities. The number of dissenters was substantial. By the end of the seventeenth century, Presbyterians were the dominant population in counties Antrim and Down, and the majority population of Ulster as a whole.[141] Presbyterians, in other words, were the largest community wherever protestants were most numerous. And their numbers continued to grow. Towards the end of the seventeenth century, successive waves of migration from Scotland brought refugees from persecution and from the environmental difficulties that created widespread dearth.[142] As numbers grew, the Presbyterian community became less religiously monolithic. Looking back on his childhood in the 1650s, William King, who abandoned his Presbyterian roots to become the Anglican archbishop of Dublin, remembered that he had been given very little instruction in Christian faith.[143] And yet, by the end of the century, there seems to have been a problem with clerical oversupply. Francis Makemie, an ordinand from county Donegal, graduated from the University of Glasgow in 1682, but could not find a pastoral charge in Ireland, and travelled to Maryland to establish the first Presbyterian Church in the new world.[144]

The growth of the Presbyterian community was being winked at by the Dublin government, which recognized the importance of building protestant numbers as a way to counter the ongoing Catholic threat. After 1662, as dissenters were expelled from the national church, the Irish government made special efforts to encourage protestant refugees from elsewhere in Europe to find a home in its established church.[145] French Huguenots established communities in locations such as Portarlington, county Laois, where they created a small society that retained its distinctive French culture into the nineteenth century, and that continues to celebrate that culture to the present day.[146] By the end of the century, similar 'stranger' churches were established in Cork, Waterford, Carlow, and Castleblaney, with two more being founded in the capital.[147] As their co-religionists were persecuted elsewhere, Irish dissenters were indulged in surprising ways. In 1663, the king prohibited the performance of a play, John Wilson's *The cheats*, which had made fun of a dissenting minister.[148] Other protections were advanced in legislation. While the Irish Act of Uniformity (1665) gave bishops power over the provision of education, required all school teachers to adhere to the established church, and imposed a fine of £100 upon a dissenting clergyman overseeing the administration of the eucharist, MPs decided not to enforce the attendance at parish worship that was still required by the similar legislation of 1560.[149] Quakers were given a great deal of leniency, perhaps because, like refugee protestants, they represented no threat to the government.[150] Baptists were largely ignored, and their already small base continued to erode.[151] The largest dissenting community, with their close connection to the ongoing rebellion by Covenanters in Scotland, did not fare so well. At first, Presbyterians were bought off. From 1672, the crown succeeded in buying their loyalty in the *regium donum*—an annual payment to Presbyterian ministers that was known as the 'king's gift'. But, even though Irish Presbyterians played no part in the Rye House Plot (1683), the Monmouth rebellion (1685), or in other acts of anti-governmental violence, they were still pushed to the social and political margins. If their religious society was weakened, however, their political power continued to be significant, and as long as they were inspired by the Scottish constitutional settlement, they were as 'little likely to welcome an indulgence, when they thought themselves entitled to an establishment'.[152] In fact, the promise of toleration was something they found appalling—mostly because that it promised greater freedoms for Catholics, too. For the competing groups of protestants agreed on one proposition, at least—that the Catholic Church could never be trusted.

This sectarian prejudice explains much of the panics of the 1670s and 1680s, the 'popish plots' that were driven by fantasists, fabricators, and agents provocateurs, like Titus Oates, whose false testimony brought fifteen men to death. Among the most famous victims was Oliver Plunkett, the Catholic archbishop of Armagh, whom Charles II knew to be innocent of the charges that were laid against him, but whose life the king could not save. Of course, Plunkett had enemies among his co-religionists, too. He was disliked after his complaints of abuses among his clergy. Discovering that the vicar apostolic of the diocese of Derry had been living with a woman for thirty years, and that the vicar general in Clogher was well known for drunkenness and might have impregnated two of his servants, Plunkett had set about a bitterly resented programme of radical reforms.[153] These were unsuccessful—and deeply unpopular. It was telling that among those to give evidence against Plunkett in the trial that led to his death in 1681 were several Irish Franciscans.[154] Speaking from the scaffold, Plunkett insisted that he would never have been convicted by an Irish jury. He may well have been right. There were no executions connected to the Popish Plot in Ireland, where protestant juries were much more sceptical of the prosecution's claims.[155]

When James II came to the throne in 1685, as an openly Catholic monarch, his efforts to advance the cause of religious toleration were soundly resisted by his Irish protestant subjects. Presbyterians realized that the king's purpose was not to make life easier for dissenters, but to liberate, and perhaps even to enfranchise, his co-religionists. For James had succeeded to the throne as an unapologetic Catholic, the first Catholic monarch since Mary, and the birth of his son, in 1688, was a powerful signal that the protestant reformation might be coming to an end. This was certainly how Irish protestants, from established and dissenting churches, understood the efforts of Richard Talbot, the earl of Tyrconnell, to effect a Catholic 'counter-revolution' under the auspices of the king.[156] Tyrconnell purged protestants from crown offices in local government, and greatly expanded the number of Catholic officers in the Irish army. His proposal to unpick the Cromwellian land settlement threatened to return large tracts of Irish land to Catholic ownership.[157] His direct attack on the viability of Ireland's protestant community ensured that Anglicans and dissenters would work together to preserve their economic gains.

Faced with the overturning of the Restoration land settlement—and with the loss of their status and power—Irish protestants responded in a show of strength. Anglicans and dissenters alike lined up behind James's son-in-law and nephew, William of Orange, who had been invited by Members of Parliament at Westminster to intervene in the deteriorating situation in order to maintain protestant liberties. For all that William's intervention has become an iconic moment in protestant memory, its constitutional status was ambiguous: while he had been invited into England by a small group of English MPs, his landing without invitation on the separate kingdom of Ireland can only have been an invasion. The Glorious Revolution that followed proceeded quietly enough in England, and with some bloodshed in Scotland, but in open war in Ireland.[158] Defeat for James at the Boyne and elsewhere led to his abandoning the field, with the result that William and Mary were proclaimed as king and queen. The island's religious divisions were consolidated at the end of the 1680s, when protestants set aside their differences to defend William of Orange against James II and his attempts to reverse the reformation and the land transfers it had made possible. But dissenters could hardly have anticipated how little they would gain as a consequence of the Glorious Revolution.

IV

Throughout the sixteenth and seventeenth centuries, the religious reformation that was promoted by successive English governments represented sustained but ultimately ineffective efforts to make Ireland protestant. Policy-makers and preachers who embraced this agenda for change expected to create a single national religious community by political, legal, administrative, and only eventually doctrinal means, promoting the ideal of a religious nation, if not yet the ideal of religious nationalism.[159] Their efforts were met by an equally resolute attempt to maintain a single national religious community of Catholics. Protestant reform was pursued inconsistently and with some hesitation until the late sixteenth century, when the established church identified with explicitly reformed convictions, and adopted one of the most stringently Calvinist of the reformed confessions of faith. But the Irish Articles marked the high-water-mark of Calvinist reform within the church. Within twenty years, they had been effectively replaced, as changing theological priorities within the Church of England combined with the political and cultural pressures that drove the three kingdoms towards civil war. The independent government that was established by the Catholic Confederation as part of its pursuit of confessional politics was followed by a republican government that was established in pursuit of policy goals that included a broad religious toleration for orthodox protestants. Cromwell never gained in Ireland his Scottish reputation as the saviour of the Catholic Church: in Scotland, Cromwell permitted the private exercise of Catholic religion while Presbyterians attempted to eradicate it.[160] But, in abandoning the expectation that the nation should share a single faith, he stepped away from the religious monopolies imagined by the leaders of the largest denominations, and may have done more than any other early modern ruler of Ireland to imagine a religiously plural society. The Cromwellian regime never made the Irish protestant—but it might have had the best chance of doing so.

After the Restoration, the persecution of religious dissenters was not as ferocious in Ireland as it was in England, where in the 1660s and early 1670s there continued a persecution of protestants by protestants that was without parallel in early modern Europe.[161] Nevertheless, the Church of Ireland occupied a very privileged position. Strictly speaking, all other forms of worship were made illegal. The legal elevation of the Church of Ireland promoted common interests among the elite Anglicans, as well as shared frustrations among Catholics and dissenters, whose social, economic, and political lives were increasingly restricted. English dissenters benefited from the Toleration Act (1688) and the Bill of Rights (1689), by means of which they were allowed to worship in public as long as their preachers obtained a government licence. But the terms of the Toleration Act were not extended to dissenters in Ireland, who had to wait until 1714 to benefit from similar legislation, nor to Catholics, whose religion would not be officially tolerated until the 1780s. Catholics would only gain the right to vote in 1829, while mixed marriages that were celebrated by a Presbyterian minister would not be legally valid until 1844.[162] In the complex and bloody aftermath of a failed reformation, the Anglican state made a determined effort to re-imagine Christian Ireland.

4

Revivals

The Irish state that was established in the aftermath of the Glorious Revolution (1689–1690) consolidated its ascendency by excluding from its benefits the overwhelming majority of the island's population—including the almost half of its protestants.[1] Throughout the eighteenth century, membership of the Church of Ireland never amounted to much more than 10 per cent of the inhabitants of the island. Although its adherents took control of parliament, the army, and the offices of the crown, and were deeply divided by arguments about such issues as the optimal method of containing the Catholic Church and the ideal relationship with the English parliament, the church by law established was so unrepresentative of the wider population that it 'more nearly resembled a sect'.[2] In this sense, Ireland was a typical *ancien régime* society, in which landowners presided over a confessional state, wielding enormous power in a deeply conservative and high stratified society, 'in which vertical ties of patronage and clientship were more important than horizontal bonds of shared economic or social position, and in which even popular protest was conducted within the assumptions that underlay the existing social order'.[3] Despite the narrowly sectional interests of the Church of Ireland, its constitutional pre-eminence determined the state's political and economic structure. But the future of the protestant establishment, with its roots in the 1530s, was only secured in 1714, when George I, a German-speaking Lutheran, acceded to the throne, seeing off the possibility of accession by James III and a long line of Catholic kings. Serious challenges continued, including the Jacobite conspiracies that attracted emotional if not military support among Irish Catholics throughout the first half of the eighteenth century.[4] There are no hard statistics to reveal the size of each religious community in eighteenth-century Ireland. A surprising number of individuals moved between these communities, like the Gaelic-speaking Scots who, in the 1690s, assimilated into the Catholic cultures of the north-east, attracted by their common language.[5] Catholics probably accounted for between 75 and 80 per cent of the total population.[6] But the power of the Anglican elite consolidated as its minority status became increasingly obvious.

In the eighteenth century, Irish society passed through some very significant changes. A rapidly growing population experienced major environmental challenges between the war of the two kings (1689–1690) and the Act of Union (1800). The island's population increased from around 2 million in 1700 to 6.8 million people in 1821.[7] As the population increased, so too did the difficulty of feeding it. *A proposal for the universal use of Irish manufactures* (1721) by the dean of Dublin's St Patrick's cathedral, Jonathan Swift, was a carefully calculated attempt to intervene in public discussion about how best to improve economic conditions. Swift became frustrated by the lassitude of the authorities, and his *Modest proposal for preventing the children of poor people from being a burthen to the parents or the country, and making them beneficial to the public* (1729) proposed a more radical solution to the problems of over-population and poverty—it suggested that Catholic youngsters should be cannibalized. Swift's satire was bitterly prescient, for the famine of 1741 was the worst in the island's history. Up to 20 per cent of the island's population may have died of dearth and the diseases that followed, with disproportionate effects among the Catholic rural poor.[8] From the mid-eighteenth century, the Irish economy expanded as a result of linen manufacturing and changes in agricultural practice. The adoption of the potato as a reliable stable for an expanding population stabilized the situation in the short term but would come to have unpredictable consequences one century later.

In the mid-eighteenth century, the devastation of the Catholic rural poor contributed to what may have been the most significant cultural change in early modern Ireland. The decline of the Irish language became a powerful symbol of the victory, if not the hegemonic power, of English culture. This process of linguistic change was long-standing.[9] By the late seventeenth century, even Queen Elizabeth's enthusiasm for Irish-language printing had been forgotten. When, in 1675, plans were hatched to publish a complete Irish Bible, Robert Boyle had to pay for the manufacture of a new font. But these Bibles did not sell, and some of the surplus stock was 'dumped' in Scotland.[10] Demand for these publications was extremely low, even among the small community of Irish-speaking protestants.[11] Of the 6,000 editions of the Book of Common Prayer and Church of Ireland catechism that were produced by the Society for the Promotion of Christian Knowledge (1709), for example, only five were sold in the first few years after publication.[12] Of course, huge numbers of Irish-speaking Catholics lived west of the Shannon. But apart from a few clergy with antiquarian interests in the language, parishes in this poorest of regions were not provided with much in the way of appropriate pastoral oversight. Catholic priests tended to be recruited from the mercantile and agricultural middle class, which had tended to embrace the shift to English. Those seminarians who did have a background in the Irish language often lost that facility while attending the continental colleges. By the time of the foundation of the seminary at Maynooth (1795), which raised the possibility that seminarians could be taught in an environment that affirmed their Gaelic identity, it was too late to reverse the trend.[13] Outside of a few regions, and apart from a few individuals, both the established church and the Catholic Church were losing interest in the vernacular.[14]

If, across the seventeenth and eighteenth centuries, the most significant cultural change was the loss of Irish, the most significant demographic change may have been in religion. For as the population increased, and language shift continued, the population of the island became less Catholic. In 1600, Scots and English protestants had accounted for less than 2 per cent of the island's population, but by the early eighteenth century, they represented around 27 per cent of the whole.[15] Nevertheless, even as their numbers grew to around 10 per cent of the total population, dissenters—like their Catholic neighbours—found Ireland's *ancien régime* to be a very cold house.[16] Introduced over five decades, and in almost haphazard fashion, penal laws excluded Catholics and dissenters from participation in the new state.[17] Similar laws existed elsewhere in Europe, of course, where national churches clamped down on the religious practice of those minorities who refused to submit to their demands. But in Ireland the situation was reversed. In Ireland, it was the established church that represented the minority population, and its members protected their status through laws, institutions, and cultures that repressed the majority—including those large numbers of dissenters upon whose loyalty to the regime, whose hostility to Catholicism, and whose willingness to bear arms the security of the state depended.[18] While there were certainly regional variations, the laws regarding landowning were more vigorously pursued than were the laws against religious practice, especially after Pope Pius VI withdrew his support for the Jacobite cause in 1766, though they could be more robustly enforced in moments of crisis. The implementation of the penal laws revealed that their true purpose was to impoverish those Catholic landowners whose land holdings had somehow survived the massive confiscations of the previous century in order to protect the Anglican elite from the threat of renewed rebellion. Despite their sectarian character, the penal laws were designed to uphold the privileges of the minority of Anglicans and were not intended to persuade members of other denominations to convert. This lesson became apparent to those who did transfer their loyalties to the established church and the vision of society that it represented: an act passed in 1728 limited the number of converts from Catholicism who could practise at the bar. The penal laws appeared to police religious difference, but they worked to protect the interests of a social and economic elite, even as a new Catholic middle class began to consolidate around interests in trade.

The Irish establishment rested on such a narrow social base that, at least in the minds of many of its leaders, it remained vulnerable. While Irish Catholics did not rise in support of the Jacobite rebellions in 1715 and 1745, the Dublin parliament felt sufficiently concerned about the security of the state that it continued to pass new penal legislation throughout this period. Designed to support the security of the establishment, these laws actually undermined it—first by frustrating the Catholic population, whose economic, political, and religious freedoms these laws curtailed, and second by encouraging conditional loyalty among dissenters, who found themselves positioned as a buffer between their Catholic neighbours and the Anglican elite, with both of which parties at different times and for different reasons they made common cause. Ironically, as their participation in the war of the two kingdoms and the rebellion of United Irishmen proved, Presbyterians determined the viability of Ireland's *ancien régime*. In some respects, the laws offered these dissenters the balance of power: the Anglican state was secure only insofar as Presbyterians supported it, and Catholic attempts to gain political and economic equality were viable only when they gained significant Presbyterian support. Yet, while the state attempted to control the Presbyterian community, it could not curtail their growth.[19] Successive waves of immigration in the 1680s and 1690s caused the number of Presbyterians to swell, while their industry and connections within the trans-Atlantic Scottish diaspora enabled them also to increase in influence and wealth. As Ireland became less Catholic, the numbers of dissenters continued to grow.

These changes meant that the religious—and therefore political—situation could never be taken for granted. The Irish Act of Uniformity (1666) made it illegal for anyone other than a clergyman of the Church of Ireland to administer communion, and required that all school teachers should take the sacrament according to the rites of the church by law established. While Irish Catholics and dissenters made small gains in James's declaration of indulgence (1687), and took advantage of its limited provisions for public worship, their legal situation was unchanged as a consequence of the English Toleration Act (1689). Dissenters won more freedoms under the Irish Toleration Act (1719), and were involved in a limited way in trade, commerce and the professions before the repeal of the Test Act in 1780.[20] Their marriage rites were not fully recognized until 1844. Catholics also remained subservient. They made significant gains under James, and dominated the parliament that he called in 1690, but in the aftermath of his defeat these achievements were rapidly reversed. The promises of religious freedom that were made in the Treaty of Limerick (1691), which brought an end to the war of the two kings, were never fulfilled, despite the Irish parliament's ratifying of the treaty—albeit some six years after it was signed—and the repeated protestations of loyalty to the crown from influential leaders of the growing Catholic mercantile class. While their marriages never lacked official recognition, in contrast to the marriages of dissenters, the achievement of political rights for Catholics was painfully slow. They maintained a network of more than 500 schools, entirely illegally, which would certainly have contributed to their resilience.[21] Catholics gained voting rights in 1793, but were still precluded from sitting as MPs. When full emancipation was offered in 1829, it came in a bill that actually reduced the numbers of those who could vote.

The penal laws demonstrated the risks that the establishment would tolerate in order to remain a minority that positioned itself as an elite. If the establishment had treated dissenters more generously, Presbyterians could have abandoned their conditional loyalty to the Irish *ancien régime* and have more effectively consolidated the 'protestant interest' before the repeal of the Test Act in 1780. Similarly, if middle-class Catholics had been welcomed into the functions of the state, they could have legitimized its rule, as Edmund Burke and other reformers realized—and this incorporation of Catholic interests would have been constitutionally beneficial after the papacy swung away from the Stuarts to encourage support for George III. But neither of these possibilities were seriously explored before the late 1770s. The Anglican establishment recognized its vulnerability but chose to preserve its privileges by retaining its minority status, suppressing opportunities for those outside the established church in the expectation that dissenters would always defend the protestant constitution and those who most benefitted from it. This was a dangerous gamble. The successful revolution of protestant dissenters in the American colonies (1776) and the bloody end of the *ancien régime* in France (1789) showed that religious communities that were repressed in Ireland could pursue radical actions in order to win significant political gains. And, at the end of the eighteenth century, this is what happened. The militarization of political opposition that resulted in a short but effective rebellion of Catholics in the south and west, and Presbyterians in the north-east, blew up in the summer and autumn of 1798 into a series of regional conflicts that resulted in spectacular sectarian brutality, war crime, and massive loss of life.[22] The rebellion revealed the serious threat posed by a secret society of Catholics and dissenters with a membership that represented 10 per cent of the island's population, that had linked up with fellow-travellers in England and that had coordinated military support from revolutionary France.[23] With a vast number of members, thousands of weapons, and the support of a hostile foreign power, the United Irishmen looked set to achieve their revolution. But the revolution, when it came, was a bloody failure, undermined by the sectarian hatreds that the movement had set out to overcome. It also illustrated the failure of the newly independent Irish parliament, which had shown itself unable to preserve the security of the island, and therefore also threatening the security of the British state. In the aftermath of the rising, the ascendancy closed in upon itself, as Westminster plotted an end to the short-won legislative independence of the Dublin parliament. Members of the newly formed Orange Order were strongly opposed to the plans for a union that they believed would lead to Catholic emancipation. Patriot MPs feared that Westminster politicians could not be trusted to defend Irish protestant interests. The Dublin parliament rejected a motion for union in 1799, but, in 1800, through effective 'management'—including the award of peerages and other honours—a majority in favour of union was created.

Even if the union did little to change the political mathematics of the early nineteenth century, it changed everything in the long term. Its political logic was clear. The collapsing of the Dublin into the Westminster parliament proposed a British solution for an Irish problem. The union was designed to minimize the impact of newly enfranchised Catholic voters. Catholics would be given political rights in a structure in which they were re-framed as a minority, for, in the much larger political culture of the

United Kingdom, Irish Catholic voters could express their political opinions without the threat of constitutional upheaval. The leaders of the ascendency discovered that they had been right to worry about the effects of the
union. They had given up their most effective means to resist the more
progressive policies of the Westminster parliament, which seemed determined to address the issue of Catholic exclusion without paying any heed
to their advice.

In the aftermath of union, protestant political interests consolidated as their
denominational landscape became more diverse. From the mid-eighteenth
century, the monopoly of the established church and its principal Presbyterian
rival had been challenged by the emergence of new communities associated
with a trans-Atlantic religious revival. Emphasizing personal religious
experience, and downplaying distinctive ecclesiological claims, evangelicalism offered a religious identity that successfully transcended denominational
boundaries.[24] Pioneered in the mid-eighteenth century by John Cennick
and other Moravians, as well as conservative Presbyterians, and supported
among Anglicans by John Wesley, George Whitefield, and others who would
become known as Methodists, the new movement provided converts with
a sometimes dramatic experience of salvation, and rapidly grew: Wesley
made his first of more than twenty visits to Ireland in 1747, and 15,000 had
identified with his new movement by the time of his death 1791.[25] Some
Methodist preachers were outrageously flamboyant. Gideon Ouseley sang
and preached in Irish at markets and fairs throughout the country. 'One-
eyed, barrel-chested and with a liberal dose of native humour and agrarian
metaphor', his anti-clericalism resonated in the years after the United
Irishmen rising.[26] Driven by enthusiasm to share their faith, evangelicals
were relentlessly entrepreneurial. After 1814, missionaries of the Baptist Irish
Society itinerated around the midlands, setting up Irish-language schools to
provide basic literacy and Bible education, working from the tiny handful
of congregations that had survived from the Cromwellian period to establish almost forty new churches by the end of the 1840s. These activities
became 'remarkable' for the goodwill that existed between Baptist missionaries and the rural poor.[27] Among the 'Bible gentry' of the Church of
Ireland, pious landlords supporting a more aggressive 'second reformation'
did what they could to promote this generic protestantism among their
Catholic tenants, combining religious instruction with special opportunities
in education or welfare, a strategy of 'souperism' to which critics pointed to

explain apostasy from the Catholic Church—sometimes exaggerating the significance of the practice in order to do so.[28] The pursuit of these ends became extraordinarily controversial during the catastrophe of the potato famine. In the mid-1840s, after the failure of the potato crop, the death from starvation and disease of 1 million of the mainly Catholic rural poor was accompanied by the emigration of 1 million survivors.[29]

Evangelicalism did best in the industrialized north-east, where protestant communities were strongest, and where the famine had made least impact.[30] In 1859, and after several years of sectarian tensions, a major revival of religious enthusiasm broke out in the north-east counties.[31] As in similar phenomena in the United States, Scotland, and Wales, the revival promoted an intense and individual evangelical spirituality at the same time that it collapsed barriers between clergy and laity as well as barriers between protestant denominations.[32] As thousands of people reported dramatic spiritual experiences, there developed for the first time in the Ulster counties a credible alternative to clerically driven dissent. There was no doubting the movement's extraordinary impact. In its immediate aftermath, it was estimated that around 100,000 individuals had experienced evangelical conversion.[33] Promoting an intense but generic spirituality, and largely avoiding questions of denominational difference, the revival united northern protestants. In its aftermath, evangelicals nevertheless understood themselves as a distinct community, which reaffirmed denominational identities while also transcending them. Evangelicals prized religious ideas such as justification by faith alone above the political doctrines by which their ancestors had been drawn into common cause with Catholics. This triumph of religious over political identities consolidated a new set of social and electoral divisions that survived the disestablishment of the Church of Ireland. The effect of the 1859 revival was that the communities of Irish protestants became both more denominationally diverse and more politically united. Protestants who not been brought together by the economic compulsion of the penal laws were instead combined by the powerful effects of evangelical faith and by fears about the possibility of Home Rule—and by the possibility that their submersion into an overwhelmingly Catholic electorate would lead to 'Rome rule'.

In the same period, Catholic religion was similarly transformed. While never promoting the emotionalism that characterized the revivalist piety of the evangelicals, the Catholic 'devotional revolution' drew upon several generations of changes in popular belief and behaviour to promote, in the aftermath of the potato famine, catechism, regular confession, and weekly mass attendance.[34] Paul Cullen, the archbishop of Dublin, pushed for the Romanization of local piety and practice, becoming the first Irish cardinal in 1866 and helping to formulate the doctrine of papal infallibility at the First Vatican Council (1869–1870). His programme of renewal was extraordinarily effective, especially among the poor who migrated into Belfast, for example, where newly constructed parish churches did so much to rebuild the more familiar structures of rural life.

By the 1870s, in urban centres and rural towns, as well as in Ireland's 'spiritual empire', in England, Australia, and the United States, the power of the Catholic Church was at its height. By the end of the century it was sending out large numbers of missionaries, with varying degrees of training, enthusiasm, commitment and success. All Hallows College had been forming priests for work in the English-speaking world since 1842. The Maynooth mission to India was founded in the same period.[35] The impact of these missionary projects was felt especially in the new world: the Catholic cathedral in New York, the first building for which was opened in 1815, was called after St Patrick.[36] But the reach of the Irish Church was global, too: almost one-third of the 730 bishops attending the First Vatican Council were Irish or of Irish descent.[37]

The power of these religious communities became increasingly important at home. In the early nineteenth century, the complexities of the *ancien régime* were radically simplified, as the multiple identities of the eighteenth century gave way to the differentiation of Catholics and nationalists versus protestants and unionists. This religious and political calculus dominated events at the end of the century and drove the balkanization of culture in the run-up to successive Home Rule crises. By the end of the nineteenth century, and partly as a consequence of the rise of evangelicalism and the Catholic devotional revolution, the complex and unstable 'protestant interest' that had provided a common purpose for elite Anglicans and dissenters was giving way to a much more straightforward and sometimes overtly sectarian politics. The 'national question' continued to haunt Irish society as protestant and Catholic churches were revitalized. Through the eighteenth and nineteenth centuries, Irish Catholics had grown enormously in confidence and success under protestant rule. As another crisis beckoned, protestants identified with the constitution and Catholics with the nation. The stage was set—again—for war.

I

The history of eighteenth-century Ireland begins and ends in a bloodbath. The political machinations that followed upon the accession of William and Mary and the defeat of the armies of James II set the agenda for the century of legislative experiment, trans-confessional cooperation, and social and political instability that marked the Irish experience of enlightenment as well as its horrific climax in the summer of 1798.[38] But this train of events was not inevitable. Irish Presbyterians could have supported James, as some dissenters did in England, at least until his counter-revolution disbarred them from crown offices and the birth of his son in 1688 signalled the prospect of a Catholic dynasty. Despite his packing the Irish army and judiciary with Catholics, and the possibility that he would overturn the Restoration land settlement, James was neither a constitutional revolutionary nor a supporter of Irish independence. In fact, paying attention to how events in Ireland would be perceived in his other kingdoms, he quashed an attempt in the overwhelmingly Catholic parliament that he called in Dublin in 1690 to repudiate Henry VII's Poyning's law and to assert the institution's legislative autonomy. (It was fortunate for later generations of Catholics that the Dublin parliament was unsuccessful in gaining its legislative independence, for Poyning's law radically restricted its ability to invent new kinds of religious persecution.[39]) Neither, despite his well-known zeal as a relatively recent convert, was James any kind of religious bigot. Irish dissenters had a great deal to gain from his policy of religious toleration. Presbyterians would have benefited from the indulgence that he promised, whatever their concern that their Catholic neighbours might do the same. Some Presbyterians recognized the opportunity that his intervention represented, and seized the opportunity of his indulgence to withhold their tithes to the established church. By the same token, there was every reason for Catholics to support William. After all, the Prince of Orange had received the blessing of the pope, largely because his efforts to resist James coincided with the Vatican's efforts to stymie the strategy of James's ally, Louis XIV of France, who was attempting to make the French church independent of Rome. But these opportunities for a more creative politics were not widely taken up. The crisis of the late 1680s was too easily represented as a struggle between religions and competing political claims. As the crisis deepened, Catholics lined up behind James and protestants behind William, and the war of the two kings became a zero-sum sectarian contest. The conflict resulted in 25,000 deaths in combat, including 7,000 deaths in combat at the battle of Aughrim on 12 July 1691—the highest death toll recorded on any day in Irish history.[40] Whatever the experience elsewhere, in Ireland, the Glorious Revolution was a long experience of slaughter.

Just as Presbyterians could have supported James in conflict, so Irish Catholics could have supported William in peace. After all, the Treaty of Limerick (1691) that was agreed after William's victory promised that Irish Catholics should 'enjoy such privileges in the exercise of their religion as are consistent with the laws of Ireland, or as they did enjoy in the reign of King Charles the Second'.[41] But, in the next of many reminders that Irish prot- estants tended to have narrower views of religious pluralism than did their English counterparts, the Dublin parliament, dominated again by members of the Church of Ireland, disagreed. For the next sixty years, this parliament passed at least one penal law at its every session.[42] By eroding those Catholic landholdings that had survived the massive transfers of the previous century, the penal laws, enacted between 1692 and 1756, were intended to ensure that the protestant minority would never experience the revolutionary reversal that it had faced under James II.

This raft of legislation began to be enacted in 1692, when the Irish parlia- ment compelled its members to repudiate the mass, transubstantiation, and papal authority, with the effect that seats in parliament were reserved for protestants until Catholics were re-admitted to Westminster in 1829.[43] The first of the penal laws forbade Catholics bearing arms, from enjoying crown offices, from careers in the legal profession or army, and removed the right to vote; required that priests should be registered, and bishops, monks, and friars expelled; that Catholics could neither buy land, rent it for more than thirty-one years, nor inherit it from a protestant; and that when Catholic landowners did die, their land was to be equally divided among all their sons, unless one converted to the established church, in which case he could claim the entire holding, even during his father's lifetime.[44] These laws were rolled out in stages and in changing circumstances. In 1697, the Banishment Act formally ejected from Ireland all bishops and regular clergy. In 1703, further legislation prohibited the arrival into Ireland of any foreign priest. In 1704, the Registration Act required priests to provide a substantial bond for their good behaviour and to remain within the county in which they had been registered. The expansion of the Registration Act in 1709 increased the financial value of the reward—or bribe—that priests would receive upon their conversion to the established church.[45] But, with the exception of the latter item, these laws were not intended to promote conversions. Converts were objects of suspicion, as illustrated in the 1728 act that limited the number of Catholics-turned-Anglicans that could be called to the bar. Whatever the debate among historians, the Irish governing class seem to have understood by the early eighteenth century that there was no real prospect of mass conversions. As early as 1711, William King, the Anglican archbishop of Dublin, recognized that the protestant strategy was not designed to achieve religious change.[46] For the laws of inheritance aimed at economic rather than religious goals. The penal laws were designed to weaken and impoverish Catholics rather than to persuade them away from their faith. As the constant division of Catholic landholdings suggests, with the inevitable reduction of individually owned acreage as one generation followed upon another, the penal laws were especially focused on perpetuating and exacerbating economic disadvantage. The cumulative effect of this legislation was the steady erosion of a Catholic landowning class (as well as the transfer of what remained of Catholic political power to the growing mercantile middle class). This explains why the economic provisions of the laws were enforced more often than were their religious provisions. This also explains why, when the proportion of land held by Catholics fell to around 5 per cent, restrictions on Catholic worship fell into disuse.[47] As the Anglican establishment achieved their economic goals, and consolidated their political power, they began to relax restrictions on religion.

Not everyone was content to live within the religious and economic binary that the penal laws presupposed. Some moments of cross-confessional friendship suggested the possibility of alternative futures. In 1708, for example, several protestants provided bail for a Catholic priest who had protected them during the reign of King James.[48] In other instances, protestants held property in trust for Catholic neighbours.[49] While some evaded the law, others set about resisting it. In the early eighteenth century, a new Catholic middle class emerged, with its wealth based not upon land but upon trade.[50] As this community grew in confidence, Catholic religious institutions began to revive. Five new bishops were appointed in 1707, and all episcopal vacancies were filled within thirty years.[51] By 1720, several communities of friars and two convents had been established in Dublin.[52] From the 1730s, Dublin newspapers carried respectful obituaries of Catholic priests.[53] By the middle of the eighteenth century, the church had made a 'good recovery' from the initial impact of the penal laws, for 'its worship was uninterrupted, its hierarchy was intact and it was provided with an adequate supply of priests'.[54] Catholic entrepreneurs took advantage of the decline of religious persecution to establish a vigorous print culture in which to promote their faith. Their experience was uneven. In 1707, two Catholic booksellers were fined for having published a devotional manual, but protestants were delighted when Cornelius Nary, a Dublin priest, published an edition of the New Testament in 1718. Catholic readers had a growing appetite for Scripture. The first complete edition of a Douai Bible appeared in five volumes in Dublin in 1763–1764, while an edition of the Bible published in Cork in 1816 attracted 2,000 subscribers.[55] Between 1817 and 1852, over 300,000 Douai Bibles were printed in Ireland.[56] But some of these entrepreneurs faced other kinds of difficulties. Nary's New Testament was banned by Roman authorities, apparently because it bore the imprimatur of French theologians who had fallen out of favour with the pope. By the 1750s, friars were more at risk from the reforms that were being promoted by Pope Benedict XIV than from any suppression by the Irish government.[57] Ironically, Benedict's ability to intervene in the Irish church was in some ways enabled by the consequences of penal legislation. In the absence of a functioning conciliar system, the Irish hierarchy was forced to look to the papacy for guidance.[58] The anxious Anglicans who framed and continued to enlarge the scope of the penal laws could never have imagined that their efforts served only to strengthen their foremost denominational rivals. For, despite their reputation, it has been claimed, the penal laws did not lead to the destruction of the Catholic Church in Ireland, but to its revival.[59]

Dissenters were disadvantaged in other ways. The 1704 act to prevent the growth of popery included a sacramental test that required all holders of crown offices to take communion within the Church of Ireland.[60] This act excluded dissenters from the Irish parliament and crown offices, even as they were compelled to maintain the Church of Ireland through tithes, which could be forcibly collected: in the 1730s, the archdeacon of Raphoe required the help of sixty-two mounted assistants to prise his tithe of barley from the cold hands of local Presbyterians.[61] These compelled payments were necessary for the survival of the established church: in 1818, a Church of Ireland survey demonstrated that only two of the eighty-seven parishes in the diocese of Meath were economically self-sufficient, and that several of these parishes did not have any protestant residents.[62] As this compulsory tithing suggests, the cooperation between Anglicans and dissenters that made possible the Glorious Revolution had not long survived it. Having supplied significant manpower in the Williamite forces, Presbyterians expected that their sacrifices would be rewarded, and began to hope that the established church would move from an episcopal to a Presbyterian model, just as had happened in Scotland. Their claims grew ever more urgent in the 1690s, as a new wave of migration from Scotland increased their numbers, much to the concern of Anglican authorities.[63] Presbyterians now represented almost half of the protestant population of Ireland, and were a clear majority in large parts of Ulster.[64] But they were excluded from full participation in the state that they had fought to defend. The benefits of the 1689 Toleration Act were not extended to Ireland until 1719, when dissenters gained limited legal rights for public worship.[65] But other disadvantages continued—most obviously in terms of marriage. In the later seventeenth century, the ecclesiastical courts of the Church of Ireland had routinely denied the legitimacy of any marriage that had been conducted by a Presbyterian minister. In 1711, the Convocation of the Church of Ireland formalized this view in a ruling that prohibited recognition of any marriage of protestants that had not been celebrated by an Anglican clergyman. This decision allowed those Presbyterians who had been married according to the rites of their own church to be prosecuted for fornication, and declared that the children of these unions were to be regarded as illegitimate, which in turn made it impossible for these children to inherit property from their parents. Only in 1737 did a Relief Act legalize the marriage of Presbyterians by a Presbyterian minister.[66] But marriages of couples of mixed denominations carried out by Presbyterian ministers faced the stigma of illegitimacy and the compounding difficulties of inheritance until these unions were recognized in the Marriage Act of 1844. Other disadvantages continued in education. Throughout the eighteenth century, dissenters remained excluded from Trinity College, and pursued higher education either in short-lived dissenting academies, such as that established by Francis Hutcheson in Dublin, or at the University of Glasgow, where they studied with some of the brightest lights of the European enlightenment.[67] It might have been easier to travel to Dublin, but the educational experience did not compare to that on offer in Scotland. Between 1722 and 1753, while Scottish intellectuals refined the core ideas of enlightenment in a series of groundbreaking publications, not a single fellow of Trinity College Dublin published anything.[68] In unexpected ways, the penal laws offered some advantages to dissenters. Just as they contributed to the organizational revival of the Catholic Church, so too the penal laws pushed Presbyterians to fully engage with the most exciting intellectual trends of the enlightenment as they benefited from ministerial formation in the institutions of the Church of Scotland.

Nevertheless, whatever their later reputation for brutality and oppression, the penal laws could be honoured more in the breach than in the observance. Over time, laws relating to economic and legal power were most effectively enforced, while those penalizing religious practice were generally overlooked. The penal laws made no real effort to promote conversion, other than in the financial incentives—some might say bribes—that were offered to priests and those eldest sons who might be persuaded to convert. Catholic clergy continued to be trained in the continental seminaries, moved fairly freely in society, and certainly outnumbered their Anglican counterparts.[69] Those Anglicans who did want to promote conversion were obviously frustrated. John Wesley showed no surprise that so few Catholics joined the Church of Ireland when 'the Protestants can find no better ways to convert them than Penal Laws and Acts of Parliament'.[70] The confessional state sustained the economic advantages of members of the established church, but they did little to encourage anyone to join it.

While the penal laws were not always vigorously enforced, they were, in comparative terms, quite reasonable. They made sense of the presuppositions of those who framed them. The Irish legislature was determined to maintain social stability, and to curtail any possibility of a return to the civil war and horrific violence that had marked successive episodes of conflict in the previous century. Protestants were pragmatic. They may not have particularly admired Charles II, William and Mary, Anne, or any of the Georges that followed, but they always preferred the security of a strong state, and supported any monarch who would protect them and effectively support their interests.[71] This is why Irish protestant loyalty to Westminster—like Presbyterian loyalty to the Anglican elite—was always conditional. It was in the name of constitutional stability that the penal laws excluded from the state those individuals who were most likely to be Jacobites, and therefore those who are most likely to foment another civil war. In this, at least, they succeeded. While Scotland and England were convulsed in 1715 and 1745, when Jacobite incursions profoundly destabilized British society, Ireland remained untroubled. It was only after the Pope ceased to recognize Jacobite claims, in 1766, that discussions about the inclusion of Catholics within the apparatus of the state could be seriously considered.

And, if the penal laws were reasonable, they were also comparatively moderate. While, in Ireland, Catholic landowners could be impoverished, and priests could be expelled from the country, in France, in the same period, any Reformed minister who was discovered leading worship could be executed, and his parishioners sent to the galleys for life.[72] In a European context, the Irish situation was exceptional only insofar as its persecution of religious minorities was less severe than it was elsewhere. As C. D. A. Leighton has noted, those parts of the penal code that where enforced 'inflicted no extraordinary hardships' on Irish Catholics—although obviously the impact on Catholic landholding was disastrous.[73] However sporadically they were enforced, and however lenient they may have been in European perspective, nevertheless, the Irish penal laws succeeded in protecting the privileges of Anglicans.

The longer-term effect of the penal laws was to establish two distinct communities on the island. Those who were members of the Anglican ascendancy were granted privileges that protected their minority status and that allowed them to prosper. Those who were excluded from this minority looked elsewhere for support, either to the largely Catholic court of the exiled Jacobites or to the Presbyterian establishment of Scotland. These out-groups had distinct cultures, languages, loyalties, and religions. While Dublin sustained a large Church of Ireland population, Presbyterians dominated the north-east and Catholics the rest of the island. Protestants found Irish-speaking Gaelic Catholics both linguistically and politically incomprehensible. This inability to understand the conversation of the majority population undoubtedly contributed to the paranoia that coursed through protestant opinion in this period. For as a tiny minority struggling to control or at least contain a population whose every day conversation they could not easily understand, and weakened by a pragmatic and unstable alliance with a community of dissenters who drew inspiration from the destruction of a similar establishment in Scotland, the situation of the Anglican ascendancy class was simply untenable—and they knew it. Whether in holding dissenters at a distance, or in refusing to see the benefits of the incorporation of Catholics into the apparatus of the state, those who supported the penal laws suffered from a critical failure of imagination.

For Anglicans certainly felt vulnerable. The establishment that was reconfigured in the aftermath of the Glorious Revolution was only too aware of its weakness. After all, the counter-revolution that had been advanced under James had captured central institutions and, in reconsidering the land settlement, threatened to undermine the economic stability of the state. Christ Church cathedral had been requisitioned from the Church of Ireland to become a centre for Catholic worship, which had been attended by James.[74] In the parliament that he called in 1690, only six of the 230 MPs who were returned could be identified as protestants.[75] The Jacobite revolution had been an anxious time for many members of the Church of Ireland. Some had turned to determined prayer: 'knots of private Christians would weekly meet together, and spend whole days in mighty wrestlings with God', in an intense expression of personal piety that anticipated the rise of the evangelical movement one generation later.[76] Nor did this anxiety recede after the Williamite triumph, the confirmation of the land settlement, and the construction of a perpetually unsettled political normality. The Church of Ireland added a commemorative day to the liturgical calendar that they shared with their co-religionists in England, institutionalizing their memory of Catholic perfidy in 1641.[77] But the established church was in a poor state. Queen Mary had put it bluntly in 1690, when she described the Church of Ireland as 'the worst in Christendom'.[78] As T. C. Barnard has observed:

> Englishmen, tempted to Ireland by impressive-sounding dignities, suffered on arrival a cultural shock that too often snapped shut their minds. Their palaces turned out to be little better than thatched cabins or derelict shells; the trip into remoter dioceses as disorientating as a journey in Transylvania; and their congregations small and cantankerous. Newcomers preferred to lodge in Dublin.[79]

Some newcomers were surprised to find their new family home to be in poor repair, or parish church constructed as a fortified redoubt.[80] Clergy who had not advanced through the ranks were more likely to be of Irish extraction, and trained in the cheap but generally effective Trinity College.[81] Bishops could not always be relied upon to maintain orthodox doctrines. By the 1730s, their number included three reputedly guilty of heresy.[82] But even in the capital, fears that Irish protestants were lowering their standards led to concerted efforts in the 1690s to police moral behaviour. Concerns were directed at the abuse of alcohol. Then, as now, Ireland was suspected of supporting a vigorous culture of drinking. Sir William Petty estimated that 'a quarter of houses in Dublin and a third of those in the provinces sold alcohol'.[83] Other forms of vice were targeted. In the 1690s, voluntary groups with an interest in promoting a reformation of manners pushed for the criminalization of sabbath-breaking and swearing—though these laws turned out to be rather difficult to enforce—while others engaged in vigilante action against prostitutes.[84]

The anomalous nature of the Irish constitution was exemplified in its treatment of Presbyterians and members of other small religious movements. From 1672, Presbyterian ministers had shared in the *regium donum*—a grant from the king that augmented the livings of a clerical body whose work his ministers simultaneously forbade.[85] The grant was in some respects an invitation for the denomination to exercise better social control. But Presbyterian leaders struggled to demonstrate that they could control the opinions of their people. One of the down-sides of exposure to enlightened thinking in the Scottish universities was that a number of ministers came to doubt the necessity of subscription to a confession of faith. An increasing number of Presbyterians felt that they could safely move beyond the claims of the Westminster Confession. Its scholastic Calvinism did not suit the mood of the times. John Toland, a Donegal Catholic who converted to Presbyterianism and studied at the University of Glasgow, published *Christianity not mysterious* (1696) to argue that the claims of Christianity were entirely rational, only to be prosecuted for blasphemy and to have his book publicly burned in Dublin by order of the courts. Also in the capital, the Presbyterian minister Thomas Emlyn published *An humble inquiry into the Scripture account of Jesus Christ* (1702) to set out views that he would shortly describe as 'unitarian'.[86] For this challenge to traditional Trinitarian formularies he was imprisoned for blasphemy and fined £1,000. Along with another blasphemer, the Irish MP John Asgill, who wrote to defend his belief that death could be evaded, these individuals were forced to flee to England, where blasphemy laws were less rigidly enforced.[87] These men were lucky to get off so lightly. In Edinburgh, in 1697, facing similar charges, and despite having recanted, Thomas Aikenhead had been executed.[88] But the number of Presbyterians who doubted the need for confessional subscription continued to grow.[89]

Conversion offered an escape route for some scrupulous minds. After the subscription crisis of the 1720s, Presbyterian laypeople who wished for a more strenuous defence of Westminster theology took refuge in such new bodies as the Seceders (from 1746) and the movement of Covenanters that became known as the Reformed Presbyterian Church (from 1757). And dissent continued to diversify.[90] In the 1750s, John Cennick worked to establish around 200 short-lived Moravian communities, mainly in county Antrim, with strong links to central European pietism, producing a body of hymnody that would do much to shape evangelical piety. John Wesley and

George Whitefield led similar developments among Anglicans, and led a community that eventually developed its own identity as Methodist, which throughout the later eighteenth century remained relatively small. Quakers held their own, though their numbers were never large, consolidating their power in industry and banking. But the older and smaller dissenting groups continued to decline. By the end of the eighteenth century, the Baptist community, which was never large, was on the verge of extinction.[91] Many protestants continued to move between dissenting groups. Others converted to Catholicism, including the grandson of Edmund Spenser, who was pros- ecuted for his new faith. Luke Joseph Hooke, the great-grandson of the Cromwellian general John Lambert, became a leading thinker in the Catholic enlightenment.[92]

For the situation of the Catholic Church, and the lot of its members, was beginning to improve. As the penal laws came to be more sporadically enforced, a Catholic middle class began to form, dominating merchant life in locations such as Waterford, Cork, Limerick, and Galway. With a newly acquired stake in the *status quo*, these middle-class Catholics began to push for the reform of the system, rather than its overthrow. Building on efforts by Catholic gentry to proclaim loyalty to George II upon his accession in 1727, the leaders of the Catholic Committee in 1756 attempted to find a form of words that would demonstrate their loyalty to the Hanoverian regime, though on neither occasion did their work gain clerical approval.[93] The committee's concerns were focused upon a payment required of mer- chants who could not or would not become full members of trade guilds. It sought to give a united voice to Catholic opinion, but its grievances were clearly those of the urban mercantile elite.[94] From this committee, and iron- ically from those Catholics who had a stake in the economic system, there grew the institutions that would work most effectively to resist hegemony. For the threat to the ascendency system came not from the margins but from the centre of Catholic financial power. The committee's agenda pre- sented the first serious alternative to Jacobitism for Irish Catholics, with the emphasis no longer upon the installation of an alternative dynasty but now upon the rights of subjects within the Hanoverian regime. This marked the transformation—even the radicalization—of Irish Catholic opinion. The competition between competing brands of monarchism give way to conflict between the dominant view of society and the claims of those upon its margins. The Catholic middle class became aware of the possibilities raised by the Québec Act of 1774, which provided the Catholic Church with an

establishment status within the British realm. This act was all the more symbolic in that it rewarded those Catholics who were loyal to the British
crown and who would support its conflict with those American colonists
holding Presbyterian and Congregational views. Irish critics began to realize that British policy was more interested in strategic than confessional
goals. The stage was set for the effective incorporation of Catholics within
the Irish state—even as British politicians raised questions about the loyalty
of dissenters.

These worries came to a head in the 1770s, when Ulster Presbyterians
were given a surprising political education—an American revolution.[95] The
context for their action was unlikely. Ireland was heavily militarized. In
1775, over 12,000 soldiers—one-quarter of the entire British army—were
stationed on the island.[96] These troop numbers declined rapidly as a consequence of the American war of independence. In their absence, and concerned by a breakdown in law and order, middle-class Presbyterians formed
militias. There was good reason for their concern about public safety.
Presbyterians in the north-east had very strong links with the rebellious
American colonies. As many as 200,000 Ulster people may have emigrated
to north America between 1717 and 1776.[97] Many of these emigrants participated in the American revolution, which, one observer claimed, was
'nothing more or less than a Scotch Irish Presbyterian rebellion'.[98] That was
certainly how many Irish Presbyterians understood the war. The Battle of
Bunker Hill (1775) was celebrated with bonfires on the hills of county
Antrim.[99] The *Belfast Newsletter* was the first newspaper in Europe to print
the text of the Declaration of Independence in full. These attitudes reflected
the enduring character of dissenting culture in the north-east. In 1787, the
duke of Rutland was astonished to discover that 'the province of Ulster is
filled with Dissenters, who are in general very factious—great levellers and
republicans...The dissenting ministers are for the most part very seditious,
and have great sway over their flocks.'[100] His claim was not much of an
exaggeration. For the American revolution was not much celebrated elsewhere in Ireland. While Presbyterians applauded American rebels, and supported their political objectives, Catholic bishops proclaimed their loyalty
to the crown.[101]

As the crisis continued, the Volunteers, as the landowners' militias were
known, played a critical role in providing security. As a trans-confessional
movement, which brought together Anglicans, dissenters and a smaller
number of Catholics, the Volunteers began as a markedly conservative force,

but quickly developed an energetic and surprisingly democratic culture of their own.[102] Leaders of the Volunteers had never agreed upon how the Catholic question should be resolved, but that ambiguity had not much mattered while the most pressing problems related to the ambitions of rebellious colonists. Representatives of the Volunteers met to debate policy and drew up a raft of legislative proposals. A small group among the membership began to argue for more radical ends, including Catholic emancipation. Some Volunteer companies sponsored the construction of Catholic church buildings in counties Antrim, Derry, and Down.[103] But the end of the American conflict saw 20,000 soldiers return home, giving the government greater power to resist this kind of radical action.[104] Still, the government offered concessions. The relief acts of 1778 and 1782 improved the lot of Catholics and protestant dissenters. In 1782, the striking down of Poyning's law granted legislative independence to the Irish parliament, and created the space for the 'patriot politics' of Henry Grattan. Members of the Church of Ireland increasingly identified as Irish as MPs in College Green took advantage of the parliament's autonomy. But this was 'an illusory independence for an imaginary people'.[105] For the question haunted political debate: exactly who comprised the Irish political nation? By the early 1780s, this question dominated Irish politics. Some radicals, like the Belfast Presbyterian William Drennan, kept alive the ideal of cross-confessional cooperation for the shared goal of progressive politics. In 1784, he appealed to

> Churchmen, Presbyterians, and Catholics to embrace each other in the mild spirit of Christianity and to unite as a secret compact in the cause of your sinking country—For you are all Irishmen—you are nurtured by the same material earth...show that it is your religion to be free.[106]

If Ulster Presbyterians had been radicalized by the American revolution, Catholics in the rest of the island were more obviously radicalized by events in France. Drennan's vision was renewed after the French revolution proved that Catholics could rise to overturn a repressive social order. In the 1790s, the 'politics of the Catholic and Presbyterian mercantile classes began for the first time to converge'.[107] In 1791, Drennan and other middle-class Presbyterians founded the Society of United Irishmen.

As momentum gathered for radical action, the Irish government continued to grant concessions. In 1793, a Relief Act granted legal toleration to the Catholic Church, which then became 'the largest voluntary association in the British Isles'.[108] New laws permitted Catholics to carry arms and serve on juries. They could vote on the same terms as protestants, although they still could not be returned as MPs.[109] In 1795, the House of Commons agreed to fund a Catholic seminary that would be built at Maynooth, granting the church a semi-establishment status, to the horror of protestants everywhere. But these initiatives satisfied no one. Many protestants felt the legislation conceded too much, while many Catholics felt it had not gone far enough. Managing a failing strategy, British policy turned again towards repression. The crisis peaked in the summer of 1795, when religious violence suddenly escalated in county Armagh. Following a long tradition of rural secret societies, including the Defenders, whose interests in local agrarian conflict escalated towards a national political agenda, protestants banded together to form a new society, which became known as the Orange Order. Within three years, the new movement had a membership of over 12,000.[110] It continued to grow as the threat from the United Irishmen also increased. By 1798, the United Irishmen claimed a membership of half a million— around one-tenth of the total population of the island.[111]

As their numbers grew, the United Irishmen continued to press their agenda. In December 1795, Wolfe Tone, who had been convicted of plotting, was exiled to France, where he attempted to bring in the revolutionary government on the side of the Society. In December 1796, he returned with a French fleet carrying 15,000 soldiers, sailing to Bantry Bay before adverse winds prevented the landing of the troops.[112] The British government woke up to the impending threat of invasion. As the situation spiralled out of control, United Irishmen leaders responded to the imposition of martial law by agreeing that the time for revolution had come.

The leaders of the United Irishmen were not able to agree upon much else. As the Society expanded throughout Ireland, it had become more politically, economically, and religiously diverse. Its leaders did not agree either on the ends to pursue or the optimal means of achieving them. Some combined enlightened political thinking with strongly anti-Catholic instincts. Drennan, for example, admitted that he did not like 'the Catholic mind...it is a churlish soil, but it is the soil of Ireland and must be cultivated or we must emigrate'.[113] For all that these ideologues claimed the mantle of enlightenment and 'thought like radicals', David A. Wilson has noted, many of them 'felt like settlers'.[114] This lack of unity among their leaders explains why the United Irishmen made competing kinds of arguments. They valorized 'a secular, democratic liberalism and a nationalism that quickly became defined in racial and religious terms'.[115] Middle-class and Presbyterian

members understood the problem as the failure of the British government
to live up to its own ideals, to which they appealed as they worked for constitutional change. But the poor and Catholic members that were attracted
to the movement looked for more fundamental changes that might reverse
centuries of landowning rights. When—quite literally—push came to shove,
the United Irishmen were 'anything but united'.[116]

The movement's ambiguities and contradictions became evident when
the rising began on 23 May 1798, and as it continued into early September.
In Wexford, where former members of the Defenders dominated the
Society, the rebellion took the form of sectarian war. Beginning on 5 June,
United Irishmen proclaimed a republic in Wexford town, summarily executed loyalists on a bridge over the river Slaney, and burned to death over
100 protestants who had been corralled in a barn.[117] Government forces
responded in kind, executing up to 500 United Irish prisoners at the
Curragh, county Kildare.[118] In the north-east, where rebellion broke out on
7 June, United Irishmen were overwhelmingly Presbyterian, but were
markedly less effective in resisting British troops, and were brutally put
down.[119] In Mayo, where rebellion broke out on 22 August, United Irishmen
were assisted by the French troops, who 'came too late and landed on the
wrong side of Ireland'.[120] Despite years of planning, and support from
France, the rising was a spectacular failure.

It was also a bloodbath. The summer of 1798 was, as Roy Foster put it,
'probably the most concentrated episode of violence in Irish history', and
remarkable even in European terms.[121] The comparisons can be instructive.
The reign of terror that followed upon the French revolution offers a telling
comparison: it lasted three years, in a population six times larger than that
of Ireland, and led to 15,000 deaths. The United Irish rebellion lasted three
months, and left 30,000 dead. None of the movement's aims were achieved,
for 'instead of becoming an independent, democratic republic, Ireland was
incorporated into the United Kingdom…instead of bringing Protestants
and Catholics together, the revolutionary movement had driven them even
further apart'.[122]

The rebellion provoked yet another reconfiguration of religious politics.
A group that inclined towards republicanism retained the movement's
hopes of revolutionary change, realizing that the doing away with the Irish
establishment required doing away with monarchy too. As they did so,
those dissenters who feared that the rising had unleashed terrible atavistic
violence lined up to support the union.[123] Everyone lost in the failed

rebellion—including the ostensibly victorious establishment. The violent summer of 1798 showed that the protestant 'patriots' who had argued for and won the autonomy of the Irish parliament could not guarantee the security of their kingdom—or prevent its being invaded from France. But the security of Ireland was a British problem too. MPs at Westminster were convinced that the Dublin parliament could not be trusted with freedom. In this graveyard of failed hopes, the Irish enlightenment perished.

II

Like the rebellion that provoked it, the legislation that united the kingdom of Ireland to the kingdom of Great Britain changed everything while satisfying no one. While a large part of the population looked on with a disinterested air, MPs in College Green were extremely concerned by the prospect of union. Among their number, Francis Dobbs rose to deliver one of the most unusual of parliamentary orations, predicting the imminent end of the age, when the messiah would appear in Dublin and Armagh would become the site of Armageddon, and all this before union could take effect.[124] Others were cautiously optimistic. Many Catholics supported the Act of Union in the hope that it would lead to their being granted electoral rights. They were bitterly disappointed when promises to that effect were undercut by George III, who feared that this extension of the franchise would be in breach of his coronation oath. Meanwhile, those protestants who had rejected the project of union realized that they had lost their ability to leverage Irish policy. They were now at the mercy of the large majority of Westminster MPs who had little knowledge of Ireland and less interest in protecting what they regarded as the constitutionally unsustainable privileges of its elite. The cross-confessional aspirations of the United Irishmen were not to be revived. Communities in nineteenth-century Ireland would continue to be divided by their political and religious goals.[125]

In the early years of the nineteenth century, the combined effects of the American and European revolutions and their consequences for the Irish legislature encouraged some within the collapsing ascendency to disengage from political questions. The disappearance of the Dublin parliament, the growth of popular democracy, and the intention of Westminster MPs to settle the question of Catholic rights apparently at the expense of the privileges of Irish protestants led some within the established church to understand events in apocalyptic terms.[126] Looking back on the early part of the nine-teenth century, J. N. Darby, an Anglican priest who went on to become a key leader of one of the period's most significant new religious movements, was candid about this fact:

> I, a conservative by birth, by education and by mind; a Protestant in Ireland into the bargain; I had been moved to the very depths of my soul on seeing that everything was going to be shaken. The testimony of God made me see and feel that all should be shaken, but...that we have a kingdom that cannot be shaken...Now all institutions are being assaulted, if they are not already thrown down; and the great whore, without strength unless given to it by the beast, loudly proclaims her intention to ride upon the beast. Here, as well as elsewhere, these men proclaim it aloud. It is a plot, well organised at Rome, and systematically carried out. But if the floods rise, the Lord is above the flood, mightier than the noise of many waters.[127]

Darby feared that the 'national apostasy' that was represented by the government's movement towards Catholic emancipation in 1829 would call down the judgement of God. His commentary upon the convulsions of the first few decades of the nineteenth century reflected the fears of those who had grown up sharing the privilege and self-confidence of those at the top of the *ancien régime*. Their concerns were real enough—for they were, in fact, watching the end of their world. But Darby and those who shared his views were wrong to foresee political collapse. Catholics and protestants were about to experience a sequence of religious, social, and political revivals.[128]

After the Act of Union, Irish protestants became more diverse and more united. The spectacular failure of the United Irishmen rebellion suggested that their enlightened hopes of cross-community cooperation had simply been naïve. Having stared into the abyss of sectarian civil war in 1798, protestants came increasingly to recognize that their safety lay in their working across denominational boundaries. The ways in which denominational communities cooperated in local areas were highlighted by the Irish Ordnance Survey, which was carried out between 1825 and 1846, which noticed the religious backgrounds of children in local schools, as well as the endurance of a very different kind of cosmology: in Tullynamullan townland, in the strongly Presbyterian parish of Connor, county Antrim, for example, locals pointed to an old whitethorn tree on a small rise in the middle of an excavated peat bog, where fairies appeared to play music. The tree was venerated by the country people, and 'no one would be so impious as to cut it down'.[129] Despite the endurance of these traditional beliefs, denominational distinctives were still extremely important. In 1834, the first reliable analysis of religious affiliation reported that 81 per cent of the population was Catholic, 11 per cent was Church of Ireland, and 8 per cent was Presbyterian.[130] Some Anglicans tried to shore up the old divisions—as when Archbishop Magee of Dublin called his fellow churchmen to action by describing Catholics as adhering to a 'church without a religion' and dissenters as supporting 'a religion without a church'.[131] But differences between Anglicans and dissenters were becoming less important. As evangelical piety encouraged a generic faith, and in its promotion of creedless Bible reading simultaneously encouraged experimentation in forms of worship and organizational structures, protestants came to understand how much they had in common. Never being certain of support from Westminster, and now with no Irish parliamentary structure to control, Irish protestants could only depend upon themselves. Peering across the no-man's-land between establishment and dissent, they wondered what really held them apart. Evangelical piety impacted upon Anglican absenteeism. While, in 1806, most Church of Ireland clergy were not living in their parishes, a revival of evangelical piety emphasized seriousness, attention, duty, and common purpose.[132] And so, while protestant religion became increasingly variegated, protestant politics were simplified as communities were brought together by what they agreed to remember, as well as what they preferred to forget.[133] Westminster could never be trusted, but it would protect protestant interests far better than would a Catholic-majority parliament in Dublin. And so, by the end of the century, while a small number of protestants identified with the so-called 'Celtic literary revival', and supported projects in cultural and then political nationalism, including the Rev. Richard Rutledge Kane, an Irish-language enthusiast and grand master of the Orange Order in Belfast, most protestants resisted any attempt to resurrect a parliament in Dublin, realizing that changes in electoral law meant that this was an institution that they could no longer control.[134] Home Rule would now be 'Rome rule'. Even those small religious bodies that took no part in constitutional politics swung to defend the union, when, in the early years of the twentieth century, protestant social attitudes consolidated against the forces of Catholic nationalism, and the island teetered on the brink of yet another civil war.[135]

In the early nineteenth century, even as evangelicalism promoted denominational revival, protestants from dissenting communities and the church by law established were brought together through the promotion of an

energetic and individualistic faith. The evangelical revival that had begun in
the 1730s worked its way slowly through the Church of Ireland. From the
1820s, those pious landowners who became known as the 'Bible gentry'
took the lead in promoting evangelical religion. Lady Theodosia Wingfield,
Viscountess Powerscourt (1800–1836), renewed her religious commitment
after the death of her husband in 1823. Her letters reflect the gradual intensi-
fication of her spirituality, as well as her search to find like-minded individuals at conferences for Bible study such as those that she convened on
the Powerscourt estate in Wicklow, where evangelical clergy from across the
United Kingdom gathered to debate recent manifestations of extraordinary
spiritual gifts as well as signs of the end of the age. Fearing that her wealth
kept her at a distance from the workers on her estate, whose faith she wanted
to inspire, she moved into a small cottage, an action that met her need for
self-denial, however much it puzzled some of her correspondents.[136] Sir
Richard Annesley O'Donel was also associated with the Plymouth Brethren,
for whom he built a chapel on his estate, along with another meeting house
for Presbyterians.[137] A rather unusual absentee landlord, he spent much of
the early 1840s in Switzerland, preaching alongside Darby, and leading a
secession from one of the dissenting congregations in Geneva, during which
period he also published a commentary on the New Testament epistle to
the Hebrews, which has since been lost.[138] But O'Donel was good at preserving other books. In 1843, he donated the Cathach of Columba, a sixth-
century psalter that is supposedly in the saint's own hand, and which had
been in the possession of his family for several centuries, to the Royal Irish
Academy, where it is exhibited as Ireland's oldest manuscript.[139]

The power relationships that landlord evangelism concealed were made
obvious during the last major famine in western Europe, the years of horror
between 1845 and 1851. During the first half of the century, the Irish population had grown from 5 million in 1800 to 8.2 million in 1841, while continuing to be extremely poor.[140] The 1841 census demonstrated that 51 per
cent of dwellings were single-room mud cabins.[141] Consequently, the Irish
economy was entirely unprepared for the failure of the potato crop, and the
social collapse that followed. In the decades preceding the famine, the rural
poor had been experiencing repeated failures of the potato crop, but with
no viable alternatives to feed large families of small plots of land they
remained 'poised on the brink of disaster'.[142] And disaster soon unfolded. In
the ten years after 1841, the Irish population shrank by one-quarter. In 1851,
it had fallen to 6.5 million: around 1 million had died of starvation, exposure

and disease, while many others emigrated. Over 900,000 Irish people landed in NewYork between 1845 and 1855.[143] The government failed to adequately address these desperate social needs. During the famine, £9.5m was spent on relief efforts, while £14m was invested in security.[144] Religious leaders of all backgrounds threw themselves into assistance efforts, sometimes in cross-confessional ventures, and often at enormous personal cost. William Crolly, the Catholic archbishop of Armagh, died of cholera in 1849, after distributing aid to the starving.[145] Charles Hardcastle, pastor of the Waterford Baptist Church, died of typhus in similar circumstances.[146] Relief efforts organized by Quakers spanned the Atlantic.[147] Joseph Bewley, partner in the famous Dublin tea business, led the Quaker committee that raised over £200,000 for relief that was distributed without religious partiality, and died in 1851 as a consequence of exhaustion from his efforts.[148] But many pious landowners, like the 'home mission' organizations that supported their second reformation, gained a less wholesome reputation by offering special support to those who would convert to evangelical religion. For many of those it promised to help, this 'souperism' left a very bitter taste.

There were some serious challenges to the growth of evangelicalism within the Church of Ireland. Its status as the church by law established created serious anomalies. In the 1830s, a proposal to create a national school system that would replace denominational provision led to fierce debate about the place of religion in the classroom, and about whether Catholic teachers could be trusted to shape young protestant minds. The link between the established church and the state could be deleterious to the church. In 1833, the Church Temporalities Act reduced by ten the number of Irish bishops, and reconfigured the church's financial support, in an effort to address some of the demands that had been raised by Catholics and dissenters in the 'war' against compulsory payment of tithes.[149] This decision was taken by the Westminster parliament, rather than by the convocation of the Irish church, the weakness of which it exposed. The lessons were obvious: the fabric of the Church of Ireland would be at the mercy of English politicians for as long as it remained the church by law established. Evangelicals came only slowly into positions of influence: the first evangelical bishop in the Church of Ireland was appointed in 1842.[150]

The dissenting communities also faced some serious challenges as they negotiated the rise of evangelicalism. In the 1820s, the Presbyterians, whose membership rivalled that of the established church, endured a second major theological crisis. Led by Henry Cooke (1788–1868), evangelicals within the

Figure 7. Lizzie Gillan, Brethren missionary to China

Synod of Ulster gradually pushed out those among their ministerial colleagues who could not subscribe their belief in the Trinity, and established a
regime that held tenaciously—almost without exception—to conservative
protestant orthodoxy.[151] The Arian party that was the subject of these efforts
dismissed compulsory confessional subscription as inhibiting unfettered
intellectual inquiry, which, they claimed, was of the essence of protestant
religion. Nevertheless, as Cooke's campaign continued, and as support grew
for traditional Trinitarian formularies, evangelicals captured the Synod of
Ulster's central ground. Those who could not subscribe to the Westminster
Confession were pushed towards, and eventually beyond, the denomination's edge. In 1830, seventeen ministers and congregations left to form the
Remonstrant Synod, which in time became known as the Non-subscribing
Presbyterian Church, and developed strong links with English Unitarians.
In 1835, the main body of Presbyterians formally adopted the requirement
for ministers to subscribe to the Westminster Confession of Faith. Buoyed
up by this victory, Cooke proclaimed 'marriage banns' between Presbyterians
and the established church, who, he claimed, were now fighting together
against the influence of rationalism in theology and Catholic influences in

politics.[152] Other protestants consolidated in this common cause of religious and political conservatism. In 1840, the Seceders joined the main Presbyterian body, which became known as the General Assembly of the Presbyterian Church in Ireland. Presbyterians were consolidating as a religion of political force.

Some small communities, with more distinctive views of church and state, were happy to remain outside the mainstream denominations. In the early decades of the nineteenth century, Baptists looked to share their faith among rural Catholics.[153] Never a large movement, hardly any of their congregations had survived into the early years of the nineteenth century, and most children born into these congregations were not remaining within them.[154] In the late 1790s and early 1800s, visits by prominent English preachers, including Samuel Pearce and Andrew Fuller, encouraged a renewal of evangelical orthodoxy and a concern among the English churches to do what they could to support their Irish brethren. In 1811, John West arrived from England to take up pastoral responsibilities in Waterford and then Dublin, from which congregation he sent out the itinerant preachers that, by 1813, had recorded seventy evangelical conversions. Encouraged by this initial response, the English Baptist churches established a Society for Promoting the Gospel in Ireland in 1814, enabling Isaac McCarthy and other missionaries to begin an extraordinary campaign of preaching around the south-east and the midlands, establishing a network of schools that may have been the first protestant educational institutions to use Irish as their principal medium of instruction.[155] Given the relatively small numbers of those involved, the project was extraordinarily successful. Baptist churches were planted at a rate of almost one per annum for a period of forty years until their work among the rural poor was devastated by the effects of the famine. But, with few exceptions, these congregations made little impact upon Ulster, where protestant culture was still dominated by Presbyterians.[156]

While rejoicing in any effort to spread the gospel, other evangelicals chose to remain apart from any form of denominational or political life. In the 1820s, some individuals from the Anglo-Irish elite withdrew from organized religion and committed themselves to meet in informal circles for Bible study and prayer in which they developed a reading of the New Testament that connected the end of their socially privileged world with the second coming of Christ. 'It is a time to be entirely heavenly', one of their most influential leaders intoned, 'for the earth is far from God, and daily its darkness closes in.'[157] The explanatory theory developed by these so-called 'Plymouth Brethren'—an end-of-the-world-view known as 'dispensational premillennialism'—made little longer-term impact upon British or Irish evangelicalism, but it was widely adopted by North American evangelicals who had little sense of its Irish political significance, whose large numbers have ensured that it has become the foundation for the foreign policy of almost every president since Jimmy Carter. These believers were certainly heavenly minded—so much that in their writing they paid hardly any attention to the famine.

But if the eschatological values of the Brethren did not shape Irish evangelicalism, their anti-creedal and anti-clerical view of the church certainly did—not least in the aftermath of the blistering religious revival that began in 1859. Presbyterians had been preparing for such an event since the early 1840s. In 1844, the General Assembly formed a 'State of Religion' committee in order actively to promote revitalization by encouraging the strict observance of personal and congregational piety. These interests continued into the 1850s.[158] Some of the laymen who were influenced by this emphasis upon revival met as a small group in Kells, county Antrim, and began to pray for conversions—not conversions from one denomination to another, but conversions of individuals from lives of wickedness and apathy to lives of vigorous spiritual life. This kind of enthusiasm among laypeople was normalized in protestant popular culture. Within the space of a few months, large parts of the north of the island were swept up in the religious excitement. One supporter of the revival reported an instance of open-air preaching that was followed, 'as usual', by several individuals engaging in 'violent and irresistible screaming'. With emotions at fever pitch, those who were overcome with religious feeling were

> reduced to a helpless condition. Presently, this state of things subsides, and with subdued voice, a call 'for Jesus' escapes their lips, the body becomes quiet, and, in due time, (varying very much as to its duration) our full confession of His blessed name flows from their hearts and lips, and they stand up, declaring they have found peace with God through the atoning blood of His beloved son.[159]

Another supporter of the revival described the effect of preaching 'in a field in front of my own house':

> an immense work of God, and that in wonderful power, was presented to the astonished eyes and hearts of a vast concourse of beholders; not less than one hundred souls were brought under conviction of sin, the greater part being

'*struck down*' to the ground. Some of the women and children were conveyed into the house; others followed to assist them, and, shortly, nearly every room was crowded with persons, crying out, and praying for mercy. The lawn was literally strewed, like a battle field, with deeply wounded—sin-stricken ones, under conviction of sin by the holy spirit, who was revealing Christ to their souls, and giving them victory over the enemy, by the blood of the Lamb. But who can describe what was going on in the house? In one large room where are gathered no less than thirty persons, on their knees, waiting and calling upon God in silent prayer for the remission of their sins; while the other rooms were filled with souls either calling out for mercy, praying, or singing praises to God for mercy received. This was going on in all parts of the house.[160]

While Presbyterians had done most of the planning for the revival, and consolidated around it, many of their ministers took a dim view of the attitudes towards ordained ministry that seemed to drive some of the revival's activity, and that contributed in its aftermath to the sudden growth of Baptist congregations and the more informal meetings of Brethren.[161] Classically trained theologians threw up their hands in horror as they reported the baneful effects of what they regarded as unbalanced hyper-spirituality. They had no doubt that this religious episode had significant social implications. Some Brethren rejoiced in this fact:

the most illiterate men have been taken up, by the Holy Ghost, and used in the glorious work of turning sinners from darkness to light. The writer has seen assembled thousands hanging on the lips of persons who, literally, could not utter a sentence of good grammar. He has seen persons smitten down without any apparent reference to ordinary ministration...Let the professing church observe the fact. The Holy Ghost has used illiterate men. He used them, in apostolic times; He used them, in the middle ages; He is using them, now. An illiterate ploughman, with Christ in his heart, is better far than a Christ-less scholar with all the learning of the schools at his fingers' ends.[162]

Recognizing the challenge of this anti-clericalism, many Presbyterians took a more cautious approach to their assessment of the revival. Some, like John Weir, author of *The Ulster awakening* (1860), hailed the movement as a harbinger of the long-awaited millennium, and a promise that 'Christianity shall become the dominant power in the world'.[163] James McCosh, professor of logic and metaphysics at Queen's College, Belfast, and future president of Princeton Theological Seminary, believed that tens of thousands had been converted, and that the movement would do enormous good.[164] Others, like William Hamilton, were more sceptical. In *An inquiry into the*

Scriptural character of the revival of 1859 (1866), Hamilton condemned the methods and ideas of leading revivalists, which he deemed entirely incompatible with Presbyterian norms. Fundamental to his concern was the revival's levelling effect and its promotion of hysteria dressed up as spirituality:

> merchants leaving their business to teach the things of Scripture, shop-boys leaving the counter to comfort distressed souls...some are struck dumb, others see visions, others are rendered blind or paralytic, and females even of the worst character become converts, and soon take a part in extending the movement.[165]

Buoyed with enthusiasm, nevertheless, apologists for the revival estimated that around 100,000 people had been converted.[166] The revival bolstered the Presbyterians, reinforced their conservative theological direction, and created an evangelical mainstream. It was heralded as a marker of the success of popular protestantism, but also marked its failure, both in highlighting the low figures for church membership before this period of unusual excitement and the rapid decline of religious observance in its aftermath.

With the rise of evangelicalism came the symbolic end of the long-weakening protestant ascendancy. Eleven years after the revival, in 1870, the Church of Ireland was disestablished, and the legal provision for the tithe in its support was finally abandoned. Newly constituted as a voluntary society, the Church of Ireland was now compelled to live within its own financial resources. As its finances contracted, the church became responsible for the upkeep of an infrastructure that included 1,630 churches and 1,400 graveyards. A programme of economic rationalization was inevitable.[167] The church struggled to keep pace with migration into the larger towns, so that in 1898, for example, the 92,000 Church of Ireland inhabitants of Belfast had to make do with 21,000 seats in churches.[168]

Irish protestants were revived and brought together as a coherent political community alongside similar trends among Catholics. By the beginning of the nineteenth century, several varieties of Catholicism were in existence. The religion of the church was largely untouched by rationalism and enlightenment, and did not tolerate the heterodoxy that was being advocated by a minority of Presbyterians. The official faith was being taught by a declining number of priests. This was not an effect of the penal laws. Instead, it was a consequence of the decision by Pope Benedict XIV (1740–1758) to reduce the number of priests in Ireland, which he achieved by forbidding bishops to ordain any more than twelve priests during their lifetime.[169] This decision made little sense in the context of the massive population growth that occurred in the second half of the eighteenth century, during which the island's population doubled, from 2.2 million in 1753 to 4.4 million in 1791.[170] As pastoral provision contracted, popular devotional practice took on new and compensating forms. The church sanctioned 'stations', for example, permitting secular clergy to itinerate between private houses, in which they would hear confessions and celebrate mass.[171] Catholics were not expected to attend mass on every Sunday and holy day, but were merely required to confess and share communion at Easter—an obligation that was sometimes omitted.[172] Naturally, this practice weakened the importance of the church building as the centre of parish life. It also increased long-standing rivalries between secular and regular priests, for friars lost their monopoly on raising support by means of helping with household piety. As stations became more common, they made the Irish church distinct, and put it at some variance with Tridentine norms.[173] Other elements of popular religion were not authorized by the church—as was the case in many other parts of Europe. Some of these customs had been handed down from time immemorial, and appeared to some critics to reflect aspects of pre-Christian religious practice.[174] (Of course, reports of popular beliefs and behaviours in the Ordnance Survey minutes show that this division between what was once distinguished as 'official' religion and 'popular' cosmology was not unique to Catholics.)

The rich, if often idiosyncratic, devotional culture of the rural poor was put under enormous pressure by the work of Catholic reformers. Under the leadership of the growing number of priests who had been trained at Maynooth, as well as Jesuits, Vincentians, and Redemptorists, with influence of members of female religious orders and in parish missions, the Irish Catholic Church experienced what used to be described as a 'devotional revolution'. Over the best part of a century, Irish Catholic practice changed, if it was not quite transformed, to shape the pious national self-image that the church promoted. If religious practice in the early nineteenth century was marked by low and irregular attendance at mass and by often unconventional folk pieties, the religious practice of the later part of the century was focused on weekly mass attendance, with energetic participation in confraternities and other pious associations, and was overseen by well-trained clergy. Archbishop Cullen was extremely wary of radical politics, which he connected with the anti-papal revolt in Italy in 1848–1849, when the pope had been compelled to flee from Rome, and which he saw as inevitably hostile to the interests of the church.[175] Nevertheless, in creating this disciplined Catholic community, the devotional revolution that he sponsored made a powerful contribution to the sense of nationhood that would underlie the achievements of cultural and political nationalists, and so would determine much of the religious, political, and cultural experience of twentieth-century Ireland.

The revolution can be quantified. A survey in 1834 established that only around 40 per cent of Catholics were in the habit of attending mass.[176] This proportion was soon to markedly increase.[177] Between 1770 and 1845, the number of clergy increased by more than 1,000. Between 1793 and 1815, as a consequence of the French Revolution, bishops could not send candidates for the priesthood to any of the Irish colleges on the continent.[178] Increasing numbers of candidates were being trained at Maynooth.[179] By 1845, the new seminary was graduating around 100 men each year, though demand continued to outstrip supply.[180] The number of parish clergy increased from 1,614 in 1800 to almost 3,000 in 1900.[181] But more remarkable growth occurred among female religious. In 1800, there were over 100 nuns in Irish institutions but, by 1900, that number had risen to over 8,000.[182] Between 1790 and 1845, the number of chapels increased by 2,000, while a major effort to construct new buildings meant that, by the mid-1840s, almost every diocese had provided two chapels in each of its parishes.[183] The growth could not come fast enough. Even in the 1830s, the Catholic community of Portrush, county Antrim, was meeting for mass in a private house during winter and during summer on the shore.[184] On the eve of the famine, the Catholic Church was 'still unable to provide the Catholic community with adequate pastoral care because the economic resources available were simply not sufficient'.[185]

This growing confidence reflected in part increasing political gains. In 1823, as agitation for electoral rights continued, Daniel O'Connell founded the Catholic Association. This name was well chosen, for in addition to representing the concerns of the Catholic middle class, O'Connell developed his movement around the structures of the church, encouraging priests to take an active role in winning it support, and made explicit the connection between religious identities and political goals.[186] Many priests were more than happy to participate, and permitted collections of the 'Catholic rent'—a membership payment of one penny per month—at church gates. O'Connell's efforts were rewarded when he was elected as a member of parliament in 1828—a position from which he was debarred by his religion.

His effective leveraging of the situation created a constitutional crisis and was generously rewarded. Catholic emancipation came in 1829. One year later, O'Connell was finally allowed to take up his seat in the mother of parliaments. Catholic emancipation had really been achieved. It made Britain 'one of the most religiously liberal states in Europe'.[187] But not everyone was impressed. George Beresford, the Church of Ireland archbishop of Armagh, described Catholic emancipation not as the sharing but as the transfer of political power.[188] He was right. The growing Catholic electorate came to demand reform and even redress. Many changes came slowly, particularly as changes to the electoral roll assisted landlords' interests, so that Conservative MPs won around or just under half of the Irish seats at elections throughout the 1850s and 1860s. Specific instances of discrimination continued. Catholics were only admitted as scholars and fellows of Trinity College Dublin in 1854 and 1873, for example.[189] But, by the 1870s, the direction of travel was clear. One by one, the bastions of protestant privilege were falling. The Irish 'nation'—at least in its guise as the state— was no longer protestant.

The Catholic Church was changing too—especially in the aftermath of the famine. Important devotional practices had been established by the mid-eighteenth century, including the rosary, and confraternities were well established by the century's end.[190] While the roots of the devotional revolution can be traced in earlier decades, the new habits of piety were popularized after the famine. The 'great hunger' had decimated the overwhelmingly Catholic rural poor. This was, as S. J. Connolly has noted, the class that the church had found most difficult to control, a cultural sphere in which were tolerated secret societies, irregular marriages and boisterous rites of passage, in which 15,000 people could congregate at a holy well for a day of festive fun.[191] While internal reforms were being promoted from the 1830s, the death and emigration of hundreds of thousands of individuals from this background accelerated the 'modernization' of Catholic practice from the 1850s onwards. At different speeds in different locations and among different classes, Irish Catholic devotion was enriched by a new aesthetic and new activities: music, incense, and devotional images assisted practices like benediction, the stations of the cross, and sacred heart piety.[192]

These reforms were driven forward after the Synod of Thurles (1850), the first Catholic synod in Ireland since 1642, which Archbishop Cullen convened. Having been appointed as an apostolic delegate, and so having been given by the pope complete power over the Irish church, Cullen set about implementing an ambitious programme of reform. The goal of his 'ultra-montanism' was to eradicate the difference of the Irish church. Clamping down on pastoral irregularities, and pushing religious practice back into church buildings, Cullen's reforms increased the distance between the people and their priests, and encouraged the development of a new and formally confessional Catholic university in Ireland.[193] His reforms were resisted in some regions—the archdiocese of Tuam somehow preferred to continue to permit the old practices of piety—and for a while older and newer religious practices co-existed.[194] In 1879, at Knock, for example, over a dozen local people reported the apparition of the Blessed Virgin Mary that is celebrated to the present day.[195] In 1895, the husband of Bridget Cleary, convinced that his wife had been abducted by fairies and replaced by a changeling, committed one of the most gruesome murders in modern Irish history.[196] But Cullen's reforms standardized religious belief and behaviour, controlling as well as giving opportunity to women, providing increasing amounts of pastoral oversight to the middle class if also some-times overlooking the pastoral needs of the poorest.[197] The wealth of the church was displayed in its most impressive building projects—the pro-cathedral in Dublin (1825), the cathedrals at Enniscorthy (1843), Thurles (1879), Armagh (built between 1840 and 1904) and Cobh (built between 1869 and 1919), and the University Church on St Stephen's Green, in Dublin (1856). But many smaller church buildings needed a great deal of investment.[198]

Over the first half of the nineteenth century, there emerged a growing division between the rural poor and the rest of the Catholic community.[199] That division became especially pronounced with significant urbanization in the later part of the century, and especially in cities such as Belfast. In 1800, the city had a population of 20,000; a century later, this had risen to almost 350,000.[200] The Catholic population in the city grew from 4,000 in 1816 to 40,000 by 1861.[201] In 1885, the city's Catholic population had reached 65,000 individuals—who were organized as a single parish.[202] With pastoral care stretched to the limit, it was hardly surprising that, as Catholic numbers grew, religious practice appeared to decline. In Belfast, in the mid-1830s, only around half of the city's 20,000 Catholic inhabitants were attending mass. In 1900, Catholics represented around one-quarter of the city's population.[203] But they were being served by an increasing number of priests.

Belfast's rapid growth provided an important context for the zero-sum sectarian politics of the later nineteenth century. The tensions that kicked off into violence in Belfast in the later 1850s set the stage for the 'Home Rule' crises that carved up the island's population into unionists and nationalists. There was nothing inevitable about the political-religious tensions that emerged. The Home Government Association was founded by a protestant lawyer, Isaac Butt, in 1870, and the Irish Parliamentary Party that best came to represent these interests was led by another protestant, Charles Stuart Parnell, from 1882 until 1891. As the 'uncrowned king of Ireland', Parnell had an uneasy relationship with its churches. His first school—to which he had been sent at the age of six—had been operated by Plymouth Brethren. John Vesey Parnell, the second baron Congleton, his distant cousin, had been a leading brother in the movement's early years. Parnell confessed that he appreciated the quietness of their worship.[204] But he found little peace and quiet anywhere else. Having led the Irish Parliamentary Party through the first Home Rule crisis of 1882, he fell afoul of the denomination upon which he most depended when it was revealed in 1890 that he was the father of three of the children of Kitty O'Shea, the wife of a party colleague. The Catholic bishops turned on Parnell, and vilified his reputation.[205] The most credible nationalist leader was not being backed by the church, whose priests, James Joyce remembered, 'broke Parnell's heart and hounded him into his grave'.[206] Another attempt to legislate for Home Rule failed in 1893. But, as pressure continued to grow, the House of Commons responded by passing a number of land acts from the 1880s to the 1900s, changing the nature of Irish land ownership in radical ways, trying to kill Home Rule with kindness. This strategy was not successful.

One hundred years after the United Irishmen rebellion, the religious and political landscape had been transformed.[207] Three generations after their great-grandfathers had fought side by side in the cause of freedom, Catholics were pressing for the rights of the 'imagined community' of the Irish nation, while dissenters lined up with Anglicans in defence of the United Kingdom. The Orange Order, which had been established to defend one Dublin parliament, now marched to resist the imposition of another. The Catholic middle class, which had welcomed the union in the hope of winning electoral rights, now largely supported a return to Home Rule. Nationalist politicians co-opted the support of the Catholic Church while unionist politicians appealed to the protestant denominations for their electoral warrant. By the end of the nineteenth century, the struggle to determine the island's constitutional future would be determined by competition between two large blocs of religious votes.

Hardly any voices cut through the religious binary. Some protestants who were greatly concerned by Catholic political advances were nevertheless not convinced that the union had any kind of future. Darby, studying biblical prophecy, became convinced that the British Empire would break up, and that the United Kingdom would be reduced to its constituent parts—in other words, although he never said as much or as bluntly, that independence for Ireland (and Scotland) was inevitable.[208] But this was a minority position.

The protestant churches continued to grow in numbers. In 1861, the census reported that the 5.8m inhabitants of the island were divided into 4.5m Catholics (77.69 per cent), 693,357 Anglicans (11.96 per cent), 523,291 Presbyterians (9.02 per cent), 45,399 Methodists (0.79 per cent), 4,257 Baptists (0.07 per cent), 3,695 Quakers (0.06 per cent), and 393 Jews (0.01 per cent). The impact of enlightened thinking might be gauged by the fact that hardly any individuals registered themselves outside the standard denominational categories.[209] In 1871, another census recorded that the 5.4m inhabitants of the island were divided into 4.15m Catholics (76.69 per cent), 667,998 Anglicans (12.34 per cent), 497,648 Presbyterians (9.2 per cent), 43,441 Methodists (0.8 per cent), 4,957 Baptists (0.09 per cent), 3,814 Quakers (0.07 per cent), and 285 Jews (0.01 per cent). Religious changes were most marked in Ulster, where throughout this period sectarian tensions remained high. From 1861 to 1911, as the population of Ulster declined from 1.9m to 1.58m, Catholics declined from 50.5 per cent to 43.87 per cent of the population; Anglicans increased from 20.4 per cent to 23.19 per cent of the population; Presbyterians increased only slightly from 26.3 per cent to 26.64 per cent of the population; Methodists increased from 1.7 per cent to 3.09 per cent of the population; and the number of religious 'others' increased from 1.1 per cent to 3.41 per cent of the population. In numerical terms, this meant that, by 1911, the population of Ulster included 691,816 Catholics, 421,410 Presbyterians, 366,773 Anglicans, 48,816 Methodists and 53,881 members of other denominations and religious groups, including 3,122 Baptists, 696 Jews, one Muslim, one druid, one member of the Order of the Golden Age, and one worshipper of Iris (or, perhaps, a mis-recorded Isis?).[210] Perhaps the biggest success story of these religious 'others' was the growth of the Plymouth Brethren. In 1871, the community (members of which self-reported under several descriptors) may have numbered little more than 4,000.[211] In 1911, it had grown to over 10,000, and represented the fourth-largest of Ulster's protestant communities.[212] Of course, numbers are not everything, nor were denominational divisions necessarily determinative or explanatory. We should recognize that individuals from very different religious cultures could have very similar habits or points of view.[213] But that complexity was among the first victims of the pressure for Home Rule.

III

Throughout much of Europe, the eighteenth and nineteenth centuries were often regarded as an age of enlightenment and doubt—but in Ireland, during the same period, the churches experienced enlightenment and religious revival. Shut out of the apparatus of the state as a consequence of the Glorious Revolution, Catholics and dissenters found themselves affected in different ways by expanding body of inconsistently applied penal laws. These laws targeted the religion of Presbyterians by denying the legality of their ordinations and marriage ceremonies, while leaving their wealth largely intact. They targeted the wealth of Catholic landowners, while recognizing the validity of their church's ordinations and marriage rites.[214] But, despite the calls of reformers for the broadening of the political nation, these laws that protected the social, cultural, economic, and religious privileges of the Anglican elite were only slowly dismantled. Eventually the restlessness of those shut out from the state boiled over into action. Towards the end of the eighteenth century, Presbyterians gained a political education during the American revolution, while Catholics were influenced by events in France. When it realized that one-tenth of the island's population had combined in a religiously pluralist but politically radical oath-bound society, with strong links to a hostile foreign power, the state responded with repression. The ideals of the enlightenment were abandoned as the rebellion of the United Irishmen led to horrific sectarian violence. While their Church condemned 'the French disease', many Catholics turned to republican theory in order to plot out their political future. Dissenting protestants recognized the danger, and came to terms with the state. The British government realized it had to take radical action in order to avoid further episodes of violence. In the Act of Union, the Dublin parliament was incorporated into that of Westminster. Many middle-class Catholics supported the union in the hope that they would be given the vote. Many protestants resisted the union on the basis that their political power would now be diluted. Both expectations were fulfilled in the early nineteenth century—even as Catholics turned against the union and protestants came to support it.

By the middle of the nineteenth century, Catholic and protestant communities had consolidated as a consequence of revivals and reformations. Archbishop Cullen standardized the practice of piety and suppressing local idiosyncrasies while pulling the Irish church more closely into alignment with Rome. Among protestants, clergymen as well as anti-clerical revivalists preached a generic evangelicalism that may have led to 100,000 conversions. Ulster was made distinctive by high levels of church attendance that were a 'by-product of the deep sectarian divisions that dominated Irish public life'.[215] For all their differences, evangelical ministers and ultramontanist priests had created strong religious communities by exploiting fears of the other.

As their communities consolidated, protestants and Catholics began to engage more fully with the wider world. This 'spiritual empire' provided denominational leaders in the United States as well as the many single women and married couples that took up opportunities for missionary work in Ireland's urban centres as well in Africa and the far east.[216] But this global vision did not often transcend local prejudices. By the end of the century, almost without exception, religious identities encoded political commitments, so that Catholics were expected to be nationalists and protestants to support the union. These identities were thrown into relief during successive Home Rule crises in the 1880s and 1890s. The fall of Parnell removed the last significant protestant voice from nationalist ranks—and showed that the Catholic Church would uphold its morals even if doing so meant loss to the nationalist cause. Census records in 1901 and 1911 demonstrated how precarious was the protestant hold outside the north-east counties. Some peered nervously over the sectarian division, wondering whether religious others could share a common political cause. For the vast majority of protestants, the moment of betrayal had come. A third Home Rule crisis—and the prospect of further violence—loomed on the horizon, as unionists and nationalists geared up to fight for their vision of Christian Ireland.

5

Troubles

At the end of the nineteenth century—at least in the eyes of its advocates—the Irish nation was born again. In the 1890s, as crisis engulfed the Irish Parliamentary Party after the failure of the second Home Rule bill and the death of Parnell, an unlikely combination of artists, academics, aristocrats, and activists developed new strategies for a recovery of the Irish language as the first step towards national rebirth.[1] During the nineteenth century, the language had passed almost into oblivion, not least because the decimation of the rural poor during and after the famine occurred as the Catholic middle class embraced the language shift in order to win respectability within an increasingly Anglophone culture—efforts that their hierarchy generally supported—and embraced new forms of popular devotion as they did so.[2] Only a handful of clergy had resisted the decline of the vernacular—among their efforts, the attempt by John MacHale, archbishop of Tuam, to translate the *Iliad* into Irish (1844–1871) might not have been the most strategic intervention. At the end of the nineteenth century, the campaign to recover Ireland's Gaelic inheritance had become a campaign for national cleansing, an attempt to wash away the 'sordid' effects of 'English imperialism' so that (in the often heavily gendered language of this kind of politics) Ireland's true beauty might be finally revealed.[3] The cultural revival became a purity cult, in which the idealized values of a resurrected Irish-ness were compared with the seedy, mercantile values of England and its commercial empire. 'There are other worthier things between heaven and earth than English music halls', the nationalist journalist D. P. Moran intoned—even if he had to allude to Shakespeare in order to make his point.[4]

In the 1890s, arguments for Irish nationhood took on a religious and sometimes mystical air. Some of the most important work in the early stages of the cultural revival was developed by protestants. In 1892, Douglas Hyde,

son of a Church of Ireland clergyman, and soon to become a founder of the
Gaelic League, delivered an influential address about the necessity of de-
Anglicizing Ireland. His fellow countrymen halted between two opinions,
he feared, having lost confidence in local traditions while imitating the
English culture they wanted to reject. Those who followed Hyde made his
arguments with greater force and much less religious nuance. The 'idea of
the national being... is not earth born', suggested George Russell, who
published his rather theosophical account of the national ideal under the
pseudonym Æ, arguing that combat with English cultural power was an
element of spiritual warfare against principalities and powers.[5] Using
another eschatological metaphor, Lady Augusta Gregory, who coordinated
much of the early stages of the revitalization movement from her home in
county Galway, drew upon her mother's evangelical piety in imagining that
the return of the Fianna would herald the 'thousand years' peace'.[6] Some
cultural nationalists moved beyond allusion and metaphor to argue that
cultural revival should have explicitly confessional ends. Some of their
arguments were easily co-opted. Catholic bishops joined their campaign
against 'evil'—that is to say, English—literature, and promoted the Catholic
Truth Society and the Pioneer Total Abstinence Association, which were
founded in 1899 to encourage intelligent piety and self-control. In 1901,
D. P. Moran published an essay on 'The battle of two civilisations' in *Ideas
in Ireland* (1901), a volume edited by Lady Gregory that included work by a
roster of protestant writers associated with the Celtic revival, which argued
that native traditions should be protected in an almost hegemonic English
cultural sphere. Moran's essay set out a broader cultural, political and
religious agenda that he would take up in his most influential book, *The
philosophy of Irish Ireland* (1905). For Moran, the Celtic revival was a wispy
chimera, and the nation would be saved only as its language and culture
were brought together in Gaelic sports and Catholic faith.[7] Many Catholics
did not find these arguments convincing. While many younger priests were
Irish-language enthusiasts, others were not.[8] Some Catholics were offended
by the ways in which the literary revivalists represented Irish mores. There
were riots at the earliest performances of *The playboy of the western world*
(1907) at the Abbey Theatre in Dublin. The play made few concessions to
Catholic sensitivities: its author, John Millington Synge, whose aesthetic
agenda does not appear to have been influenced by his family background
in the Church of Ireland and the Plymouth Brethren, offered a sympathetic
portrayal of the rural poor that depicted their worldview as essentially pagan.[9]

Some of the most pious Catholic nationalists were not appalled by this kind of claim. Pádraic Pearse, a young but influential teacher, writer and nationalist activist, believed that traditional culture, even in its pre-Christian forms, might be sanctified for the national cause. Gaelic culture revealed Christ, he argued, recycling claims from the sixth and seventh centuries that pagan storytellers could be prophets of Christian faith. After all, he considered, thinking about one of the classic Irish sagas, even *The Táin* could be seen to symbolize 'the redemption of man by a sinless God':

> The curse of primal sin lies upon a people; new and personal sin brings doom to their doors; they are powerless to save themselves; a youth, free from the curse, akin with them through his mother but through his father divine, redeems them by his valour; and his own death comes from it. I do not mean that the Tain is a conscious allegory: but there is the story in its essence, and it is like a retelling (or is it a fore-telling?) of the story of Calvary.[10]

But how could old Irish stories bear witness to Christian truth? Only because the culture that produced them was exceptional, Pearse explained. 'Ireland possesses a more ancient, a more extensive, and a better literature, *wholly of native growth*, than any other European country, with the single exception of Greece', he claimed, and 'there is absolutely nothing like it in the world's literature'.[11] 'We have struggled as no other nation has struggled', he continued. 'We have bled as no other nation has bled; we have endured an agony compared with which the agonies of other nations have been as child's play.'[12] Having experienced its own passion, Ireland uniquely witnessed to Christ. But Ireland's future would be exceptional too. Renewed by the cultural nationalist agenda, and therefore revived in its Catholic faith, the island would have a 'destiny more glorious than that of Rome, more glorious than that of Britain'. It would become the 'saviour of idealism in modern intellectual and social life, the regenerator and rejuvenator of the literature of the world, the instructor of the nations, the preacher of the gospel of nature-worship, hero-worship, God-worship'.[13] Pearse's almost millennial vision concluded with a vision of the peoples of the world flocking to Ireland as the 'fountain-head of their Christianity'.[14] Traditional culture could be recovered, he believed, because the struggle for the nation was a struggle for the future of the Christian faith.

As the advocates of Celtic revival turned their attention to politics, competing campaigns of religious nationalism came to be dominated by contrasting religious themes. In the north-east, after extensive consultation with the churches, unionist leaders campaigning against Home Rule chose

Figure 8. Signing the Ulster Covenant, 1912

to fashion their movement around symbols that resonated in the religious history of Scotland. The Ulster Covenant (1912) evoked the struggle of seventeenth-century Presbyterians to resist liturgical changes that were to be imposed by royal fiat upon the Scottish church. In the mid-seventeenth century, the Solemn League and Covenant (1643) had brought together a wide range of grievances, which were combined in the language of religious complaint. Over 250 years later, the Ulster Covenant attempted to do the same. In 1912, Sir Edward Carson, the leader of unionism, signed the Covenant amid almost hysterically patriotic scenes in Belfast, and in the presence of leading protestant churchmen, including the Presbyterian moderator and the archbishop of Down, Connor, and Dromore.[15] Over 237,000 men and 234,000 women signed similar declarations.[16] The Covenant brought together Ulster protestants as a collective religious and political body, with a shared Scottish heritage and a common commitment to maintaining the union with Britain. The irony of the occasion was that the only denomination that still saw the original Solemn League and Covenant as binding—the small but never insignificant Reformed

Presbyterian Church of Ireland—took no part in the event. As protestant ranks consolidated, the Home Rule crisis put extraordinary pressure on religious communities that refused to take part in politics.[17] After all, the leaders of unionism and the protestant churches agreed that they were standing 'for God and Ulster'. This religious rationale warranted their opportunistic and risky turn towards non-constitutional forms of politics and the threat of civil war. But it provoked nationalists to respond in kind. They too formed a militia, which was much stronger in numbers than its northern rival, if less well provided with weapons. And nationalists also developed a covenant, drawn up to resist military conscription for the war effort. Ironically, while presenting visual imagery that was designed to appeal to Catholics, 'Ireland's Solemn League and Covenant', steered closer to the language of Scottish Presbyterian tradition than the unionist document had earlier managed to do. Drawing upon the language of covenant, with all of its Old Testament associations, the crises of the 1910s encouraged competing groups to identify themselves as chosen peoples of God.

In the tense and unsettled aftermath of the third Home Rule bill of 1912, the formation of rival militias pushed Irish society towards the brink of another civil war. The rival militias had large memberships. By 1914, one Ulster protestant male in every three and one Catholic Irishman in every five was a member of a paramilitary organization.[18] Ulster and Irish Volunteers engaged in military-style drilling, and began to import arms from Germany. An armed clash between these militias was avoided only because in the autumn of 1914 the world fell into an unprecedented conflict, in which soldiers from both religious and political backgrounds fought for the honour of the empire and for the rights of small nations, on the continent and at home.[19] While the experience of world war undermined religious practice throughout much of the rest of Europe, the Irish churches benefited from the crisis, which consolidated their rival religious identities.

For nationalists, the war created 'Ireland's opportunity'—and facilitated the attempt by a body of revolutionaries to mount an 'Easter rising'. On 24 April 1916, some 1,200 men and women seized control of key sites in and around Dublin and announced themselves as representatives of the provisional government of the Irish Republic. Steeped in romantic notions of blood-sacrifice, and claiming the 'protection of the Most High God, Whose blessing we invoke upon our arms', they abandoned the commitment of several generations of nationalists to constitutional politics, and turned towards grand gestures of symbolic violence.[20] The insurrection led to almost 500 deaths—including the deaths of 260 civilians, as well as the deaths, mostly by execution, of sixteen rebel leaders. While protestant church leaders had lined up to support the militia culture of the north, the Catholic hierarchy could not support the republican rebels. The Easter Rising did not meet the criteria for 'just war', according to their teaching. The bishops condemned the rising, and priests tended not to support it: Father Paddy Flanagan was the only priest arrested for participation in the rising.[21] After all, Home Rule was already on the statute books, where the enabling legislation was to sit until the end of the war before coming into effect. The rising did nothing to accelerate its implementation. Of course, the rebels wanted more than Home Rule within the empire—they wanted to establish an independent republic, which some among their number insisted should have a socialist order.[22] But in the short term, their most significant achievement may have been to sanctify the revolutionary cause and to validate the trend towards extra-constitutional violence that had begun with the arming of the Ulster volunteers. The unofficial canonization of the rebel leaders was the result of a powerfully successful propaganda campaign in which the suffering of the Irish nation and those who fought to defend it was compared to the agonies of Christ.

While some rebels linked the cause of Ireland to Catholic piety, they were not all persuaded by the appeal to a specifically religious nationalism. The hagiography that came to surround the leaders of the rising represented them as facing death with fervent devotion. The Catholic bishops were more cautious about the rising, and refused to warrant its violence. But protestants participated in political nationalism on their own terms. Their numbers included W. B. Yeats, who found his Church of Ireland background less compelling than the occult societies with which he increasingly identified; Jack White, who followed his career as an officer in the British army by founding the Irish Citizen Army; Roger Casement, who helped in shipping German guns to republicans before taking a leading role in the Easter Rising; Bulmer Hobson, who resigned from the Quakers in order to engage in the acts of violence that their pacifist creed forbade; and Constance Markievicz, the first woman elected to the Westminster parliament, in 1918, who escaped execution as a participant in the Easter Rising only on account of her sex.[23]

The experience of war was traumatic, and politically destabilizing for many years after the armistice.[24] Ideas of redemptive sacrifice became pervasive. Just weeks after the Easter Rising, on 1 July 1916, the soldiers of the 36th (Ulster) Division, most of them former Ulster Volunteers, went over the top on the first day of the battle of the Somme, gaining ground in long hours of fierce fighting, during which they won four of the nine Victoria Crosses awarded for actions in the battle, before being instructed to abandon their territorial gains. It was the anniversary of the battle of the Boyne—and the day in which the British army recorded its highest ever causalities.[25] As they won the war, they lost their home. One month after the cessation of hostilities, a general election returned a landslide victory for Sinn Féin, and a mandate for independence. Only the unionist constituencies in the northeast withstood the electoral tsunami. In January 1919, the Sinn Féin MPs, who had been backed by the overwhelming majority of the Irish electorate to win 73 of the 105 Irish seats, made good on their electoral promises and announced the formation of Dáil Éireann, a revolutionary parliament in Dublin. Northern unionists looked to Westminster for defence. An Anglo-Irish War began, as the British army and the Royal Irish Constabulary combined against the forces of the new Republic. Former soldiers of the British army fought on both sides of the war. Many ex-servicemen were recruited into the 'Black and Tans', a division of the Royal Irish Constabulary that was raised to put down the Irish Republican Army, as the republican military wing was known, but which gained a reputation for vigilantism, brutality, and extra-judicial violence.[26] In June 1922, as violence spilled across the Irish Sea, IRA volunteers Joseph O'Sullivan and Reginald Dunne, who had served on the western front, assassinated Field-Marshall Sir Henry Wilson, who had served during the conflict as Chief of the Imperial General Staff.[27] Modern Ireland was born in the chaos of never-ending war.

Of course, the constitutional consequences of the third Home Rule bill, the Easter Rising, and the war of independence were something that neither nationalists nor unionists could have expected. Although these rival political factions were committed to competing views of Ireland's future, which they dressed up in rival religious nationalisms, neither party anticipated that the island would be partitioned. The treaty that brought an end to the Anglo-Irish War divided the island in two. On either side of the border, the new jurisdictions developed around very different religious cultures. Northern Ireland was to be governed, and not only in the eyes of its critics, by a 'protestant parliament for a protestant people', while Southern Ireland, which became a Free State in 1922, and a Republic in 1949, would come to privilege in constitutional law the special status of the Catholic Church, and to formulate policy that reflected Catholic teaching. While the north continued to be governed by British constitutional customs—though for the first several years of its existence the newly devolved parliament was convened in the Belfast seminary of the Presbyterian Church—leaders in the southern jurisdiction, grasping the opportunity to pursue an unprecedented political experiment, thought hard about the kind of state that they wished to create.[28] The two jurisdictions represented the religious and political aspirations of their 'imagined communities'—or at least their dominant majorities.[29] Over eight decades, the Catholic Church validated the southern state, and provided much of the infrastructure of its institutions. While the small population of protestants rapidly declined, from 11 per cent of the population in 1911 to less than 5 per cent in 1961, the Catholic Church held the state together by setting a cultural agenda, until, in the final third of the century, in one of the most striking examples of sudden-onset secularization, and after horrific revelations of neglect and abuse in religious institutions, its claims were suddenly rejected.[30] In their declining numbers—and in their increasing distance from their co-religionists in the north—southern protestants never sought to over-turn the state. But a radical overhaul of the constitutional settlement did become a strategic goal of nationalist politics in the north, which Catholics largely supported. North of the border, in the 'Ulster protestant nation', the much larger proportion of Catholics grew from representing around one-third of the population of Northern Ireland at partition to around half of the population of Northern Ireland one century later.[31] Provoked by the structural inequalities that were the responsibility of the unionist politicians who governed Northern Ireland from 1922 until 1972, as well as by enduring sectarian tensions, a series of outbreaks of violence that were euphemistically known as 'troubles' extended, intermittently, from partition to the ceasefire that was announced in Belfast on Good Friday 1998.[32] Yet even this was not an end to violence. Four months later there occurred the worst single loss of life during the troubles, in which twenty-nine people were killed by a bomb in Omagh, county Tyrone. And sectarian killings continued. Ireland's twentieth century began on Easter Monday 1916 and ended on Good Friday 1998—as if the bright hope of national resurrection would be followed inevitably by suffering and death.

I

The aspirations of the new Free State were brought together in Sir John Lavery's painting, *The blessing of the colours* (1922).[33] Having hosted the Irish delegation during the Treaty negotiations in London, Lavery returned home to witness key events in the formation of the new state, and to represent the moment when, in St Mary's Pro-Cathedral, Edward Byrne, the archbishop

Figure 9. Sir John Lavery, *The Blessing of the Colours* (1922).

of Dublin, blessed the new national flag.[34] Its colours were symbolic, with
the orange, white, and green panels representing the peaceful co-existence of
the island's protestant and Catholic populations. This represented a real aspir-
ation on the part of the architects of the Free State. The first Senate was
designed to be as inclusive as possible of religious minorities, so that its membership included thirty-six Catholics, twenty protestants, three Quakers, and

POBLACHT NA H EIREANN.

THE PROVISIONAL GOVERNMENT
OF THE
IRISH REPUBLIC
TO THE PEOPLE OF IRELAND.

IRISHMEN AND IRISHWOMEN In the name of God and of the dead generations from which she receives her old tradition of nationhood, Ireland, through us, summons her children to her flag and strikes for her freedom.

Having organised and trained her manhood through her secret revolutionary organisation, the Irish Republican Brotherhood, and through her open military organisations, the Irish Volunteers and the Irish Citizen Army, having patiently perfected her discipline, having resolutely waited for the right moment to reveal itself, she now seizes that moment, and, supported by her exiled children in America and by gallant allies in Europe, but relying in the first on her, own strength, she strikes in full confidence of victory.

We declare the right of the people of Ireland to the ownership of Ireland, and to the unfettered control of Irish destinies, to be sovereign and indefeasible. The long usurpation of that right by a foreign people and government has not extinguished the right, nor can it ever be extinguished except by the destruction of the Irish people. In every generation the Irish people have asserted their right to national freedom and sovereignty, six times during the past three hundred years they have asserted it in arms. Standing on that fundamental right and again asserting it in arms in the face of the world, we hereby proclaim the Irish Republic as a Sovereign Independent State, and we pledge our lives and the lives of our comrades-in-arms to the cause of its freedom, of its welfare, and of its exaltation among the nations.

The Irish Republic is entitled to, and hereby claims, the allegiance of every Irishman and Irishwoman. The Republic guarantees religious and civil liberty, equal rights and equal opportunities to all its citizens, and declares its resolve to pursue the happiness and prosperity of the whole nation and of all its parts, cherishing all the children of the nation equally, and oblivious of the differences carefully fostered by an alien government, which have divided a minority from the majority in the past.

Until our arms have brought the opportune moment for the establishment of a permanent National Government, representative of the whole people of Ireland and elected by the suffrages of all her men and women, the Provisional Government, hereby constituted, will administer the civil and military affairs of the Republic in trust for the people.

We place the cause of the Irish Republic under the protection of the Most High God, Whose blessing we invoke upon our arms, and we pray that no one who serves that cause will dishonour it by cowardice, inhumanity, or rapine. In this supreme hour the Irish nation must, by its valour and discipline and by the readiness of its children to sacrifice themselves for the common good, prove itself worthy of the august destiny to which it is called.

Signed on Behalf of the Provisional Government,
THOMAS J. CLARKE.
SEAN Mac DIARMADA,   THOMAS MacDONAGH,
P. H. PEARSE,   EAMONN CEANNT,
JAMES CONNOLLY.   JOSEPH PLUNKETT.

Figure 10. The proclamation of the Irish Republic, 1916

one Jew. But the fact that the Free State's flag—and the ideal it represented—was being blessed in a Catholic cathedral revealed much about how the new state's high-minded aspirations were likely to be worked out.[35] The island's principal religious communities would be brought together in a single jurisdiction under the moral and social oversight of the Catholic Church.

Of course, in 1922, there were more immediate causes for anxiety. The Easter Rising and the end of the First World War had been followed by a war of independence, and the offer of partition in the Government of Ireland Act of 1920 and the Anglo-Irish Treaty of 1921. The Black and Tans committed outrages, and tested the credibility of British justice. Severe sectarian violence broke out in Belfast. After Catholic workers were 'evicted' from the shipyards, in 1920, there commenced a period of troubles that left almost 500 people dead and around 2,000 people wounded.[36] South of the border, the decision by Michael Collins and other negotiators to accept something less than a thirty-two-county republic provoked a civil war between Free State and anti-treaty IRA forces, led among others by Éamon de Valera, a former school teacher and future taoiseach and president, for whom republican ideals remained sacrosanct.[37] The Irish revolution that continued from 1916 until 1923 was brutal, and led to an unknown number of fatalities, with estimates ranging as high as 4,000. This violence between competing communities of republicans was never sanctified in the same way as had been the violence of 1916. In popular culture, the martyr-status that was granted to the sixteen dead leaders of the Easter Rising was never extended to the seventy-seven republicans who were summarily executed by Free State forces six years later—some without trial.[38] And, despite the hopes of the 1916 rebels, the republican struggle continued to highlight the importance of religious difference. While the Easter proclamation had engaged the rebels to cherish 'all the children of the nation equally, and oblivious of the differences carefully fostered by an alien government, which have divided a minority from the majority in the past', reality soon fell short of these ecumenical ideals.[39] As violence spiralled out of control, especially in the south-west, where fighting was hardest, it was never absolutely clear as to whether attacks on isolated communities of protestants were motivated by long-standing local rivalries, by the need of irregulars to acquire weapons, or simply by sectarian hatred.[40] The killing of thirteen protestant boys and men around Dunmanway, county Cork, in 1922, prompted fears that the Free State's religious minority would be subject to a campaign of sustained religious terror.[41] Protestants became increasingly unsure of their place in the new state. As the British

army withdrew, and other institutions responded to the new political landscape, between 1911 and 1926, the number of protestants fell by around one-
third, with the total number of Anglicans, Presbyterians, and Methodists in
the twenty-six counties decreasing from around 310,000 in 1911 to around
206,000 in 1926.[42] Nevertheless, the Catholic Church made clear its opposition to continued republican violence. The bishops denounced the anti-
Treaty campaign as 'murder before God', and priests, almost without
exception, warned the faithful against any involvement with the IRA.[43] But
the leaders of the anti-Treaty forces did not allow this to define their relationship with the church. Republican leaders were often extremely devout.
Their forces split in 1926, when members of Sinn Féin who were unhappy
with its policy of abstentionism formed a new party, Fianna Fáil, which
sought to achieve similar goals within the institutions of the state. The new
party was led by de Valera, a man of deep and enduring piety, who had been
saved from being executed with other leaders of the Easter Rising on account
of his American citizenship, the late timing of his proposed execution, and
the changing mood of the Irish public in response to earlier executions. 'No
famous statesman of our time', intones his official biography, 'can have cen-
tered his life more completely, or perhaps so completely, on religion'.[44] The
treaty had created two new jurisdictions, and had split the republican movement over the vital issue of Irish sovereignty.[45] On both sides of the border,
the people of Ireland launched out in grand, exclusive and sometimes violent
experiments in religious nationalism.

In some respects, the Catholic Church made the Free State possible. After
all, the church and the Gaelic Athletic Association were the only bodies that
could appeal to transcendent loyalties, and so heal the wounds of civil war.[46]
Taking their lead from recent papal encyclicals, new organizations were
established to inculcate the values of the church's social teaching. This
project of 'Catholic Action' worked in different social contexts, but with
shared goals. Its agenda protested against various forms of modernism,
including Pope Pius X's *Lamentabili sane exitu* (1907) and *Pascendi Dominici
gregis* (1907), which were interpreted by the Irish church as condemning any
departure from theological or exegetical tradition.[47] In 1909, the Irish
bishops had introduced an anti-modernist oath, which all clergy were
required to swear until the 1960s. The oath demonstrated the power of
conservative ideas as well as their impressive hold: upon its first imposition,
only forty priests refused to subscribe.[48]

The programme for Catholic Action in Ireland stepped up a gear in the
annus mirabilis of cultural modernism. In 1922, in the year in which were

published James Joyce's *Ulysses*, T. S. Eliot's *The waste land*, and the earliest lyrics of Hugh MacDiarmid, Pope Pius XI issued *Ubi arcano Dei consilio*, a call for Catholic laypeople to work under the supervision of bishops to promote the social theory of the church. A wide range of voluntary organizations were formed, or re-constituted, in response to this call. As they extended religious influence through civil society, in youth organizations, devotional fraternities, and movements for farmers, businessmen, and mothers, they paved the way for enduring problems of clerical over-reach and unchecked power. Some of these organizations worked at arm's length from the hierarchy—like the Legion of Mary, for example, which was founded by Frank Duff in 1921, and which was never the servant of the bishops in the way that it was sometimes represented. The Legion of Mary became one of the most visible and enduring agents of Catholic Action. Duff promoted the organization in an effort to encourage Catholic piety by emulating the tactics of protestant proselytists. Its aggressive techniques were not widely appreciated: Seán Ó Faoláin, several of whose books were later banned in Ireland, turned on their heads criticisms of nineteenth-century pious landlords to describe the tactics of the Legion as 'snooperism'.[49] The organization was never formally approved in the archdiocese of Dublin, partly because the archbishop was concerned that it represented lay over-reach.[50] In 1922, the Knights of St Columbanus were re-formed in an effort to protect Catholic business interests. Modelled on the Freemasons, whose influence it was designed to combat, the movement grew in prestige, until by 1933 it had a membership of almost 5,500 business-men, politicians, and judges.[51] Piety was often public: around 10,000 members of the temperance organization, the Pioneers, marched through Dublin in 1924.[52] In some locations, the effort to promote Catholic social teaching was taken to extremes. In the popular campaign against evil literature, English newspapers, some of which advertised contraceptive devices, were publicly burned.[53] In their place, Catholic Action organizations made massive efforts to ensure the circulation of appropriate religious periodicals. A campaign by members of the Catholic Truth Society ensured that 95 per cent of the Catholic households in Roscrea, county Tipperary, were receiving approved religious reading by 1929.[54]

In the aftermath of civil war, these new organizations built much-needed social capital—but also narrowed the potential of the state. The Free State turned in upon itself, with some of its most influential intellectual agendas set by church teaching. The Censorship of Films Act (1923) was followed by the Censorship of Publications Act (1929) and the Public Dance Halls Act

(1935). Catholic people were steered towards conservative forms of piety. Large numbers entered the religious life, with the greatest numbers of those involved in missionary work serving between 1916 and 1937. The 'faith of our fathers' was most obviously exhibited to the world during the Eucharistic Congress (1932), which marked what was thought to be the 1,500th anniversary of the arrival of St Patrick. After a decade of preparation by Catholic Action groups, the 'government participated in a massive public demonstration of Catholic ascendency throughout the country', in a clear demonstration of the 'religious ethos of the Irish Free State'.[55] Dublin was festooned with Vatican colours. Around one million people attended the open air mass in Phoenix Park—almost one-third of the island's population— where they were addressed by Pope Pius XI in a broadcast from Rome. The event was celebrated by G. K. Chesterton, in *Christendom in Ireland* (1932), and in a commemorative feature film by Father Frank Browne. Suddenly, Ireland was at the centre of the global Catholic imagination. The Catholic Film Society of London seized upon the opportunity, and produced *Aran of the saints* (1932) to advertise the piety and authenticity of Irish faith—not in the capital, which had been the centre of Eucharistic Congress, but in isolated communities on the west coast, in a trope that would echo in R. L. Benson's *Lord of the world* (1909) and Brian Moore's *Catholics* (1972) before being reduced to absurdity in *Father Ted* (1995–1998).[56] The Congress was a stunning success. Catholic Action had been the making of Catholic Ireland. The devotional revolution was complete.

These demonstrations of public piety marked out the growing differences between the jurisdictions on either side of the border. In the early 1920s, worried by the rising tide of immorality that it associated with protestants, Freemasons and English culture, the church was concerned that the Irish nation had lost its 'moral fibre'. Even in Ireland's rather timid experience of the 'Roaring Twenties', Catholic leaders feared that wholesome and traditional pastimes were being replaced by the materialistic hedonism that was evident in new fashions in music and dance. In 1925, the bishops issued a stern warning against these modern trends: 'The surroundings of the dancing hall, withdrawal from the hall for intervals, and the back ways home have been the destruction of virtue in every part of Ireland'.[57] Traditional Irish dancing was innocuous, the bishops believed, but the tendency of Irish young people to follow fashions from London and Paris would lead to their adopting the moral habits of alien, degenerate cultures. The moral panic regarding dancing was one of the earliest indicators of the fears of religious leaders that traditional culture, and the conservative social mores it

represented, was facing a precipitous decline. There was some evidence that
social attitudes were changing, not least in the rise in illegitimate births,
which, at their peak of 3.5 per cent in 1933–1934, were still comparatively
small.[58] In their worries about dancing, as well as in their response to
modern trends in fashion, music, and literature, Catholic clergy denounced
pastimes that were regarded as more or less unremarkable by all but the
most extreme protestant fundamentalists in the north.

The church's influence over sexual matters was tested in 1925, when the
Free State government legislated to make divorce impossible. For some
nationalists, this was a betrayal of the values of the long struggle for Irish
freedom, and raised questions about the place of the protestant minority in
the new state. W. B. Yeats, who was then sitting in the Senate, insisted that
he and his fellow protestants, whose churches in certain circumstances
permitted divorce, were discovering that their fight for freedom had to
continue. Irish protestants were 'no petty people', he insisted:

> We are one of the great stocks of Europe. We are the people of Burke; we are
> the people of Grattan; we are the people of Swift, the people of Emmet, the
> people of Parnell. We have created the most of the modern literature of this
> country. We have created the best of its political intelligence.[59]

But protestants in the Free State, he complained, could no longer take their
religious freedoms for granted. And this concern about the impossibility of
divorce was enduring. Three decades after it was made illegal, Paul Smith,
who remembered his own father's inability to deal with the horrors of service
in the First World War, and the misery and terror that his abusive behaviour
brought upon his mother, insisted that this ban on divorce was immoral. In his
semi-autobiographical novel, *The countrywoman* (1961), he offered a damning
vision of the ways in which this insistence upon the indissolubility of marriage, irrespective of the dangers that compelled cohabitation might represent,
could destroy the lives of the gentle and the good: 'the Church would not
release her from Pat; she would not, sinning, release herself; only death would
free her'.[60] In the mid-1920s, these concerns about dancing and the sanctity
of marriage developed alongside fears about new trends in fashion. In 1927,
the Modest Dress and Deportment Crusade attracted a membership of 1,000
within a few months of its being founded. Its membership had grown to
12,000 by the end of 1929.[61] Catholic Action was charting Ireland's future—
and, with the banning of divorce, the moral panic continued.

For all their relentless activity, Catholic Action organizations were interpreting a sophisticated and carefully articulated social theory. These ideas

were worked out in an Irish context by individuals such as Father Denis Fahey, whose study of *The kingship of Christ* (1931) included a preface by John Charles McQuaid, the future archbishop of Dublin; Father Edward Cahill, author of *The framework of the Christian state* (1932); and Father George Clune, author of *Christian social reorganisation* (1940).[62] Cahill was perhaps the most significant of these social theorists. His ambition was to bring Irish culture more closely into line with Catholic social teaching. The stakes were very high: whatever the constitutional changes, he feared, current trends were 'leading directly towards the final extinction of the historic Irish nation'.[63] Cahill announced his social theory as a plan for national salvation. A Christian state, he argued, should be 'one in which the laws and administration as well as the organized activities and general outlook of the citizens are in accordance with Christian principles'.[64] The effect of this change in outlook would be that the 'rules of the State' would be more closely conformed to 'natural and divine law'.[65] Those who broke these laws should be punished. In 1926, he founded An Ríoghacht ('The kingdom') as a think-tank and propaganda machine. Providing a receptive audience for his lectures on social theory, An Ríoghacht was comprised of a deliberately revolving membership, through which its ideals could circulate into the broader culture. As his thinking developed, Cahill worried that the Criminal Law Amendment Act (1935), which, among other things, prohibited the sale or advertisement of contraceptives, was too weak on implementing Catholic social teaching, and, in a letter to de Valera, who by then had been elected as president of the executive council (a position more or less equivalent to prime minister), suggested that breaches of the law with respect to the use of contraceptives should be met with imprisonment.[66] In another letter to de Valera, in 1936, he recognized that the state was not likely to adopt a fully Catholic constitution—though he hoped that this situation might eventually change.[67] But he made some notable gains: in his magnum opus, *The framework of the Christian state*, he described the family as the 'natural and primary' social unit, some five years before article 41 of the new constitution referred to the family as the 'natural, primary and fundamental unit group of Society'.[68] While northern protestants continued to work 'for God and Ulster', Cahill and the theorists of Catholic Action worked 'for the glory of God and the honour of Ireland', as the title page of his book put it, recycling a well-known expression that reappeared in the conclusion of the 1937 constitution.[69]

The moral panic about evil literature provided a context for dramatic restrictions on the circulation of printed matter. In 1929, a censorship act allowed for books to be placed upon a list of forbidden titles. Titles on this list—which existed apart from the Vatican's *Index librorum prohibitorum*— were most often identified after complaints from the public. The number of titles added to the list grew annually until it peaked in the 1950s, before winding down in 1967.[70] The Irish list seemed at times to be more restrictive than the *Index*. *Laws of life* (1935), by Halliday Sutherland, a Scottish Catholic doctor and opponent of artificial birth control, whose work was appreciated by Cahill, was approved by Catholic bishops in England but fell afoul of the Irish censors.[71] The new censorship regime, and the concern about evil literature that it reflected, offered another demonstration of the subordinate status of protestants in the south, even though southern protestants often approved of censorship's goals. In 1930, Letitia Dunbar-Harrison, a graduate of Trinity College Dublin, was appointed as the Mayo county librarian. Her appointment became a focus of struggle between the government, which insisted that she be allowed to take up the role, and the library committee of Mayo County Council, which, citing her lack of ability in Irish, claimed that Dunbar-Harrison should be disbarred. As the debate continued, and with the decision of the library committee now supported by a bishop, it became clear that other factors were involved in the decision-making—including blatant religious prejudice. One contributor to the discussion asked whether a protestant could be 'trusted to hand out books to Catholics'.[72]

While these relatively isolated instances of discrimination paled into insignificance in comparison with the structural dynamics of discrimination in the north, they did raise questions about the inclusive character of the Free State. Were Irish protestants, after all, to be a 'petty people'? Many Catholics thought not. Some groups reached across the confessional divide to incorporate protestants in their work. Muintir na Tíre ('People of the land'), founded by Canon John Hayes in 1937, sought to include protestants in its efforts to achieve rural cooperation.[73] Members agreed to promote the 'love of God and of country and to strive and secure peace and prosperity for all through the observances of the principles held sacred by everyone bearing the name of Christian'.[74] Even the IRA was prepared to take a stand against anti-protestant prejudice. In 1933, Robert Bradshaw was appointed as town clerk of Sligo, in a decision that the Minister for Local Government reversed. Bradshaw was an IRA member—and a protestant. *An Phoblacht* condemned his removal as the result of religious discrimination.[75] The vast majority of southern protestants remained within the new state, accepted its authority, and, increasingly, identified with its institutions.

Nevertheless, as the church adopted clearer views of the economic arrangements that ought to underlie an ideal Christian constitution, the advocates of Catholic Action circulated their ideals. *Quadragesimo anno* (1931), an encyclical from Pope Pius XI, condemned the excesses of free-market capitalism while warning against socialism. The Irish bishops and the Free State government coordinated this rejection of the left. In two consecutive days in October 1931, bishops condemned the IRA for its socialism, and prohibited the faithful from joining it, while the government proscribed the IRA and various communist groups.[76] In place of socialism, the church emphasized its commitment to corporatism, a theory of social organization that became an enduring strain in Catholic Action theory, which these organizations preferred to describe as 'vocationalism' to avoid the other term's fascistic connotations.[77] Some political leaders took the idea of corporatism very seriously—and were less concerned by unflattering comparisons with the European far-right. During the later 1920s and 1930s, Eoin O'Duffy, commissioner of An Garda Síochána, led pilgrimages to religious sites across Europe, as a consequence of which he came to admire the social agenda of the fascists whom he encountered. O'Duffy planned for radical action, and, in 1932, considered how he might replace the Dáil with a parliament elected not by constituencies but by vocational and professional groups.[78] But the *coup* never happened, and democratic politics normalized when Fianna Fáil formed their first government and began more obviously to court Catholic opinion. Under the leadership of de Valera, future taoiseach and president of Ireland, whose political career extended into the 1970s, the southern jurisdiction pursued its most ambitious quest for an authentically Christian political order. De Valera sought to consolidate these gains in a new constitution. As they cemented church teaching into law, the republicans who had been denounced by the Catholic bishops during the civil war now became their political saviours. It was time for Ireland to become a proper Christian state.

De Valera's project to renew the constitution took advantage of the fact that over 92 per cent of Irish citizens shared a common Catholic faith. As discussions of draft texts continued, he studied recent trends in Catholic social teaching. Some Catholic Action movements spotted an opportunity to realize their ideals. In 1934, Cahill gained de Valera's ear. With help from Fahey, he began to push for arrangements that might have represented an ecclesiastical establishment in all but name.[79] Their agenda had serious implications for protestant civil rights. An Ríoghacht publications referred to mixed-religion marriages as 'invalid and merely legalized concubinage'—a position similar to Cahill's description of civil marriages.[80] These views threatened Presbyterians with a status in the Free State comparable to that of their forefathers under the penal laws, when the legal status of their marriages had been similarly impaired, and would have confirmed the darkest fears of those northern protestants who had taken up arms to resist 'Rome rule'. But de Valera checked this move towards denominational triumphalism. As discussions about the content of the constitution continued, de Valera backed away from Cahill and Fahey, and turned for advice to McQuaid, in an effort to design a constitution that could find room to include—even if it would never appeal to—northern protestants.[81] But even McQuaid remained unpersuaded by the constitution's eventual separation of church and state.[82]

Much of the debate about the new constitution centred on the text of its preamble.[83] De Valera had no doubt about the denominational character of the state. In his St Patrick's day address in 1935, he insisted that Ireland 'remains a Catholic nation'.[84] But, at the same time, he consulted on the text of the new constitution with the leaders of other religious communities, including the chief rabbi, Dr Isaac Herzog, and the Anglican archbishops of Armagh, C. F. D'Arcy, and Dublin, John Gregg.[85] Brushing aside arguments by Jesuits that the preamble should refer to 'Christ the universal king', as Cahill had done in *The framework of a Christian state*, the preamble invoked 'the Name of the Most Holy Trinity, from Whom is all authority and to Whom, as our final end, all actions both of men and States must be referred'.[86] The preamble represented 'the people of Éire' as 'humbly acknowledging all our obligations to our Divine Lord, Jesus Christ, Who sustained our fathers through centuries of trial'. This was a powerful projection of the document's idealized 'imagined community': the Irish nation could be known by its devotion to the Holy Trinity and its gratitude to Jesus Christ.[87] The state's religious parameters were clarified in article 44, which recognized the 'special status' of the Catholic Church, along with the Church of Ireland, the Presbyterian Church in Ireland, Methodists, Quakers, Jews, and the smaller religious communities that existed at the state's formation (this article was annulled after a referendum in 1972). But this article appeared to be something of an afterthought. Defined by the preamble, the Irish nation was an 'imagined community' from which Dublin's small community of Jews was necessarily excluded. The constitution also claimed jurisdiction over the six counties that made up Northern

Ireland. This claim was also hard to take at face value—much like the gesturing towards corporatism, the principles of which were only put into effect in the composition of the senate. Whatever de Valera's principles and preferences, partition made his religious politics possible: the incorporation into the Free State of hundreds of thousands of northern protestants would have imperilled the 'special status' that had been granted to the Catholic Church by raising the protestant population from less than 10 to around 25 per cent of the whole.[88] Read in connection with the document's religious politics, therefore, de Valera's irredentism was little more than politics by gesture. Nevertheless, the text of the constitution cut both ways: it excluded from Ireland's 'imagined community' the very small number of Jews who lived happily within it, and included, if only in principle, hundreds of thousands of northern protestants whose forcible incorporation within the state would have challenged, if not overturned, its Catholic pretensions. The final text of the constitution was 'theocratic in precept' if also 'democratic in practice'.[89] But the state that it defined was more inclusive of its religious minorities than its critics might have expected: in 1938, Douglas Hyde, a protestant and much-admired nationalist stalwart, was installed as Ireland's first president (Erskine Hamilton Childers, another protestant, would follow as the fourth president of Ireland in 1973).[90]

In the new constitution, as in the legislation of morality that pre-dated it, the politicians of the Free State offered the church an extraordinary opportunity. Irish values would be shaped by the church's views on gender, the economy, trade union–employer relations, education, health, media, freedom of thought, sexual health, and appropriate literature. As clerical influence grew, only a handful of spheres within the state would remain independent of clerical power—including Trinity College, which was seen as 'dark and outrageously Protestant in its gloomy withdrawal', and from which, after 1944, students from the Dublin diocese and, after 1956, Catholic students from across the island were forbidden entry by their own bishops until 1970;[91] the *Irish Times*, which remained a protestant opinion-former until re-inventing itself as Ireland's newspaper of record, and which was edited by protestants until the 1980s; and those businesses controlled by protestant families and networking organizations such as the Freemasons, through which that control was often exercised; as well as in enclaves of left-wing thought, in trades unions and in the Labour Party (and its schisms), as well as in the dissident republican movement, which was drifting away from its roots in religious nationalism to embrace the social and economic analysis that was being provided by the revolutionary movements of the 1960s.[92] The church worried about these separate spheres, and determined to see off the threats that were represented by protestant networks and international socialism. In developing its own social programme, it won the admiration of some of the new state's most reactionary forces—including individuals and corporatist movements that lionized the achievements of Salazar's Portugal and fascist organizations elsewhere.

For all that partition offered new opportunities for the implementation of Catholic social theory, it was, in many respects, a disaster for the communities that it divided. The southern jurisdiction was stabilized by the fact that its religious minority was privileged, if also having gone through a period of rapid decline in the early 1920s, with few substantial links to protestant communities in the north apart from those provided by the island-wide infrastructures of the larger protestant denominations. In the decades after partition, southern protestants made their peace with the new political realities and developed an identity apart from that of their co-religionists in the north. But the northern jurisdiction was destabilized by the fact that its religious minority was large, growing, well-connected with a cultural hinterland on the other side of a porous and fairly arbitrary border, and increasingly resentful of being stuck in second place. While the Free State consolidated around the almost hegemonic power of the Catholic Church, the government of Northern Ireland had to come to terms with the fact that around one-third of its population remained unreconciled to the values and institutions of the state and were (mostly) determined to see it replaced. Of course, the dissatisfaction of many northern Catholics was caused by the fact that they tended to compare their economic and political situation with that of their protestant neighbours rather than with the often poorer living standards of their co-religionists in the south. Northern protestants may have been more aware than their Catholic neighbours of the economic contrasts that were represented by the border. With one eye on developments in the south, and recognizing that Home Rule had indeed turned out to be a very emphatic form of 'Rome rule', the first Prime Minister of Northern Ireland, James Craig, the first viscount Craigavon, met one style of confessional government with another. While working within British constitutional norms, and never having the opportunity to re-fashion the nation and the apparatus of the state from the ground up, he clearly understood his role as leading a 'protestant parliament for a protestant people'—a frequently quoted phrase that he seems never to have used.

In 1934, responding to an objection that his government favoured protestants, he made his position clear: 'All I boast of is that we are a Protestant Parliament and a Protestant State.' He figured the economic argument in religious terms: 'It would be rather interesting for historians of the future to compare a Catholic State launched in the South with a Protestant State launched in the North and to see which gets on the better and prospers the more.'[93] While de Valera had to make a virtue of rural poverty, Craigavon could take advantage of the strongly industrial base of the north-east counties, from the large conurbations of which, as a result of the trade war, the Free State had cut itself off.

By 1937, large parts of the southern state and society had been more or less aligned with the teachings of the church. Its power was projected in popular culture, too: clergy directed much of the early cinema industry.[94] As the world edged towards a second global conflict, and the United Kingdom led the struggle against Nazi aggression, the south pursued a policy of neutrality, and turned in upon itself. De Valera valorized the nation that he was imagining into existence. In a broadcast in 1943, he meditated upon the 'Ireland that we would have, the Ireland that we dreamed of', as the

> home of a people who valued material wealth only as a basis for right living, of a people who, satisfied with frugal comfort, devoted their leisure to the things of the spirit—a land whose countryside would be bright with cosy homesteads, whose fields and villages would be joyous with the sounds of industry, with the romping of sturdy children, the contest of athletic youths and the laughter of happy maidens, whose firesides would be forums for the wisdom of serene old age. The home, in short, of a people living the life that God desires that men should live.[95]

It was an idealized representation that bore little comparison to the seedy underworld of the larger cities, in which during the 1940s missionaries like Eva Stuart Watt reached out to prostitutes and alcoholics.[96] It was also an idealized representation of a nation that was almost but never quite at war. For Ireland's wartime neutrality was sometimes ambiguous, both in the practical assistance that the government provided to the Allies and in the respect it paid to Nazi opinion, as when de Valera went to the German legation to express his condolences upon the death of Adolf Hitler. During the 'emergency', as the war was known, a media black-out meant that Irish citizens could not easily follow the course of the conflict, but those who were aware of Nazi atrocities waited in vain for their government to denounce them. The Catholic Church had no hesitation in doing so. In fact, throughout the conflict, the church often spoke more clearly than the state regarding the moral causes and consequences of the war.[97]

The campaign to legislate a Catholic Ireland into being continued in the first few years of peace. The church's precepts continued to be widely respected. Even at the state funeral for Douglas Hyde, in 1949, Catholic members of government, observing their bishops' exhortation not to participate in a protestant worship, stood outside the church to wait for the emergence of the cortege (the ban on attending protestant funerals was lifted in 1966).[98] But some activists wanted to see much faster progress in creating a confessional state. In the late 1940s and 1950s, members of a small integralist group known as Maria Duce ('With Mary as our leader') began a long campaign to have article 44 recognize the status of the 'one true church'.[99] Their efforts succeeded only in Westmeath, where, in 1950, the county council passed a resolution to the effect that the constitution should recognize the Catholic faith as being above the 'man-made religions of the world'—a resolution that was almost immediately rescinded. As their efforts continued, in the early 1950s, Maria Duce fell out of favour with Archbishop McQuaid and was forced to change its name.[100] The organization was highly secretive. In 1946, when Special Branch had investigated the organization, it had been unable to establish its membership.[101] Its reputation was not helped when, in 1957, one member, Sean South, was killed as he participated in a republican paramilitary attack on a police station in Northern Ireland.[102] These links between confessional politics and religious nationalism reappeared in Ailtirí na hAiséirghe ('The architects of the resurrection'), a political party that in the early 1940s emerged out of the language revival movement, which drew members from protestant and Catholic backgrounds, and which wanted Ireland to become the source of a global religious revival.[103] In *Aiséirge says* (1944), the organization advertised its goal of securing the 'independence of our country as an essential preliminary towards the establishment of a state which, in the Christian perfection of its social and economic systems, will be a model for the whole world'.[104] This mission would have very particular beginnings, members believed, as Ailtirí na hAiséirghe worked for the restoration of the Irish language, in order to prevent the circulation of immoral literature and films from overseas. 'Co-operating with destiny, co-operating in the development of a divine plan', Ailtirí na hAiséirghe would establish a 'Christian, social and economic order in a free, democratic, Gaelic Ireland'.[105] But these goals were complicated by the perception that leaders of the movement sympathized with governments that were waging war against the Allies. Sinn Féin campaigned against anti-Catholic and foreign literature, while even publications of the IRA continued to project this ideal image of Ireland in strongly conservative tones, advertising anti-Semitic books by Father Denis Fahey, exposing Masonic influence within the European Economic Community, and warning emigrants to England of the 'irreligious completely materialistic atmosphere' that they would there encounter.[106] These statements were, in a way, recycling the claim of Paul Blanshard, the American secularist journalist, who spent several months on the island in the early 1950s, that the Irish border was a 'barrier in time between the spirit of the modern democratic state and the medieval spirit of Rome'.[107]

Efforts of these movements notwithstanding, the Catholic Church continued to shape the moral life of the nation. The tensions that had been emerging between integralist and more conventionally liberal political traditions were brought to a head in 1950, when the health minister announced plans for 'Mother and Child scheme', which would offer welfare support to large numbers of struggling families.[108] This seemingly innocuous proposal was met with fierce resistance from doctors, concerned about their losing private practice, who allowed resistance to the proposal to be led by Archbishop McQuaid and the Catholic hierarchy, who, in good corporatist style, feared that the state was encroaching on the charitable sphere of the church. As Seán Ó Faoláin observed, 'the Dáil proposes; Maynooth disposes'.[109] Unable to face down the opposition of the church, the health minister abandoned the scheme. McQuaid had struck an early blow in what would over the next few decades become a crisis between church and state. But the politics of the family, and the church's guidance on mixed marriages, continued to be a source of tension. In 1957, the decision by one protestant mother in a mixed marriage not to raise her children in the Catholic faith—a decision that resisted the demands of *Ne temere* (1907), the papal decree that required that children of mixed marriages should be raised within the Catholic faith—led to a boycott of every protestant shop in Fethard-on-Sea, county Wexford.[110] More radical activists explored a return to terror as the continuation of religious nationalism by other means. During the later 1950s and the early 1960s, the IRA and some splinter republican groups mounted a 'border campaign', in which they attacked the infrastructure of British rule in mainly republican areas. Despite the condemnation of the Catholic bishops, some units engaged in conflict after receiving absolution from a local priest.[111]

But the southern state was modernizing too. In the 1950s and 1960s, protestant intellectuals like Hubert Butler played a brave and critical role in challenging assumptions that the Catholic majority should permit free speech as long as protestants never requested it.[112] In 1963, the celebrations that attended the visit of John F. Kennedy, the first Irish-American and Catholic president of the United States, disguised a more significant structural change. By the early 1960s, it was no longer clear either that the Catholic Church could depend upon the submission of the state, nor indeed that it expected it: the edifice of Catholic Ireland was beginning to crumble.[113] Paul Smith's observations that 'the priests were always on the winning side' and that 'somebody ought to be able to abolish the power of the priests over the minds of the people' reflected an increasingly popular opinion.[114] Ireland was undergoing a minor cultural revolution.[115] In 1961, RTE made its first television broadcast, during which Cardinal D'Alton insisted that the organization's chairman and director-general could be 'depended upon' to present high-minded material rather than social critique.[116] But broadcasts began to expose Irish viewers to other ways of life: households on the east coast and around the border could keep up to date with the 'Swinging Sixties' by tuning in to the BBC.

The Irish media began to reflect and simultaneously create the changing social realities. Irish political parties appeared to be moving to the left.[117] Even the church began acknowledged the changing mood. Two papal encyclicals, *Mater et magistra* (1961) and *Populorum progressio* (1967), seemed to question traditional notions of property rights. From 1962 to 1965, almost 3,000 delegates at the Second Vatican Council sought to re-think at a fundamental level the relationship between the church and the modern world. The changes that followed were foundational, so that Latin liturgy became less common and vernacular Bible reading more frequently encouraged. Protestants were no longer outside the pale of salvation, and the sexual revolution was not entirely to be rejected. Women were no longer required to wear a head-covering at mass. This issue paled into insignificance beside other trends in gender politics. For, with the publication of *Humanae vitae* (1968), the liberalizing trends were almost stopped in their tracks. In 1966, the Pontifical Commission on Birth Control had agreed that the Catholic faithful could use oral contraceptives. Two years later, Pope Paul VI overturned its recommendation. *Humanae vitae* confirmed the church's traditional teaching on the sanctity of life with a finality that shocked the large constituency of Irish Catholics who had quietly ignored its admonitions.

'For the first time, a significant majority in Ireland chose to disregard a central teaching' of the church.[118] Or, as one of the feminist activists involved in the campaign later put it, 'the Pill did more than control fertility: it sowed sedition: it evangelized for autonomy'.[119] As an emerging movement of feminists pushed for reproductive rights, the opinions of Irish Catholics divided. Faced with the opportunity to regulate pregnancy through means that were both accessible and discreet, an increasing number of Irish Catholics began to make their own moral choices.[120] Their decision to do so presented the church with an existential challenge. As in Britain, though with less immediately visible effects, the 1960s were a watershed for Irish religion.[121] But not everyone understood the direction of travel. Missionaries were among those who found it most confusing. If salvation could be found in protestant denominations—and even, as some of the more radical theologians suggested, in non-Christian religions—what was the point of the missionary life?[122] One of the first signs that trouble was on the horizon was a declining number of vocations.[123] But the cultural mood was impacting the northern jurisdiction too, where, inspired by civil rights campaigners in the United States, a cross-community movement took to the streets to protest against housing, employment, and electoral inequalities. On both sides of the border, and in two very different jurisdictions, the battle was on for the soul of Christian Ireland.

II

As the Catholic Church gained increasing control over key institutions in the Free State, and then the Republic, residents of Northern Ireland found themselves in a jurisdiction that took religion seriously without ever making it central to the workings of government or to the shaping of law.[124] If the southern state was revolutionary, in that it designed its laws and institutions *de novo*, the northern jurisdiction was conservative, in that it moved very slowly to liberalize the laws and institutions that it had inherited. For the first several decades of Northern Ireland's existence, its religious demographics did not encourage such gestures of religious symbolism or fundamental constitutional experiments. The six counties that comprised Northern Ireland contained a population that was approximately two-thirds protestant and one-third Catholic. While Catholics made up a small minorities of the populations of counties Antrim (20 per cent) and Down

(30 per cent), and almost half of the populations of counties Armagh (45 per cent) and Derry (48 per cent), they constituted small majorities in counties Fermanagh and Tyrone (both 55 per cent).[125] The decision by the architects of partition to include Fermanagh and Tyrone within the new jurisdiction ensured that it remained perpetually unstable. Like independent Ireland, the north sustained separate spheres between protestants and Catholics—but, while southern protestants maintained their own domains of influence and power, northern Catholics were largely disempowered and became victims of structural discrimination. The demographic split meant that the government of Northern Ireland could not operate along confessional lines, even if it wanted to do so. North of the border, religious politics did not make as much sense as it did in the larger but more cohesively ethno-national society of the south. Northern politicians, in a devolved jurisdiction, had fewer choices to make than did politicians in the independent south.

From partition until the early 1970s, the unionist government of Northern Ireland made gestures in religious rhetoric that it never fulfilled in policy terms. The north had no protestant equivalent of the movement for Catholic Action. The Church of Ireland had been disestablished in 1870, and the new jurisdiction showed no interest in inviting any denomination to take up the position of social and cultural privilege that the Catholic Church was being offered in the south. This was partly because protestants in the north were much more denominationally varied than were southern protestants, who were overwhelmingly Anglican. But—at least in the eyes of its critics—this ostensibly secular public sphere did make religious claims. Its non-denominational system of education was seen by many Catholics as discriminatory, especially during the debate about compulsory Bible reading in schools in the 1920s.[126] Catholics also worried about the sustainability of the Mater Hospital in Belfast, which had been established by the Sisters of Mercy and which worked hard to retain its religious ethos after partition, so that it operated outside the National Health Service from 1948 until 1973.[127] Of course, the government of Northern Ireland did not consistently represent itself as confessional. And yet in some respects its parliament was more closely linked to ecclesiastical influences than was its counterpart in the south. The proximity was symbolized in the new parliament's first home: between 1921 and 1932, while the new parliament building at Stormont was being completed, members met in the Belfast seminary of the Presbyterian Church.[128] The link between church and state was most obvious in terms of elected officials. The Catholic Church forbade its priests from accepting political office, but protestant denominations applied no similar ruling. And so a number of protestant clergymen were elected as unionist politicians—including Rev. James Little, a Presbyterian minister who entered the House of Commons in 1939 at the age of seventy-one, who as an independent unionist suggested that Irish unity would be a price worth paying to bring the Free State into the Allied war effort; Rev. Robert Bradford, a Methodist minister and member of the Vanguard Unionist party, who was assassinated by the IRA in 1981; Rev. Martin Smyth, a Presbyterian minister and member of the Ulster Unionist Party; and Rev. Ian Paisley, a Free Presbyterian minister and member of the Democratic Unionist Party, whose late-career change of heart took him into a power-sharing government with Sinn Féin.[129] Huge numbers of unionist politicians became members of protestant fraternal organizations, such as the Orange Order. There was no movement of protestant integralists, even if the small community of Reformed Presbyterians continued to argue that the state should accept the claims of the Solemn League and Covenant and legislate according to biblical law. Already small in number, their influence was much reduced by their principled refusal to vote. In Northern Ireland, the relationship between church and state may have been less visible than in the south, but it may have been just as immediate.

For its first fifty years, the government of Northern Ireland was controlled by the Ulster Unionist Party.[130] Its largely patrician leadership was not always trusted by working-class or rural voters. Despite their occasional sectarian asides, and links to protestant fraternal organizations, the leaders of unionism governed to ensure the prosperity of the region, while protecting the interests of the landed class that they perceived to be its natural leaders. This was—almost—an *ancien régime* revival. In the 1960s, Prime Minister Terence O'Neill made determined efforts to normalize the relationship with the minority population and with the southern state. In 1964, he made the first ever visit of a unionist politician to a Catholic school. In 1965, he invited the taoiseach, Seán Lemass, to Belfast for talks about trade.[131] This beginning of strategic links between the governments of the two jurisdictions was an important moment of mutual recognition. For many unionist voters, however, O'Neill's recognition of Catholic education and his willingness to cooperate with the government of the Republic signalled his betrayal of the protestant and unionist cause. For many nationalist voters, his gestures were too little, too late, and had to be balanced against O'Neill's support for the location of Northern Ireland's new university in the mainly protestant

Coleraine rather than in the mainly Catholic Derry (among other things). From the middle of the decade, many of those who were most concerned about the political and religious future of the province gathered around the leadership of a young, ambitious, and energetic fundamentalist minister. For the previous twenty years, Ian Paisley had been preaching across the province, building a tiny movement that became known as the Free Presbyterian Church of Ulster, and which emphasized a highly conservative iteration of evangelical religion alongside an unflinching commitment to the union. O'Neill was appalled by the new movement, which he dismissed as fascist.[132] In 1966, amidst growing tensions in the city and renewed violence by protestant paramilitaries, Paisley led a march through the centre of Belfast to protest at what he perceived to be ecumenical tendencies within the main Presbyterian Church. His marchers encountered a hostile stone-throwing crowd, and in the chaos that followed Paisley was arrested and jailed. It was the moment that his small religious movement had been waiting for. Suddenly, for thousands of rural and working-class protestants, Paisley was identified as a hero, and they gathered to support his distinctive style of preaching and political agitation.[133]

In the later 1960s, the most conservative strains of unionism and evangelicalism were coalescing around Paisley as northern Catholics were making similar decisions to take to the streets to demand their rights. Their claims had obvious merit. For forty years, since the inception of the state, Catholics had faced discrimination in the allocation of jobs and housing, and as voters in gerrymandered constituencies they struggled to project their political will.[134] Catholics did suffer discrimination—though not always on account of their religion—for the difficulties that they faced could sometimes be explained by other factors, including poverty or lack of education, which civil rights advocates often attributed to the invisible sectarianism that was cemented into the structures and institutions of the north.[135] With some exceptions, Catholics were not well represented in the professions or in higher education: Queen's University had hardly any Catholic staff in the 1950s, for example, even though Catholics comprised 20 per cent of its students. Catholics made up around one-third of the student body in the late 1960s, when Bernadette Devlin emerged as a vocal proponent of civil rights and, at the age of twenty-one, became the youngest MP ever elected to Westminster.[136] But other Catholic students had very different experiences of university life. The historian Marianne Elliot, who was a student at Queen's in the late 1960s, did not experience any sectarian discrimination.[137] When unionists did gesture towards the inclusion of Catholics, it was often from a position of confidence and security, as when, in 1963, the Ulster Unionist-controlled Belfast City Council flew its flag at half-mast to mark the death of Pope John XXIII.[138] Some groups wanted to enshrine this respect in legislation. In the mid-1960s, pressure groups came together to form the Northern Ireland Civil Rights Association, which pushed for changes in UK law rather than for Irish unification.[139] Early civil rights marches were supported by socially progressive protestants, so that Ivan Cooper worked alongside John Hume to draw attention to the situation in the north-west.[140] But the struggle for civil rights came to be interpreted through a religious lens. Of course, as in the United States in the same period, civil rights were demanded in protest marches that led inevitably to confrontations with the police and Paisley's supporters. Tensions mounted from the summer of 1968. By the late summer of 1969, sectarian rioting left large sections of Derry out of control. Pogroms drove minority populations out of some of the larger urban areas, and many Catholic families fled across the border, in what became the 'largest refugee crisis in western Europe since the Second World War'.[141] As this religious cleansing continued, loyalist paramilitaries, who had begun a campaign of murder in 1966, were countered by the revitalized IRA, which coordinated island-wide efforts towards a military solution, with alleged assistance from senior figures in the military and government of the Republic, before the institutions of the southern state turned towards the repression of paramilitaries.[142] The IRA movement split, as leaders of the Official movement moved increasingly to the left while leaders of the new Provisional movement promoted their idea of a 'free Ireland' organized around 'Christian principles'.[143] By the middle of August, the British army had deployed. Paramilitary violence escalated as demands for civil rights increased. In February 1971, republican paramilitaries murdered their first British soldier.[144] In January 1972, and in circumstances that remain highly controversial, Parachute Regiment soldiers who may have believed themselves to be under fire shot at anti-internment marchers in Derry.[145] One of the iconic images of the 'Bloody Sunday' massacre was that of Father Edward Daly, who became bishop of Derry, waving a white handkerchief as he escorted a mortally wounded victim to safety. Fifteen people were killed by the soldiers. Then the situation exploded. Six months later, one 'bloody Friday' in July, eleven people were killed by IRA bombs in Belfast. The largest single loss of life in a single day occurred in May 1974, when thirty-three people were killed by

Figure 11. Father Edward Daly on Bloody Sunday, 1972

loyalist bombs in Dublin and Monaghan. In November 1974, twenty-one people were killed by republican bombs in Birmingham. 'Ireland may soon be united in nothing but a common chaos', worried J. C. Beckett, a Queen's University historian, in a letter to *The Times* in March 1972.[146] He was right—it was.

The Northern Ireland troubles lasted three decades and led to more than 3,000 deaths in Northern Ireland, Ireland, England, Germany, and in locations elsewhere. This was not strictly speaking a religious war, though religion played an important role in validating the continuation of violence.[147] After all, according to one set of calculations, the body responsible for killing the largest number of Catholics was not the British army, but the IRA.[148] But, if religion was not a cause of the conflict, it certainly kept it going. Actors on both sides of the conflict drew on their faith in critically symbolic moments. In 1981, for example, IRA volunteer Bobby Sands and other hunger strikers sought to renew the cause of republicanism by means of redemptive death. Their actions met with mixed approval in the Church. Cardinal Basil Hume criticized the Irish bishops for not condemning the hunger strikers' deaths as suicide, but it was the intervention of a prison chaplain, Father Denis Faul, that brought the protests to an end.[149] In 1988, Ian Paisley, who was now sitting as a Member of the European Parliament, interrupted a speech by John Paul II, announcing before his baffled and horrified Strasbourg colleagues that the pope was antichrist. This kind of denunciation became a commonplace in unionist culture, but it's not clear that everyone who invoked the slogan really believed that they were engaged in an apocalyptic battle.[150] Some terrorists were obviously motivated by religion. In 1983, for example, republicans attacked a Pentecostal congregation in Darkley, county Armagh, killing three men standing in the foyer, and in 1987 a bomb at a Remembrance Sunday commemoration in Enniskillen left eleven protestants dead. In the mid-1990s, Billy Wright, a former evangelical preacher, was expelled from the UVF for continuing to wage a war against Catholics—a war that he believed could damn his soul.[151] He gained a notorious reputation for religious violence, before being assassinated in prison by members of the INLA.[152] Religion mattered in different ways to loyalist and republican paramilitaries. Loyalists drew on the religious imagery of the evangelical religion that very few of them took seriously. Republicans often drew strength from personal piety but fought ostensibly for political and economic ends. Paramilitaries forged surprising alliances. In 1974, meetings between the Official IRA and UVF leadership led to some unlikely friendships. During the loyalist feud that followed upon these meetings, it has been reported, Billy Mitchell hid out in the home of Official IRA leader Harry McKeown.[153] On both sides of the conflict, competing variants of religious nationalism were giving way to left-wing politics, and old enemies recognized how much they now had in common.[154]

As the troubles continued in the north, the influence of the Catholic Church in the Republic peaked and began to decline. In 1979, over one-third of the state's population gathered in Phoenix Park for an open-air mass with Pope John Paul II. That was approximately the same proportion of the population that, the magazine *Magill* estimated in 1980, were living below the poverty line.[155] Building on the momentum of his visit, a movement of conservative Catholic laypeople began a campaign to copper-fasten the illegality of abortion in Irish law. In 1983, their campaigning resulted in another constitutional referendum, in which two-thirds of voters supported the proposal to guarantee the equal right to life of the pregnant mother and the unborn child. While many protestants lined up to support the amendment, some church leaders did not: Victor Griffin, dean of the Church of Ireland's St Patrick's cathedral, insisted that voters should prefer secular republicanism to any continuation of the confessional state.[156]

This referendum led, in Tom Hesketh's memorable phrase, to the 'second partitioning of Ireland', in which rural and conservative voters lined up against their urban and more socially progressive fellow citizens.[157] The tragedies to which the attitudes that lay behind this tightening legislation could lead were illustrated in 1984, when the body of a fifteen-year-old girl was found along with her new-born son at a Marian grotto in county Longford. Many Catholics hoped for miracles. In summer 1985, observers reported over thirty instances of moving statues—promoting an ecstatic personal piety that the bishops did everything to undermine.[158] In 1986, a referendum on the question of whether divorce should be legalized returned 935,843 votes (63 per cent of the total) in favour of retaining the special status of Catholic social teaching. The majority was smaller than it had been in the referendum on abortion, three years before, when 841,223 votes (67 per cent of the total) had supported the copper-fastening of Catholic teaching within the constitution, but the result continued to point to the existence of significant cultural differences between the two jurisdictions. The strength of Catholic Ireland mattered enormously to many protestants in the north. After all, the Anglo-Irish Agreement, which the British and Irish governments had signed in 1985, provided the southern state with an advisory role in Northern Ireland's government—and was met with protests by up to 100,000 unionists at a mass rally at Belfast City Hall.[159] Even though the Provisionals had by this time followed the Official IRA on their move away from religious nationalism to socialist internationalism, loyalists still represented 'Home Rule' as 'Rome rule'. But, as conflict continued in the north, Catholic Ireland was quietly decreasing in confidence.[160]

Religious faith comforted victims and encouraged those who worked for peace, just as much as religious ideas contributed to the chaos, and sometimes guided the perpetrators of violence. Even as the troubles traumatized northern society—at the height of the conflict, huge numbers of women became dependent upon sedatives—courageous souls found in their faith the resources by which to reach beyond sectarian barriers.[161] From 1973, representatives of the Irish Council of Churches—a protestant body—met with their Catholic counterparts in the Irish Episcopal Conference at Ballymascanlon, county Louth.[162] At the height of the troubles, in 1974, leaders from the Church of Ireland, Presbyterian, and Methodist churches met secretly with paramilitary leaders and passed on their offer of peace to the British government. In 1976, Mairead Corrigan and Betty William founded the Women's Peace Movement, in an effort to bring protestants

Figure 12. Protest against the Anglo-Irish Agreement, 1985

and Catholics together, and were awarded a Nobel Peace Prize for their efforts.[163] In 1979, John Paul II begged for an end to terrorist violence as he celebrated mass before the 1 million people who gathered in Phoenix Park, at the end of a visit in which his rallies had been attended by 2.7 million people—an appeal for peace that the IRA explicitly rejected.[164] Gordon Wilson, whose daughter was one of eleven people killed at a Remembrance Day commemoration service in Enniskillen in 1987, called not for revenge but for forgiveness and reconciliation, and promised to pray for her murderers.[165] Charismatic renewal, while never fully embraced by the Irish Catholic bishops, brought together evangelicals on both sides of the reformation divide.[166] Those Catholics and evangelicals who could unpick the tangled treads of religious nationalism participated in movements like Corrymeela and ECONI to promote the reconciliation that, increasingly, prevailed.[167]

Eventually the violence ended. On Good Friday, 10 April 1998, an agreement between the Irish and British governments and eight Northern Ireland political parties accepted that the province was a constituent part of the United Kingdom, and that it would remain such until a majority of voters on both sides of the border expressed their preference for that constitutional situation to change. The agreement was ratified by referenda in both jurisdictions. The Republic abandoned its constitutional claim to the

Figure 13. John Paul II's visit to Ireland, 1979

six counties, and for the first time recognized the existence of Northern Ireland in international law. Eighty years after the end of the First World War, it seemed that the rights of small nations mattered after all. So much of the tragedy of the troubles was that the principle by which the violence ended was so utterly banal.

III

While the Good Friday Agreement brought a formal end to most of the violence of the troubles, and undoubtedly saved lives, it offered a very unsettled prospect of peace. It constructed a system of devolved government that did away with the ideal of parliamentary opposition in favour of compulsory power-sharing, and promoted single-identity politics by enforcing so-called 'parity of esteem'.[168] This mechanism offered the unionist and nationalist blocs within Stormont an effective veto on the continued existence of government—and gave a significant strategic advantage to those parties who contend that the state of Northern Ireland cannot work and should not exist. After John Hume and David Trimble were awarded the Nobel Peace Prize for their role in ending the troubles, their parties were

Figure 14. Ian Paisley denouncing Pope John Paul II, 1988

squeezed by the inevitable rush to the political extremes. As the influence of the UUP and SDLP receded, Sinn Féin and the DUP took up the reins of power, and Ian Paisley and Martin McGuinness were installed as the First and Deputy First Ministers. In a warm and enduring friendship, former enemies became the poster boys of peace.

The search for peace was never likely to end on Good Friday. Not many people could understand what was going on. If the troubles were complicated, peace was harder to explain. The conflict had presented the irony, complexity, and tragedy of Ireland's competing religious nationalisms to an often bewildered world. Over thirty years, commentators had done their best to explain what the violence might mean, and to suggest how it could be resolved. Few approached the clarity of the historian, A. T. Q. Stewart: 'during the last thirty years of the twentieth century, all the irreconcilables of Irish history came to dwell in the North', he argued. 'The Northern Ireland conflict remains in essence a war between two religious cultures', he explained, as he pointed to the sweep of Irish history to make his most important claim: the religious violence of the troubles was 'not just a clash of cultures; it is a culture in itself'.[169] Moving beyond violence would require a cultural revolution—and that would bring an end to Christian Ireland.

Conclusion

Losing faith in Ireland?

Father Michael Cleary had everything. Born in Dublin in 1934, and an energetic advocate for traditional Catholic teaching, he committed himself to pastoral work in his home town as a radical social activist who campaigned on behalf of the poor. The 'Dirty Harry of the Irish church', as journalists dubbed him, he developed into a media personality, publishing a book, releasing two number-one albums, becoming the host of the most popular evening radio show in Ireland, and owning a racehorse, the aptly named Chancy Man. As his work continued, in the 1960s, Father Mick began to push the boundaries of his pastoral calling. In a documentary film, *Rocky road to Dublin* (1967), he spoke about how much he would have wanted a wife and a family of his own, and of how he had found alternative ways to channel those ambitions through his work as a priest. In the 1970s, his fame grew as his influence within the church continued to increase, until, in 1979, he was invited to sing to one of the largest crowds in the island's history, as it waited in Galway for the arrival by helicopter of Pope John Paul II. At the pinnacle of his career, Father Mick had everything. But he had something else that hardly anyone suspected—a lover, who was also his housekeeper, and a son.

Father Mick's secret was revealed only weeks after his death in 1993. News of his clandestine family tumbled out in a disastrous slew of bad publicity for the church, to become one of the first of a long sequence of scandals that would shatter the reputation of the Catholic Church, undermine the moral consensus it had promoted, and contribute to sudden-onset secularization on both sides of the border. Father Mick had everything—but his secret life would contribute to the collapse of Christian Ireland.[1]

I

The Irish experience of secularization was sudden, shocking, and decisive.[2] On both sides of the border, the tipping point may have occurred in the mid-1990s. In the north, the peace process led to sustained efforts to de-politicize religious identity, as weekly church attendance declined from over 60 per cent in 1968 to just over 40 per cent in 2004.[3] In the Republic, where, during the 1970s, 91 per cent of the population was attending mass on a weekly basis, popular culture internationalized, reflecting stronger links with the USA, an influence that was noticed in the changing accents of middle-class young people as much as in the cosmopolitan values they increasingly espoused.[4]

The grip of Catholic social teaching began to relax. This relaxation was symbolized by the changing status of contraception. While in the southern state it had never been illegal to use contraceptives, it had been illegal to import or to sell them, which in practical terms meant that means for 'family planning' was not available to Irish citizens. Change came slowly. In 1980, pharmacists were permitted to sell contraceptive devices, but, until 1985, they could only be offered to those who could furnish a doctor's prescription. This 'Irish solution to an Irish problem', as taoiseach Charlie Haughey put it, was both a consequence and a cause of slowly liberalizing social norms. But when the dam burst, in the 1990s, the Irish Catholic consensus, which had developed over centuries, gave way because of internal weakness, not external pressure. The moral authority of the church, which had so profoundly shaped the self-consciousness of the Republic as to become almost invisible—and so almost beyond challenge—was shattered by a devastating sequence of scandals. In a religious community that valorized its celibate priesthood and affirmed strict sexual mores even inside marriage, these revelations were devastating.[5]

Even some of those involved in the scandals struggled to respond to displays of iniquity that were almost flamboyant in their hypocrisy. Father Mick had been berated by his friend and confessor, Eamonn Casey, the bishop of Galway and Kilmacduagh, when he had privately acknowledged in confession the existence of his secret family. But, it soon turned out, to Father Mick's astonishment, and fury, Bishop Casey had a secret family of his own—and one that he had supported by diverting church funds. Media thrived on this breathtaking exhibition of clerical arrogance and double-dealing, and, as the decade continued, news of these secret families refused to go away. Baited in the media, and threatened by members of the public, the partners of these eminent churchmen chose to defend themselves in print. *Forbidden fruit: The true story of my secret love for the Bishop of Galway* (1993), by Annie Murphy, was followed by Phyllis Hamilton's *Secret love: My life with Father Michael Cleary* (1995). These books established a new genre of confessional writing—but their authors found little forgiveness.

Then public opinion began to change. The Cleary and Casey affairs were shocking enough, but after the mid-1990s, priests were no longer so easily given the benefit of the doubt. Revelations of secret families were embarrassing to the church, especially when they were linked to allegations of financial misconduct, but these stories paled in comparison to the increasing numbers of testimonies, stretching back over decades, from abused children and single mothers. The allegations became darker and ever more horrific. As the decade continued, the respectable façade of Catholic Ireland was peeled back to reveal corruption, complicity, and criminality in state as well as church, reaching to the highest echelons of society. And the impact of these stories was staggering—for in December 1994, the scandals brought down the government.

The trouble began with Father Brendan Smyth. In 1991, Smyth had been arrested by police in Belfast on charges of child molestation, but he had escaped over the border, and remained on the run in the Republic for three years, until his arrest by An Garda Síochána. His detention created a political crisis. In October 1994, the Irish state broadcaster, RTÉ, aired a television documentary that reconstructed his long history of abuse, and revealed that warrants requesting his extradition to face trial in Northern Ireland had been held without being processed in the office of the Attorney General for seven months. There was no clear explanation for this delay, or why Smyth had been allowed to continue on the run from the northern justice system and as a continuing risk to the public in the south. The failure of justice was weaponized in the tensions that were emerging between the taoiseach, Albert Reynolds, and his partner in the coalition government, Dick Spring, the Labour Party leader. Several weeks later, Reynolds acknowledged in the Dáil that the Irish legal system had failed to confront corruption within the church, 'with ghastly and specific consequences for the children of the country'.[6] But he never got the chance to correct his mistake. Two days later, on 17 November 1994, after pressure from media and politicians made it impossible for him to continue in office, Reynolds resigned. Under a new government, and with his extradition papers finally processed, Smyth was taken north, imprisoned in Magilligan prison, after which he was returned to the Republic, where he stood trial on further charges of child abuse, and was handed down an additional twelve-year sentence. He died, still in prison, in August 1997. His body was taken back to Holy Trinity Abbey, in Kilnacrott, county Cavan, where he had hidden from the police, and where, in the early hours of a late summer morning, his colleagues celebrated his funeral mass and attended his internment. Smyth's coffin was covered in concrete, but the problem he represented could not be so easily disposed of.

For, in the mid-1990s, with the state in turmoil, the Catholic Church in Ireland began to implode. As police forces on both sides of the border developed their investigation into Smyth's crimes, it became apparent that authorities within the Catholic Church had been aware of his long history of abuse and had worked hard to conceal it. Media reports suggested that the Norbertine order, of which Smyth had been a member, had known of allegations about his sexual misconduct since the late 1970s, but had not referred these allegations to police forces on either side of the border. Instead, when it became impossible for him to continue in any individual location, Smyth had been moved between parishes, dioceses, and even countries. And those with knowledge of this abuse reached to the top of the hierarchy. Seán Brady, the Catholic archbishop of Armagh who became a cardinal, was reported to have admitted that in the mid-1970s he had witnessed two boys being sworn to silence after testifying against Smyth's abusive behaviour in a secret church inquiry. But, as these gagging orders showed, authorities in the church had chosen to protect themselves and the institution instead of the most vulnerable of those whom they served. The consequences were horrific. Over a period of forty years, their evasions and incompetence, together with inefficiencies within key institutions in the state, had enabled Smyth to abuse more than 140 children.[7]

At first, this appeared to be an isolated case. After all, between 1975 and 2011, only six priests had been convicted of abuse. But, it soon emerged, over the same period, hundreds of priests had been abusing thousands of vulnerable people in their care. The scale of the crisis became apparent when, in 2002, eighteen religious orders signed up to create a fund of €128 million for victims' compensation. The money would be awarded on one condition—that claimants would agree not to resort to legal action and that the names of alleged abusers would never be revealed. Even then, the €128 million fund was not big enough. For nothing could have prepared the church for the extraordinary scale of the horrors that had been perpetrated under its oversight. And nothing could have prepared the state for the social, political, and diplomatic crises that would be created by these failures in the church.[8]

The results of this long investigation into institutional failure, the criminality of Catholic clergy and the complicity of religious organizations were released in the Ferns Report (2005) and the Ryan and Murphy Reports (both 2009).[9] These reports described a world of malevolence, brutality, and despair. The problems seemed to begin in the seminaries, where, reports suggested, there were well-established cultures of sexual abuse and coercion. Again, the reports implicated those at the top. In 1994, for example, Micheál Ledwith, vice-president of Maynooth College, resigned after allegations that he had sexually harassed his students.[10] The problems continued through other religious institutions, and throughout the welfare system that the church had established to parallel that of the state. After all, Smyth's abuse had been made possible by the access to children and vulnerable adults that he shared with many other members of the clergy. Again, the culture was well established. Since the earliest years of the Free State, the Catholic Church had contributed to the provision of social welfare by running over 200 institutions. These orphanages, hostels, and industrial schools were intended to reform those in their charge, to turn 'delinquents' and single mothers into productive members of a Catholic society. But these were also sites of systemic exploitation, trafficking, malnutrition, sexual abuse, and death.[11] These were problems that the hierarchy had not been prepared adequately to address. Instead, religious leaders had created a 'culture of secrecy and cover-up designed to protect the reputation of the Church and its assets', the reports concluded, pursuing a 'policy of double avoidance', in which those involved in the cover-ups flouted both the law of the church and the law of the land.[12] In a letter to the Irish church in 2010, Pope Benedict acknowledged the church's failure to address 'serious sins committed against defenceless children', and published a formal apology to the victims.[13]

Irish society was by then awake to the monster it had helped to create. One of the worst of these institutions was described by Enda Kenny as a 'chamber of horrors'. The Bon Secours Mother and Baby Home, in Tuam, county Galway, which had provided accommodation for unmarried mothers and their children from the 1920s until the 1960s, had long been the subject of local rumours, especially after skeletons were discovered on the site in the mid-1970s. But the home became the focus of intense media scrutiny in

2012. Writing for a local heritage journal, the historian Catherine Corless recovered inspection reports that documented the large number of children who had died of malnutrition while under the care of the Bon Secours Sisters. But hardly any of these infants had been interred in local graveyards. Corless concluded that hundreds of babies born to single mothers had been buried on site or had otherwise disappeared. In 2015, the Health Service Executive suggested that around 1,000 children who had been born in the home had been illegally trafficked to North America, where they had been adopted without the consent of their mothers. And worse was to come. For, in 2016, the remains of a large number of babies and small children were discovered in an underground structure, where they apparently had been deposited thirty years earlier. Perhaps only taoiseach Enda Kenny, speaking in the Dáil in March 2017, knew how to articulate an adequate sense of grief, pain, anger, shame, and national complicity:

> we took their babies and gifted them, sold them, trafficked them, starved them, neglected them or denied them to the point of their disappearance from our hearts, our sight, our country and, in the case of Tuam and possibly other places, from life itself.[14]

Throughout the crisis, the Taoiseach had few equals in describing the scale of clerical depravity and the horror of the society that had enabled it. In the absence of credible religious leadership, Enda Kenny seemed to embody a genuinely moral vision. His speech in response to the Cloyne Report (2011) was one of the most powerful in the history of the Irish state—and one in which he visibly struggled to give adequate expression to the frustration, horror, and rage that was warranted by the ecclesiastical obstruction of justice. 'It's fair to say that after the Ryan and Murphy Reports Ireland is, perhaps, un-shockable when it comes to the abuse of children', he began, but revelations of the church's obstructive behaviour had 'brought the Government, Irish Catholics and the Vatican to an unprecedented juncture.' The Cloyne Report revealed the extent to which church authorities had enabled and then covered up the 'rape and torture of children', and had recorded the horror of those victims who had to live alongside abusers who were 'held in high regard by their families and the community...In one case, the abuser even officiated at the victim's own wedding'. For, Kenny explained, some 'calculated, withering' members of the hierarchy had shown a 'frankly brazen disregard for protecting children' by undermining the institutions of the state. Authorities within the church had 'downplayed' the significance of these crimes in order to uphold the 'primacy of the institution, its power, standing and "reputation"'. This was an assault on the state as much as on its children, he insisted. For attempts to investigate the scale of the exploitation and abuse of children by Catholic clergy and religious had been impeded by the 'dysfunction, disconnection, elitism [and] narcissism' of the Vatican, which represented an unprecedented 'attempt by the Holy See to frustrate an inquiry in a sovereign, democratic republic'.

Kenny argued that, in defending its own institutions, the church had undermined Irish democracy.

> I am making it absolutely clear, that when it comes to the protection of the children of this State, the standards of conduct which the Church deems appropriate to itself cannot and will not be applied to the workings of democracy and civil society in this republic.

The Ireland of 2011 was not 'industrial-school or Magdalene Ireland, where the swish of a soutane smothered conscience and humanity'. Liberated from this kind of religious tyranny, Ireland had become 'a Republic of laws, of rights and responsibilities, of proper civic order, where the delinquency and arrogance of a particular version of a particular kind of "morality" will no longer be tolerated or ignored'. The church could not be trusted to safe-guard Irish children. Now it was the job of the government to 'protect the sacred space of childhood and to restore its innocence'.[15] Recycling themes that echoed from the war of religion through the Ulster Covenant, Paul Blanshard, and Ian Paisley, Kenny's speech announced the end of Christian Ireland. At the end of the year, and in a deeply symbolic gesture, the Irish government closed its embassy in the Vatican. The institutions that had been inspired by Catholic religious nationalism had betrayed both church and nation. And the story continues to shock the general public. The most recent report into the mother and baby homes, released in early 2021, qualified some of the earlier claims, including the assertion that thousands of children had been trafficked to the United States. But it did more than any other report to document the scale of the horror. Christian Ireland was dead and gone, and Catholic politicians had buried it.

As the crisis continued, Irish society suddenly transformed. In the Republic, secularization took hold in a morally conservative society, but advanced at a rapid pace.[16] Weekly mass attendance collapsed, plummeting from 91 per cent of the general population in 1972 to 30 per cent in 2011, with some striking regional variation: in 2016, over one-third of the population of Dublin and Galway identified as being non-Catholic.[17] The decriminalization of same-sex sexual activity in 1993 and of divorce in 1995 set in motion a radical reformulation of ethics in public policy, so that, after a referendum in 2015, the state became the first in the world to legalize same-sex marriage on the basis of a national popular vote, and, in 2017, Leo Varadkar became the country's first openly gay taoiseach. Popular attitudes to LGBT+ people in the Republic are among the most liberal in the world, with progressive policies being overwhelmingly supported by the very large number of younger voters. The emergence of this key electoral demographic illustrates how seriously the Catholic Church failed to instil its moral values in a generation whose education it virtually monopolized, with the result that a culture that never embraced protestant reformation lives with what one Catholic critic of the protestant reformation describes as its 'unintended consequences'.[18] Reflecting this general decline, Irish priests decreased in number and increased in average age, with catastrophic effects on recruitment.[19] The church could not close its seminaries fast enough to cope with decreasing demand. St Patrick's, Carlow, shut its doors in 1993, and was followed by St Kieran's, Kilkenny, in 1994, St Peter's, Wexford, and St John's, Waterford, in 1999, Clonliffe College, Dublin, in 2000, St Patrick's, Thurles, in 2002, All Hallows, Dublin, in 2015, and St Malachy's, Belfast, in 2018. These closures left two seminaries to provide training for Irish clergy— St Patrick's College in Maynooth, which, in September 2018, enrolled only five new students, the smallest number of seminarians in its long and venerable history, and the Irish College in Rome, which in June 2020 announced that it would stop training clergy, in order to shore up recruitment in Ireland.[20] The collapse in recruitment was absolutely unprecedented. And the astonishingly low numbers of Catholics who turned out to see Pope Francis during his visit to Ireland tell their own story too. One-and-a-half million of the faithful attended John Paul II's mass in Phoenix Park in 1979, but less than one-tenth of that number attended mass with Pope Francis in 2018.[21]

The Catholic Church lost, but the protestant churches did not win, the battle for religious adherence in the Republic. The last survey of Irish religious attitudes, in 2016, showed that the earlier growth of non-denominational and Pentecostal churches has stalled, while membership of the Church of Ireland and the Presbyterian Church has begun to decline.[22] Eastern Orthodox Christians now represent the only growing branch of Christianity in Ireland, thanks largely to immigration from eastern Europe, with a 37 per cent growth bringing their membership to over 65,000. Some other religious communities are growing, including Hindus and Muslims, but almost 10 per cent of the population now claim to have no religion at all. Catholic thinkers have responded cautiously to the new situation, but they cannot turn the tide of the sea of faith.[23] These changes are so foundational that the Catholic culture of even the early 1990s can now hardly be imagined.[24]

II

In Northern Ireland, the scale of the crisis and the speed of secularization have been less dramatic. Since the paramilitary ceasefire, the region has become one of the most deprived parts of the United Kingdom. Its households have a disposable income that is half that of the United Kingdom average. Children in these households experience one of the worst rates of child poverty in the United Kingdom and some of the worst child health in western Europe. This deprivation can be plotted along religious lines. Many more children from Catholic than protestant backgrounds enter higher education. Protestants have significantly worse educational achievements than Catholics, and boys from working-class protestant backgrounds share the worst educational achievements of any group in the United Kingdom, apart from Roma and Traveller children. The region has the highest suicide rate in the United Kingdom. If the unionist politicians must be held accountable for the structural discrimination against Catholics that continued under the oversight of the Northern Ireland Parliament, from partition to 1972, successive power-sharing administrations must be held accountable for the systemic failure of government that has followed the Good Friday Agreement.[25]

The social and moral conservatism of the large community of Catholics and evangelical protestants has been divided in the cross-fire of debates about the border, and weakened by the slow corrosion of modernity. But here too a tipping point appears to have occurred in the 1990s. The Good Friday Agreement (1998) brought an end to the troubles, which, whatever else they achieved, had worked to reinforce religious identities. This may explain why, although the scandals within the church crossed the border, northern Catholics have tended to remain more conservative than their southern counterparts. But it is difficult for them to express that conservatism in politics, for Catholics who wish to vote in support of their church's social teaching lack viable opportunities to do so. Sinn Féin has dropped its long-standing opposition to abortion, losing some members in the process, while the SDLP, a much smaller political party, campaigned for same-sex marriage before its eventual imposition on the province by Westminster MPs. Catholic bishops continue to exhort the faithful not to support these positions in the ballot box.[26] But when the traditional leaders of nationalism no longer support Catholic moral teaching, the faithful are left to choose between nationalist politics and Catholic faith. And some—including some high-profile republicans—are doing what was once unthinkable, in voting for parties like the hard-line Traditional Unionist Voice, as a way to express their morally conservative views.[27] If these instances represent a genuine realignment, northern politics may be swinging towards another single issue.

This political realignment reflects a conservative response to dramatic shifts in public opinion. In the north, as in the Republic, the decline in religious influence has been particularly marked in public policy. While same-sex sexual acts were decriminalized in Northern Ireland in 1982, and while the age of homosexual consent was reduced from twenty-one to seventeen, in 2000, and to sixteen, in 2008, same-sex marriage was only legalized in October 2019. Future legislation will almost certainly keep pace with declining commitment to traditional moral values. And the scale of this religious decline could be significant. In Northern Ireland, one of the most rapidly expanding religious categories is that of non-belief. This is particularly pronounced in unionist constituencies, around south Belfast and in county Down, which areas have the highest numbers of those reporting no religion in polling returns. Whatever else this collapse of religious commitment represents, it will present a challenge to the religiously orientated identity politics that the defenders of Ulster unionism have, for a very long time, assumed. What will unionism look like when its supporters are no longer uncomplicatedly protestant? Can unionist politics survive the move away from protestant religious nationalism? Evangelicals are resisting the legal impact of secularization even as their numerical, social and political significance continues to decline. On both sides of the border, lobbying groups like the mainly protestant Christian Institute and the mainly Catholic Iona Institute have grown, but demand for their services is a mark of the failure rather than of the success of faith-based social action.

The structures of religion may differ on either side of the border, but the issues that challenge believers are oddly similar, as two states, with semi-confessional foundations, struggle to create a civil society that will not depend upon the religious convictions and behaviours upon which they were established. While the 2016 census indicated that over 78 per cent of the population of the Republic identified as Catholic, the results of the referenda on same-sex marriage and abortion demonstrated that a majority of the electorate has not been persuaded by the claims of Catholic moral teaching.[28] In some respects Irish Catholic practice has become more European, in that religious practice has become more selective.[29] In other respects the Irish experience of secularization was not like that of other western societies, which observed the phenomenon of 'believing without belonging', for the Irish were belonging without attending. The civilization that was established by fifth-century missionaries, and that developed over a millennium-and-a-half to shape in profound ways the experience of being Irish and of living on the island, has been transformed. The collapse of religious nationalism cuts both ways, for the Irish may be losing faith in Christianity at the same time as many Christians may be losing faith in Ireland. North and south of the border, the two cultures that evolved through the twentieth century to support rival but equally committed visions of Christian society are disappearing—gradually but inevitably, in the north, and with such astonishing rapidity in the Republic that some social commentators now wonder whether any real piety ever lay behind the façade of Catholic Ireland.[30] With this record of division, sorrow, and exploitation, almost all the criticisms of the Irish churches are warranted— but I will add one more. To the extent that the Catholic and protestant churches attempted to dominate and control the peoples of the island, they undermined the Christian faith.

III

Failure has not only marked modern Catholic social institutions, or efforts at protestant reformation, of course—it has marked the entire history of Christian Ireland. By definition, it could not be otherwise. 'Christian Ireland' was never all that it should have been. As the French sociologist and historian Jacques Ellul recognized, everything that Jesus said about the future of his disciples assumed that they would remain a 'little flock', while acting as 'salt' and 'light' in their host societies.[31] Jesus's teachings made no provision for the elaboration of Christian culture, and gave no warrant for that culture to co-opt the structures of pagan religion or the strategies of earthly power. Measured by the standards of the gospels and epistles, the church was in ruins long before it became the religion of the Roman empire, or crossed beyond its boundaries into Ireland. This ruin was caused by distortions and even denials of the gospel, was manifest in the development of architectural forms, sacramental theories and structures of governance that elevated clergy over laity, and in the turns to persecution that shored up competing quests for power. The source of this failure may be traced to the possibility that culture—rather than Scripture—set so much of the church's agenda. Early missionaries aligned the structures of the church with local and regional kingdoms. The Gregorian reforms of the later medieval period drew the Irish church to adopt the structures of an empire. The protestant reformation replaced one problematic authority structure with another, and moved from an initial indifference to specific theological claims to the persecution of those who would not accept them. Penal laws impoverished those whose religious opinions would not be forced. In the later twentieth century, preaching politicians and politically active priests brought this long tradition to a head. Loyalists gave their lives 'for God and Ulster' just as much as republicans gave theirs '*dochum glóire Dé agus onóra na hÉireann*' ('for the glory of God and the honour of Ireland'). Again and again, throughout 1,500 years of history, the community of believers that Jesus described as being 'not of this world' committed themselves to competing struggles for power. Of course, this history contains inspiring examples of faith and self-sacrifice. Yet, in many respects, as discoveries of abuse and violence attest, cultures that were built up in the name of Jesus Christ turned out to be doing the 'works of the devil'.[32] For, as William Kelly, the nineteenth-century county Down biblical scholar, put it, 'Christendom fell away … into the dream of the church triumphant'.[33] What passed as Christian Ireland is finally over—and Christians should be glad.

For Christians should not be astonished at this long history of failure, or the horrors to which it has given birth. After all, the letter that Paul wrote to the Celtic Christians in Galatia warned that the gospel would be manipulated as much as it would be denied.[34] Paul predicted that leaders within the church would distort the gospel with horrific consequences for everyone who accepted their teaching. Their distortion of the gospel would be marked by a powerful and hypocritical religious moralism, he warned, in which believers would 'fall from grace' by attempting to earn their salvation.[35] Against these dangers, Paul called for Christians to remember that 'a person is not justified by works of the law but through faith in Jesus Christ', who came to 'deliver us from the present evil age', rather than to dominate it.[36] Paul encouraged the Galatians to look beyond their ethnic and cultural particulars to recognize the identity that their baptism revealed, an identity that transcended earthly differences, in which believers from every background would find themselves 'one in Christ', and set free to serve one other in love.[37] Paul's letter suggests some new approaches to the history of the Irish church—and suggests what its prospects might be. So what might come next? What should come next? How will Ireland change as its once-dominant Christian culture continues to erode? And how will this erosion of traditional values affect the thinking and behaviour of Irish Christians?

IV

These questions are particularly acute in terms of the Republic, where it is not clear what will replace the Catholic Church as the principal arbiter of morality. After the collapse of the Catholic consensus, and by means of referenda, the Republic has been feeling its way towards a new moral centre. Without the guidance of clergy or institutional religion, either pushing for or effectively resisting this broader cultural change, the new moral centre is being constructed by other means. As elsewhere in the post-Christian West, Ireland's new moral consensus is proving to be flexible, adaptable, and malleable, an 'Overton window' that will move without a fixed centre and far beyond what were once impermissible boundaries. And the boundaries of permissible opinion are moving fast. Same-sex sexual activity was only decriminalized in 1993 in the Republic, for example, although gay identities continued to be stigmatized—but little more than twenty-five years later, an openly gay man was serving as taoiseach, and practitioners of 'gay conversion therapy' could face up to one year in prison and a very hefty fine. Leo Varadkar may be criticized for many things—but his sexuality is not up for discussion. As younger people make up an increasing proportion of voters, their hashtags dismantle what remains of the Irish Catholic consensus.

As this example suggests, Ireland's new moral consensus will not likely be constructed by politics or by means of democratic institutions. As elsewhere in the West, as religious organizations retreat from cultural formation, the new moral centre will be shaped by a constantly changing culture. But

Figure 15. Abortion debate in Northern Ireland, Rally For Choice, Belfast, 2017

political change, like any other change led by majorities, occurs as a consequence of culture and in response to those who shape it, and so the cultural brokers who will determine the moral expectations of post-Christian Ireland will be those who can most effectively disseminate their opinions through media, either by means of editorial control or through buying some form of advertising. This new hegemony should worry the churches. Not for nothing does one leading Catholic theologian describe the Irish media as 'the most hostile...in the developed world'.[38] And, as elsewhere in the post-Christian West, those who obtain influence over public opinion will be those who are wealthy enough to purchase it. The corruption of church and state will be replaced by the authority of an unaccountable financial elite, whose preferences become the preferences of the majority, and eventually those of their legislators. In terms of the evolution of ethics, there is everything to play for—and pay for.

This marketization of ethics represents not so much the liberalization as the neo-liberalization of Irish public opinion. In other words, the moral centre that will emerge in post-Christian Ireland will be created not by the hegemony of religious or philosophical organizations but by the creativity and enterprise of international business with the support of major philanthropic organizations. In recent referenda, business and philanthropic organizations demonstrated their capacity to make significant and effective political interventions. In the referenda of 2015 and 2018, debates about same-sex marriage and abortion were energized by interventions from ostensibly non-political organizations. During the abortion referendum, for example, Amnesty International received a donation of €137,000 from George Soros's organization, Open Society Foundations, which was ruled illegal by the Standards in Public Office Commission under the terms of the Electoral Act, which prohibits overseas organizations and individuals from making political donations in Ireland—but not before that money had bought some significant public influence.[39] The 'long march through the institutions' that was proposed by an older generation of Marxists has now more or less succeeded, as advocates of various forms of social change have taken up positions of leadership in education, law, and politics, through which their once revolutionary commitments have been normalized in popular culture and have—perhaps unexpectedly—become neo-liberal commodities.[40] The logic of late capitalism means that even criticisms of its system can be bought and sold. Capitalism commodifies even its discontents, and turns liberation into a product. This explains why one element of Irish secularization has been the adoption of liberation theories and certain strains of identity politics by supermarkets and distilleries who seek to do well while doing good. During the referenda, businesses entered the arena of public debate to an unprecedented degree, advocating in favour of constitutional change on the sides of buses and advertising hoardings. And when big business begins to project its social conscience, no other institution can afford to be left behind. This explains why non-political institutions, including universities, came out publicly in favour of same-sex marriage during the referendum in 2015. Across what might in other circumstances be regarded as a political spectrum, organizations combined to promote progressive causes, disagreeing about the speed but not about the direction of social change, while consolidating the new consensus that public opinion, politics, and law should contribute to the fashioning of a post-national and post-religious future. The referenda agreed new social mores at the same time as they established the means by which those convictions would be shaped. Of course, after it had enabled over decades the systemic abuse and exploitation of children and vulnerable adults, voters agreed, what passed as Christian Ireland did not deserve to continue to exist. But, if the marketization of ethics continues, and if public opinion does in fact become a neo-liberal commodity, to be bought and sold by the highest and most influential bidder, it is not clear that any real improvement will have been made. The revolution will have corporate sponsorship. But it is not clear that the opinion formers who will create a new social consensus will be any more representative of or accountable to the people than were the religious organizations whose influence they have so effectively replaced, shaping decision-making in the name of progress and freedom.

V

Of course, cultural change is nothing new, in Ireland or elsewhere, and as Irish society continues to evolve so it is likely that Irish Christianity will continue to evolve with it. Christianity will survive in post-Christian Ireland, but, as long as believers keep on praying and reading their Bibles, it will be radically transformed: as Ellul argued, institutional Christianity cannot long survive an encounter with Jesus Christ. And, ironically, as Christianity evolves so the erosion of confidence in denominational structures is only likely to continue.

Irish Christians will require new kinds of commitment. For the state that once recognized the 'special status' of the church may soon become more aggressively critical of the faithful. If current trends in public opinion continue, some of the traditional moral claims of Christianity will cease to be socially acceptable, and, in the absence of robust free speech legislation, the public statement of these claims may no longer be permitted. As a new consensus emerges, and as hostility to same-sex sexual activity becomes as unthinkable as racism, for example, believers will come under increasing social pressure to abandon the moral claims that have been promoted throughout the history of the church. It is likely that denominations such as the Church of Ireland, which has a long tradition of liberalism, will find it easier to move with the times than will denominations such as the Catholic Church or the Presbyterian Church in Ireland, in which liberal causes have been weakened and in some cases decisively outflanked. Those churches who refuse to liberalize their moral teaching will suffer the inevitable consequences, with a reducing number of adherents facing increasing social opprobrium and, if they make their convictions public, declining social prospects. To some extent, this is already taking place. The Presbyterian Church in Ireland has faced extraordinary pressure to tone down its teaching on sexuality, especially after the General Assembly in May 2018 passed resolutions against same-sex relationships—a decision that led to a media outcry, condemnation from prominent politicians, and demands for the termination of the long-standing relationship between the denominational seminary and Queen's University Belfast. This academic divorce highlighted the difference between the values agreed upon in the highest court of the Presbyterian Church in Ireland—which is, after all, the largest democratic organization in the northern jurisdiction—and those of another institution that exists to serve the community in which that denomination operates.

An inevitable consequence of this kind of social disapproval is that Irish churches will find it increasingly difficult to recruit new leaders. The Catholic clergy, who are noticeably more liberal in the south than north of the border, are not likely to be able to resist the coming cultural revolution. South of the border, where the Catholic Church has lost the moral high ground, a large group among its clergy will, almost inevitably, follow its adherents as they move towards accommodation with the emerging status quo, while maintaining for as long as possible basic positions on the sanctity of life, although there are already indications that some southern priests would be happy to reconsider even this once foundational claim. The slump in recruitment into the priesthood, and declining numbers attending mass, will work its way through the system to result in smaller parishes and diminishing membership. In the short term, the church will need to recruit priests from overseas, many of whom will bring with them a stronger commitment to traditional Catholic teaching, and conservatives will continue to organize around groups such as the Iona Institute, an organization that lobbies in favour of traditional Christian moral teaching, and publications such as *Alive!*, a widely distributed free newspaper that promotes a stringently conservative Catholic faith. But the long-term trend seems clear. The Irish Catholic Church will no longer be led by Irish priests—and perhaps it may not be led by priests at all.

In Northern Ireland, where traditional moral positions are shared between conservative Catholic and the evangelicals who still make up the majority of members in the main protestant denominations, change will happen more slowly, but with equal inevitability. After all, the collapse in clerical recruitment in the Catholic Church compares to declining recruitment into the ministry of the principal protestant denominations. As among Catholics, membership of those communities will decline to the hardcore, to those believers whose commitment to their faith makes it possible for them to rationalize the negativity of the outside world through strong social bonds within the group.

In terms of politics, the overall social impact of these believers will continue to be undermined by their divisions with respect to the border and for as long as the border continues to be a significant political issue. But it is not clear how long this division will matter. Recent analyses of northern politics suggest that unionism is growing softer, while analyses of the demographics of northern protestants suggest that they will continue to decline as a percentage of the overall population, and that after 2021 they will form a definite minority, reflecting the fact that for the first time since partition the province now has more nationalist than unionist MPs.[41] In any case, as public opinion continues to liberalize, the border will represent less and less of an ontological barrier: if Northern Ireland no longer represents a 'protestant state for a protestant people', and the Republic no longer recognizes the 'special status' of the Catholic Church or conforms to its moral teaching, there may exist no real rationale for the continued division of the six and twenty-six counties. If earlier unionists had opposed Home Rule as 'Rome rule', their successors will need to discover a less sectarian rationale for continued partition—something that will call for more imagination than simply rehearsing the benefits of the National Health Service. And, without this competition between different varieties of Christian Ireland, there might not exist a compelling warrant for partition. This may explain the very different responses from northern leaders to the visit of Pope Francis in summer 2018: unionist leaders refused to meet him, while the leaders of the largest and most conservative protestant churches took the opportunity to welcome this outspoken defender of traditional Christian morality.

But there will be some resistance to secularization and the marginalization that will inevitably follow. The renewal of Christianity in the Republic, if it is to occur, will most likely occur without the leadership of the Catholic clergy. Demoralized, and declining in number, they are not in a position to offer a credible critique of their culture—and they are certainly not yet in a position to be taken seriously by the general public. Instead, as several indicators already suggest, the renewal of Irish Christianity will most likely be achieved among the laity. Even at the present moment, a substantial body of opinion retains its commitment to traditional Catholic teaching without much leadership from the church. This became apparent during the referendum on blasphemy in October 2018. None of the mainstream churches campaigned to retain the law. In fact, in 2013, a joint statement from Churches in Ireland, an ecumenical body representing the largest denominations, had rejected the Republic's constitutional rejection of blasphemy as being 'largely obsolete'.[42] But when they came to cast their ballots, and entirely without any leadership from churches or any other religious body, over 35 per cent of voters supported a retention of the blasphemy laws. This substantial group of religious conservatives does not have a leader, a spokesperson, or even, apparently, an agenda. Without representation or organization, Ireland's hidden Catholics are not forming an underground, but they are registering their discontent. As Irish society has secularized, on both sides of the border, some believers continue to resist it, as new forms of cultural politics trump older religious differences.

This new cultural politics is being led most effectively by lobbying groups. Based in England, the Christian Institute convenes a large number of public meetings in evangelical churches in Northern Ireland, where among its *causes célèbres* it successfully defended the right of a bakery to refuse to decorate a cake with a message promoting same-sex marriage, several years before Westminster MPs reformed marriage law in Northern Ireland. The case had been brought against the bakery with the support of the Northern Ireland Equality Commission, headed, ironically, by a theologian who had formerly taught at one of Belfast's most prominent evangelical Bible colleges. The Christian Institute supported the bakery as the case passed through the British legal system, attracting increasing international attention, as well as some unexpected support from such esteemed advocates of gay rights as Peter Tatchell, and as it was eventually referred to the Supreme Court of the United Kingdom. There, after a protracted and complicated hearing, and apparently to everyone's astonishment, the judges unanimously ruled in favour of the bakery, concluding that the equal provision of goods and services could not require compelled speech. For now, in Northern Ireland, those who continue to support traditional Christian teaching on sexuality cannot be forced to say otherwise.

While similar cases have arisen in the Republic, none have resulted in controversial legal landmarks. The Iona Institute, which offers the traditionalist moral clarity that the church can no longer provide, has taken a leading role in public debates relating to the recent referenda, providing participants for television debates of the quality of Maria Steen, a barrister and home educator, who clashed with prominent advocates of abortion rights. The Institute was founded in 2007 by David Quinn, who now acts as its director, but his experience may be less encouraging than has been that of his counterparts in the north. On Twitter, Quinn responded to the result of the abortion referendum by suggesting that the time had come for the preamble to the Irish constitution to be removed. It was no longer tenable, he believed, for the Irish state to confess 'the Name of the Most Holy Trinity, from Whom is all authority and to Whom, as our final end, all actions both of men and States must be referred'.[43] The state, he recognized, was now acting without any regard for its final end, and it ought to have the honesty to say so.[44]

Perhaps he is right—and perhaps it is those believers who have given up on the state who are best prepared for the future. For not everyone is persuaded that this kind of lobbying is likely to sustain the legislative privilege of traditional Christian teaching. Some believers are abandoning any expectation of affirmation or support from broader society and have begun to explore new and sometimes radical expressions of faith. Some of these experiments have taken place among the Catholic faithful, where they make it their aim to strengthen the cause of that church. Inspired by American journalist, Rod Dreher, whose book of the same title has become a *New York Times* best-seller, some believers are pursuing 'Benedict options', cultivating intentional communities in which to live out their faith in parallel with, if not by actually engaging with, the broader culture. Developing themes in a broader conversation about the shape of the church after Christendom, including important work by the American theologian Stanley Hauerwas, this new monasticism recognizes the status of believers as 'pilgrims and strangers', and encourages its adherents to think creatively and with ambition about what Christians acting without the affirmation of broader society can nevertheless achieve.[45]

Rod Dreher's work has been central to this agenda. When he spoke in Dublin in January 2019, at the invitation of the Iona Institute, Dreher encouraged his audience of more than 300 to form new kinds of communities in which to live out their faith, with weakened economic dependence upon outsiders and, ironically, upon the institutions of the church. Emphasizing the value of home schooling, Dreher in effect encouraged his listeners to withdraw their children from denominational schools, which could no longer be trusted for the spiritual formation of the children in their care. The text of his talk contained no reference to protestants or to non-denominational Christians, perhaps because he did not expect many of these believers to attend his presentation in the ornate surroundings of the University College Dublin chapel. But evangelicals are paying careful attention to his arguments.

For Dreher's argument is protestant at its core. His agenda may name-check St Benedict of Nursia, the father of monasticism, as well as Pope Benedict XVI, one of the most conservative of modern church leaders, but Dreher's agenda reflects his own movement from Methodism through Catholicism and into the Russian Orthodox Church. In his account, believers may need to fend for themselves, if necessary without the support of an institutional church. And this message finds its most obvious home among those religious individualists who make up what is sometimes inappropriately homogenized or collectivized as the evangelical movement.

Some evangelicals have always pursued a variety of the 'Benedict option'. While other believers have set out to pursue wider political influence, in parts of county Antrim, for example, groups such as the Plymouth Brethren exist in such numbers and concentrations as to make possible the formation of a feasible parallel society, in which believers can provide for each other so many of the necessities of modern life that they can insulate themselves from the wider world, developing what Alasdair MacIntyre described as 'local forms of community within which civility and the intellectual and moral life can be sustained'.[46] Participants in these communities are often easily recognized, identifiable by distinctive habits in fashion and hairstyle, maintaining traditional preferences in hymnody and an intellectual air in public worship, while refusing to engage in any way in the political process. Without withdrawing from the wider world, but living unobtrusively within it, these emerging communities of faith offer an improvising alternative to the discredited structures of Christian Ireland.

VI

What has passed as Christian Ireland is dead. But its critics cannot relax any more than believers ought to despair. After all, things looked bleak in 410, when the Visigoths sacked Rome, and brought an end to Christian civilization. For many Christians, the decline of the Roman empire was cata-strophic. Since the conversion of Constantine, and the state's official backing of the new religion, many believers had identified Roman civilization as the kingdom of God on earth. After all, it had been by means of the state, and with the support of its emperor, that Christians had moved from being a small and persecuted minority to having an outsized influence on the empire. The sudden end of the political system that had supported the church was, for many believers, shattering. But, despite the fears of the faithful, the decline of the empire did not herald the end of the Christian faith. After the sack of Rome, Christian thinkers considered the implications of their church's dependence upon imperial power. Augustine's *City of God* was the most significant, and certainly the most enduring, result of this enquiry. His argument was simple: that Christians should refuse to identify any earthly political power as the expression of God's kingdom. The events of history would continue to be contingent and unpredictable, he insisted, as the fortunes of the church continued to wax and wane. His measured and careful reflections supported the work of Ireland's first Christians.

The conditions within which Christianity emerged in Ireland reflect in some ways those of the present time. As Vincent Twomey, emeritus professor of theology at Maynooth, has argued, 'the Church on earth is by its very nature a Church lurching from one crisis to another'.[47] And these crises are likely to continue. But the dramatic collapse of the older religious structures, which shaped the experience of Irish Christianity, and sudden movements in political and cultural norms, have created opportunities for new kinds of religious expression. After the failure of religious nationalism, what looks like irredeemable failure might actually be a second chance. For the old Augustines still point to a heavenly kingdom, as new Patricks shape the rise of another Christian Ireland.

Notes

PREFACE AND ACKNOWLEDGEMENTS

1. S.J. Connolly, *Priests and people in pre-famine Ireland, 1740–1845*, second edition (Dublin: Four Courts, 2000), pp. 112–129.
2. While a great deal of work investigates divisions within individual communities, some of the most exciting studies of the religious history of Ireland have documented commonalities between religious 'others'; see Raymond Gillespie, *Devoted people: Belief and religion in early modern Ireland* (Manchester: Manchester University Press, 1997); Donald Akenson, *Small differences: Irish Catholics and Irish Protestants, 1815–1922* (Kingston, ON: McGill-Queen's University Press, 1998); Andrea Ebel Brożyna, *Labour, love and prayer: Female piety in Ulster religious literature, 1850–1914* (Kingston, ON: McGill-Queen's University Press, 1998).

EPIGRAPH

1. Scripture quotations are from the ESV® Bible (The Holy Bible, English Standard Version®), copyright © 2001 by Crossway Bibles, a publishing ministry of Good News Publishers. Used by permission. All rights reserved.

INTRODUCTION

1. Thomas Bartlett, *Ireland: A history* (Cambridge: Cambridge University Press, 2010), p. 3. All names cited in the main text are as represented in the *Dictionary of Irish biography*.
2. Ireland's Christian history has been surveyed in W.D. Killen, *The ecclesiastical history of Ireland*, 2 vols (London: Macmillan, 1875); Clement Pike, *The story of religion in Ireland* (London: The Sunday School Association, 1895), which reflects its author's interest in Unitarianism; Michael Staunton, *The illustrated story of Christian Ireland: From St Patrick to the peace process* (Dublin: Emerald Press, 2001); and Brendan Bradshaw and Dáire Keogh (eds), *Christianity in Ireland: Revisiting the story* (Blackrock: Columba Press, 2002).
3. See, for extended discussion of one aspect of this story, P.J. Corish (ed.), *A history of Irish Catholicism*, 6 vols (Dublin: Gill, 1968).
4. Kevin Whelan, *Religion, landscape and settlement in Ireland: From Patrick to present* (Dublin: Four Courts, 2018), p. 220.
5. Crawford Gribben, *Evangelical millennialism in the trans-Atlantic world, 1500–2000* (New York: Palgrave Macmillan, 2011), pp. 71–91.

6. See especially Salvador Ryan (ed.), *Treasures of Irish Christianity*, vol. III: *To the ends of the earth* (Dublin: Veritas Publications, 2015).

7. See, for example, John Carey, 'The Old Gods of Ireland in the later middle ages', in Katja Ritari and Alexandra Bergholm (eds), *Understanding religion: Revisiting the pagan past* (Cardiff: University of Wales Press, 2015), pp. 51–68; James G. Schryver, 'Converting the land of the Irish: Saint Patrick, the Church, and the Irish landscape', in James Lyttleton and Matthew Stout (eds), *Church and settlement in Ireland* (Dublin: Four Courts, 2018), pp. 1–16.

8. Estyn Evans, *Prehistoric and early Christian Ireland: A guide* (London: Batsford, 1966), p. 21. For more recent work on the artistic achievement of high crosses, see Tasha Gefreh, 'Sun of understanding: The iconographic programme of Iona's free-standing crosses', in Conor Newman et al. (eds), *Islands in a global context: Proceedings of the seventh international conference on Insular art, held at the National University of Ireland, Galway, 16–20 July 2014* (Dublin: Four Courts, 2017), pp. 75–83.

9. A.T.Q. Stewart, *The shape of Irish history* (Belfast: Blackstaff Press, 2001), p. 24; Michael P. Carroll, *Irish pilgrimage: Holy wells and popular Catholic devotion* (Baltimore, MD: Johns Hopkins University Press, 1999); Louise Nugent, *Journeys of faith: Stories of pilgrimage from medieval Ireland* (Dublin: Columba Press, 2020). For the distribution of *Lúnasa* celebrations, see Whelan, *Religion, landscape and settlement in Ireland*, p. 122.

10. Peter O'Dwyer, *Mary: A history of devotion in Ireland* (Dublin: Four Courts, 1988).

11. For the history of this practice, see Whelan, *Religion, landscape and settlement in Ireland*, pp. 7, 218.

12. There may be institutional explanations for some of the difficulties they face; S.J. Connolly, 'The moving statue and the turtle dove: Approaches to the history of Irish religion', *Irish Economic and Social History* 31 (2004), pp. 2–3.

13. Seamus Heaney, 'Whatever you say, say nothing' [1975], in Seamus Heaney, *New selected poems 1966–87* (London: Faber, 1990), p. 79.

14. Connolly, 'The moving statue and the turtle dove: Approaches to the history of Irish religion', pp. 1–22, shows how the revival of interest in Irish religious history after the 1980s coincided with the beginnings of the recent crisis in religious institutions.

15. John Bossy, *Christianity in the west, 1400–1700* (Oxford: Oxford University Press, 1985), p. vii.

16. Evans, *Prehistoric and early Christian Ireland*, p. 5.

17. Stewart, *The shape of Irish history*, p. 31.

18. The outputs of this project included such important work as Hallam L. Movius, *The Irish Stone Age: Its chronology, development and relationships* (Cambridge: Cambridge University Press, 1942). For a discussion of the project's theoretical basis, see Mairead Carew, *The quest for the Irish Celt: The Harvard Archaeological Mission to Ireland, 1932–1936* (Newbridge: Irish Academic Press, 2018).

19. Evans, *Prehistoric and early Christian Ireland*, p. 1.

20. Dáibhí Ó Cróinín, *Early medieval Ireland, 400–1200* (London: Longman, 1995), p. 9.

21. T.M. Charles-Edwards, 'Prehistoric and early Ireland', in Dáibhí Ó Cróinín (ed.), *A new history of Ireland,* vol. 1: *Prehistoric and early Ireland* (Oxford: Oxford University Press, 2005), p. lxi.

22. J.P. Mallory, *The origins of the Irish,* second edition (London: Thames & Hudson, 2017), pp. 296–299.

23. Stewart, *The shape of Irish history,* p. 33.

24. Mallory, *The origins of the Irish,* pp. 37, 40, 296–297.

25. This point is contested: compare M.J. O'Kelly, 'Ireland before 3000 B.C.', in Dáibhí Ó Cróinín (ed.), *A new history of Ireland,* vol. 1: *Prehistoric and early Ireland* (Oxford: Oxford University Press, 2005), pp. 66–67, with Mallory, *The origins of the Irish,* pp. 32–58.

26. Movius, *The Irish Stone Age,* p. 132.

27. Lara M. Cassidy et al., 'A dynastic elite in monumental Neolithic society', *Nature* 582 (2020), pp. 384–388.

28. O'Kelly, 'Ireland before 3000 B.C.', pp. 59–65; Mallory, *The origins of the Irish,* pp. 40–70.

29. Mallory, *The origins of the Irish,* pp. 71–104.

30. A radical re-dating of the Céide fields has been proposed by, among others, Andrew Whitefield, 'Neolithic "Celtic" fields? A reinterpretation of the chronological evidence from Céide Fields in north-western Ireland', *European Journal of Archaeology* 20:2 (2017), pp. 257–279.

31. Stewart, *The shape of Irish history,* p. 18.

32. Federico Sánchez-Quinto et al., 'Megalithic tombs in western and northern Neolithic Europe were linked to a kindred society', *Proceedings of the National Academy of Science of the United States of America* 116 (2019), pp. 9469–9474.

33. Mallory, *The origins of the Irish,* pp. 74–77.

34. P.J. Stooke, 'Neolithic lunar maps at Knowth and Baltinglass, Ireland', *Journal for the History of Astronomy* 25 (1994), pp. 39–55.

35. Bartlett, *Ireland: A history,* p. 1.

36. Sánchez-Quinto et al., 'Megalithic tombs in western and northern Neolithic Europe were linked to a kindred society', pp. 9469–9474.

37. See, for a report on the construction of the monument, Michael J. O'Kelly, *Newgrange: Archaeology, art and legend* (London: Thames & Hudson, 1985).

38. Cassidy et al., 'A dynastic elite in monumental Neolithic society', pp. 384–388.

39. 'Further details of Brú na Bóinne aerial survey released', available at https://www.archaeology.ie/news/bru-na-boinne-aerial-survey, accessed 20 June 2020.

40. Mallory, *The origins of the Irish,* p. 194.

41. For this paragraph, see O'Kelly, *Newgrange,* passim.

42. Mallory, *The origins of the Irish,* pp. 105–128.

43. Mallory, *The origins of the Irish,* p. 123.

44. Mallory, *The origins of the Irish,* p. 117.

45. Geraldine Stout and Matthew Stout, 'Early landscape: From prehistory to plantation', in F.H.A. Aalen et al. (eds), *Atlas of the Irish rural landscape* (Cork: Cork University Press, 1997), pp. 31–63.

46. Nollaig Ó Muraíle, 'Settlement and place-names', in Patrick J. Duffy et al. (eds), *Settlement and place-names in Gaelic Ireland, c. 1250–c. 1650: Land, lordship and settlement* (Dublin: Four Courts, 2004), p. 223.
47. John Haywood, *The historical atlas of the Celtic world* (London: Thames & Hudson, 2009), p. 28.
48. Caesar, *The Gallic war*, trans. H.J. Edwards, The Loeb Classical Library (London: Heinemann, 1917), 1.1.
49. A more sceptical view of the possibility of Celtic culture in Ireland is represented in Roy Flechner, *Saint Patrick retold* (Princeton, NJ: Princeton University Press, 2019), pp. 61–63.
50. For this paragraph, see Haywood, *The historical atlas of the Celtic world*, pp. 32–44.
51. Mallory, *The origins of the Irish*, p. 199.
52. Donnchadh Ó Corráin, 'Prehistoric and early Christian Ireland', in R.F. Foster (ed.), *The Oxford history of Ireland* (Oxford: Oxford University Press, 1989), p. 2. See also L.M. Cassidy et al., 'Neolithic and Bronze Age migration to Ireland and establishment of the insular Atlantic genome', *Proceedings of the National Academy of Sciences of the United States of America* 113 (2016), pp. 368–373; E. Gilbert et al., 'The Irish DNA Atlas: Revealing fine-scale population structure and history within Ireland', *Nature Scientific Reports* 7 (2017), article 17,199; M. Furholt, 'Massive migrations? The impact of recent aDNA studies on our view of third millennium Europe', *European Journal of Archaeology* 21 (2018), pp. 159–191.
53. Charles-Edwards, 'Prehistoric and early Ireland', p. lxvi.
54. Barry Raftery, 'Iron-Age Ireland', in Dáibhí Ó Cróinín (ed.), *A new history of Ireland,* vol. 1: *Prehistoric and early Ireland* (Oxford: Oxford University Press, 2005), p. 141.
55. Mallory, *The origins of the Irish*, pp. 129–156.
56. J.P. Mallory, *In search of the Irish dreamtime: Archaeology and early Irish literature* (London: Thames & Hudson, 2016), passim.
57. Mallory, *The origins of the Irish*, p. 158.
58. Ó Cróinín, *Early medieval Ireland*, p. 45; Mallory, *In search of the Irish dreamtime*, p. 68.
59. Evans, *Prehistoric and early Christian Ireland*, p. 5.
60. Proinsias Mac Cana, *The cult of the sacred centre: Essays on Celtic ideology* (Dublin: Dublin Institute for Advanced Studies, 2011).
61. Mallory, *In search of the Irish dreamtime*, p. 227; Jacqueline Borsje et al. (eds), *Celtic cosmology: Perspectives from Ireland and Scotland*, Papers in Mediaeval Studies 26 (Toronto: Pontifical Institute of Mediaeval Studies, 2014); Elizabeth Dawson, 'Paganism, Celtic', in *The Oxford dictionary of late antiquity*, s.v.
62. Caesar, *The Gallic war*, 6.16.
63. Phyllis Fray Bober, reviewing Réne Magnen, *Epona, Déesse Gauloise des Chevaux, Protectrice des Cavaliers*, *American Journal of Archaeology* 62:3 (July 1958), pp. 349–350.

64. Ronald Hutton, *Blood and mistletoe: The history of the druids in Britain* (New Haven, CT: Yale University Press, 2011), pp. 1–5.

65. Caesar, *The Gallic war*, 6.13–14.

66. Mark Williams, *Fiery shapes: Celestial portents and astrology in Ireland and Wales, 700–1700* (Oxford: Oxford University Press, 2010), and Hutton, *Blood and mistletoe*, argue that the druids in Irish texts from this period should not be confused with druids described in Roman writing. On Patrick and the druids, see John Carey, 'Saint Patrick, the druids, and the end of the world', *History of Religions* 36:1 (1996), pp. 42–53.

67. Lucan, *Pharsalia (The civil war)*, trans. J.D. Duff, The Loeb Classical Library (Cambridge, MA: Harvard University Press, 1962), 3. 400–425.

68. Caesar, *The Gallic war*, 6.16; Strabo, *Geography*, trans. Horace Leonard Jones, The Loeb Classical Library (Cambridge, MA: Harvard University Press, 1923), 4. 4. 5.

69. Pliny, *Natural history*, vol. 4, trans. H. Rackham, The Loeb Classical Library (Cambridge, MA: Harvard University Press, 1960), 16: 249. For more, see Barry Cunliffe, *The ancient Celts*, second edition (Oxford: Oxford University Press, 2018), passim.

70. Philip Freeman, *Ireland and the classical world* (Austin: University of Texas Press, 2001), pp. 56–57.

71. Mallory, *The origins of the Irish*, p. 213.

72. Mallory, *The origins of the Irish*, p. 177.

73. 'Iron Age "bog man" used imported hair gel', *National Geographic* 17 January 2006.

74. Ó Corráin, 'Prehistoric and early Christian Ireland', p. 3.

75. F.F. Bruce, *The epistle to the Galatians: A commentary on the Greek text*, New International Greek Testament Commentary (Grand Rapids, MI: Eerdmans, 1982), pp. 3–12.

76. James D.G. Dunn, *The partings of the ways between Christianity and Judaism and their significance for the character of Christianity*, second edition (London: SCM, 2006).

77. Michael J. Kruger, *Christianity at the crossroads: How the second century shaped the future of the church* (London: SPCK, 2017), passim.

78. Justin Martyr, 'First apology', in *Ante-Nicene Fathers*, ed. Alexander Roberts and James Donaldson (Buffalo, NY: Christian Literature Publishing Company, 1885), 1: 185–186.

79. Harlow Gregory Snyder, '"Above the bath of Myrtinus": Justin Martyr's "school" in the city of Rome', *Harvard Theological Review* 100:3 (2007), pp. 335–362. See also 'The martyrdom of the holy fathers', in *Ante-Nicene Fathers*, 1: 305.

80. Tertullian, *Against the Jews*, 7, in *Ante-Nicene Fathers*, 3: 158. Conversely, Henry Chadwick argues in *The early Church* (London: Penguin, 1993), p. 63, that Christianity arrived in Britain in the third century.

81. David Potter, *Constantine, the emperor* (Oxford: Oxford University Press, 2013), pp. 150–162.

82. Augustine, *Confessions*, trans. R.S. Pine-Coffin (London: Penguin, 1961), 8: 2–3.

83. 'The "Nicene" creed', in Henry Bettenson and Chris Maunder (eds), *Documents of the Christian Church*, fourth edition (Oxford: Oxford University Press, 2011), pp. 27–28.

84. Evans, *Prehistoric and early Christian Ireland*, p. 31.

85. Clare Downham, *Medieval Ireland* (Cambridge: Cambridge University Press, 2017), p. 9.

CHAPTER 1

1. D.N. Dumville, 'Some British aspects of the earliest Irish Christianity', in P. Ní Chatháin and M. Richter (eds), *Irland und Europa/Ireland and Europe: Die Kirche im Frühmittelalter/The early church* (Stuttgart: Klett-Cotta, 1984), p. 17; Clare Stancliffe, 'Christianity amongst the Britons, Dalriadan Irish and Picts', in Paul Fouracre (ed.), *The New Cambridge medieval history* (Cambridge: Cambridge University Press, 2005), 1: 426–461.

2. Williams, *Fiery shapes*, p. 2, reports that 'an eschatological focus on the apocalypse was one of the most dominant themes and characteristics of the early Irish Church'. For further exploration of this theme, see Carey, 'Saint Patrick, the druids, and the end of the world', pp. 42–53.

3. Flechner, *Saint Patrick retold*, pp. 29–58.

4. Barbara Yorke, *The conversion of Britain: Religion, politics and society in Britain, 600–800* (London: Routledge, 2006), pp. 98–114.

5. Mallory, *The origins of the Irish*, pp. 196–198.

6. Tertullian, *Against the Jews*, 7.

7. I follow the Britonnic spelling of Alt Clud; Norman Davies, *Vanished kingdoms: The history of half-forgotten Europe* (London: Penguin, 2012). Compare this with the Old Irish version, Ail Chluathe; Flechner, *Saint Patrick retold*, p. 44.

8. Bede, *Ecclesiastical history of the English people*, trans. Leo Sherley-Price, ed. D.H Farmer (London: Penguin, 1990), p. 58; David Petts, *Christianity in Roman Britain* (Dublin: History Press, 2003).

9. Downham, *Medieval Ireland*, p. 12. On border and permeable boundaries, see Elva Johnston, 'Ireland in late antiquity: A forgotten frontier?' *Studies in Late Antiquity* 1:2 (2017), pp. 107–123.

10. Flechner, *Saint Patrick retold*, p. 43.

11. Bede, *Ecclesiastical history of the English people*, p. 55.

12. Ó Cróinín, *Early medieval Ireland*, p. 17.

13. Bede, *Ecclesiastical history of the English people*, pp. 61–62.

14. Peter Brown, *Through the eye of a needle: Wealth, the fall of Rome, and the making of Christianity in the west, 350–550 AD* (Princeton, NJ: Princeton University Press, 2014), pp. 293–294.

15. Freeman, *Ireland and the classical world*.
16. T.M. Charles-Edwards, *Early Christian Ireland* (Cambridge: Cambridge University Press, 2000), pp. 145–148.
17. Charles-Edwards, *Early Christian Ireland*, p. 151; Aidan O'Sullivan et al., *Early medieval Ireland, AD 400–1100: The evidence from archaeological excavations* (Dublin: Royal Irish Academy, 2014), pp. 74–76.
18. N.B. Aitchison, *Armagh and the royal centres in early medieval Ireland: Monuments, cosmology and the past* (Woodbridge, UK: Boydell and Brewer, 1994), pp. 131–198; Charles-Edwards, *Early Christian Ireland*, p. 147; Mallory, *The origins of the Irish*, p. 165.
19. Mallory, *The origins of the Irish*, p. 186.
20. Tacitus, *Agricola*, trans. Maurice Hutton, The Loeb Classical Library (Cambridge, MA: Harvard University Press, n.d.), *c.* 24, p. 211.
21. Mallory, *The origins of the Irish*, pp. 196–198; Flechner, *Saint Patrick retold*, pp. 52–53.
22. Donnchadh Ó Corráin, 'St Patrick and the kings', in Seán Duffy (ed.), *Princes, prelates and poets in medieval Ireland: Essays in honour of Katherine Simms* (Dublin: Four Courts, 2013), pp. 211–220.
23. Downham, *Medieval Ireland*, p. 20.
24. Charles-Edwards, *Early Christian Ireland*, p. 175.
25. David Finkelstein and Alistair McCleery, *An introduction to book history* (London: Routledge, 2005), p. 30.
26. *The new Oxford book of Irish verse*, ed. and trans. Thomas Kinsella (Oxford: Oxford University Press, 1986), p. 3.
27. Downham, *Medieval Ireland*, p. 19. Contra Thomas Cahill, *How the Irish saved civilisation* (New York: Doubleday, 1995).
28. For an excellent survey of scholarship, see Roy Flechner, 'Conversion in Ireland: Reflections on the state of the art', in Roy Flechner and Máire Ní Mhaonaigh (eds), *The introduction of Christianity into the early medieval insular world* (Turnhout, Belgium: Brepols, 2016), pp. 41–55, and Colmán Etchingham, 'Conversion in Ireland', in Roy Flechner and Máire Ní Mhaonaigh (eds), *The introduction of Christianity into the early medieval insular world* (Turnhout, Belgium: Brepols, 2016), pp. 181–204.
29. Ó Cróinín, *Early medieval Ireland*, p. 20. John Carey disputes this claim, noting that the reference in the letter is to 'the Irish believing in Christ'; John Carey, 'Learning, imagination and belief', in Brendan Smith (ed.), *The Cambridge history of Ireland, vol. 1: 600–1550* (Cambridge: Cambridge University Press, 2018), p. 47. See also Downham, *Medieval Ireland*, p. 48. For details of the Bettystown excavations, see *Mapping death: Peoples, boundaries and territories in Ireland*, available at http://www.mappingdeathdb.ie/idlocs, accessed 20 June 2020.
30. Charles-Edwards, *Early Christian Ireland*, pp. 15, 173.
31. Ó Cróinín, *Early medieval Ireland*, p. 14, with reference.
32. Ó Cróinín, *Early medieval Ireland*, p. 14; 'Palladius', *Dictionary of Irish biography*, s.v.

33. This traditional view of the contribution made by Pelagius has been challenged by Ali Bonner, *The myth of Pelagianism* (Oxford: Oxford University Press, 2018).
34. Bede, *Ecclesiastical history of the English people*, p. 65.
35. Bede, *Ecclesiastical history of the English people*, pp. 65–66.
36. Bede, *Ecclesiastical history of the English people*, p. 71.
37. Charles-Edwards, *Early Christian Ireland*, p. 2101.
38. Quoted in Ó Cróinín, *Early medieval Ireland*, p. 21.
39. Charles-Edwards, *Early Christian Ireland*, pp. 202–214.
40. Charles Thomas, *Christianity in Roman Britain to AD 500* (Berkley, CA: University of California Press, 1981), p. 306; see 'Auxilius', 'Iserninus', and 'Secundinus' in *Dictionary of Irish biography*, s.v.
41. Charles-Edwards, *Early Christian Ireland*, p. 234.
42. Tim Clarkson, *Columba* (Edinburgh: John Donald, 2011), p. 25. On Patrick, see D.A. Binchy, 'Patrick and his biographers', *Studia Hibernica* 2 (1962), pp. 7–173; R.P.C. Hanson, *Saint Patrick: His origins and career* (Oxford: Clarendon Press, 1968); E.A. Thomson, *Who was Saint Patrick?* (Woodbridge, UK: Boydell, 1985); Liam de Paor, *St Patrick's world: The Christian culture of Ireland's apostolic age* (Notre Dame, IN: University of Notre Dame Press, 1993); Philip Freeman, *St Patrick of Ireland: A biography* (New York: Simon & Schuster, 2004). A controversial revisionist account is provided in Flechner, *Saint Patrick retold*. Mallory, *The origins of the Irish*, p. 195, assumes that Patrick's arrival in Ireland can be dated to 432, but Colmán Etchingham, in 'Conversion in Ireland', p. 182, describes this date as 'wholly artificial'.
43. Charles-Edwards, *Early Christian Ireland*, p. 239, suggests that Auxilius, Iserninus, and Secundinus are more easily associated with Palladius, working in the middle third of the fifth century, than with Patrick, working in the later part of the fifth century, with whose mission they have traditionally been identified. This is not surprising, in that many aspects of Palladius's mission were later ascribed to that of Patrick.
44. Flechner, *Saint Patrick retold*, p. 65.
45. Thomson, *Who was Saint Patrick?*, pp. xi, 17.
46. Thomson, *Who was Saint Patrick?*, pp. xi–xii.
47. Charles-Edwards, *Early Christian Ireland*, p. 219.
48. Charles-Edwards, *Early Christian Ireland*, p. 233.
49. Thomson, *Who was Saint Patrick?*, pp. 36–37. For a summary of Patrick's theology, see Thomas O'Loughlin, *Celtic theology: Humanity, world, and God in early Irish writings* (London: Continuum, 2000), pp. 25–46.
50. Davies makes this claim in *Vanished kingdoms*, pp. 49–52. Flechner, *Saint Patrick retold*, pp. 31–32, suggests that Bannavem Taburniae should be located closer to Carlisle. Other historians prefer a location in Wales.
51. 'Saint Patrick's Confessio', available at https://confessio.ie/etexts/confessio_english#, accessed 12 August 2020.
52. Etchingham, 'Conversion in Ireland', pp. 188–189.

53. Ludwig Bieler, 'The problem of "Silua Focluti"', *Irish Historical Studies* 3:12 (1943), pp. 351–364.

54. 'Saint Patrick's *Confessio*', available at https://confessio.ie/etexts/confessio_english#, accessed 12 August 2020.

55. 'Saint Patrick's *Confessio*', available at https://confessio.ie/etexts/confessio_english#, accessed 12 August 2020.

56. Thomson, *Who was Saint Patrick?*, p. 43; Flechner, *Saint Patrick retold*, pp. 12–17.

57. 'Saint Patrick's *Confessio*', available at https://confessio.ie/etexts/confessio_english#, accessed 12 August 2020.

58. Thomson, *Who was Saint Patrick?*, p. 80.

59. On Patrick's view of the end times, see Thomson, *Who was Saint Patrick?*, p. 106; Carey, 'Saint Patrick, the druids, and the end of the world'.

60. Ó Cróinín, *Early medieval Ireland*, p. 25; Etchingham, 'Conversion in Ireland', p. 190.

61. 'Saint Patrick's *Confessio*', available at https://confessio.ie/etexts/confessio_english#, accessed 12 August 2020.

62. M. Pepperdene, 'Baptism in the early British and Irish churches', *Irish Theological Quarterly* 22 (1955), pp. 110–123.

63. 'Saint Patrick's *Confessio*', available at https://confessio.ie/etexts/confessio_english#, accessed 12 August 2020.

64. Charles-Edwards, *Early Christian Ireland*, p. 239.

65. 'Saint Patrick's *Confessio*', available at https://confessio.ie/etexts/confessio_english#, accessed 12 August 2020.

66. Aitchison, *Armagh and the royal centres in early medieval Ireland*, p. 7. On the history of early Christian burial practice, see Nancy Edwards, *The archaeology of early medieval Ireland* (London: Routledge, 1996), pp. 129–131; Whelan, *Religion, landscape and settlement in Ireland*, pp. 13–15.

67. Hutton, *Blood and mistletoe*, and Williams, *Fiery shapes*, emphasise that the 'druids' in Christian writing should not be identified with the druids that were described by, for example, Julius Caesar.

68. Charles Plummer, 'Introduction', in *Vitae Sanctorum Hiberniae*, ed. Charles Plummer, 2 vols (Oxford: Clarendon Press, 1910), I: cxxxiv.

69. Sharpe, *Medieval Irish saints' lives*, p. 9; Elizabeth Dawson, 'Brigit and Patrick in *Vita Prima Sanctae Brigitae*: Veneration and jurisdiction', *Peritia* 28 (2017), pp. 35–50.

70. Ó Cróinín, *Early medieval Ireland*, p. 38; Williams, *Fiery shapes*, p. 5.

71. Downham, *Medieval Ireland*, p. 117.

72. Ó Cróinín, *Early medieval Ireland*, pp. 31–33.

73. Downham, *Medieval Ireland*, p. 115.

74. Richard Sharpe, *Medieval Irish saints' lives: An introduction to Vitae Sanctorum Hiberniae* (Oxford: Clarendon Press, 1991).

75. W.B. Yeats, 'Preface', in Lady Gregory, *Gods and fighting men: The story of the Tuatha De Danaan and of the Fianna of Ireland* (London: John Murray, 1905), p. xix.

76. Charles-Edwards, *Early Christian Ireland*, pp. 188, 240.

77. Clarkson, *Columba*, p. 26.

78. Colmán Etchingham, *Church organisation in Ireland, A. D. 650 to 1000* (Maynooth, Ireland: Laigin Publications, 1999).

79. Rob Meens, *Penance in medieval Europe, 600–1200* (Cambridge: Cambridge University Press, 2014), p. 38.

80. Charles-Edwards, *Early Christian Ireland*, p. 239.

81. Colmán Etchingham, 'Bishops in the early Irish church: A reassessment', *Studia Hibernica* 28 (1994), pp. 35–62; Etchingham, *Church organisation in Ireland, A. D. 650 to 1000*, pp. 455–458.

82. Charles-Edwards, *Early Christian Ireland*, p. 421.

83. Ó Cróinín, *Early medieval Ireland*, p. 151.

84. Ó Cróinín, *Early medieval Ireland*, p. 162.

85. Catherine Thom, *Early Irish monasticism: An understanding of its cultural roots* (London: T&T Clark, 2006).

86. Christina Harrington, *Women in a Celtic church: Ireland, 450–1150* (Oxford: Oxford University Press, 2002), pp. 23–48.

87. Kathleen Hughes and Ann Hamlin, *The modern traveller to the early Irish church* (1977; rpr. Dublin: Four Courts, 1997), p. 8.

88. Charles-Edwards, *Early Christian Ireland*, p. 275.

89. Clarkson, *Columba*, p. 26.

90. Westley Follett, *Céli Dé in Ireland: Monastic writing and identity in the early middle ages* (Woodbridge, UK: Boydell and Brewer, 2006), pp. 171–219.

91. Charles-Edwards, *Early Christian Ireland*, p. 250.

92. Michelle P. Brown, *Art of the islands: Celtic, Pictish, Anglo-Saxon and Viking visual culture, c. 450–1050* (Oxford: Bodleian Library, 2016).

93. Jonathan M. Wooding, '*Peregrini* in the ocean: Spirituality and reality', in Emer Purcell et al. (eds), *Clerics, kings and Vikings: Essays on medieval Ireland in honour of Donnchadh Ó Corráin* (Dublin: Four Courts, 2015), pp. 411–417; Stephanie Hayes-Healy, ' "Irish pilgrimage": A romantic misconception', in Seán Duffy (ed.), *Princes, prelates and poets in medieval Ireland: Essays in honour of Katherine Simms* (Dublin: Four Courts, 2013), pp. 241–260; Tim Severin, *The Brendan voyage* (London: Arrow Books, 1979).

94. Charles-Edwards, *Early Christian Ireland*, p. 2.

95. Charles-Edwards, *Early Christian Ireland*, p. 277.

96. Edel Bhreathnach, 'Communities and their landscapes', in Brendan Smith (ed.), *The Cambridge history of Ireland*, vol. 1: *600–1550* (Cambridge: Cambridge University Press, 2018), p. 29.

97. Hughes and Hamlin, *The modern traveller to the early Irish church*, p. 30.

98. Lisa Bitel, *Isle of the saints: Monastic settlement and Christian community in early Ireland* (Ithaca, NY: Cornell University Press, 1990); Howard B. Clarke, 'Quo vadis? Mapping the Irish "monastic town"', in Seán Duffy (ed.), *Princes, prelates and poets in medieval Ireland: Essays in honour of Katherine Simms* (Dublin: Four Courts, 2013), pp. 261–278; J. Soderberg, 'Anthropological *civitas* and the possibility of monastic towns', *Journal of the Royal Society of Antiquaries of Ireland* 144–145 (2014–15), pp. 45–59; Whelan, *Religion, landscape and settlement in Ireland*, p. 6.

99. Donnchadh Ó Corráin, *The Irish church, its reform and the English invasion* (Dublin: Four Courts, 2017), pp. 12–13.

100. For these details of construction, see Hughes and Hamlin, *The modern traveller to the early Irish church*, pp. 55–60; Tomás Ó Carragáin, *Churches in early medieval Ireland: Architecture, ritual and memory* (New Haven, CT: Yale University Press, 2010).

101. Hughes and Hamlin, *The modern traveller to the early Irish church*, p. 84.

102. Heather King, 'Late medieval Irish crosses and their European background', in Colum Hourihane (ed.), *From Ireland coming: Irish art from the early Christian to the late Gothic period and its European context* (Princeton, NJ: Princeton University Press, 2001), pp. 333–350.

103. Charles-Edwards, *Early Christian Ireland*, pp. 326–343; Jennifer O'Reilly, 'The art of authority', in Thomas Charles-Edwards (ed.), *After Rome* (Oxford: Oxford University Press, 2003), pp. 141–190; Jane Hawkes, 'Art and society', in Brendan Smith (ed.), *The Cambridge history of Ireland*, vol. 1: *600–1550* (Cambridge: Cambridge University Press, 2018), p. 81.

104. Hughes and Hamlin, *The modern traveller to the early Irish church*, p. 95.

105. Hughes and Hamlin, *The modern traveller to the early Irish church*, p. 97. See, more recently, Griffin Murray, 'Viking influence in Insular art: Considering identity in early medieval Ireland', in Cynthia Thickpenny et al. (eds), *Peopling Insular art: Practice, performance, perception* (Havertown, PA: Oxbow, 2020), pp. 51–57.

106. Brian Lalor, *The Irish round tower: Origins and architecture explored* (Dublin: Collins Press, 1999).

107. Hughes and Hamlin, *The modern traveller to the early Irish church*, p. 69.

108. Quoted in Hughes and Hamlin, *The modern traveller to the early Irish church*, p. 3. On Columba's penitential teaching, see Meens, *Penance in medieval Europe*, pp. 64–69.

109. Quoted in Hughes and Hamlin, *The modern traveller to the early Irish church*, p. 5. Charles-Edwards, *Early Christian Ireland*, p. 152.

110. Hughes and Hamlin, *The modern traveller to the early Irish church*, p. 3.

111. Hughes and Hamlin, *The modern traveller to the early Irish church*, p. 38.

112. Ó Corráin, *The Irish church, its reform and the English invasion*.

113. Hughes and Hamlin, *The modern traveller to the early Irish church*, p. 10.

114. Fintan O'Toole, *A history of Ireland in 100 objects* (Dublin: Royal Irish Academy, 2013).

115. For a survey of this literature, see O'Loughlin, *Celtic theology*.

116. Charles-Edwards, *Early Christian Ireland*, p. 181. See also Martin McNamara, *The Bible and the apocrypha in the early Irish church (AD 600–1200): Collected essays*, Instrumenta Patristica et Medievalia (Turnhout, Belgium: Brepols, 2015).

117. Ó Cróinín, *Early medieval Ireland*, p. 219.

118. *The Hibernensis: A study and edition*, ed. Roy Flechner (Washington, DC: The Catholic University of America Press, 2019), pp. 48–53.

119. Charles-Edwards, *Early Christian Ireland*, p. 181.

120. Charles-Edwards, *Early Christian Ireland*, p. 239; Noel Kissane, *Saint Brigid of Kildare: Life, legend and cult* (Dublin: Four Courts, 2017).

121. Charles-Edwards, *Early Christian Ireland*, p. 177.

122. Bede, *Ecclesiastical history of the English people*, p. 143.

123. Charles-Edwards, *Early Christian Ireland*, p. 9.

124. Charles-Edwards, *Early Christian Ireland*, p. 180.

125. Bede, *Ecclesiastical history of the English people*, p. 154.

126. Jennifer O'Reilly, *Early medieval text and image*, vol. 1: *The insular Gospel books* (London: Routledge, 2019); Jennifer O'Reilly, *Early medieval text and image*, vol. 2: *The Codex Amiatinus, the Book of Kells and Anglo-Saxon art* (London: Routledge, 2019).

127. Gerald of Wales, *The history and topography of Ireland*, trans. John O'Meara (London: Penguin, 1982), pp. 84–85.

128. Downham, *Medieval Ireland*, p. 39.

129. *The new Oxford book of Irish verse*, p. 8.

130. Thomas Kinsella, 'Introduction', in *The new Oxford book of Irish verse*, p. xxiii.

131. Herbert, *Iona, Kells and Derry*, pp. 151–179.

132. David Woods, 'Under the abbot's cloak: The symbolism of Columba's clothing in Adomnán's *Vita Columbae*' in Emer Purcell et al. (eds), *Clerics, kings and Vikings: Essays on medieval Ireland in honour of Donnchadh Ó Corráin* (Dublin: Four Courts, 2015), pp. 341–351, considers the symbolism of clothing in hagiographical writing—which Adomnán may have emphasised in order to validate the developing cult associated with Columba's relics, which included his clothing (p. 350).

133. Máire Herbert, *Iona, Kells, and Derry: The history and hagiography of the monastic familia of Columba* (Oxford: Clarendon Press, 1988).

134. Clarkson, *Columba*, p. 14.

135. Lahney Preston-Matto, 'Saints and fosterage in medieval Ireland: A sanctified social practice', *Eolas: The Journal of the American Society of Irish Medieval Studies* 5 (2011), pp. 62–78.

136. Clarkson, *Columba*, p. 37.

137. Clarkson, *Columba*, p. 83.

138. Clarkson, *Columba*, pp. 48–51.

139. Clarkson, *Columba*, p. 110; Meens, *Penance in medieval Europe*, p. 66.

140. Clarkson, *Columba*, pp. 57–62, 125.

141. For a summary of recent scholarship on 'Picts', see Alex Woolf, 'On the nature of the Picts', *Scottish Historical Review* 96:2 (2017), pp. 214–217.

142. Clarkson, *Columba*, p. 150.

143. Clarkson, *Columba*, p. 140.

144. James Bruce, *Prophecy, miracles, angels, and heavenly light? The eschatology, pneumatology, and missiology of Adomnán's Life of St. Columba* (Carlisle: Paternoster, 2004); Thomas O 'Loughlin, *Adomnán and the holy places* (London: T&T Clark, 2007).

145. Séamus Mac Mathúna, 'The relationship of the chthonic world in early Ireland to chaos and cosmos', in Jacqueline Borsje et al. (eds), *Celtic cosmology: Perspectives from Ireland and Scotland*, Papers in Mediaeval Studies 26 (Toronto: Pontifical Institute of Mediaeval Studies, 2014), pp. 53–76.

146. Charles-Edwards, *Early Christian Ireland*, p. 194.

147. Charles-Edwards, *Early Christian Ireland*, p. 8; Alex Woolf, 'Columbanus's Ulster education', in Alexander O'Hara (ed.), *Columbanus and the peoples of post-Roman Europe* (Oxford: Oxford University Press, 2018), pp. 91–101.

148. Columbanus, 'A boat song', in *The new Oxford book of Irish verse*, ed. and trans. Thomas Kinsella (Oxford: Oxford University Press, 1996), pp. 9–10.

149. Quoted in Hughes and Hamlin, *The modern traveller to the early Irish church*, p. 1.

150. Charles-Edwards, *Early Christian Ireland*, p. 348; Tomás Ó Carragáin, 'The architectural setting of the cult of relics in early medieval Ireland', *Journal of the Royal Society of Antiquaries of Ireland* 133 (2003), pp. 130–176. The relics cult was linked to the 'Romanisation' of the Irish church: see Niamh Wycherley, *The cult of relics in early medieval Ireland*, Studies in the Early Middle Ages 43 (Turnhout, Belgium: Brepols, 2015), p. 193.

151. Alexander O'Hara, *Jonas of Bobbio and the legacy of Columbanus: Sanctity and community in the seventh century* (Oxford: Oxford University Press, 2018), pp. 68–88, 261; Alexander O'Hara, 'Introduction: Columbanus and Europe', in Alexander O'Hara (ed.), *Columbanus and the peoples of post-Roman Europe* (Oxford: Oxford University Press, 2018), pp. 3–18. For a detailed study of the Easter controversy, see Olive M. Cullen, 'A question of time or a question of theology: A study of the Easter controversy in the insular church' (unpublished PhD thesis, Pontifical University, St Patrick's College, Maynooth, 2007), available at http://mural.maynoothuniversity.ie/1331/1/PHD_Thesis_corrected_copy_1st_July_08.pdf, accessed 20 June 2020.

152. Downham, *Medieval Ireland*, p. 127.

153. For a recent discussion of the Easter controversy, see Caitlin Corning, 'Columbanus and the Easter controversy: Theological, social and political contexts', in Roy Flechner and Sven Meeder (eds), *The Irish in early medieval Europe* (New York: Palgrave Macmillan, 2016), pp. 101–115.

154. Bede, *Ecclesiastical history of the English people*, pp. 109–110.

155. Bede, *Ecclesiastical history of the English people*, p. 138. It is possible that these papal letters to the Irish are not genuine: Michael Herren, 'The "Papal letters to the Irish" cited by Bede: How did he get them?' in Emer Purcell et al. (eds), *Clerics, kings and Vikings: Essays on medieval Ireland in honour of Donnchadh Ó Corráin* (Dublin: Four Courts, 2015), pp. 3–10.

156. Bede, *Ecclesiastical history of the English people*, p. 138. On the context to this possibility, see Joseph Kelly, 'Pelagius, Pelagianism and the early Christian Irish', *Mediaevalia* 4 (1978), pp. 99–124; Dáibhí Ó Cróinín, '"New heresy for old": Pelagianism in Ireland and the papal letter of 640', *Speculum* 60 (1985), pp. 505–516; Gilbert Márkus, 'Pelagianism and the "Common Celtic Church"', *Innes Review* 56 (2005), pp. 165–213.

157. Bede, *Ecclesiastical history of the English people*, p. 139.

158. Charles-Edwards, *Early Christian Ireland*, pp. 320, 409–410.

159. Clarkson, *Columba*, pp. 178–181. See also Charles-Edwards, *Early Christian Ireland*, pp. 391–415.

160. Bhreathnach, 'Communities and their landscapes', p. 36.

161. Bhreathnach, 'Communities and their landscapes', p. 41; Elizabeth O'Brien, *Mapping death: Burial in late Iron Age and early medieval Ireland* (Dublin: Four Courts, 2020).

162. Carey, 'Learning, imagination and belief', pp. 49–51.

163. Carey, 'Learning, imagination and belief', p. 64.

164. Carey, 'Learning, imagination and belief', p. 68.

165. Carey, 'Learning, imagination and belief', p. 66.

166. Carey, 'Learning, imagination and belief', p. 63.

167. Carey, 'Learning, imagination and belief', p. 51.

168. Thomas O'Loughlin, ' "Celtic spirituality", ecumenism, and the contemporary religious landscape', *Irish Theological Quarterly* 67 (2002), p. 167.

169. Quoted Charles-Edwards, *Early Christian Ireland*, p. 182.

CHAPTER 2

1. Ó Carragáin, *Churches in early medieval Ireland*; Whelan, *Religion, landscape and settlement in Ireland*, p. 2.

2. I.N. Wood, 'The Irish in England and on the continent in the seventh century: Part II', *Peritia* 27 (2016), pp. 189–214; *Dictionary of Irish biography*, s.v.

3. I.N. Wood, 'The Irish in England and on the continent in the seventh century: Part I', *Peritia* 26 (2015), pp. 171–198.

4. *Dictionary of Irish biography*, s.v.

5. Quoted in Carey, 'Learning, imagination and belief', p. 73.

6. This echoed an earlier dismissal of Pelagius. John Healy, *Insula sanctorum et doctorum, or Ireland's ancient schools and scholars*, sixth edition (Dublin: Sealy, Bryers and Walker, 1912), pp. 582–583; *Dictionary of Irish biography*, s.v.

7. Ó Corráin, *The Irish church, its reform and the English invasion*, p. 37. John Scotus of Mecklenburg is sometimes identified as a Scot.

8. Charles-Edwards, *Early Christian Ireland*, p. 586.

9. Wycherley, *The cult of relics in early medieval Ireland*, p. 194.

10. Pádraic H. Pearse, *Songs of the Irish rebels*, Collected Works of Pádraic H. Pearse (Dublin: The Phoenix Publishing Company, n.d.), p. 196.

11. Charles-Edwards, *Early Christian Ireland*, p. 586.

12. See, for example, Donnchadh Ó Corráin, 'Viking Ireland: Afterthoughts', in Howard Clarke et al. (eds), *Ireland and Scandinavia in the early Viking age* (Dublin: Four Courts, 1998), pp. 485–498; David Griffiths, *Vikings of the Irish Sea: Conflict and assimilation, AD 790–1050* (London: History Press, 2010); Gwendolyn Sheldon, 'The conversion of the Vikings of Dublin', in Seán Duffy (ed.), *Medieval Dublin XIV* (Dublin: Four Courts, 2014), pp. 51–97; Howard Clarke et al., *Dublin and the Viking world* (Dublin: O'Brien Press, 2018).

13. On the difficulty of naming the invaders, see Robin Frame, ' "Les Engleys nées en Irlande": The English political identity in medieval Ireland', *Transactions of the Royal Historical Society* 3 (1993), pp. 83–103; Sparky Booker, 'Intermarriage in fifteenth-century Ireland: The English and Irish in the "four obedient shires"', *Transactions of the Royal Irish Academy* 113C (2013), pp. 219–223. I have followed Booker and others in allowing the colonists to name themselves as 'English'.

14. Flanagan, *The transformation of the Irish church in the twelfth century*, argues that Gregorian reform was well advanced before the Anglo-Norman invasion.

15. Anne Duggan has argued that Pope Adrian IV's bull *Laudabiliter* was forged by Gerald of Wales: Anne J. Duggan, 'The power of documents: The curious case of *Laudabiliter*', in Brenda Bolton and Christine Meek (eds), *Aspects of power and authority in the middle ages* (Turnhout, Belgium: Brepols, 2007), pp. 251–275.

16. Ó Corráin, *The Irish church, its reform and the English invasion.*

17. Whelan, *Religion, landscape and settlement in Ireland*, p. 11.

18. For the history of the institution that became Christ Church cathedral, see Kenneth Milne (ed.), *Christ Church Cathedral Dublin: A history* (Dublin: Four Courts, 2010).

19. Henry A. Jefferies, *The Irish church and the Tudor reformations* (Dublin: Four Courts, 2010), pp. 15–69. For an authoritative study of the mendicants in Ireland, see Colmán Ó Clabaigh, *The Friars in Ireland, 1224–1540* (Dublin: Four Courts, 2011).

20. For recent discussions of Irish marriage customs, see Salvador Ryan (ed.), *Marriage and the Irish: A miscellany* (Dublin: Wordwell Press, 2019); Maria Luddy and Mary O'Dowd, *Marriage in Ireland, 1660–1925* (Cambridge: Cambridge University Press, 2020).

21. Ó Cróinín, *Early medieval Ireland*, p. 11.

22. Quoted in Davies, *Vanished kingdoms*, p. 66.

23. For a discussion of this mission, see Dagmar Ó Riain-Raedeland Pádraig Ó Riain, 'Irish saints in a Regensburg litany', in Emer Purcell et al. (eds), *Clerics, kings and Vikings: Essays on medieval Ireland in honour of Donnchadh Ó Corráin* (Dublin: Four Courts, 2015), pp. 55–66.

24. Alex Woolf, 'The Scandinavian intervention', Brendan Smith (ed.), *The Cambridge history of Ireland*, vol. 1: *600–1550* (Cambridge: Cambridge University Press, 2018), p. 125.

25. Ó Cróinín, *Early medieval Ireland*, p. 245.

26. Ó Cróinín, *Early medieval Ireland*, p. 236. For details of this resistance, see Darren McGettigan, *The kings of Aileach and the Vikings, AD 800–1060* (Dublin: Four Courts, 2020).

27. Ó Cróinín, *Early medieval Ireland*, pp. 236–237.

28. Bhreathnach, 'Communities and their landscapes', p. 27.

29. Downham, *Medieval Ireland*, pp. 30, 49, 53.

30. Ó Cróinín, *Early medieval Ireland*, p. 247.

31. Ó Cróinín, *Early medieval Ireland*, p. 241.

32. Ó Cróinín, *Early medieval Ireland*, p. 250; Downham, *Medieval Ireland*, p. 68.

33. Ó Cróinín, *Early medieval Ireland*, p. 250.
34. Downham, *Medieval Ireland*, p. 108.
35. Woolf, 'The Scandinavian intervention', pp. 125–126.
36. Colin Breen, 'The maritime cultural landscape in medieval Gaelic Ireland', in Patrick J. Duffy et al. (eds), *Gaelic Ireland, c.1250-c.1650: Land, lordship and settlement* (Dublin: Four Courts, 2004), pp. 431–433.
37. Bhreathnach, 'Communities and their landscapes', p. 19; *Dictionary of Irish biography*, s.v.
38. Downham, *Medieval Ireland*, p. 108.
39. Ó Cróinín, *Early medieval Ireland*, p. 251.
40. Woolf, 'The Scandinavian intervention', p. 111.
41. Hughes and Hamlin, *The modern traveller to the early Irish church*, p. 50; Downham, *Medieval Ireland*, pp. 32, 55.
42. Downham, *Medieval Ireland*, pp. 56.
43. Hughes and Hamlin, *The modern traveller to the early Irish church*, p. 14.
44. Ó Cróinín, *Early medieval Ireland*, p. 261.
45. Follett, *Céli Dé in Ireland*, pp. 171–219; Meens, *Penance in medieval Europe, 600–1200*, pp. 62–63.
46. Ó Cróinín, *Early medieval Ireland*, pp. 236–237; *Dictionary of Irish biography*, s.v.
47. Woolf, 'The Scandinavian intervention', pp. 109, 114; Whelan, *Religion, landscape and settlement in Ireland*, p. 12.
48. Woolf, 'The Scandinavian intervention', p. 126.
49. Woolf, 'The Scandinavian intervention', p. 107.
50. Ó Muraíle, 'Settlement and place-names', p. 224.
51. Woolf, 'The Scandinavian intervention', p. 127.
52. Downham, *Medieval Ireland*, p. 109.
53. John Maas, 'The Viking events of AD 902–19 and the Lough Ennell hoards', Emer Purcell et al. (eds), *Clerics, kings and Vikings: Essays on medieval Ireland in honour of Donnchadh Ó Corráin* (Dublin: Four Courts, 2015), p. 253.
54. Maas, 'The Viking events of AD 902–19 and the Lough Ennell hoards', p. 251.
55. Poul Holm, 'The naval power of Norse Dublin', in Emer Purcell et al. (eds), *Clerics, kings and Vikings: Essays on medieval Ireland in honour of Donnchadh Ó Corráin* (Dublin: Four Courts, 2015), p. 67; Downham, *Medieval Ireland*, p. 110.
56. Bhreathnach, 'Communities and their landscapes', p. 33.
57. Lesley Abrams, 'Conversion and the church in Viking-age Dublin', in John Sheehan and Donnchadh Ó Corráin (eds), *The Viking age: Ireland and the west* (Dublin: Four Courts, 2010), pp. 1–10; Lesley Abrams, 'The conversion of the Scandinavians of Dublin', *Anglo-Norman Studies* 20 (1997), pp. 1–29.
58. Downham, *Medieval Ireland*, p. 141.
59. Ó Cróinín, *Early medieval Ireland*, p. 265.
60. *Dictionary of Irish biography*, s.v.
61. Downham, *Medieval Ireland*, pp. 81, 87.
62. Downham, *Medieval Ireland*, p. 142.

63. Ó Corráin, *The Irish church, its reform and the English invasion*, p. 33.

64. *Dictionary of Irish biography*, s.v.

65. Woolf, 'The Scandinavian intervention', p. 128.

66. Woolf, 'The Scandinavian intervention', p. 108.

67. Ó Corráin, *The Irish church, its reform and the English invasion*, p. 23.

68. Stewart, *The shape of Irish history*, p. 57.

69. Downham, *Medieval Ireland*, pp. 107, 160.

70. Downham, *Medieval Ireland*, p. 120.

71. For a discussion of the early origins of 'national' feeling among the Irish, see Brendan Bradshaw, *'And so began the Irish nation': Nationality, national consciousness and nationalism in pre-modern Ireland* (Farnham, UK: Ashgate, 2015).

72. Flanagan, *The transformation of the Irish church in the twelfth century*, p. 25.

73. Colmán Etchingham, *Church organisation in Ireland, AD 650 to 1000* (Maynooth: Laigin, 1999), pp. 455–458.

74. Flanagan, *The transformation of the Irish church in the twelfth century*, p. 37.

75. Flanagan, *The transformation of the Irish church in the twelfth century*, pp. 26–27.

76. Flanagan, *The transformation of the Irish church in the twelfth century*, p. 48.

77. Flanagan, *The transformation of the Irish church in the twelfth century*, pp. xi, 33.

78. See, for example, Ó Corráin, *The Irish church, its reform and the English invasion*.

79. *The letters of Lafranc, archbishop of Canterbury*, trans. H. Clover and M. Gibson (Oxford: Clarendon Press, 1979), p. 67.

80. H.E.J. Cowdrey, *The epistolae vagantes of Pope Gregory VII* (Oxford: Clarendon Press, 1972), pp. 139–141.

81. Flanagan, *The transformation of the Irish church in the twelfth century*, p. 40.

82. See, for example, Philippians 1:1.

83. Ó Corráin, *The Irish church, its reform and the English invasion*, p. 10.

84. Ó Corráin, *The Irish church, its reform and the English invasion*, pp. 72–75; Downham, *Medieval Ireland*, p. 281.

85. Flanagan, *The transformation of the Irish church in the twelfth century*, pp. 34–35; Ó Corráin, *The Irish church, its reform and the English invasion*, pp. 91–96.

86. Flanagan, *The transformation of the Irish church in the twelfth century*, p. 35; Downham, *Medieval Ireland*, p. 83; Ó Corráin, *The Irish church, its reform and the English invasion*, p. 9.

87. Downham, *Medieval Ireland*, p. 185; Whelan, *Religion, landscape and settlement in Ireland*, pp. 18–23.

88. Ó Corráin, *The Irish church, its reform and the English invasion*, p. 79.

89. Ó Corráin, *The Irish church, its reform and the English invasion*, pp. 81–82.

90. Flanagan, *The transformation of the Irish church in the twelfth century*, p. 110; *Dictionary of Irish biography*, s.v.

91. Flanagan, *The transformation of the Irish church in the twelfth century*, pp. 64, 73, 176, 211.

92. Flanagan, *The transformation of the Irish church in the twelfth century*, p. 151.

93. Flanagan, *The transformation of the Irish church in the twelfth century*, p. 165.

94. Ó Corráin, *The Irish church, its reform and the English invasion*, p. 19.

95. Flanagan, *The transformation of the Irish church in the twelfth century*, pp. 184–195; Ó Corráin, *The Irish church, its reform and the English invasion*, pp. 43–57; Downham, *Medieval Ireland*, pp. 74–76. But see also Liam Breatnach's questioning of supposed polygamy among the Irish in Liam Breatnach, '*Cétmuinter*: The Old Irish term for spouse and its interpretation', in Salvador Ryan (ed.), *Marriage and the Irish: A miscellany* (Dublin: Wordwell Press, 2019), pp. 7–9.

96. *St Bernard of Clairvaux's life of St Malachy of Armagh*, trans. H. J. Lawlor (London: SPCK, 1920).

97. Roger Stalley, *The Cistercian monasteries of Ireland: An account of the history, art and architecture of the White Monks in Ireland from 1142–1540* (New Haven, CT: Yale University Press, 1987); Flanagan, *The transformation of the Irish church in the twelfth century*, p. 24; Maeve Brigid Callan, *The Templars, the witch, and the wild Irish: Vengeance and heresy in medieval Ireland* (New York: Cornell University Press, 2015), p. 215.

98. Ó Corráin, *The Irish church, its reform and the English invasion*, pp. 45, 47.

99. Flanagan, *The transformation of the Irish church in the twelfth century*, p. 21; Colmán Etchingham, 'The organization and function of an early Irish church settlement: What was Glendalough?' in Charles Doherty et al. (eds), *Glendalough: City of God* (Dublin: Four Courts, 2011), pp. 22–53.

100. Flanagan, *The transformation of the Irish church in the twelfth century*, p. 28.

101. Downham, *Medieval Ireland*, p. 163.

102. Flanagan, *The transformation of the Irish church in the twelfth century*, p. 23.

103. Flanagan, *The transformation of the Irish church in the twelfth century*, pp. 28–29, 32.

104. See, for example, Mallory, *In search of the Irish dreamtime*; Cassidy et al., 'A dynastic elite in monumental Neolithic society', pp. 384–388.

105. *Vitae Sanctorum Hiberniae*, ed. Plummer; Sharpe, *Medieval Irish saints' lives*, p. 14. For an example of this genre, see Adomnán of Iona, *Life of St Columba*, trans. Richard Sharpe (London: Penguin, 1995).

106. Aitchison, *Armagh and the royal centres in early medieval Ireland*, p. 32.

107. Theresa O'Byrne, 'Centre or periphery? The role of Dublin in James Yonge's *Memoriale* (1412)', in Kathleen Miller and Crawford Gribben (eds), *Dublin: Renaissance city of literature* (Manchester: Manchester University Press, 2017), pp. 16–37.

108. Flanagan, *The transformation of the Irish church in the twelfth century*, p. 12; Downham, *Medieval Ireland*, pp. 304–305.

109. Connolly, *Priests and people in pre-famine Ireland*, p. 182.

110. Downham, *Medieval Ireland*, p. 283.

111. Downham, *Medieval Ireland*, pp. 337–341; Callan, *The Templars, the witch, and the wild Irish*, p. 215.

112. On the history of St Patrick's cathedral, see John Crawford and Raymond Gillespie (eds), *St Patrick's cathedral, Dublin: A history* (Dublin: Four Courts, 2009).

113. Callan, *The Templars, the witch, and the wild Irish*, p. 18.

114. Flanagan, *The transformation of the Irish church in the twelfth century*, p. 25.

115. Downham, *Medieval Ireland*, p. 280.

116. Duggan, 'The power of documents: The curious case of Laudabiliter', pp. 251–275.

117. Sean Duffy, 'The Welsh conquest of Ireland', Emer Purcell et al. (eds), *Clerics, Kings and Vikings: Essays on medieval Ireland in honour of Donnchadh Ó Corráin* (Dublin: Four Courts, 2015), p. 114.

118. *Dictionary of Irish biography*, s.v. for both.

119. Keiran D. O'Conor, 'The morphology of Gaelic lordly sites in North Connacht', in Patrick J. Duffy et al. (eds), *Gaelic Ireland, c.1250–c.1650: Land, lordship and settlement* (Dublin: Four Courts, 2004), p. 329.

120. Ó Corráin, *The Irish church, its reform and the English invasion*, pp. 65–71.

121. Flanagan, *The transformation of the Irish church in the twelfth century*, p. 55; Ó Corráin, *The Irish church, its reform and the English invasion*, p. 70.

122. Meens, *Penance in medieval Europe, 600–1200*, pp. 2–3.

123. Flanagan, *The transformation of the Irish church in the twelfth century*, pp. xi, 3.

124. Patrick J. Duffy et al., 'Introduction: Recovering Gaelic Ireland, c. 1250–c. 1650', in Patrick J. Duffy et al. (eds), *Gaelic Ireland, c.1250–c.1650: Land, lordship and settlement* (Dublin: Four Courts, 2004), p. 65.

125. Duffy et al., 'Introduction: Recovering Gaelic Ireland, c. 1250–c. 1650', p. 40.

126. Downham, *Medieval Ireland*, p. 246.

127. For older arguments along these lines, see J.A. Watt, *The Church and the two nations in medieval Ireland* (Cambridge: Cambridge University Press, 1970); J.A. Watt, *The Church in medieval Ireland* (Dublin: UCD Press, 1998).

128. Downham, *Medieval Ireland*, p. 215.

129. Edmund Curtis, 'The English and Ostmen in Ireland', *English Historical Review* 23 (1908), p. 210.

130. Duffy et al., 'Introduction: Recovering Gaelic Ireland, c. 1250–c. 1650', p. 38.

131. Downham, *Medieval Ireland*, p. 215.

132. Downham, *Medieval Ireland*, pp. 217, 252.

133. Downham, *Medieval Ireland*, p. 219.

134. Elizabeth Fitzpatrick, 'Assembly and inauguration places of the Burkes in late medieval Connacht', in Patrick J. Duffy et al. (eds), *Gaelic Ireland, c.1250–c.1650: Land, lordship and settlement* (Dublin: Four Courts, 2004), p. 357.

135. Ó Corráin, *The Irish church, its reform and the English invasion*, p. 88. This view is confirmed by Sparky Booker, 'Irish clergy and the diocesan church in the "four obedient shires" of Ireland, c. 1400–c. 1540', *Irish Historical Studies* 39: 154 (2014), pp. 190, 195.

136. K.W. Nicholls, *Gaelic and Gaelicised Ireland in the middle ages*, second edition (Dublin: Lilliput, 2003).

137. Duffy et al., 'Introduction: Recovering Gaelic Ireland, c. 1250–c. 1650', pp. 22, 34; Caitriona MacKenzie and Eileen Murphy, *Life and death in medieval Gaelic Ireland: The skeletons from Ballyhana, co. Donegal* (Dublin: Four Courts, 2018).

138. O'Conor, 'The morphology of Gaelic lordly sites in north Connacht', p. 329.

139. Stewart, *The shape of Irish history*, p. 62.

140. Martin Browne and Colmán Ó Clabaigh, 'Introduction', in Martin Browne and Colmán Ó Clabaigh (eds), *Soldiers of Christ: The Knights Templar and the Knights Hospitaller in medieval Ireland* (Dublin: Four Courts, 2016), p. xvii.

141. Helen J. Nicholson, 'A long way from Jerusalem: The Templars and Hospitallers in Ireland, c. 1172–1348', in Martin Browne and Colmán Ó Clabaigh (eds), *Soldiers of Christ: The Knights Templar and the Knights Hospitaller in medieval Ireland* (Dublin: Four Courts, 2016), p. 2.

142. Nicholson, 'A long way from Jerusalem', pp. 2, 7. See, more generally, Callan, *The Templars, the witch, and the wild Irish.*

143. Nicholson, 'A long way from Jerusalem', p. 11.

144. Nicholson, 'A long way from Jerusalem', p. 13.

145. Nicholson, 'A long way from Jerusalem', p. 1.

146. Nicholson, 'A long way from Jerusalem', p. 17.

147. Nicholson, 'A long way from Jerusalem', pp. 2, 10, 11; Callan, *The Templars, the witch, and the wild Irish*, pp. 45, 69.

148. Nicholson, 'A long way from Jerusalem', p. 18; Helen Nicholson, 'The Hospitallers' and Templars' involvement in warfare on the frontiers of the British Isles in the late thirteenth and early fourteenth centuries', *Ordines Militares Colloquia Torunensia Historica: Yearbook for the Study of the Military Orders* 17 (2012), pp. 105–119.

149. Nicholson, 'A long way from Jerusalem', p. 17.

150. Edel Bhreathnach, 'The mendicant orders and vernacular Irish learning in the late medieval period', *Irish Historical Studies* 37:147 (2011), pp. 357–375.

151. Clabaigh, *The Friars in Ireland*, p. 1.

152. See Salvador Ryan and Anthony Shanahan, 'How to communicate Lateran IV in 13th century Ireland: Lessons from the *Liber Exemplorum* (c. 1275)', *Religions* 9:3 (2018), pp. 1–14.

153. Whelan, *Religion, landscape and settlement in Ireland*, p. 26.

154. Ó Clabaigh, *The Friars in Ireland, 1224–1540*, p. 1; Annejulie Lafaye, 'The Dominicans in Ireland: A comparative study of the east Munster and Leinster settlements', *Journal of Medieval Monastic Studies* 4 (2015), pp. 79–108.

155. Ó Clabaigh, *The Friars in Ireland, 1224–1540*, pp. 2, 3, 6, 7, 10, 16, 18. See also the essays contained in Martin Browne and Colmán Ó Clabaigh (eds), *Households of God: The regular canons and canonesses of St Augustine and of Prémontré in medieval Ireland* (Dublin: Four Courts, 2019).

156. Bhreathnach, 'The mendicant orders and vernacular Irish learning in the late medieval period', pp. 357–375; Ó Clabaigh, *The Friars in Ireland, 1224–1540*, p. xix.

157. Ó Clabaigh, *The Friars in Ireland, 1224–1540*, pp. 143, 245, 260.

158. Ó Clabaigh, *The Friars in Ireland, 1224–1540*, p. 302.

159. Diane Hall, *Women and the church in medieval Ireland, c. 1140–1540* (Dublin: Four Courts, 2003); Ó Clabaigh, *The Friars in Ireland, 1224–1540*, pp. 112–117.

160. Ó Clabaigh, *The Friars in Ireland, 1224–1540*, pp. 22–23.

161. E.B. Fitzmaurice and A.G. Little (eds), *Materials for the history of the Franciscan province of Ireland, 1230–1450* (Manchester: Manchester University Press, 1920), pp. 52–53.

162. Fitzmaurice and Little (eds), *Materials for the history of the Franciscan province of Ireland*, p. 64; Callan, *The Templars, the witch, and the wild Irish*, p. 215.

163. Seán Duffy, 'Ireland and the Irish Sea region, 1014–1318' (unpublished PhD thesis, Trinity College Dublin, 1993), p. 218; Callan, *The Templars, the witch, and the wild Irish*, p. 141.

164. Ó Clabaigh, *The Friars in Ireland, 1224–1540*, p. 36.

165. *Irish historical documents, 1172–1922*, ed. E. Curtis and R.B. McDowell (London, 1943), p. 43; Walter Bower, *Scotichronicon*, ed. Norman F. Shead, 9 vols (Edinburgh: Aberdeen University Press, 1987–1998), 6: 397; Callan, *The Templars, the witch, and the wild Irish*, pp. 78, 188–189, 214.

166. See Callan, *The Templars, the witch, and the wild Irish*.

167. Bernadette Williams, 'Heresy in Ireland in the thirteenth and fourteenth centuries', in Seán Duffy (ed.), *Princes, prelates and poets in medieval Ireland: Essays in honour of Katharine Simms* (Dublin: Four Courts, 2013), pp. 345–346; Downham, *Medieval Ireland*, p. 226.

168. Callan, *The Templars, the witch, and the wild Irish*, pp. 117–147.

169. Ó Clabaigh, *The Friars in Ireland, 1224–1540*, p. 91.

170. Flanagan, *The transformation of the Irish church in the twelfth century*, p. 169.

171. Callan, *The Templars, the witch, and the wild Irish*, pp. 188–234. See also Williams, 'Heresy in Ireland in the thirteenth and fourteenth centuries', pp. 339–351.

172. Callan, *The Templars, the witch, and the wild Irish*, p. xx.

173. Downham, *Medieval Ireland*, p. 188; Whelan, *Religion, landscape and settlement in Ireland*, p. 29.

174. Callan, *The Templars, the witch, and the wild Irish*, p. xx; Williams, 'Heresy in Ireland in the thirteenth and fourteenth centuries', p. 349.

175. Callan, *The Templars, the witch, and the wild Irish*, p. 184.

176. Ó Clabaigh, *The Friars in Ireland, 1224–1540*, p. 46.

177. This is the argument of Callan, *The Templars, the witch, and the wild Irish*, particularly pp. 1–28, 31–33.

178. Booker, 'Irish clergy and the diocesan church in the "four obedient shires" of Ireland, c. 1400–c. 1540', p. 186; Sparky Booker, *Cultural exchange and identity in late medieval Ireland: The English and Irish of the four obedient shires* (Cambridge: Cambridge University Press, 2018), pp. 97–142.

179. Booker, *Cultural exchange and identity in late medieval Ireland*, p. 97.

180. Jefferies, *The Irish church and the Tudor reformations*, p. 32; Booker, 'Irish clergy and the diocesan church in the "four obedient shires" of Ireland, c. 1400–c. 1540', pp. 190, 195.

181. Ó Clabaigh, *The Friars in Ireland, 1224–1540*, p. 50; Downham, *Medieval Ireland*, p. 295.

182. Ó Clabaigh, *The Friars in Ireland, 1224–1540*, pp. 138–142.

183. Ó Clabaigh, *The Friars in Ireland, 1224–1540*, p. 26.

184. Ó Clabaigh, *The Friars in Ireland, 1224–1540*, p. 30.

185. Connolly, *Contested island*, p. 53.

186. Ó Clabaigh, *The Friars in Ireland, 1224–1540*, pp. 54, 68.

187. Ó Clabaigh, *The Friars in Ireland, 1224–1540*, p. 307.

188. Ó Clabaigh, *The Friars in Ireland, 1224–1540*, pp. 311–314.

189. Quoted in Ó Clabaigh, *The Friars in Ireland, 1224–1540*, p. 79.

190. Connolly, *Contested island*, pp. 57–58.

191. Simon Kingston, 'Delusions of Dál Riada: The co-ordinates of Mac Domnaill power, 1461–1550', in Patrick J. Duffy et al. (eds), *Gaelic Ireland, c.1250–c.1650: Land, lordship and settlement* (Dublin: Four Courts, 2004), pp. 101, 104.

192. Steven G. Ellis, *Tudor Ireland: Crown, community and the conflict of cultures, 1470–1603* (London: Longman, 1985), pp. 77–78; Steven G. Ellis, *Tudor frontiers and noble power: The making of the British state* (Oxford: Oxford University Press, 1995).

193. Watt, *The Church and the two nations in medieval Ireland*; Watt, *The Church in medieval Ireland*.

194. Jefferies, *The Irish church and the Tudor reformations*, pp. 25–28.

195. Jefferies, *The Irish church and the Tudor reformations*, pp. 15–69; Rachel Moss et al. (eds), *Art and devotion in late medieval Ireland* (Dublin: Four Courts, 2006). For some examples of the spirituality of the late medieval period, see Salvador Ryan, '"Scarce anyone survives a heart wound": The wounded Christ in Irish bardic religious poetry', in Larissa Tracy and Kelly de Vries (eds), *Wounds and wound repair in medieval culture* (Leiden: Brill, 2015), pp. 291–312; Salvador Ryan, 'Christ the wounded lover and affective piety in late medieval Ireland and beyond', in Henning Laugerud et al. (eds), *The materiality of devotion in late medieval northern Europe: Images, objects and practices* (Dublin: Four Courts, 2016), pp. 70–89.

196. Brendan Scott, *Religion and reformation in the Tudor diocese of Meath* (Dublin: Four Courts, 2006), pp. 29–38.

197. Booker, *Cultural exchange and identity in late medieval Ireland*, p. 258.

198. D. George Boyce, *Nationalism in Ireland*, third edition (London: Routledge, 1991), p. 19.

CHAPTER 3

1. P.J. Corish, *The Irish Catholic experience* (Dublin: Gill and Macmillan, 1985); Alan Ford, *The protestant reformation in Ireland, 1590–1641* (Dublin: Four Courts, 1997); Samantha Meigs, *The reformation in Ireland: Tradition and confessionalism, 1400–1690* (Dublin: Gill and Macmillan, 1997); Henry A. Jefferies, *The Irish church and the Tudor reformations* (Dublin: Four Courts, 2010); Tadhg Ó hAnnracháin, *Catholic Europe, 1592–1648: Centres and peripheries* (Oxford: Oxford University Press, 2015).

2. See, for example, Mary O'Dowd, *A history of women in Ireland* (London: Routledge, 2004), pp. 153–186.

3. For a discussion of the strength of Irish language cultures in the sixteenth century, see Vincent Carey, 'Bi-lingualism and identity formation in sixteenth-century Ireland', in Hiram Morgan (ed.), *Political ideology in Ireland, 1541–1641* (Dublin: Four Courts, 1999), pp. 45–61.

4. Whelan, *Religion, landscape and settlement in Ireland*, p. 70.

5. For this debate, see Benedict Anderson, *Imagined communities: Reflections on the origin and spread of nationalism*, second edition (London:Verso, 1991);E.J. Hobsbawm, *Nations and nationalism since 1780*, second edition (Cambridge: Cambridge University Press, 1990); Boyce, *Nationalism in Ireland*. For a specifically Irish discussion, see the debate between Steven G. Ellis, 'Nationalist historiography and the English and Gaelic worlds in the late middle ages', *Irish Historical Studies* 25:97 (1986), pp. 1–18, and Brendan Bradshaw, 'Nationalism and historical scholarship in modern Ireland', *Irish Historical Studies* 26 (1989), pp. 329–351.

6. Connolly, *Contested island*, p. 342. See also Bernadette Cunningham, *The annals of the four masters: Irish history, kingship and society in the early seventeenth century* (Dublin: Four Courts, 2010);Thomas O'Connor, 'Towards the invention of the Irish Catholic *natio*:Thomas Messingham's *Florilegium*', *Irish Theological Quarterly* 64:2 (1999), pp. 157–177;Thomas O'Connor, 'Custom, authority and tolerance in Irish political thought: David Rothe's *Analecta sacra et mira* (1616)', *Irish Theological Quarterly* 65:2 (2000), pp. 133–156.

7. Whelan, *Religion, landscape and settlement in Ireland*, p. 70.

8. For an excellent exploration of this theme, see Gillespie, *Devoted people*.

9. Ó Clabaigh, *The Friars in Ireland*, p. 320.

10. Frederick M. Jones, 'Canonical faculties on the Irish mission in the reign of Queen Elizabeth, 1558–1603', *Irish Theological Quarterly* 30 (1953), pp. 152–171.

11. Jefferies, *The Irish church and the Tudor reformations*, pp. 71–87.

12. Roy Foster, *Modern Ireland, 1600–1972* (London:Allen Lane, 1988), p. 29.

13. Bernadette Cunningham, ' "Zeal for God and for souls": Counter-reformation preaching in early seventeenth-century Ireland', in Alan J. Fletcher and Raymond Gillespie (eds), *Irish preaching, 700–1700* (Dublin: Four Courts, 2001), pp. 108–126; Salvador Ryan, 'From late medieval piety to Tridentine pietism? The case of 17th century Ireland', in FredVan Lieburg (ed.), *Confessionalism and pietism: religious reform in the early modern period* (Göttingen:Vandenhoeck and Ruprecht, 2006), pp. 51–69; Salvador Ryan, ' "New wine in old bottles": Implementing Trent in early modern Ireland', in Thomas Herron and Michael Potterton (eds), *Ireland in the Renaissance, c.1540–1660* (Dublin: Four Courts Press, 2007), pp. 122–137.

14. Whelan, *Religion, landscape and settlement in Ireland*, p. 44; Jefferies, *The Irish church and the Tudor reformations*, pp. 246, 258.

15. Connolly, *Contested island*, pp. 335–336.

16. Connolly, *Contested island*, pp. 337–338.

17. Nicholas Canny, 'Why the reformation failed in Ireland: *Une question mal posée*', *Journal of Ecclesiastical History* 30 (1979), pp. 423–450; Karl Bottigheimer, 'The failure of the reformation in Ireland: *Une question bien posée*', *Journal of Ecclesiastical History* 36 (1985), pp. 196–207; James Murray, *Enforcing the English reformation in Ireland: Clerical resistance and political conflict in the diocese of Dublin, 1534–1590* (Cambridge: Cambridge University Press, 2009); Jefferies, *The Irish church and the Tudor reformation*, pp. 241–283; Henry A. Jefferies, 'Elizabeth's reformation in the Irish Pale', *Journal of Ecclesiastical History* 66:3 (2015), pp. 524–542;

Henry A. Jefferies, 'Why the reformation failed in Ireland', *Irish Historical Studies* 40 (2016), pp. 151–170; Colm Lennon, 'Mass in the manor house: The counter-reformation in Dublin, 1560–1630', in James Kelly and Daire Keogh (eds), *History of the Catholic diocese of Dublin* (Dublin: Four Courts, 2000), pp. 112–126. On the success of protestant reformation in Scottish Gaelic culture, see Jane Dawson, 'Calvinism and the Gaidhealtachd in Scotland', in Andrew Pettegree et al. (eds), *Calvinism in Europe, 1540–1620* (Cambridge: Cambridge University Press, 1996), pp. 231–253.

18. Ute Lotz-Heumann, 'Confessionalisation in Ireland: Periodisation and character, 1534–1649', in Alan Ford and James McCafferty (eds), *The origins of sectarianism in early modern Ireland* (Cambridge: Cambridge University Press, 2005), pp. 24–53.

19. Ian W.S. Campbell, *Renaissance humanism and ethnicity before race: The Irish and the English in the seventeenth century* (Manchester: Manchester University Press, 2013), pp. 53–82; Micheál Mac Craith, '"Do chum glóire Dé agus an mhaitheasa phuiblidhe so / For the glory of God and the public good": The reformation and the Irish language', *Studies* 106:424 (2017–18), pp. 476–483.

20. Alan Ford, *James Ussher: Theology, history and politics in early modern Ireland and England* (Oxford: Oxford University Press, 2007).

21. Murray, *Enforcing the English reformation in Ireland*, p. 317; Whelan, *Religion, landscape and settlement in Ireland*, p. 38.

22. Alan Ford, 'Martyrdom, history and memory in early modern Ireland', in Ian McBride (ed.), *History and memory in modern Ireland* (Cambridge: Cambridge University Press, 2001), pp. 50–54.

23. Brendan Bradshaw, *The Irish constitutional revolution of the sixteenth century* (Cambridge: Cambridge University Press, 1979).

24. Ellis, *Tudor Ireland*.

25. Nicholas Canny, *Making Ireland British, 1580–1650* (Oxford: Oxford University Press, 2001), pp. 165–241; R.J. Hunter, *Ulster transformed: Essays on plantation and print culture, c. 1590–1641* (Belfast: Ulster Historical Foundation, 2012). See also Gerard Farrell, *The 'mere' Irish and the colonisation of Ulster, 1570–1641* (London: Palgrave, 2017).

26. For population statistics, I follow S.J. Connolly, *Divided kingdom: Ireland, 1630–1800* (Oxford: Oxford University Press, 2008), p. 164.

27. Raymond Gillespie, 'Traditional religion in sixteenth-century Gaelic Ireland', in Tadhg Ó hAnnracháin and Robert Armstrong (eds), *Christianities in the early modern Celtic world* (London: Palgrave Macmillan, 2014), pp. 29–41.

28. Canny, *Making Ireland British*, pp. 121–163.

29. Edmund Spenser, *A view of the state of Ireland*, eds Andrew Hadfield and Willy Maley (Oxford: Blackwell, 1997), p. 103.

30. Alan Gailey, 'The Scots element in North Irish popular culture', *Ethnologica Europeae* 11:1 (1975), pp. 2–22.

31. Rachel Moss, 'Continuity and change: The material setting of public worship in the sixteenth century', in Thomas Herron and Michael Potterton (eds), *Dublin and the Pale in the Renaissance, 1494–1660* (Dublin: Four Courts, 2011), pp. 182–206.

32. Duffy et al., 'Introduction: Recovering Gaelic Ireland, c. 1250-c. 1650', p. 44; Campbell, *Renaissance humanism and ethnicity before race*, pp. 23–52.
33. Ó Clabaigh, *The Friars in Ireland*, pp. 322–323.
34. On the semiotics of beheading, see Patricia Palmer,' "An headlesse lady" and "a horses loades of heades": Writing the beheading', *Renaissance Quarterly* 60:1 (2007), pp. 25–57.
35. Brendan Bradshaw, *The dissolution of the monastic orders in Ireland in the reign of Henry VIII* (Cambridge: Cambridge University Press, 1976).
36. John H. Andrews, 'The mapping of Ireland's cultural landscape, 1550–1630', in Patrick J. Duffy et al. (eds), *Gaelic Ireland, c.1250–c.1650: Land, lordship and settlement* (Dublin: Four Courts, 2004), p. 165.
37. Ó Clabaigh, *The Friars in Ireland*, p. 318.
38. Ó Clabaigh, *The Friars in Ireland*, pp. 318–319.
39. Ó Clabaigh, *The Friars in Ireland*, p. 327; Bronagh A. MacShane, 'Negotiating religious change and conflict: Female religious communities in early modern Ireland, c. 1530-c. 1641', *British Catholic History* 33:3 (2017), pp. 357–382.
40. Whelan, *Religion, landscape and settlement in Ireland*, p. 63. See also John McCafferty, 'A mundo valde alieni: Irish Franciscan responses to the dissolution of the monasteries, 1540–1640', *Reformation and Renaissance Review* 19:1 (2017), pp. 50–63.
41. Ó Clabaigh, *The Friars in Ireland*, p. 328.
42. Jefferies, *The Irish church and the Tudor reformations*, pp. 88–103.
43. Jefferies, *The Irish church and the Tudor reformations*, pp. 94, 98.
44. Jefferies, *The Irish church and the Tudor reformations*, pp. 89–91.
45. Jefferies, *The Irish church and the Tudor reformations*, pp. 99–101.
46. Jefferies, *The Irish church and the Tudor reformations*, p. 103.
47. Jefferies, *The Irish church and the Tudor reformations*, pp. 104–121.
48. Connolly, *Contested island*, pp. 184–199; Jefferies, *The Irish church and the Tudor reformations*, pp. 125–240.
49. Connolly, *Contested island*, pp. 172–183; Anthony McCormack, 'The social and economic consequences of the Desmond Rebellion of 1579–1583', *Irish Historical Studies* 34:113 (2004), pp. 1–15.
50. Hiram Morgan, *Tyrone's rebellion: The origins of the Nine Years War in Tudor Ireland* (Woodbridge, UK: Boydell, 1992); Connolly, *Contested island*, pp. 233–254.
51. Canny, *Making Ireland British*, pp. 461–549.
52. Marc Caball, 'Religion, culture and the bardic elite in early modern Ireland', in Alan Ford and James McCafferty (eds), *The origins of sectarianism in early modern Ireland* (Cambridge: Cambridge University Press, 2005), pp. 158–181.
53. C. Scott Dixon, *The church in the early modern age* (London: I.B. Taurus, 2016), p. 89.
54. William Camden, *Britain, Or a chorographicall description of the most flourishing kingdomes, England, Scotland, and Ireland, and the ilands adioyning, out of the depth of antiquitie* (1610), p. 144.
55. J. Hagan, 'Miscellanea Vaticano-Hibernia, 1580–1631', *Archivium Hibernicum* 3 (1914), pp. 300–301.

56. W. Maziere Brady, *State papers concerning the Irish church* (London: Longmans, Green, Reader, and Dyer, 1868), p. 118.

57. Ford, *The protestant reformation in Ireland*, p. 58.

58. Tadhg Ó hAnnracháin, *Catholic reformation in Ireland: The mission of Rinuccini, 1645–1649* (Oxford: Oxford University Press, 2002), pp. 40–46, argues that the Catholic Church in Ireland was pulled into closer conformity with the Council of Trent as a consequence of the mission of Cardinal Rinuccinni in the 1640s.

59. Alexander S. Wilkinson, 'Peripheral print cultures in Renaissance Europe', in Kathleen Miller and Crawford Gribben (eds), *Dublin: Renaissance city of literature* (Manchester: Manchester University Press, 2017), pp. 228–249.

60. O'Connor, 'Religious change, 1550–1800', p. 174; T.C. Barnard, 'Protestants and the Irish language, c. 1675–1725', in T.C. Barnard, *Irish protestant ascents and descents, 1641–1770* (Dublin: Four Courts, 2004), p. 180.

61. O'Connor, 'Religious change, 1550–1800', p. 175; Barnard, 'Protestants and the Irish language, c. 1675–1725', p. 183.

62. O'Connor, 'Religious change, 1550–1800', pp. 178–179.

63. O'Connor, 'Religious change, 1550–1800', p. 182.

64. O'Connor, 'Religious change, 1550–1800', p. 169.

65. Carey, ' "Neither good English nor good Irish": Bilingualism and identity formation in sixteenth-century Ireland', pp. 45–61.

66. Quoted in Nicholas M. Wolf, *An Irish-speaking island: State, religion, community, and the linguistic landscape in Ireland, 1770–1870* (Madison, WI: University of Wisconsin Press, 2014), p. 8; Connolly, *Contested island*, p. 341.

67. *Dictionary of Irish biography*, s.v.

68. Jefferies, *The Irish church and the Tudor reformations*, p. 256.

69. Alan Ford, 'Scottish protestant clergy and the origins of dissent in Ireland', in David Edwards and Simon Egan (eds), *The Scots in early Stuart Ireland: Union and separation in two kingdoms* (Manchester: Manchester University Press, 2015), p. 118.

70. Francis J. Bremer, *John Winthrop: American's forgotten Founding Father* (Oxford: Oxford University Press, 2015), pp. 138–140.

71. Ford, 'Scottish protestant clergy and the origins of dissent in Ireland', pp. 118–120.

72. Ford, 'Scottish protestant clergy and the origins of dissent in Ireland', p. 128; Jefferies, *The Irish church and the Tudor reformations*, p. 258.

73. John Livingstone, *A brief historical relation of the life of Mr John Livingstone*, ed. Thomas Houston (Edinburgh: John Johnstone, 1848), pp. 76–77.

74. Alan Ford, 'The Church of Ireland, 1558–1641: A puritan church?' in Alan Ford et al. (eds), *As by law established: The Church of Ireland since the reformation* (Dublin: Lilliput Press, 1995), pp. 52–68.

75. Alan Ford, 'Dependent or independent? The Church of Ireland and its colonial context, 1536–1649', *The Seventeenth Century* 9 (1995), p. 169.

76. Elizabethanne Boran, 'An early friendship network of James Ussher, archbishop of Armagh, 1626–1656', in H.H.W. Robinson-Hammerstein (ed.), *European universities in the age of reformation* (Dublin: Four Courts, 1998), pp. 116–134;

Ian W.S. Campbell, 'Calvinist absolutism: Archbishop James Ussher and royal power', *Journal of British Studies* 53:3 (2014), pp. 588–610.

77. Andrew Stewart, 'History of the Church of Ireland', in Patrick Adair, *A true narrative of the rise and progress of the Presbyterian Church in Ireland* (Belfast: Aitchison, 1870), p. 313.

78. Stewart, 'History of the Church of Ireland', p. 317.

79. Colm Lennon, 'Taking sides: The emergence of Irish Catholic ideology', in Vincent P. Carey and Ute Lotz-Heumann (eds), *Taking sides? Colonial and confessional mentalities in early modern Ireland* (Dublin: Four Courts, 2003), pp. 78–93; David Edwards, 'A haven of popery: English Catholic migration to Ireland in the age of plantations', in Alan Ford and James McCafferty (eds), *The origins of sectarianism in early modern Ireland* (Cambridge: Cambridge University Press, 2005), pp. 95–125; Alison Forrestal, *Catholic synods in Ireland, 1600–1690* (Dublin: Four Courts, 1998).

80. *Calendar of the State Papers relating to Ireland… 1625–30*, ed. R.P. Mahaffy (London, 1900), pp. 661–662.

81. S.J. Connolly, 'Religion and society, 1600–1914', in Liam Kennedy and Philip Ollerenshaw (eds), *Ulster since 1600: Politics, economics and society* (Oxford: Oxford University Press, 2012), p. 76.

82. *A full confutation of the Covenant, lately sworne and subscribed by many in Scotland* (1639), p. 4.

83. For more on this context, see John McCafferty, *The reconstruction of the Church of Ireland: Bishop Bramhall and the Laudian reforms, 1633–1641* (Cambridge: Cambridge University Press, 2007).

84. T.C. Barnard, 'The protestant interest, 1641–1660', in Jane Ohlmeyer (ed.), *Ireland from independence to occupation, 1641–1660* (Cambridge: Cambridge University Press, 1995), pp. 218–240.

85. Connolly, 'Religion and society, 1600–1914', p. 75.

86. Brian Mac Cuarta, 'The Catholic Church in Ulster under the plantation', in Éamonn Ó Ciardha and Micheál Ó Siochrú (eds), *The plantation of Ulster: Ideology and practice* (Manchester: Manchester University Press, 2012), pp. 119–142.

87. Eamon Darcy, *The Irish rebellion of 1641 and the wars of the three kingdoms* (Woodbridge, UK: Boydell, 2013); John Gibney, *The shadow of a year: The 1641 rebellion in Irish history and memory* (Madison, WI: University of Wisconsin Press, 2013). See also David Edwards, 'Out of the blue? Provincial unrest in Ireland before 1641', in Jane Ohlmeyer and Micheál Ó Siochrú (eds), *Ireland 1641: Contexts and reactions* (Manchester: Manchester University Press, 2013), pp. 99–114; Brian Mac Cuarta, 'Religious violence against settlers in south Ulster, 1641–2', in David Edwards et al. (eds), *Age of atrocity: Violence and political conflict in early modern Ireland* (Dublin: Four Courts, 2007), pp. 154–175; Kenneth Nicholls, 'The other massacre: English killings of Irish, 1641–3', in David Edwards et al. (eds), *Age of atrocity: Violence and political conflict in early modern Ireland* (Dublin: Four Courts, 2007), pp. 176–191.

88. Gibney, *A short history of Ireland*, pp. 61–62.

89. TCD MS 815 fol. 322r, Deposition of John Fortune, 21 June 1643.

90. David A. O'Hara, *English newsbooks and Irish rebellion, 1641–1649* (Dublin: Four Courts, 2006).

91. Connolly, *Religion, law and power*, p. 16.

92. O'Hara, *English newsbooks and Irish rebellion, 1641–1649*.

93. Kirsteen M. MacKenzie, *The Solemn League and Covenant of the three kingdoms and the Cromwellian Union, 1643–1663* (London: Routledge, 2018), p. 9.

94. TCD MS 837 fol. 36v, Deposition of Peter Hill, 29 May 1645.

95. TCD MS 836, ff. 101r–105v, Deposition of Elizabeth Price, 26 June 1643.

96. TCD MS 833, fol. 282v, Deposition of Audrey Carington, 27 October 1645. I am grateful to Elaine Murphy for her advice on the Depositions.

97. TCD MS 838, ff. 3r–4v, Deposition of Arthur Gore, 3 June 1644; TCD MS 838 ff. 5r–6v, Deposition of Theophilus Jones, 3 June 1644; TCD MS 838, ff. 9r–10v, Deposition of Randall Domville, 3 June 1644.

98. MacKenzie, *The Solemn League and Covenant of the three kingdoms and the Cromwellian Union*, p. 16; *The minutes of the Antrim ministers' meeting, 1654–8*, ed. Mark S. Sweetnam (Dublin: Four Courts, 2012).

99. Alan Ford, 'The origins of Irish dissent', in Kevin Herlihy (ed.), *The religion of Irish dissent, 1650–1800* (Dublin, 1996), pp. 9–30.

100. Robert Armstrong, *Protestant war: The 'British' of Ireland and the wars of the three kingdoms* (Manchester: Manchester University Press, 2005).

101. See, generally, Crawford Gribben, *God's Irishmen: Theological debates in Cromwellian Ireland* (New York: Oxford University Press, 2007).

102. *Dictionary of Irish biography*, s.v.

103. Robert Armstrong, 'The Scots of Ireland and the English Republic, 1649–60', in David Edwards and Simon Egan (eds), *The Scots in early Stuart Ireland: Union and separation in two kingdoms* (Manchester: Manchester University Press, 2015), pp. 251–278.

104. Micheál Ó Siochrú, *Confederate Ireland, 1642–1649: A constitutional and political analysis* (Dublin: Four Courts, 1999); Pádraig Lenihan, *Confederate Catholics at war, 1642–49* (Cork: Cork University Press, 2001); Ó hAnnracháin, *Catholic reformation in Ireland*.

105. Ó Siochrú, *Confederate Ireland*, p. 11.

106. Ian W. S. Campbell, 'Truth and calumny in Baroque Rome: Richard O'Ferrall and the *Commentarius Rinuccinianus, 1648–1667*', *Irish Historical Studies* 38:150 (2012), pp. 211–229.

107. Ó Siochrú, *Confederate Ireland*, p. 240.

108. Armstrong, *Protestant war*.

109. See, generally, Gribben, *God's Irishmen*.

110. James Scott Wheeler, *Cromwell in Ireland* (Dublin: Gill and Macmillan, 1999); Micheál Ó Siochrú, *God's executioner: Oliver Cromwell and the conquest of Ireland* (London: Faber and Faber, 2008).

111. John Cunningham, 'Oliver Cromwell and the "Cromwellian" settlement of Ireland', *Historical Journal* 53:4 (2010), pp. 919–937.

112. Padraig Lenihan, 'War and population, 1649–52', *Irish Economic and Social History* 24 (1997), pp. 1–21; John Morrill, 'The Drogheda massacre in Cromwellian context', in David Edwards et al. (eds), *Age of atrocity: Violence and political conflict in early modern Ireland* (Dublin: Four Courts, 2007), pp. 242–265; Cunningham, 'Oliver Cromwell and the "Cromwellian" settlement of Ireland', pp. 919–937.

113. Gribben, *God's Irishmen.*

114. Blair Worden, 'Toleration and the Cromwellian Protectorate', in W.J. Sheils (ed.), *Persecution and toleration*, Studies in Church History 21 (Oxford: Blackwell, 1984), p. 219; John Coffey, 'Puritanism and liberty revisited: The case for toleration in the English revolution', *Historical Journal* 41:4 (1998), pp. 961–985.

115. T.C. Barnard, *Cromwellian Ireland: English government and reform in Ireland, 1649–1660*, second edition (Oxford: Oxford University Press, 2000), p. 99; Crawford Gribben, *John Owen and English puritanism: Experiences of defeat* (Oxford: Oxford University Press, 2016), pp. 111–114.

116. Crawford Gribben, 'Angels and demons in Cromwellian and Restoration Ireland: Heresy and the supernatural', *Huntington Library Quarterly* 76:3 (2013), pp. 377–392.

117. Jane Shaw, *Miracles in Enlightenment England* (New Haven, CT: Yale University Press, 2006).

118. John Owen, *Works*, 16 vols, ed. William H. Goold (Edinburgh: Johnstone & Hunter, 1850–1855), 8: 236.

119. John Rogers, *Ohel or Bethshemesh* (1653).

120. Walter Gostelo, *Charls Stuart and Oliver Cromwel united* (1655), p. 45.

121. William Penn, *The new witnesses proved old heretics* (1672), pp. 61–62.

122. Oliver Cromwell, *Declaration of the Lord Lieutenant of Ireland for the undeceiving of deluded and seduced people* (1650).

123. Stefanio Tutino, *Thomas White and the Blackloists: Between politics and theology during the English Civil War* (Aldershot, UK: Ashgate, 2008).

124. Ó Siochrú, *God's executioner*, pp. 204–210.

125. Connolly, *Religion, law and power*, p. 19.

126. Whelan, *Religion, landscape and settlement in Ireland*, p. 134.

127. *Dictionary of Irish biography*, s.v.

128. Stewart, *The shape of Irish history*, p. 94.

129. Owen, *Works*, 8: 237.

130. Rogers, *Ohel or Bethshemesh.*

131. Cecile O'Rahilly (ed.), *Five seventeenth-century political poems* (Dublin: Dublin Institute for Advanced Studies, 1952), p. 75.

132. Aidan Clarke, *Prelude to Restoration in Ireland: The end of the Commonwealth, 1659–1660* (Cambridge: Cambridge University Press, 1999); Connolly, *Divided kingdom*, pp. 119–171.

133. This data is derived from *The Down Survey of Ireland: Mapping a century of change*, available at http://downsurvey.tcd.ie, accessed 20 June 2020.

134. William Petty, 'The political anatomy of Ireland', in *The economic writings of Sir William Petty*, ed. C. H. Hull, 2 vols (London, 1899), 2: 155–157.

135. Eoin Kinsella, *Catholic survival in protestant Ireland, 1660–1711: Colonel John Browne, landownership and the Articles of Limerick* (Woodbridge, UK: Boydell and Brewer, 2018).

136. Robin Usher, *Protestant Dublin, 1660–1760: Architecture and iconography* (Basingstoke: Palgrave Macmillan, 2012).

137. See, generally, Phil Kilroy, *Protestant dissent and controversy in Ireland, 1660–1714* (Cork: Cork University Press, 1994).

138. Richard L. Greaves, *God's other children: Protestant nonconformists and the emergence of denominational churches in Ireland, 1660–1700* (Stanford, CA: Stanford University Press, 1997); Kathryn Rose Sawyer, 'A "disorderly tumultuous way of serving God": Prayer and order in Ireland's church and state, 1660–89', *Irish Historical Studies* 42:162 (2018), pp. 207–224.

139. Connolly, 'Religion and society, 1600–1914', p. 77.

140. Raymond Gillespie, 'Dissenters and nonconformists, 1661–1700', in Kevin Herlihy (ed.), *The Irish dissenting tradition, 1650–1750* (Dublin: Four Courts, 1995), pp. 11–28; Jacqueline R. Hill, 'Dublin Corporation, protestant dissent, and politics, 1660–1800', in Kevin Herlihy (ed.), *The politics of Irish dissent, 1650–1800* (Dublin: Four Courts, 1997), pp. 28–39; James McGuire, 'Ormond and Presbyterian nonconformity, 1660–63', in Kevin Herlihy (ed.), *The politics of Irish dissent, 1650–1800* (Dublin: Four Courts, 1997), pp. 40–51.

141. Robert Whan, *The Presbyterians of Ulster, 1680–1730* (Woodbridge, UK: Boydell, 2013), p. 1.

142. J.C. Beckett, *Protestant dissent in Ireland, 1687–1780* (London: Faber and Faber, 1948), p. 23.

143. *ODNB*, s.v.

144. *ODNB*, s.v. On Presbyterian fortunes in the new world, see Peter Gilmore, *Irish Presbyterians and the shaping of western Pennsylvania* (Pittsburgh, PA: University of Pittsburgh Press, 2018).

145. T.C. Barnard, 'Identities, ethnicity and tradition among Irish dissenters, c. 1650–1750', in Kevin Herlihy (ed.), *The Irish dissenting tradition, 1650–1750* (Dublin: Four Courts, 1995), pp. 29–48.

146. Ruth Whelan, 'Sanctified by the word: The Huguenots and Anglican liturgy', in Kevin Herlihy (ed.), *Propagating the word of Irish dissent* (Dublin: Four Courts, 1998), pp. 74–94; Raymond Pierre Hylton, 'The less-favoured refuge: Ireland's nonconformist Huguenots at the turn of the eighteenth century', in Kevin Herlihy (ed.), *The religion of Irish dissent, 1650–1800* (Dublin: Four Courts, 1996), pp. 83–99; G. Andrew Forrest, 'Religious controversy within the French protestant community in Dublin, 1692–1716: An historiographical critique', in Kevin Herlihy (ed.), *The Irish dissenting tradition, 1650–1750* (Dublin: Four Courts, 1995), pp. 96–110.

147. Beckett, *Protestant dissent in Ireland*, p. 127; Vivien Hick, ' "As nearly related as possible": Solidarity amongst the Irish Palatines', in Kevin Herlihy (ed.), *The Irish dissenting tradition, 1650–1750* (Dublin: Four Courts, 1995), pp. 111–125.

148. Stephen Austin Kelly, 'Anglo-Irish drama? Writing for the stage in Restoration Dublin', in Kathleen Miller and Crawford Gribben (eds), *Dublin: Renaissance city of Literature* (Manchester: Manchester University Press, 2017), pp. 206–227.

149. Beckett, *Protestant dissent in Ireland*, p. 40.

150. Richard S. Harrison, ' "As a garden enclosed": The emergence of Irish Quakers, 1650–1750', in Kevin Herlihy (ed.), *The Irish dissenting tradition, 1650–1750* (Dublin: Four Courts, 1995), pp. 81–95; Richard L. Greaves, *Dublin's merchant Quaker: Anthony Sharp and the community of Friends, 1643–1707* (Stanford, CA: Stanford University Press, 1998); Sandra Hynes, 'Becoming convinced: The use of Quaker testimonies in late seventeenth-century Ireland', in Michael Brown et al. (eds), *Converts and conversions in Ireland, 1650–1850* (Dublin: Four Courts, 2005), pp. 107–127; Naomi Pullin, *Female Friends and the making of trans-Atlantic Quakerism, 1650–1750* (Cambridge: Cambridge University Press, 2018).

151. Kevin Herlihy, ' "The faithful remnant": Irish Baptists, 1650–1750', in Kevin Herlihy (ed.), *The Irish dissenting tradition, 1650–1750* (Dublin: Four Courts, 1995), pp. 65–79; Kevin Herlihy, ' "A gay and flattering world": Irish Baptist piety and perspective, 1650–1780', in Kevin Herlihy (ed.), *The religion of Irish dissent, 1650–1800* (Dublin: Four Courts, 1996), pp. 48–67.

152. Beckett, *Protestant dissent in Ireland*, p. 24.

153. *The letters of Saint Oliver Plunkett, 1625–81*, ed. J. Hanly (Dublin: Colin Smythe, 1979), quoted in Connolly, 'Religion and society, 1600–1914', p. 77.

154. Connolly, 'Religion and society, 1600–1914', p. 77.

155. Connolly, *Religion, law and power*, pp. 31–32.

156. John Miller, 'The earl of Tyrconnell and James II's Irish policy', *Historical Journal* 20:4 (1997), pp. 803–823; Connolly, *Religion, law and power*, pp. 33–39.

157. Kevin McKenny, 'The Restoration land settlement in Ireland: A statistical interpretation', in Coleman A. Dennehy (ed.), *Restoration Ireland: Always settling and never settled* (Aldershot, UK: Ashgate, 2007), pp. 35–52.

158. John Childs, 'The laws of war in seventeenth-century Europe and their application during the Jacobite War in Ireland, 1688–91', in David Edwards et al. (eds), *Age of atrocity: Violence and political conflict in early modern Ireland* (Dublin: Four Courts, 2007), pp. 283–300.

159. Joep Leerssen, *Mere Irish and Fíor-Ghael: Studies in the idea of Irish nationality, its development and literary expression prior to the nineteenth century* (Cork: Cork University Press, 1996); Declan Downey, 'Purity of blood and purity of faith in early modern Ireland', in Alan Ford and James McCafferty (eds), *The origins of sectarianism in early modern Ireland* (Cambridge: Cambridge University Press, 2005), pp. 217–227.

160. R. Scott Spurlock, 'Cromwell and Catholics: Towards a reassessment of lay Catholic experience in Interregnum Ireland', in Mark Williams and Stephen P. Forrest (eds), *Constructing the past: Writing Irish history, 1600–1800* (Woodbridge, UK: Boydell, 2010), pp. 157–179.

161. John Coffey, *Persecution and toleration in protestant England, 1558–1689* (London: Pearson, 2000), p. 169.
162. Beckett, *Protestant dissent in Ireland*.

CHAPTER 4

1. Edward Brynn, *The Church of Ireland in the age of Catholic emancipation* (New York: Garland, 1982); Thomas Bartlett, *The fall and rise of the Irish nation: The Catholic question, 1690–1830* (Dublin: Gill and Macmillan, 1992); S.J. Brown, *The national churches of England, Ireland and Scotland, 1801–1846* (Oxford: Oxford University Press, 2001); Connolly, *Divided kingdom*, pp. 249–285; Nigel Yates, *The religious condition of Ireland, 1770–1850* (Oxford: Oxford University Press, 2006); David Dickson, *New foundations: Ireland, 1660–1800*, second edition (Dublin: Irish Academic Press, 2000); Toby Barnard, *A new anatomy of Ireland: The Irish protestants, 1649–1770* (New Haven, CT: Yale University Press, 2003); D.W. Hayton, 'Anglo-Irish attitudes: Shifting perceptions of national identity', in D.W. Hayton, *The Anglo-Irish experience, 1680–1730: Religion, identity and patriotism* (Woodbridge, UK: Boydell, 2012), pp. 25–48.
2. Dickson, *New foundations*, pp. 1–29; Connolly, *Religion, law and power*, p. 3; T.C. Barnard, 'Reforming Irish manners: The religious societies in Dublin during the 1690s', in T.C. Barnard, *Irish protestant ascents and descents, 1641–1770* (Dublin: Four Courts, 2004), p. 144.
3. Connolly, *Religion, law and power*, p. 2.
4. Dickson, *New foundations*, pp. 67–69; Daniel Corkery, *The hidden Ireland: A study of Gaelic Munster in the eighteenth century* (1925; rpr. Dublin: Gill and Macmillan, 1975); Breandán Ó Buachalla, '"James our true king": The ideology of Irish royalism in the seventeenth century', in D.G. Boyce et al. (eds), *Political thought in Ireland since the seventeenth century* (London: Routledge, 1993), pp. 9–14; Breandán Ó Buachalla, 'From Jacobite to Jacobin', in Thomas Bartlett et al. (eds), *1798: A bi-centenary perspective* (Dublin: Four Courts, 2003), pp. 75–96; Éamonn Ó Ciardha, *Ireland and the Jacobite cause, 1685–1766: A fatal attachment* (Dublin: Four Courts, 2002); David Dickson, 'Jacobitism in eighteenth-century Ireland: A Munster perspective', *Éire-Ireland* 39 (2004), pp. 38–99.
5. John Richardson, *A proposal for the conversion of the popish natives of Ireland to the establish'd religion* (London, 1712), pp. 13–14.
6. Connolly, *Religion, law and power*, p. 145.
7. Connolly, *Divided island*, p. 164.
8. Dickson, *New foundations*, pp. 90–91; Michael Brown, *The Irish Enlightenment* (Cambridge, MA: Harvard University Press, 2016), p. 164.
9. Carey, '"Neither good English nor good Irish": Bi-lingualism and identity formation in sixteenth-century Ireland', pp. 45–61.
10. Barnard, 'Protestants and the Irish language', pp. 183–186.
11. Wolf, *An Irish-speaking island*, p. 4.

12. Dickson, *New foundations*, pp. 64–65; Barnard, 'Protestants and the Irish language', p. 192.

13. Aidan Doyle, *A history of the Irish language: From the Norman invasion to independence* (Oxford: Oxford University Press, 2015), pp. 90–92.

14. Barnard, 'Protestants and the Irish language', p. 196.

15. Foster, *Modern Ireland*, p. 14. See, more recently, *Catholics and protestants in eighteenth-century Ireland: Irish religious censuses of the 1760s*, ed. Brian Gurrin et al. (Dublin: Irish Manuscript Commission, 2016).

16. Toby C. Barnard, 'The government and Irish dissent, 1704–1780', in Kevin Herlihy (ed.), *The politics of Irish dissent, 1650–1800* (Dublin: Four Courts, 1997), pp. 9–27; Andrew R. Holmes, 'Protestant dissent in Ireland', in Andrew Thompson (ed.), *The Oxford history of protestant dissenting traditions,* vol. 2: *1689 to the repeal of the Test and Corporation Acts* (Oxford: Oxford University Press, 2018), pp. 119–138.

17. Connolly, *Religion, law and power*, p. 263; Connolly, *Divided kingdom*, pp. 173–207; Hilary Joyce Bishop, 'Memory and legend: recollections of penal times in Irish folklore', *Folklore* 129:1 (2018), pp. 18–38.

18. Jacqueline Hill, 'National festivals, the state, and "Protestant Ascendancy" in Ireland', *Irish Historical Studies* 24:93 (1984), pp. 31–51.

19. Holmes, 'Protestant dissent in Ireland', pp. 119–138.

20. For discussion of Presbyterian involvement in trade, see Whan, *The Presbyterians of Ulster, 1680–1730.*

21. Connolly, *Religion, law and power*, pp. 151–152.

22. Nancy J. Curtin, *The United Irishmen: Popular politics in Ulster and Dublin, 1791–1798* (Oxford: Oxford University Press, 1998); I.R. McBride, *Scripture politics: Ulster Presbyterians and Irish radicalism in the late eighteenth century* (Oxford: Clarendon Press, 1998).

23. Curtin, *The United Irishmen*, p. 11.

24. David Hempton and Myrtle Hill, *Evangelical protestantism in Ulster society, 1740–1890* (London: Routledge, 1992).

25. Connolly, *Divided island*, p. 285; Hempton and Hill, *Evangelical protestantism in Ulster society, 1740–1840*; Andrew R. Holmes, *The shaping of Ulster Presbyterian belief and practice, 1770–1840* (Oxford: Oxford University Press, 2006).

26. *The Blackwell dictionary of evangelical biography*, s.v.

27. Irene Whelan, *The Bible war in Ireland: The 'second reformation' and the polarization of protestant–Catholic relations, 1800–1840* (Dublin: Lilliput, 2005), p. 103.

28. S.J. Brown, 'The new reformation movement in the Church of Ireland, 1801–1829', in S. Brown and D. Miller (eds), *Piety and power in Ireland, 1760–1960: Essays in honour of Emmet Larkin* (Belfast: Institute of Irish Studies, 2000), pp. 180–208; Whelan, *The Bible war in Ireland*; Miriam Moffitt, *Soupers and jumpers: The protestant missions in Connemara, 1848–1937* (Dublin: Nonsuch Publishing, 2008); Whelan, *Religion, landscape and settlement in Ireland*, pp. 157–159. For an older account, see Desmond Bowen, *The protestant crusade in Ireland, 1800–70* (Dublin: Gill and Macmillan, 1978), pp. 208–258.

29. Peter Gray, *The Irish famine* (London: Thames & Hudson, 1995); Cormac Ó Gráda, *Black '47 and beyond: The Great Irish Famine in history, economy, and memory* (Princeton, NJ: Princeton University Press, 1999); John Crowley and William J. Smyth (eds), *Atlas of the Great Irish Famine* (Cork: Cork University Press, 2012); Emily Mark-Fitzgerald, *Commemorating the Irish famine: Memory and the monument* (Liverpool: Liverpool University Press, 2013).

30. D.W. Miller, 'Presbyterianism and "modernization" in Ulster', *Past and Present* 80 (1978), pp. 66–90.

31. On these tensions, see Janice Holmes, 'The role of open-air preaching in the Belfast riots of 1857', *Proceedings of the Royal Irish Academy* 102, C (2002), pp. 47–66.

32. Janice Holmes, *Religious revivals in Britain and Ireland 1859–1905* (Dublin: Irish Academic Press, 2000); Andrew R. Holmes, 'The Ulster revival of 1859: Causes, controversies and consequences', *Journal of Ecclesiastical History* 63 (2012), pp. 488–515; Andrew R. Holmes, '"Personal conversion, revival, and the Holy Spirit": Presbyterian evangelicalism in early nineteenth-century Ulster', in John Coffey (ed.), *Heart religion: Evangelical piety in England and Ireland, 1690–1850* (Oxford: Oxford University Press, 2016), pp. 191–200.

33. William Gibson, *Year of grace: A history of the Ulster revival of 1859* (Edinburgh: Andrew Elliot, 1860), p. 220.

34. D.W. Miller, 'Landscape and religious practice: A study of mass attendance in pre-famine Ireland', *Éire-Ireland* 40 (2005), pp. 90–106; C.C.P. Barr, 'The re-energising of Catholicism, 1815–1880', in Tom Bartlett and James Kelly (eds), *The Cambridge history of Ireland: 1730–1880*, vol. 3 (Cambridge: Cambridge University Press, 2018), pp. 280–304.

35. Colm Cooke, 'The modern Irish missionary movement', *Archivium Hibernicum* 35 (1980), pp. 234–246; C.C.P. Barr, *Ireland's empire: The Roman Catholic Church in the English-speaking world, 1829–1914* (Cambridge: Cambridge University Press, 2020).

36. John Loughery, *Dagger John: Archbishop John Hughes and the making of Irish America* (New York: Cornell University Press, 2018).

37. Whelan, *Religion, landscape and settlement in Ireland*, p. 220; Barr, *Ireland's empire*.

38. Ultán Gillen, 'The Enlightenment and Irish political culture in the age of revolutions', in Richard Butterwick et al. (eds), *Peripheries of the Enlightenment* (Oxford: Voltaire Foundation, 2008), pp. 163–182.

39. Dickson, *New foundations*, pp. 79–80.

40. Brown, *The Irish Enlightenment*, pp. 60–62.

41. Quoted in Stewart, *The shape of Irish history*, p. 99; Dickson, *New foundations*, pp. 38–41.

42. Brown, *The Irish Enlightenment*, p. 113.

43. Dickson, *New foundations*, pp. 45–47.

44. Dickson, *New foundations*, pp. 56–58. The standard land lease lasted for thirty-one years; Dickson, *New foundations*, p. 119.

45. Charles Ivar McGrath, 'The provisions for conversion in the penal laws, 1695–1750', in Michael Brown et al. (eds), *Converts and conversions in Ireland,*

1650–1850 (Dublin: Four Courts, 2005), pp. 35–59; Thomas P. Power, "'A weighty, serious business": The conversion of Catholic clergy to Anglicanism', in Michael Brown et al. (eds), *Converts and conversions in Ireland, 1650–1850* (Dublin: Four Courts, 2005), pp. 183–213.

46. O'Connor, 'Religious change, 1550–1800', p. 184.
47. Connolly, *Priests and people in pre-famine Ireland*, p. 51; C.D.A. Leighton, *Catholicism in a protestant kingdom: A study of the Irish ancien régime* (London: Palgrave Macmillan, 1994), p. 6.
48. Connolly, 'Religion and society, 1600–1914', p. 80.
49. Leighton, *Catholicism in a protestant kingdom*, p. 9.
50. Kevin Whelan, 'An underground gentry: Catholic middlemen in eighteenth-century Ireland', in Kevin Whelan (ed.), *The tree of liberty: Radicalism, Catholicism and the construction of Irish identity* (Cork: Cork University Press, 1996), pp. 3–56.
51. Connolly, *Priests and people in pre-famine Ireland*, p. 80.
52. Leighton, *Catholicism in a protestant kingdom*, p. 6.
53. O'Connor, 'Religious change, 1550–1800', p. 184.
54. Leighton, *Catholicism in a protestant kingdom*, p. 7.
55. O'Connor, 'Religious change, 1550–1800', pp. 185–189.
56. Marianne Elliot, *When God took sides: Religion and identity in Ireland* (Oxford: Oxford University Press, 2009), p. 81.
57. Leighton, *Catholicism in a protestant kingdom*, p. 7.
58. Brown, *The Irish Enlightenment*, p. 125.
59. Leighton, *Catholicism in a protestant kingdom*, p. 7.
60. Connolly, 'Religion and society, 1600–1914', p. 78.
61. Barnard, *A new anatomy of Ireland*, p. 95.
62. Whelan, *Religion, landscape and settlement in Ireland*, p. 142.
63. Dickson, *New foundations*, pp. 48–49, 60–61.
64. Connolly, 'Religion and society, 1600–1914', p. 78.
65. Dickson, *New foundations*, pp. 80–81.
66. Connolly, *Religion, law and power*, pp. 162–164;
67. Michael Brown, *Francis Hutcheson in Dublin* (Dublin: Four Courts, 2002).
68. Brown, *The Irish Enlightenment*, p. 212.
69. Connolly, *Religion, law and power*, pp. 149–151.
70. John Wesley, *The journal of the Rev John Wesley*, 4 vols (London, 1895), 2:67; Robin Roddie, 'John Wesley's political sensibilities in Ireland, 1747–89', in Kevin Herlihy (ed.), *The politics of Irish dissent, 1650–1800* (Dublin: Four Courts, 1997), pp. 93–103.
71. Connolly, *Religion, law and power*, p. 12.
72. Connolly, *Religion, law and power*, p. 263.
73. Leighton, *Catholicism in a protestant kingdom*, p. 15.
74. Brown, *The Irish Enlightenment*, p. 108.
75. Dickson, *New foundations*, p. 33; Brown, *The Irish Enlightenment*, p. 106.
76. Barnard, 'Reforming Irish manners: The religious societies in Dublin during the 1690s', p. 145.

77. T.C. Barnard, 'The uses of the 23rd October 1641 and Irish protestant celebrations', in T.C. Barnard, *Irish protestant ascents and descents, 1641–1770* (Dublin: Four Courts, 2004), pp. 111–142.
78. Connolly, *Religion, law and power*, p. 178.
79. Barnard, 'The uses of the 23rd October 1641 and Irish protestant celebrations', p. 133.
80. Whelan, *Religion, landscape and settlement in Ireland*, pp. 155, 161.
81. Barnard, *A new anatomy of Ireland*, pp. 88–89, 107–110.
82. Connolly, *Religion, law and power*, p. 188.
83. Barnard, 'Reforming Irish manners: The religious societies in Dublin during the 1690s', p. 163.
84. Barnard, 'Reforming Irish manners: The religious societies in Dublin during the 1690s', pp. 151–52, 158.
85. Connolly, *Religion, law and power*, p. 162.
86. Connolly, *Religion, law and power*, p. 175; Brown, *The Irish Enlightenment*, pp. 15, 57.
87. Barnard, 'Reforming Irish manners: The religious societies in Dublin during the 1690s', p. 166.
88. Connolly, *Religion, law and power*, p. 175.
89. McBride, *Scripture politics*, pp. 41–61.
90. David Stewart, *The Seceders in Ireland, with annals of their congregations* (Belfast: Presbyterian Historical Society, 1950).
91. Elizabethanne Boran, 'Education and dissemination of the word: A Baptist library in the eighteenth century', in Kevin Herlihy (ed.), *Propagating the word of Irish dissent, 1650–1800* (Dublin: Four Courts, 1998), pp. 114–131; Connolly, *Religion, law and power*, p. 160.
92. Andrew Hadfield, *Edmund Spenser: A life* (Oxford: Oxford University Press, 2021), pp. 410–411; T.C. Barnard, 'Edmund Spencer, Edmund Spenser and the problems of Irish protestants in the mid-eighteenth century', in T.C. Barnard, *Irish protestant ascents and descents, 1641–1770* (Dublin: Four Courts, 2004), p. 290–305; Thomas O'Connor, *An Irish theologian in Enlightenment France: Luke Joseph Hooke, 1714–96* (Dublin: Four Courts, 1995), p. 13.
93. Dickson, *New foundations*, pp. 86–87, 102–104; Vincent Morley, *Irish opinion and the American revolution, 1760–1783* (Cambridge: Cambridge University Press, 2009), pp. 10, 14.
94. Leighton, *Catholicism in a protestant kingdom*, p. 69.
95. Dickson, *New foundations*, pp. 157–165.
96. Morley, *Irish opinion and the American revolution*, p. 14.
97. Various estimates are outlined in Connolly, *Divided kingdom*, pp. 380–382.
98. Quoted in David A. Wilson, *United Irishmen, United States: Immigrant radicals in the early Republic* (Dublin: Four Courts, 1998), p.14.
99. Wilson, *United Irishmen, United States*, p. 14.
100. Quoted in Stewart, *The shape of Irish history*, p. 120.
101. Dickson, *New foundations*, p. 160; Morley, *Irish opinion and the American revolution*, pp. 129–137.

102. McBride, *Scripture politics*, pp. 127–133.

103. Whelan, *Religion, landscape and settlement in Ireland*, p. 132.

104. Wilson, *United Irishmen, United States*, p. 17.

105. Wilson, *United Irishmen, United States*, p. 16.

106. Quoted in Brown, *The Irish Enlightenment*, p. 388.

107. Stewart, *The shape of Irish history*, p. 105.

108. Emmet Larkin, *The pastoral role of the Roman Catholic Church in pre-famine Ireland, 1750–1850* (Dublin: Four Courts, 2006), p. 263.

109. Brown, *The Irish Enlightenment*, p. 412.

110. James Wilson, 'Orangeism in 1798', in Bartlett et al. (eds), *1798: A bicentenary perspective* (Dublin: Four Courts, 2003), p. 359.

111. Curtin, *The United Irishmen*, p. 11.

112. Wilson, *United Irishmen, United States*, p. 25.

113. Quoted in Wilson, *United Irishmen, United States*, p. 13.

114. Wilson, *United Irishmen, United States*, p. 13.

115. Curtin, *The United Irishmen*, pp. 10–11.

116. Curtin, *The United Irishmen*, p. 288.

117. Stewart, *The shape of Irish history*, p. 128.

118. Brown, *The Irish Enlightenment*, pp. 406, 439.

119. McBride, *Scripture politics*, pp. 186–206; Marianne Elliot, 'Religious polarization and sectarianism in the Ulster rebellion', in Thomas Bartlett et al. (eds), *1798: A bicentenary perspective* (Dublin: Four Courts, 2003), pp. 279–297.

120. Stewart, *The shape of Irish history*, p. 129.

121. Quoted Wilson, *United Irishmen, United States*, p. 30.

122. Wilson, *United Irishmen, United States*, pp. 30, 34.

123. Stewart, *The shape of Irish history*, p. 131.

124. Crawford Gribben, 'Introduction', in Crawford Gribben and Andrew R. Holmes (eds), *Protestant millennialism, evangelicalism and Irish society, 1790–2005* (Basingstoke: Palgrave Macmillan, 2006), pp. 11–13.

125. Connolly, *Priests and people in pre-famine Ireland*, p. 42.

126. On the broader context, see David Fitzpatrick, *Descendancy: Irish protestant histories since 1795* (Cambridge: Cambridge University Press, 2014).

127. J.N. Darby, *Letters of J.N.D.*, 3 vols, second edition (London: Morrish, n.d.), 2: 158.

128. Andrew R. Holmes, 'Protestantism in nineteenth-century Ireland: Revival and crisis', in James Kelly (ed.), *The Cambridge history of Ireland*, 4 vols (Cambridge: Cambridge University Press, 2018), 2: 331–349.

129. *Ordnance Survey memoirs of Ireland*, vol. 19: *Parishes of county Antrim VI, 1830, 1833, 1835–38*, eds Angélique Day and Patrick McWilliams (Belfast: Institute of Irish Studies, 1993), p. 20; Gillian Doherty, *The Irish Ordnance Survey: History, culture and memory* (Dublin: Four Courts, 2006).

130. Whelan, *Religion, landscape and settlement in Ireland*, p. 118.

131. Whelan, *Bible war*, p. 159.

132. Whelan, *Religion, landscape and settlement in Ireland*, p. 156.

133. See the argument of Guy Beiner, *Forgetful remembrance: Social forgetting and vernacular historiography of a rebellion in Ulster* (Oxford: Oxford University Press, 2018).

134. *Dictionary of Irish biography*, s.v.

135. T.C. Donachie, *Irish Covenanters: Politics and society in the 19th century* (privately published, 2016), pp. 167–198.

136. *Letters and papers of the late Theodosia A. Viscountess Powerscourt*, ed. Robert Daly (London, 1838).

137. Peter Mullowney, 'The expansion and decline of the O'Donel estate, Newport, county Mayo, 1785–1852' (unpublished PhD thesis, NUI Maynooth, 2002); John Eliot Howard, *'The Island of the Saints'; or Ireland in 1855* (London: Seeleys, 1855), pp. 187–189; J.N. Darby, *Letters of J.N. Darby, Supplement from French*, 2 vols (Chessington: Bible and Gospel Trust, 2016), 1: 61–62, 181.

138. Roy Coad, *History of the brethren movement* (Carlisle: Paternoster, 1976), p. 119 n, confuses the authorship of this commentary.

139. Review of George Petrie, 'The ecclesiastical architecture of Ireland, anterior to the Anglo-Norman invasion', in *The Quarterly Review* 76 (1845), p. 379; Gustav Ischebeck, *John Nelson Darby: Son temps et son oeuvre* (Yverdon/Lausanne [1937]), p. 59.

140. I extrapolate these figures from Connolly, *Divided island*, p. 164, and Captain Larcom, 'Observations on the census of the population of Ireland in 1841', *Journal of the Statistical Society of London* 6:4 (1843), p. 324.

141. Thomas Linehan, 'History and development of Irish population censuses', *Journal of the Statistical and Social Inquiry Society of Ireland* 16:4 (1991–1992), p. 103.

142. Connolly, *Priests and people in pre-famine Ireland*, pp. 46, 48.

143. Gibney, *A short history of Ireland*, p. 148; Sarah Roddy, *Population, providence and empire: The churches and emigration from nineteenth-century Ireland* (Manchester: Manchester University Press, 2014).

144. Gibney, *A short history of Ireland*, p. 145.

145. *Dictionary of Irish biography*, s.v.

146. Kingdon, *Baptist evangelism in nineteenth-century Ireland*.

147. Gibney, *A short history of Ireland*, p. 146.

148. *Dictionary of Irish biography*, s.v.

149. Whelan, *Religion, landscape and settlement in Ireland*, pp. 142–143.

150. Connolly, 'Religion and society, 1600–1914', p. 83.

151. Andrew R. Holmes, *The Irish Presbyterian mind: Conservative theology, evangelical experience, and modern criticism, 1839–1930* (Oxford: Oxford University Press, 2018), pp. 41–78.

152. Holmes, *The Irish Presbyterian mind*, pp. 90–91.

153. Crawford Gribben, *The revival of Particular Baptist life in Ireland, 1780–1840* (Louisville, KY: The Andrew Fuller Center for Baptist Studies, 2018).

154. Cork Church Book, pp. 56–7, 72–5, 79–80, 87–8, 99, 111; Backus MS, appendix pp. 4–7.

155. Wolf, *An Irish-speaking island*, p. 9.

NOTES TO PAGES 151–156 259

156. Robert Dunlop, 'Alexander Carson of Tobermore: An Ulster giant', *Irish Baptist Historical Society Journal* 9 (1976–1977), pp. 14–28.

157. Darby, *Letters*, 1: 232.

158. Holmes, *The Irish Presbyterian mind*, p. 51.

159. 'The awakening in Ulster', *Things New and Old* 2 (1859), p. 166.

160. 'The awakening in Ulster', p. 166.

161. Crawford Gribben, ' "The worst sect a Christian man can meet": Opposition to the Plymouth Brethren in Ireland and Scotland, 1859–1900', *Scottish Studies Review* 3:2 (2002), pp. 34–53.

162. 'The awakening in Ulster', pp. 163–164. For more accounts of revival, see James McCosh, *The Ulster revival and its physiological accidents: A paper read before the Evangelical Alliance, September 22, 1859* (Belfast: C. Aitchison, 1859); John Weir, *The Ulster awakening: Its origin, progress, and fruit* (London: Arthur Hall, Virtue and Co., 1860); Gibson, *The year of grace*.

163. Weir, *The Ulster awakening*, p. 7.

164. McCosh, *The Ulster revival and its physiological accidents*, pp. 10–11.

165. William Hamilton, *An inquiry into the Scriptural character of the revival of 1859* (1866), p. 9.

166. Gibson, *Year of grace*, p. 220.

167. Alan Acheson, *A history of the Church of Ireland, 1691–2001*, second edition (Dublin: APCK, 2002), pp. 205–221; Whelan, *Religion, landscape and settlement in Ireland*, p. 160.

168. Connolly, 'Religion and society, 1600–1914', p. 87.

169. Larkin, *The pastoral role of the Roman Catholic Church in pre-famine Ireland*, p. 1.

170. Connolly, *Religion, law and power*, p. 43.

171. Connolly, *Priests and people in pre-famine Ireland*, p. 71.

172. Larkin, *The pastoral role of the Roman Catholic Church in pre-famine Ireland*, p. 4; Connolly, *Priests and people in pre-famine Ireland*, p. 105.

173. Larkin, *The pastoral role of the Roman Catholic Church in pre-famine Ireland*, p. 3.

174. Connolly, *Priests and people in pre-famine Ireland*, pp. 14, 16, describes this practice as 'magic'.

175. *Dictionary of Irish biography*, s.v.

176. Connolly, 'Religion and society, 1600–1914', p. 82.

177. Connolly, *Priests and people in pre-famine Ireland*, p. 21.

178. Larkin, *The pastoral role of the Roman Catholic Church in pre-famine Ireland*, p. 4.

179. Connolly, *Priests and people in pre-famine Ireland*, pp. 66–68.

180. Larkin, *The pastoral role of the Roman Catholic Church in pre-famine Ireland*, p. 5; Connolly, *Priests and people in pre-famine Ireland*, p. 57.

181. Connolly, *Priests and people in pre-famine Ireland*, p. 26.

182. Whelan, *Religion, landscape and settlement in Ireland*, pp. 202–203. On the expansion of female religious, see Rosemary Raughter, 'Pious occupations: Female activism and the Catholic revival in eighteenth-century Ireland', in Rosemary Raughter (ed.), *Religious women and their history: Breaking the silence* (Dublin: Irish Academic Press, 2005), pp. 25–49; Cara Delay, 'Confidantes or competitors:

Women, priests and conflict in post-famine Ireland', *Éire-Ireland* 40 (2005), pp. 107–125; Deirdre Raftery, 'The "mission" of nuns in female education in Ireland, c. 1850–1950', *Pedagogica Historica* 48:2 (2012), pp. 299–313; Deirdre Raftery, '"Je suis d'aucune nation": The recruitment and identity of Irish women religious in the international mission field, c. 1840–1940', *Pedagogica Historica* 49:4 (2013), pp. 513–530.

183. Larkin, *The pastoral role of the Roman Catholic Church in pre-famine Ireland*, p. 3.

184. Connolly, *Priests and people in pre-famine Ireland*, p. 107.

185. Larkin, *The pastoral role of the Roman Catholic Church in pre-famine Ireland*, p. 259.

186. Connolly, *Priests and people in pre-famine Ireland*, p. 41.

187. Elliot, *When God took sides*, p. 171.

188. Stewart, *The shape of Irish history*, p. 150.

189. Elliot, *When God took sides*, p. 172.

190. Connolly, *Religion, law and power*, p. 155.

191. Connolly, *Priests and people in pre-famine Ireland*, p. 143.

192. Connolly, *Priests and people in pre-famine Ireland*, pp. 17–20.

193. Whelan, *Religion, landscape and settlement in Ireland*, p. 103.

194. Connolly, *Priests and people in pre-famine Ireland*, p. 90.

195. Connolly, *Priests and people in pre-famine Ireland*, p. 15; Eugene Hynes, *Knock: The Virgin's apparition in nineteenth-century Ireland* (Cork: Cork University Press, 2009), p. xiii; Whelan, *Religion, landscape and settlement in Ireland*, p. 113.

196. Angela Bourke, *The burning of Bridget Cleary* (London: Pimlico, 1999).

197. Cara Delay, *Irish women and the creation of modern Catholicism, 1850–1950* (Manchester: Manchester University Press, 2019); Larkin, *The pastoral role of the Roman Catholic Church in pre-famine Ireland*, p. 260.

198. Connolly, 'Religion and society, 1600–1914', p. 81..

199. Connolly, *Priests and people in pre-famine Ireland*, p. 25.

200. Whelan, *Religion, landscape and settlement in Ireland*, p. 205.

201. Whelan, *Religion, landscape and settlement in Ireland*, p. 100.

202. Ambrose Macauley, *Patrick McAlister: Bishop of Down and Connor, 1886–1895* (Dublin: Four Courts, 2006), p. 23; A.C. Hepburn, *Catholic Belfast and nationalist Ireland in the era of Joe Devlin, 1871–1934* (Oxford: Oxford University Press, 2008), pp. 7–29.

203. Whelan, *Religion, landscape and settlement in Ireland*, p. 206.

204. F.S.L. Lyons, *Charles Stewart Parnell* (Dublin: Gill and Macmillan, 2005), p. 15; T.P. O'Connor, *The life of Charles Stewart Parnell* (London: Ward, Lock, Bowden and Co., [1891]), pp. 170–171.

205. Jane Jordan, 'The English Delilah: Katharine O'Shea and Irish politics, 1880–1891', in Roger Swift and Christine Kinealy (eds), *Politics and power in Victorian Ireland* (Dublin: Four Courts, 2006), pp. 69–83; Macauley, *Patrick McAlister*, pp. 74–96.

206. James Joyce, *A portrait of the artist as a young man*, ed. Seamus Deane (London: Penguin, 1992), p. 35.

207. R.T.G. Holmes, 'United Irishmen and unionists: Irish Presbyterians, 1791–1886', in W.J. Sheils and Diana Wood (eds), *The churches, Ireland and the Irish: Studies in Church History* (Oxford: Blackwell, 1989), pp. 171–189.

208. J.N. Darby, *Notes & jottings*, 5 vols (London: Morrish, n.d.), 2: 69.

209. Connolly, *Priests and people in pre-famine Ireland*, p. 91.

210. *Census of Ireland, 1911: Province of Ulster: Area, houses, and population; also the ages, civil or conjugal condition, occupations, birthplaces, religion, and education of the people* (London: HMSO, 1912), pp. 37–38.

211. *Census of Ireland, 1871: Part III: General report* (Dublin: Alexander Thom, 1876), p. 107.

212. Andrew Holmes will establish this point in work that is forthcoming.

213. Brożyna, *Labour, love and prayer*; Andrea Ebel Brożyna, 'The right to labour, love, and pray: The creation of the ideal Christian woman in Ulster Roman Catholic and protestant religious literature, 1850–1914', *Women's History Review* 6:4 (1997), pp. 505–525.

214. Connolly, *Religion, law and power*, p. 156.

215. Connolly, 'Religion and society, 1600–1914', p. 88.

216. Compare Andrew R. Holmes, 'The shaping of Irish Presbyterian attitudes to mission, 1790–1840', *Journal of Ecclesiastical History* 57 (2006), pp. 711–37, with Andrew R. Holmes, 'Protestants and "greater Ireland": Mission, migration and identity in the nineteenth century', *Irish Historical Studies* 41:160 (2017), pp. 275–285. See also Myrtle Hill, 'Gender, culture and "the spiritual empire": The Irish protestant female missionary experience', *Women's History Review* 16 (2007), pp. 203–226. For the global influence of Irish Christianity, see the essays contained in Salvador Ryan (ed.) *Treasures of Irish Christianity*, vol. 3: *To the ends of the earth*; Barr, Ireland's empire.

CHAPTER 5

1. D.P. Moran, 'The battle of two civilizations', in Lady Gregory (ed.), *Ideas in Ireland* (London: Unicorn, 1901), p. 29; W.B. Yeats, 'The literary movement in Ireland', in Lady Gregory (ed.), *Ideas in Ireland* (London: Unicorn, 1901), p. 88.

2. Wolf, *An Irish-speaking island*, pp. 181–222, notes that this argument has been over-stated.

3. Æ, 'Nationality and imperialism', in Lady Gregory (ed.), *Ideas in Ireland* (London: Unicorn, 1901), p. 17.

4. Moran, 'The battle of two civilizations', p. 26; *Dictionary of Irish biography*, s.v.

5. Æ, 'Nationality and imperialism', pp. 15, 21; Nicholas Allen, *George Russell (Æ) and the new Ireland, 1905–30* (Dublin: Four Courts, 2003).

6. Editor's note, in Lady Gregory (ed.), *Ideas in Ireland* (London: Unicorn, 1901), p. 64. *Dictionary of Irish biography*, s.v. For more on the millennial theory of the Celtic revivalists, see R.F. Foster, *W. B. Yeats: A life*, vol. 1: *The apprentice mage, 1865–1914* (Oxford: Oxford University Press, 1997), pp. 162–200.

7. Fearghal McGarry, *The rising: Ireland, Easter 1916* (Oxford: Oxford University Press, 2010), p. 24.

8. McGarry, *The rising*, p. 35.

9. *Dictionary of Irish biography*, s.v.

10. Pearse, *Songs of the Irish Rebels*, p. 156.

11. Pearse, *Songs of the Irish Rebels*, pp. 164, 166.

12. Pearse, *Songs of the Irish Rebels*, p. 220.

13. Pearse, *Songs of the Irish Rebels*, p. 221.

14. Pearse, *Songs of the Irish Rebels*, p. 232.

15. Alan Megahey, ' "God will defend the right": The protestant churches and opposition to Home Rule', in D.G. Boyce and Alan O'Day (eds), *Defenders of the union: A survey of British and Irish unionism since 1801* (London: Routledge, 2001), pp. 159–175; A.R. Holmes, 'Presbyterian religion, historiography, and Ulster Scots identity, c. 1800 to 1914', *Historical Journal* 52 (2009), pp. 615–640; Andrew Scholes, *The Church of Ireland and the third Home Rule bill* (Dublin: Irish Academic Press, 2009); Nicola K. Morris, 'Traitors to their faith? Protestant clergy and the Ulster Covenant of 1912', *New Hibernian Review* 15:3 (2011), pp. 16–35.

16. A.T.Q. Stewart, *The Ulster crisis: Resistance to Home Rule, 1912–1914* (London: Faber, 1969), p. 66.

17. Donachie, *Irish Covenanters*, pp. 168, 180–183.

18. McGarry, *The rising*, p. 63.

19. Keith Jeffery, *Ireland and the great war* (Cambridge: Cambridge University Press, 2000), pp. 37–68.

20. 'Poblacht na hÉireann, The Provisional Government of the Irish Republic to the people of Ireland' (1916), single sheet.

21. McGarry, *The rising*, p. 56.

22. McGarry, *The rising*, pp. 1–3.

23. Terence Brown, *The life of W. B. Yeats* (Oxford: Blackwell, 1999), pp. 31–33; *Dictionary of Irish biography*, s.v.; Valeria Jones, *Rebel Prods: The forgotten story of protestant radical nationalists and the 1916 Rising* (Dublin: Ashfield, 2014).

24. David Fitzpatrick, 'Irish consequences of the Great War', *Irish Historical Studies* 39:165 (2015), pp. 643–658.

25. Keith Jeffery, *1916: A global history* (London: Bloomsbury, 2015), pp. 243–271.

26. D.M. Leeson, *The Black and Tans: British police and auxiliaries in the Irish war of independence, 1920–21* (Oxford: Oxford University Press, 2011).

27. Jeffery, *Ireland and the great war*, p. 65.

28. Holmes, *The Irish Presbyterian mind*, p. 30.

29. N. Cunningham and I. Gregory, 'Religious change in twentieth-century Ireland: A spatial history', *Irish Geography* 45:3 (2012), pp. 209–233.

30. J.H. Whyte, *Church and state in modern Ireland, 1923–1970* (Dublin: Gill and Macmillan, 1971), p. 3; Robin Bury, *Buried Lives: The protestants of southern Ireland* (Dublin: History Press, 2017); Ian d'Alton and Ida Milne (eds), *Protestant and Irish: The minority's search for place in independent Ireland* (Cork: Cork University Press, 2019).

31. Peter Brooke, *Ulster Presbyterianism: The historical perspective, 1610–1970*, second edition (Belfast: Athol Books, 1994), p. 201; Alan Megahey, *The Irish protestant churches in the twentieth century* (Basingstoke: Macmillan, 2000).

32. Details of the last episode of 'troubles' may be found in David McKitterick et al., *Lost lives: The stories of the men, women and children who died as a result of the Northern Ireland troubles* (Edinburgh: Mainstream, 2000).

33. The outstanding account of the history of independent Ireland is Diarmaid Ferriter, *The transformation of Ireland* (London: Profile, 2004).

34. *Dictionary of Irish biography*, s.v.

35. John Regan, *Myth and the Irish state* (Dublin: Irish Academic Press, 2014); Mel Farrell, *Party politics in a new democracy: The Irish Free State, 1922–37* (London: Palgrave Macmillan, 2017).

36. Alan F. Parkinson, *Belfast's unholy war: The troubles of the 1920s* (Dublin: Four Courts, 2004), pp. 12–13; A.C. Hepburn, *Catholic Belfast and nationalist Ireland in the era of Joe Devlin, 1871–1934* (Oxford: Oxford University Press, 2008), pp. 232–237.

37. *Dictionary of Irish biography*, s.v.

38. Gemma Clark, *Everyday violence in the Irish civil war* (Cambridge: Cambridge University Press, 2014), p. 3.

39. 'Poblacht na hÉireann, The Provisional Government of the Irish Republic to the people of Ireland', single sheet.

40. Peter Hart, *The I.R.A. and its enemies: Violence and community in Cork, 1916–1923* (Oxford: Oxford University Press, 1999). On the controversy that Hart's claims provoked, see John M. Regan, 'The "Bandon valley massacre" as a historical problem', *History* 97:325 (2012), pp. 70–98; Neil Meehan, 'Uncovering Peter Hart', *Field Day Review* 10 (2014), pp. 102–147; Andy Bielenberg et al., ' "Something of the nature of a massacre?" The Bandon valley killings revisited', *Éire-Ireland* 49 (2014), pp. 7–59.

41. R.B. McCarthy, 'The Church of Ireland in south Tipperary in the twentieth century', *Tipperary Historical Journal* (2007), pp. 145–152; Ian d'Alton, ' "A vestigial population": Perspectives on southern Irish protestants in the twentieth century', *Éire-Ireland* 44 (2009), pp. 9–42; Andy Bielenberg, 'Exodus: The emigration of southern Irish protestants during the War of Independence and Civil War', *Past and Present* 218 (2013), pp. 199–233.

42. Maurice Irvine, *Northern Ireland: Faith and faction* (London: Routledge, 1991), p. 139; Bielenberg, 'Exodus: The emigration of southern Irish protestants during the War of Independence and Civil War', pp. 199–233; David Fitzpatrick, 'Protestant depopulation and the Irish revolution', *Irish Historical Studies* 38:152 (2013), pp. 643–670.

43. Brian Hanley, *The IRA, 1926–1936* (Dublin: Four Courts, 2002), pp. 64–65.

44. The earl of Longford and Thomas P. O'Neill, *Éamon de Valera* (Boston, MA: Houghton Mifflin, 1971), p. xvii.

45. Marie Coleman, *The Irish revolution, 1916–1923* (London: Routledge, 2013).

46. J.J. Barrett, *In the name of the game* (Dublin: Dub Press, 1997); Síle de Cléir, *Popular Catholicism in twentieth-century Ireland: Locality, identity and culture* (London: Bloomsbury, 2017).

47. Maurice Curtis, *A challenge to democracy: Militant Catholicism in modern Ireland* (Dublin: The History Press, 2010), p. 28.

48. Curtis, *A challenge to democracy*, p. 30.

49. Curtis, *A challenge to democracy*, p. 68; *Dictionary of Irish biography*, s.v.; Finola Kennedy, *Frank Duff: A life story* (Dublin: Burns and Oates, 2007).

50. Curtis, *A challenge to democracy*, p. 66.

51. Evelyn Bolster, *The Knights of St Columbanus* (Dublin: Gill and Macmillan, 1979); Curtis, *A challenge to democracy*, p. 53.

52. Curtis, *A challenge to democracy*, p. 80.

53. Curtis, *A challenge to democracy*, pp. 32–33.

54. Curtis, *A challenge to democracy*, p. 82.

55. Harvey O'Brien, *The real Ireland: The evolution of Ireland in documentary film* (Manchester: Manchester University Press, 2004), p. 33; Curtis, *A challenge to democracy*, p. 46.

56. O'Brien, *The real Ireland*, p. 36.

57. Quoted in Michael Cronin, *The Blueshirts and Irish politics* (Dublin: Four Courts, 1997), pp. 188–189.

58. Whyte, *Church and state in modern Ireland*, p. 31.

59. W.B. Yeats, *The Senate speeches of W. B. Yeats*, ed. Donald Pearce (London: Faber, 1961), p. 99.

60. Paul Smith, *The countrywoman* (1961; rpr. London: Penguin, 1989), p. 141.

61. Curtis, *A challenge to democracy*, pp. 63–65.

62. For the culture that inspired these movements, see Whyte, *Church and state in modern Ireland*, pp. 72–74; Enda Delaney, 'Political Catholicism in post-war Ireland: The Revd Denis Fahey and Maria Duce, 1945–54', *Journal of Ecclesiastical History* 52:3 (2001), pp. 487–511; Thomas J. Morrissey, *The Ireland of Edward Cahill, SJ: A secular or a Christian state?* (Dublin: Messenger Publications, 2016).

63. Edward Cahill, *The framework of a Christian state: An introduction to social science* (Dublin: Gill, 1932), p. 664.

64. Cahill, *The framework of a Christian state*, p. xv.

65. Cahill, *The framework of a Christian state*, p. 290.

66. Seán Faughnan, 'The Jesuits and the drafting of the Irish constitution of 1937', *Irish Historical Studies* 26:101 (1988), p. 81.

67. Faughnan, 'The Jesuits and the drafting of the Irish constitution of 1937', p. 82.

68. Cahill, *The framework of a Christian state*, p. 278.

69. *Do cum glóire Dé agus onóra na hÉireann*, title page of Cahill, *The framework of a Christian state*.

70. For a representative sample of titles on the list by 1952, see Paul Blanshard, *The Irish and Catholic power: An American interpretation* (London: Derek Verschoyle, 1954), pp. 95–102.

71. Blanshard, *The Irish and Catholic power*, pp. 108–109; Cahill, *The framework of a Christian state*, p. 349.

72. Enda Delaney, *Demography, state and society: Irish migration to Britain, 1921–1971* (Liverpool: Liverpool University Press, 2000), pp. 74–75.

73. Curtis, *A challenge to democracy*, p. 67.
74. *The need for rural organisation* (Dublin: Muintir nà Tire, 1932), pp. 7–8.
75. Hanley, *The IRA*, p. 70.
76. Curtis, *A challenge to democracy*, pp. 103–104.
77. Curtis, *A challenge to democracy*, p. 118.
78. Fearghal McGarry, *Eoin O'Duffy: A self-made hero* (Oxford: Oxford University Press, 2005), pp. 200–233; Cronin, *The Blueshirts*, pp. 38–68; Curtis, *A challenge to democracy*, p. 115; Donal Coffey, *Drafting the Irish constitution, 1935–1937* (Basingstoke: Palgrave Macmillan, 2018), p. 4; R.M. Douglas, *Architects of the resurrection: Ailtirí na hAiséirghe and the fascist 'new order' in Ireland* (Manchester: Manchester University Press, 2009), p. 9.
79. John Cooney, *John Charles McQuaid: Ruler of Catholic Ireland* (Dublin: O'Brien, 1999), p. 94; Curtis, *A challenge to democracy*, p. 127.
80. Curtis, *A challenge to democracy*, p. 134; Cahill, *The framework of a Christian state*, p. 346.
81. Cooney, *John Charles McQuaid*, pp. 94–106; Curtis, *A challenge to democracy*, p. 132; Coffey, *Drafting the Irish constitution*, p. 19.
82. Cooney, *John Charles McQuaid*, p. 101.
83. Coffey, *Drafting the Irish constitution*, pp. 41–54.
84. Quoted in Coffey, *Drafting the Irish constitution*, p. 47.
85. Cooney, *John Charles McQuaid*, p. 100; Faughnan, 'The Jesuits and the drafting of the Irish constitution of 1937', pp. 79–109; Coffey, *Drafting the Irish constitution*, p. 16.
86. Coffey, *Drafting the Irish constitution*, p. 43.
87. This concept was developed by a Waterford protestant: Benedict Anderson, *Imagined communities: Reflections on the origins and spread of nationalism*, second edition (London: Verso, 1991).
88. Irvine, *Northern Ireland*, pp. 148–149.
89. Curtis, *A challenge to democracy*, p. 132.
90. Janet Egleson Dunleavy and Gareth W. Dunleavy, *Douglas Hyde: A maker of modern Ireland* (Berkeley, CA: University of California Press, 1991).
91. Smith, *The countrywoman*, p. 236; Cooney, *John Charles McQuaid*, pp. 167, 319, 410–412.
92. Irvine, *Northern Ireland*, pp. 145–147, provides statistics showing over-representation of protestants in professional careers in the first few decades of the Free State. Terence Brown, *Ireland: A social and cultural history, 1922–2002*, second edition (London: Harper Perennial, 2004), pp. 91–128; Brian Hanley and Scott Millar, *The lost revolution: The story of the Official IRA and the Workers' Party* (London: Penguin, 2010), pp. 30–69.
93. *Northern Ireland House of Commons Official Report*, vol. 34, col. 1095, 24 April 1934.
94. O'Brien, *The real Ireland*, pp. 61–65.
95. Éamon de Valera, *Speeches and statements, 1917–83*, ed. Maurice Moynihan (Dublin: Gill and Macmillan, 1980), p. 466.
96. Eva Stuart Watt, *Ireland awakening* (Chicago: Moody Press, 1952).

97. Brown, *Ireland*, pp. 159–198; Clair Wills, *That neutral island: A cultural history of Ireland during the Second World War* (London: Faber, 2007); Bryce Evans, *Ireland during the Second World War: Farewell to Plato's Cave* (Manchester: Manchester University Press, 2014).

98. Dunleavy and Dunleavy, *Douglas Hyde*, p. 434; R.F. Foster, *Luck and the Irish: A brief history of change, c. 1970–2000* (London: Allen Lane, 2007), p. 56.

99. Blanshard, *The Irish and Catholic power*, pp. 197–204; Delaney, 'Political Catholicism in post-war Ireland', p. 501.

100. Delaney, 'Political Catholicism in post-war Ireland', pp. 502–507.

101. Delaney, 'Political Catholicism in post-war Ireland', p. 497; Eamonn Dunne, 'Action and reaction: Catholic lay organisations in Dublin in the 1920s and the 1930s', *Archivium Hibernicum* 48 (1994), pp. 107–118.

102. Delaney, 'Political Catholicism in post-war Ireland', p. 498.

103. Douglas, *Architects of the resurrection*, pp. 92–97.

104. *Aiséirge says: The new order in the new Ireland* (Dublin: Ailtirí na hAiséirghe 1944), p. 1.

105. *Aiséirge says*, p. 2, inside back cover.

106. Hanley and Millar, *The lost revolution*, pp. 6, 72.

107. Blanshard, *The Irish and Catholic power*, p. 36.

108. Whyte, *Church and state in modern Ireland*, pp. 196–238.

109. Blanshard, *The Irish and Catholic power*, p. 82; Cooney, *John Charles McQuaid*, p. 275.

110. Catherine O'Connor, 'Mixed marriage, "a grave injury to our church": An account of the 1957 Fethard-on-sea boycott', *History of the Family* 13 (2008), pp. 395–401; David Jameson, 'The religious upbringing of children in "mixed marriages": The evolution of Irish law', *New Hibernia Review* 18:2 (2014), pp. 65–83.

111. Hanley and Millar, *The lost revolution*, pp. 14–15.

112. Elliot, *When God took sides*, p. 233; Robert Tobin, *The minority voice: Hubert Butler and southern Irish protestantism, 1900–1991* (Oxford: Oxford University Press, 2012).

113. Brian Girvin, 'Church, state and society in Ireland since 1960', *Éire-Ireland* 43 (2008), pp. 74–98; Carole Holohan, 'Challenges to social order and Irish identity? Youth culture in the 1960s', *Irish Historical Studies* 38:151 (2013), pp. 389–405; Eleanor O'Leary, *Youth and popular culture in 1950s Ireland* (London: Bloomsbury, 2018); Carole Holohan, *Reframing Irish youth in the sixties* (Liverpool: Liverpool University Press, 2018).

114. Smith, *The countrywoman*, pp. 84, 137.

115. Brown, *Ireland*, pp. 254–296.

116. Foster, *Luck and the Irish*, p. 39.

117. Hanley and Millar, *The lost revolution*, p. 75.

118. Curtis, *A challenge to democracy*, p. 194.

119. Kenny, *Goodbye to Catholic Ireland*, p. 251.

120. Laura Kelly, 'Irishwomen United, the Contraception Action Programme and the feminist campaign for free, safe and legal contraception in Ireland,

c. 1975–81', *Irish Historical Studies* 43:164 (2019), pp. 269–297; Vincent Twomey, *The end of Irish Catholicism?* (Dublin: Veritas, 2002), p. 141.

121. Callum Brown, *The death of Christian Britain: Understanding secularisation, 1800–2000*, second edition (London: Routledge, 2009).

122. Twomey, *The end of Irish Catholicism?*, p. 37; Colin Barr and Hilary M. Carey (eds), *Religion and greater Ireland: Christianity and Irish global networks, 1750–1969* (Kingston, ON: McGill-Queen's University Press, 2015); Fiona Bateman, 'Ireland's spiritual empire: Territory and landscape in Irish Catholic missionary discourse', in Hilary M. Carey (ed.), *Empires of religion* (London: Palgrave Macmillan, 2008), pp. 267–287.

123. Whyte, *Church and state in modern Ireland*, p. 7 n 18.

124. Irvine, *Northern Ireland*, pp. 94–136; Patrick Buckland, 'A protestant state: Unionists in government, 1921–39', in D.G. Boyce and Alan O'Day (eds.), *Defenders of the union: A survey of British and Irish unionism since 1801* (London: Routledge, 2001), pp. 211–226.

125. The 1926 census of Northern Ireland is available at https://www.nisra.gov.uk/publications/1926-census-reports, accessed 12 August 2020.

126. Sean Farren, *The politics of Irish education, 1920–65* (Belfast: Institute of Irish Studies, 1995).

127. Peter Martin, '"Why have a Catholic hospital at all?" The Mater Infirmorum Hospital Belfast and the state, 1883–1972', in Donnacha Seán Lucey and Virginia Crossman (eds), *Healthcare in Ireland and Britain from 1850: Voluntary, relgional and comparative perspectives* (London: Institute for Historical Research, 2014), pp. 101–116.

128. Holmes, *The Irish Presbyterian mind*, p. 30.

129. Matthew Houston, 'Presbyterianism, unionism, and the Second World War in Northern Ireland: The career of James Little, 1939–46', *Irish Historical Studies* 43:164 (2019), p. 256; Norah Bradford, *A sword bathed in heaven: The assassination of Robert Bradford* (London: HarperCollins, 1984); Steve Bruce, *Paisley: Religion and politics in Northern Ireland* (Oxford: Oxford University Press, 2007).

130. Graham Walker, *A history of the Ulster Unionist Party: Protest, pragmatism and pessimism* (Manchester: Manchester University Press, 2004).

131. Irvine, *Northern Ireland*, p. 111.

132. Bruce, *Paisley*, p. 95.

133. Margaret O'Callaghan and Catherine O'Donnell, 'The Northern Ireland government, the "Paisleyite movement" and Ulster Unionism in 1966', *Irish Political Studies* 21 (2006), pp. 203–222.

134. Irvine, *Northern Ireland*, p. 98.

135. Irvine, *Northern Ireland*, pp. 98–100; John Whyte, 'How much discrimination was there under the unionist regime, 1921–68?' in Tom Gallagher and James O'Connell (eds), *Contemporary Irish Studies* (Manchester: Manchester University Press, 1983), pp. 1–35.

136. L.A. Clarkson, *A university in troubled times: Queen's Belfast, 1945–2000* (Dublin: Four Courts, 2004), p. 132.

137. Marianne Elliot, *The Catholics of Ulster: A history* (London: Allen Lane, 2000), p. xxxvii.

138. Bruce, *Paisley*, p. 77.

139. Foster, *Luck and the Irish*, p. 105.

140. Maurice Fitzpatrick, *John Hume in America: From Derry to DC* (Dublin: Irish Academic Press, 2017).

141. Gearóid Ó Faoleán, *A broad church: The Provisional IRA in the Republic of Ireland, 1969–1980* (Dublin: Merrion Press, 2019), p. 29.

142. Foster, *Luck and the Irish*, p. 99; Hanley and Millar, *The lost revolution*, pp. 137–138, 152; Ó Faoleán, *A broad church*, pp. viii–ix.

143. Hanley and Millar, *The lost revolution*, p. 203; Ó Faoleán, *A broad church*, p. 20.

144. Ó Faoleán, *A broad church*, p. 46.

145. Hanley and Millar, *The lost revolution*, p. 174.

146. J.C. Beckett, 'Initiatives in Ireland', letter to the editor, *The Times*, 2 March 1972.

147. Patrick Mitchel, *Evangelicalism and national identity in Ulster 1921–1998* (Oxford: Oxford University Press, 2003); Gladys Ganiel, *Evangelicalism and conflict in Northern Ireland* (Basingstoke: Palgrave Macmillan, 2008).

148. https://www.wesleyjohnston.com/users/ireland/past/troubles/troubles_stats. html, accessed 20 June 2020.

149. Irvine, *Northern Ireland*, p. 128; Elliot, *When God took sides*, p. 49.

150. Crawford Gribben, 'Protestant millennialism, political violence and the Ulster conflict', *Irish Studies Review* 15:1 (2007), pp. 51–63.

151. Chris Anderson, *The Billy Boys: The life and death of LVF leader Billy Wright* (Mainstream, 2002); Martin Dillon, *God and the gun: The church and Irish terrorism* (London: Routledge, 1999).

152. *Dictionary of Irish biography*, s.v.

153. Hanley and Millar, *The lost revolution*, p. 227.

154. Hanley and Millar, *The lost revolution*, pp. 172, 179–180, 213.

155. Foster, *Luck and the Irish*, p. 12.

156. Foster, *Luck and the Irish*, p. 58.

157. Tom Hesketh, *The second partitioning of Ireland: The abortion referendum of 1983* (Dun Laoghaire: Brandsma Books, 1990).

158. Tim Ryan and Jurek Kirakowski, *Ballinspittle: Moving statues and faith* (Dublin: Mercier, 1985); Chris Eipper, 'Moving statues and moving images: Religious artefacts and the spiritualisation of materiality', *The Australian Journal of Anthropology* 18:3 (2007), pp. 253–263.

159. Irvine, *Northern Ireland*, p. 133.

160. Foster, *Luck and the Irish*, pp. 37–66.

161. Begoña Aretxaga, *Shattering silence: Women, nationalism and political subjectivity* (Princeton, NJ: Princeton University Press, 1996), p. 115.

162. Alan Acheson, *A history of the Church of Ireland, 1691–2001*, second edition (Dublin: APCK, 2002), p. 239.

163. Irvine, *Northern Ireland*, p. 125.

164. Foster, *Luck and the Irish*, p. 61; Ó Faoleán, *A broad church*, p. 152.

165. *Dictionary of Irish biography*, s.v.

166. Twomey, *The end of Irish Catholicism?*, p. 146.

167. Joshua Searle, *The scarlet woman and the red hand: Evangelical apocalyptic belief in the Northern Ireland troubles* (Eugene, OR: Pickwick, 2014), pp. 129–178.

168. Elliot, *When God took sides*, p. 17.

169. Stewart, *The shape of Irish history*, pp. 180, 182–185.

CONCLUSION

1. Foster, *Luck and the Irish*, pp. 61–63; *Father, son and the housekeeper* (dir. Alison Millar, 2008).

2. Michael J. Breen and Caillin Reynolds, 'The rise of secularism and the decline of religiosity in Ireland: The pattern of religious change in Europe', *International Journal of Religion and Spirituality in Society* 1 (2011), pp. 195–212.

3. Bruce, *Paisley*, p. 59.

4. Connolly, *Priests and people in pre-famine Ireland*, p. 102.

5. Ferriter, *The transformation of Ireland*, pp. 341–342, 420–423, 666, 714.

6. Ferriter, *The transformation of Ireland*, p. 736; Liam Collins, 'Brendan Smyth's evil deeds can never be forgotten', *Irish Independent* 23 July 2017, available at https://www.independent.ie/irish-news/brendan-smyths-evil-deeds-can-never-be-forgotten-35958053.html, accessed 20 June 2020.

7. Brendan Boland, *Sworn to silence* (London: Random House, 2014); Gerry Moriarty, 'Cardinal Brady part of process which "silenced" abuse victim', *Irish Times* 20 January 2017, available at https://www.irishtimes.com/news/ireland/irish-news/cardinal-brady-part-of-process-which-silenced-abuse-victim-1.2945594, accessed 20 June 2020; Collins, 'Brendan Smyth's evil deeds can never be forgotten'; 'Summary of clerical sex abuse scandals in Ireland', *Belfast Telegraph* 24 August 2018, available at https://www.belfasttelegraph.co.uk/news/republic-of-ireland/summary-of-clerical-sex-abuse-scandals-in-ireland-37248116.html, accessed 20 June 2020.

8. Patsy McGarry, 'Religious congregations yet to fully honour compensation deals', *Irish Times* 11 May 2019, available at https://www.irishtimes.com/news/social-affairs/religion-and-beliefs/religious-congregations-yet-to-fully-honour-compensation-deals-1.3887870, accessed 20 June 2020.

9. Catriona Crowe, 'The Ferns Report', *Éire-Ireland* 43 (2008), pp. 50–73.

10. Luke Byrne, 'From rising star of Church to defrocked priest plagued by allegations of sex abuse', *Irish Independent* 4 August 2016, available at https://www.independent.ie/irish-news/from-rising-star-of-church-to-defrocked-priest-plagued-by-allegations-of-sex-abuse-34937398.html, accessed 20 June 2020.

11. On the history of these institutions, see James M. Smith, *Ireland's Magdalene Laundries and the nation's architecture of containment* (South Bend, IN: University of Notre Dame Press, 2007); Eoin O'Sullivan and Ian O'Donnell (eds), *Coercive confinements in post-independence Ireland: Patients, prisoners and penitents* (Manchester: Manchester University Press, 2012).

12. The National Board for Safeguarding Children in the Catholic Church, *Annual Report 2009*, p. 5, available at https://www.safeguarding.ie/images/Article_Images/NBSCCC_Report_2009.pdf, accessed 20 June 2020.

13. 'Pastoral letter of the Holy Father Pope Benedict XVI to the Catholics of Ireland', available at http://www.vatican.va/content/benedict-xvi/en/letters/2010/documents/hf_ben-xvi_let_20100319_church-ireland.html, accessed 20 June 2020.

14. Juno McEnroe, 'We did not just hide away the dead bodies of tiny human beings, we dug deep and deeper still to bury our compassion, our mercy', *Irish Examiner* 8 March 2017, available at https://www.irishexaminer.com/ireland/we-did-not-just-hide-away-the-dead-bodies-of-tiny-human-beings-we-dug-deep-and-deeper-still-to-bury-our-compassion-our-mercy-444626.html, accessed 20 June 2020.

15. 'Enda Kenny speech on Cloyne Report', *RTÉ News* 20 July 2011, available at https://www.rte.ie/news/2011/0720/303965-cloyne1/, accessed 20 June 2020.

16. Gladys Ganiel, *Transforming post-Catholic Ireland: Religious practice in late modernity* (Oxford: Oxford University Press, 2016).

17. 'Irish census (2016)', *Faith Survey*, available at https://faithsurvey.co.uk/irish-census.html, accessed 20 June 2020.

18. Brad S. Gregory, *The unintended reformation: How a religious revolution secularised society* (Cambridge, MA: Belknap Press of Harvard University Press, 2015).

19. 'Irish census (2016)', *Faith Survey*, available at https://faithsurvey.co.uk/irish-census.html, accessed 2 September 2019.

20. Patsy McGarry, 'Further drop in seminarians entering St Patrick's College, Maynooth', *Irish Times* 5 October 2018, available at https://www.irishtimes.com/news/social-affairs/religion-and-beliefs/further-drop-in-seminarians-entering-st-patrick-s-college-maynooth-1.3653247, accessed 20 June 2020; Michael Kelly, 'End of era as Rome's Irish College shuts as seminary after nearly 400 years...for now', *The Irish Catholic* 18 June 2020, available at https://www.irishcatholic.com/end-of-era-as-romes-irish-college-shuts-as-seminary-after-nearly-400-yearsfor-now/, accessed 20 June 2020.

21. Sorcha Pollak, 'Organiser "guesstimates" turnout of 200,000 for papal Mass', *The Irish Times* 27 August 2018, available at https://www.irishtimes.com/news/social-affairs/religion-and-beliefs/papal-visit/organiser-guesstimates-turnout-of-200-000-for-papal-mass-1.3609073, accessed 20 June 2020.

22. Mary Cagney, 'Ireland's evangelical moment', *Christianity Today* 13 March 2007, available at http://www.christianitytoday.com/ct/2007/april/7.21.html, accessed 20 June 2020.

23. Distinguished contributions included Daniel J. O'Leary, *Lost soul? The Catholic Church today* (Dublin: Columba Press, 1999); Louise Fuller, *Irish Catholicism since 1950: The undoing of a culture* (Dublin: Gill and Macmillan, 2002); Raymond Murray, 'A new Ireland in a new Europe', *Irish Theological Quarterly* 69:2 (2004), pp. 189–201; Twomey, *The end of Irish Catholicism?*; Niall Coll and Paschal Scallon

(eds), *A church with a future? Challenges to Irish Catholicism today* (Dublin: Columba Press, 2005); Diarmiad Ó Catháin, 'When a priest is accused of a crime', *Irish Theological Quarterly* 70:4 (2005), pp. 367–374.

24. 'Irish census (2016)', *Faith Survey*, available at https://faithsurvey.co.uk/irish-census.html, accessed 2 September 2019.

25. Crawford Gribben, 'The future of Northern Ireland: What is going wrong?' *Foreign Policy Research Institute* blog 23 August 2017, available at https://www.fpri.org/article/2017/08/future-northern-ireland-going-wrong/, accessed 20 June 2020; Simon Doyle, 'Review into why protestant boys do worse at school will be "meaningless" unless followed up by action', *Irish News* 20 January 2020, available at https://www.irishnews.com/news/northernireland-news/2020/01/20/news/new-review-into-why-protestant-boys-do-worse-at-school-will-be-meaningless-unless-followed-up-by-action-1818408/, accessed 20 June 2020.

26. 'Statement by the Catholic bishops in Northern Ireland in advance of the Assembly election on 2 March 2017', *Diocese of Down & Connor* 22 February 2017, available at http://www.downandconnor.org/press_office/press-releases/statement-catholic-bishops-northern-ireland-advance-assembly-election-2-march-2017/, accessed 20 June 2020.

27. 'Abortion debate: Bloody Sunday relative Liam Wray votes for TUV on abortion', available at https://www.bbc.co.uk/news/uk-northern-ireland-foyle-west-37796888, accessed 20 June 2020.

28. 'Irish census (2016)', *Faith Survey*, available at https://faithsurvey.co.uk/irish-census.html, accessed 2 September 2019.

29. Whelan, *Religion, landscape and settlement in Ireland*, p. 230.

30. Gerard Howlin, 'Abortion is the final nail in our old identity's coffin: Who are we now?' *The Irish Examiner* 2 January 2019, available at https://www.irishexaminer.com/breakingnews/views/abortion-is-the-final-nail-in-our-old-identitys-coffin-who-are-we-now-895034.html#.Xu3i9iFg6cw.gmail, accessed 20 June 2020; Joe Cleary, 'The Catholic twilight?' in Eamon Maher and Eugene O'Brien (eds), *Tracing the cultural legacy of Irish Catholicism: From Galway to Cloyne and beyond* (Manchester: Manchester University Press, 2017), pp. 209–225.

31. Luke 12:32; Jacques Ellul, *The subversion of Christianity*, trans. Geoffrey W. Bromiley (Grand Rapids, MI: Eerdmans, 1986).

32. 1 John 3:8.

33. William Kelly, *An exposition of the epistle to the Hebrews* (London: T. Weston, 1905), p. 196.

34. Galatians 1:7–9.

35. Galatians 5:4.

36. Galatians 1:4, 2:16.

37. Galatians 3:27–28, 5:13.

38. Twomey, *The end of Irish Catholicism?*, p. 67.

39. Wayne O'Connor, 'Simon Harris under fire for backing Amnesty despite abortion donation dispute', *Irish Times* 11 April 2018, available at https://www.independent.ie/irish-news/abortion-referendum/simon-harris-under-fire-for-backing-amnesty-despite-abortion-donation-dispute-36796015.html, accessed 20 June 2020.
40. Ingo Cornils, '"The struggle continues": Rudi Dutschke's long march', in Gerard J. DeGroot (ed.), *Student protest: The sixties and after* (London: Addison Wesley Longman, 1998), pp. 100–114.
41. '"Catholic majority possible" in NI by 2021', *BBC News* 19 April 2018, available at https://www.bbc.co.uk/news/uk-northern-ireland-43823506, accessed 20 June 2020; Freya McClements, 'North returns more nationalist than unionist MPs for first time', *Irish Times* 13 December 2019, available at https://www.irishtimes.com/news/politics/north-returns-more-nationalist-than-unionist-mps-for-first-time-1.4114260, accessed 20 June 2020.
42. Irish Inter Church Meeting, 'Removal of blasphemy from the Constitution of Ireland', 31 October 2013, available at https://www.irishchurches.org/news-blog/919/removal-of-blasphemy-from-the, accessed 20 June 2020.
43. 'Preamble', *Bunreacht na hÉireann, Constitution of Ireland*.
44. @DavQuinn, 28 May 2018. I am grateful to David Quinn for his permission to cite this tweet. Similar proposals were discussed in, for example, Patrick Hannon, 'Religion, the constitution, and the new Ireland', *Irish Theological Quarterly* 74:3 (2009), pp. 258–271.
45. See, for example, Stanley Hauerwas and William H. Willimon, *Resident aliens: Life in the Christian colony* (Nashville, TN: Abingdon Press, 1989); Stanley Hauerwas, *After Christendom: How the church is to behave if freedom, justice and a Christian nation are bad ideas* (Nashville, TN: Abingdon Press, 1991).
46. Alasdair MacIntyre, *After virtue*, third edition (London: Bloomsbury, 2007), p. 305.
47. Twomey, *The end of Irish Catholicism?*, p. 12.

Bibliography

MANUSCRIPTS

TCD MS 815, fol. 322r, Deposition of John Fortune, 21 June 1643.
TCD MS 833, fol. 282v, Deposition of Audrey Carington, 27 October 1645.
TCD MS 836, ff. 101r–105v, Deposition of Elizabeth Price, 26 June 1643.
TCD MS 837, fol. 36v, Deposition of Peter Hill, 29 May 1645.
TCD MS 838, ff. 3r–4v, Deposition of Arthur Gore, 3 June 1644.
TCD MS 838, ff. 5r–6v, Deposition of Theophilus Jones, 3 June 1644.
TCD MS 838, ff. 9r–10v, Deposition of Randall Domville, 3 June 1644.

PUBLISHED MATERIAL

'Abortion debate: Bloody Sunday relative Liam Wray votes for TUV on abortion', available at https://www.bbc.co.uk/news/uk-northern-ireland-foyle-west-37796888, accessed 20 June 2020.

Abrams, Lesley, 'The conversion of the Scandinavians of Dublin', *Anglo-Norman Studies* 20 (1997), pp. 1–29.

Acheson, Alan, *A history of the Church of Ireland, 1691–2001*, second edition (Dublin: APCK, 2002).

Adomnán of Iona, *Life of St Columba*, trans. Richard Sharpe (London: Penguin, 1995).

Æ [George Russell], 'Nationality and imperialism', in Lady Gregory (ed.), *Ideas in Ireland* (London: Unicorn, 1901), pp. 25–44.

Æ [George Russell], 'Conversion and the church in Viking-age Dublin', in John Sheehan and Donnchadh Ó Corráin (eds), *The Viking age: Ireland and the west* (Dublin: Four Courts, 2010), pp. 1–10.

Aiséirge says: The new order in the new Ireland (Dublin: Ailtirí na hAiséirghe, 1944).

Aitchison, N.B., *Armagh and the royal centres in early medieval Ireland: Monuments, cosmology and the past* (Woodbridge, UK: Boydell and Brewer, 1994).

Akenson, Donald, *Small differences: Irish Catholics and Irish protestants, 1815–1922* (Kingston, ON: McGill-Queen's University Press, 1998).

Allen, Nicholas, *George Russell (Æ) and the new Ireland, 1905–30* (Dublin: Four Courts, 2003).

Anderson, Benedict, *Imagined communities: Reflections on the origins and spread of nationalism*, second edition (London: Verso, 1991).

Anderson, Chris, *The Billy Boys: The life and death of LVF leader Billy Wright* (Edinburgh: Mainstream, 2002).

Andrews, John H., 'The mapping of Ireland's cultural landscape, 1550–1630', in Patrick J. Duffy, David Edwards, and Elizabeth Fitzpatrick (eds), *Gaelic Ireland, c.1250–c.1650: Land, lordship and settlement* (Dublin: Four Courts, 2004), pp. 153–180.

Aretxaga, Begoña, *Shattering silence: Women, nationalism and political subjectivity* (Princeton, NJ: Princeton University Press, 1996).

Armstrong, Robert, *Protestant war: The 'British' of Ireland and the wars of the three kingdoms* (Manchester: Manchester University Press, 2005).

Armstrong, Robert, 'The Scots of Ireland and the English Republic, 1649–60', in David Edwards and Simon Egan (eds), *The Scots in early Stuart Ireland: Union and separation in two kingdoms* (Manchester: Manchester University Press, 2015), pp. 251–278.

Augustine, *Confessions*, trans. R.S. Pine-Coffin (London: Penguin, 1961).

'The awakening in Ulster', *Things New and Old* 2 (1859), pp. 163–166.

Barnard, T.C., *A new anatomy of Ireland: The Irish protestants, 1649–1770* (New Haven, CT: Yale University Press, 2003).

Barnard, T.C., *Cromwellian Ireland: English government and reform in Ireland, 1649–1660*, second edition (Oxford: Oxford University Press, 2000).

Barnard, T.C., 'Edmund Spencer, Edmund Spenser and the problems of Irish protestants in the mid-eighteenth century', in T.C. Barnard, *Irish protestant ascents and descents, 1641–1770* (Dublin: Four Courts, 2004), pp. 290–305.

Barnard, T.C., 'Identities, ethnicity and tradition among Irish dissenters, c. 1650–1750', in Kevin Herlihy (ed.), *The Irish dissenting tradition, 1650–1750* (Dublin: Four Courts, 1995), pp. 29–48.

Barnard, T.C., 'Protestants and the Irish language, c. 1675–1725', in T.C. Barnard, *Irish protestant ascents and descents, 1641–1770* (Dublin: Four Courts, 2004), pp. 179–207.

Barnard, T.C., 'Reforming Irish manners: The religious societies in Dublin during the 1690s', in T.C. Barnard, *Irish protestant ascents and descents, 1641–1770* (Dublin: Four Courts, 2004), pp. 143–178.

Barnard, T.C., 'The protestant interest, 1641–1660', in Jane Ohlmeyer (ed.), *Ireland from independence to occupation, 1641–1660* (Cambridge: Cambridge University Press, 1995), pp. 218–240.

Barnard, T.C., 'The government and Irish dissent, 1704–1780', in Kevin Herlihy (ed.), *The politics of Irish dissent, 1650–1800* (Dublin: Four Courts, 1997), pp. 9–27.

Barnard, T.C., 'The uses of the 23rd October 1641 and Irish protestant celebrations', in T.C. Barnard, *Irish protestant ascents and descents, 1641–1770* (Dublin: Four Courts, 2004), pp. 111–142.

Barr, C.C.P., 'The re-energising of Catholicism, 1815–1880', in Tom Bartlett and James Kelly (eds), *The Cambridge history of Ireland: 1730–1880*, vol. 3 (Cambridge: Cambridge University Press, 2018), pp. 280–304.

Barr, C.C.P., *Ireland's empire: The Roman Catholic Church in the English-speaking world, 1829–1914* (Cambridge: Cambridge University Press, 2020).

Barr, Colin, and Hilary M. Carey (eds), *Religion and greater Ireland: Christianity and Irish global networks, 1750–1969* (Kingston, ON: McGill-Queen's University Press, 2015).

Barrett, J.J., *In the name of the game* (Dublin: Dub Press, 1997).

Bartlett, Thomas, *The fall and rise of the Irish nation: The Catholic question, 1690–1830* (Dublin: Gill and Macmillan, 1992).

Bartlett, Thomas, *Ireland: A history* (Cambridge: Cambridge University Press, 2010).

Bateman, Fiona, 'Ireland's spiritual empire: Territory and landscape in Irish Catholic missionary discourse', in Hilary M. Carey (ed.), *Empires of religion* (London: Palgrave Macmillan, 2008), pp. 267–287.

Beckett, J.C., *Protestant dissent in Ireland, 1687–1780* (London: Faber and Faber, 1948).

Beckett, J.C., 'Initiatives in Ireland', letter to the editor, *The Times*, 2 March 1972.

Bede, *Ecclesiastical history of the English people*, trans. Leo Sherley-Price, ed. D. H Farmer (London: Penguin, 1990).

Beiner, Guy, *Forgetful remembrance: Social forgetting and vernacular historiography of a rebellion in Ulster* (Oxford: Oxford University Press, 2018).

Bhreathnach, Edel, 'The mendicant orders and vernacular Irish learning in the late medieval period', *Irish Historical Studies* 37:147 (2011), pp. 357–375.

Bhreathnach, Edel, 'Communities and their landscapes', in Brendan Smith (ed.), *The Cambridge history of Ireland*, vol. 1: *600–1550* (Cambridge: Cambridge University Press, 2018), pp. 15–46.

Bielenberg, Andy, 'Exodus: The emigration of southern Irish protestants during the War of Independence and Civil War', *Past and Present* 218 (2013), pp. 199–233.

Bielenberg, Andy, John Borgonovo, and James S. Donnelly, ' "Something of the nature of a massacre": The Bandon valley killings revisited', *Éire-Ireland* 49 (2014), pp. 7–59.

Bieler, Ludwig, 'The problem of "Silua Focluti" ', *Irish Historical Studies* 3:12 (1943), pp. 351–364.

Binchy, D.A., 'Patrick and his biographers', *Studia Hibernica* 2 (1962), pp. 7–173.

Bishop, Hilary Joyce, 'Memory and legend: Recollections of penal times in Irish folklore', *Folklore* 129:1 (2018), pp. 18–38.

Bitel, Lisa, *Isle of the saints: Monastic settlement and Christian community in early Ireland* (Ithaca, NY: Cornell University Press, 1990).

Blanshard, Paul, *The Irish and Catholic power: An American interpretation* (London: Derek Verschoyle, 1954).

Bober, Phyllis Fray, reviewing Réne Magnen, *Epona, Déesse Gauloise des Chevaux, Protectrice des Cavaliers*, in *American Journal of Archaeology* 62:3 (July 1958), pp. 349–350.

Boland, Brendan, *Sworn to silence* (London: Random House, 2014).

Bolster, Evelyn, *The Knights of St Columbanus* (Dublin: Gill and Macmillan, 1979).

Bonner, Ali, *The myth of Pelagianism* (Oxford: Oxford University Press, 2018).

Booker, Sparky, 'Intermarriage in fifteenth-century Ireland: The English and Irish in the "four obedient shires" ', *Transactions of the Royal Irish Academy* 113C (2013), pp. 219–250.

Booker, Sparky, 'Irish clergy and the diocesan church in the "four obedient shires" of Ireland, c. 1400–c. 1540', *Irish Historical Studies* 39: 154 (2014), pp. 179–209.

Booker, Sparky, *Cultural exchange and identity in late medieval Ireland: The English and Irish of the four obedient shires* (Cambridge: Cambridge University Press, 2018).

Boran, Elizabethanne, 'An early friendship network of James Ussher, archbishop of Armagh, 1626–1656', in H.H.W. Robinson-Hammerstein (ed.), *European universities in the age of reformation* (Dublin: Four Courts, 1998), pp. 116–134.

Boran, Elizabethanne, 'Education and dissemination of the word: A Baptist library in the eighteenth century', in Kevin Herlihy (ed.), *Propagating the word of Irish dissent, 1650–1800* (Dublin: Four Courts, 1998), pp. 114–131.

Borsje, Jacqueline, Ann Dooley, Séamus Mac Mathúna, and Gregory Toner (eds), *Celtic cosmology: Perspectives from Ireland and Scotland*, Papers in Mediaeval Studies 26 (Toronto: Pontifical Institute of Mediaeval Studies, 2014).

Bossy, John, *Christianity in the west, 1400–1700* (Oxford: Oxford University Press, 1985).

Bottigheimer, Karl, 'The failure of the reformation in Ireland: *Une question bien posée*', *Journal of Ecclesiastical History* 36 (1985), pp. 196–207.

Bourke, Angela, *The burning of Bridget Cleary* (London: Pimlico, 1999).

Bowen, Desmond, *The protestant crusade in Ireland, 1800–70* (Dublin: Gill and Macmillan, 1978).

Bower, Walter, *Scotichronicon*, ed. Norman F. Shead, 9 vols (Edinburgh: Aberdeen University Press, 1987–1998).

Boyce, D. George, *Nationalism in Ireland*, third edition (London: Routledge, 1991).

Bradford, Norah, *A sword bathed in heaven: The assassination of Robert Bradford* (London: HarperCollins, 1984).

Bradshaw, Brendan, *The dissolution of the monastic orders in Ireland in the reign of Henry VIII* (Cambridge: Cambridge University Press, 1976).

Bradshaw, Brendan, *The Irish constitutional revolution of the sixteenth century* (Cambridge: Cambridge University Press, 1979).

Bradshaw, Brendan, 'Nationalism and historical scholarship in modern Ireland', *Irish Historical Studies* 26 (1989), pp. 329–351.

Bradshaw, Brendan, *'And so began the Irish nation': Nationality, national consciousness and nationalism in pre-modern Ireland* (Farnham, UK: Ashgate, 2015).

Brady, W. Maziere, *State papers concerning the Irish church* (London: Longmans, Green, Reader, and Dyer, 1868).

Breatnach, Liam, '*Cétmuinter*: The Old Irish term for spouse and its interpretation', in Salvador Ryan (ed.), *Marriage and the Irish: A miscellany* (Dublin: Wordwell Press, 2019), pp. 7–9.

Breen, Colin, 'The maritime cultural landscape in medieval Gaelic Ireland', in Patrick J. Duffy, David Edwards, and Elizabeth Fitzpatrick (eds), *Gaelic Ireland, c. 1250–c. 1650: Land, lordship and settlement* (Dublin: Four Courts, 2004), pp. 418–433.

Breen, Michael J., and Caillin Reynolds, 'The rise of secularism and the decline of religiosity in Ireland: The pattern of religious change in Europe', *International Journal of Religion and Spirituality in Society* 1 (2011), pp. 195–212.

Bremer, Francis J., *John Winthrop: American's forgotten Founding Father* (Oxford: Oxford University Press, 2015).

Brooke, Peter, *Ulster Presbyterianism: The historical perspective, 1610–1970*, second edition (Belfast: Athol Books, 1994).

Brown, Callum, *The death of Christian Britain: Understanding secularisation, 1800–2000*, second edition (London: Routledge, 2009).

Brown, Michael, *Francis Hutcheson in Dublin* (Dublin: Four Courts, 2002).

Brown, Michael, *The Irish Enlightenment* (Cambridge, MA: Harvard University Press, 2016).

Brown, Michelle P., *Art of the islands: Celtic, Pictish, Anglo-Saxon and Viking visual culture c. 450–1050* (Oxford: Bodleian Library, 2016).

Brown, Peter, *Through the eye of a needle: Wealth, the fall of Rome, and the making of Christianity in the west, 350–550 AD* (Princeton, NJ: Princeton University Press, 2014).

Brown, S.J., 'The new reformation movement in the Church of Ireland, 1801–1829', in S. Brown and D. Miller (eds), *Piety and power in Ireland, 1760–1960: Essays in honour of Emmet Larkin* (Belfast: Institute of Irish Studies, 2000), pp. 180–208.

Brown, S.J., *The national churches of England, Ireland and Scotland, 1801–1846* (Oxford: Oxford University Press, 2001).

Brown, Terence, *The life of W. B. Years* (Oxford: Blackwell, 1999).

Brown, Terence, *Ireland: A social and cultural history, 1922–2002*, second edition (London: Harper Perennial, 2004).

Browne, Martin, and Colmán Ó Clabaigh, 'Introduction', in Martin Browne and Colmán Ó Clabaigh (eds), *Soldiers of Christ: The Knights Templar and the Knights Hospitaller in medieval Ireland* (Dublin: Four Courts, 2016), pp. xvii–xxi.

Browne, Martin, and Colmán Ó Clabaigh (eds), *Households of God: The Regular Canons and Canonesses of St Augustine and of Prémontré in Medieval Ireland* (Dublin: Four Courts, 2019).

Brożyna, Andrea Ebel, 'The right to labour, love, and pray: The creation of the ideal Christian woman in Ulster Roman Catholic and protestant religious literature, 1850–1914', *Women's History Review* 6:4 (1997), pp. 505–525.

Brożyna, Andrea Ebel, *Labour, love and prayer: Female piety in Ulster religious literature, 1850–1914* (Kingston, ON: McGill-Queen's University Press, 1998).

Bruce, F.F., *The epistle to the Galatians: A commentary on the Greek text*, New International Greek Testament Commentary (Grand Rapids, MI: Eerdmans, 1982).

Bruce, James, *Prophecy, miracles, angels, and heavenly light? The eschatology, pneumatology, and missiology of Adomnán's Life of St. Columba* (Carlisle: Paternoster, 2004).

Bruce, Steve, *Paisley: Religion and politics in Northern Ireland* (Oxford: Oxford University Press, 2007).

Brynn, Edward, *The Church of Ireland in the age of Catholic emancipation* (New York: Garland, 1982).

Buckland, Patrick, 'A protestant state: Unionists in government, 1921–39', in D.G. Boyce and Alan O'Day (eds), *Defenders of the union: A survey of British and Irish unionism since 1801* (London: Routledge, 2001), pp. 211–226.

Bury, Robin, *Buried Lives: The protestants of southern Ireland* (Dublin: History Press, 2017).

Byrne, Luke, 'From rising star of Church to defrocked priest plagued by allegations of sex abuse', *Irish Independent* 4 August 2016, available at https://www.independent.ie/irish-news/from-rising-star-of-church-to-defrocked-priest-plagued-by-allegations-of-sex-abuse-34937398.html, accessed 20 June 2020.

Caball, Marc, 'Religion, culture and the bardic elite in early modern Ireland', in Alan Ford and James McCafferty (eds), *The origins of sectarianism in early modern Ireland* (Cambridge: Cambridge University Press, 2005), pp. 158–181.

Caesar, *The Gallic war*, trans. H.J. Edwards, The Loeb Classical Library (London: Heinemann, 1917).

Cagney, Mary, 'Ireland's evangelical moment', *Christianity Today* 13 March 2007, available at http://www.christianitytoday.com/ct/2007/april/7.21.html, accessed 20 June 2020.

Cahill, Edward, *The framework of a Christian state: An introduction to social science* (Dublin: Gill, 1932).

Cahill, Thomas, *How the Irish saved civilisation* (New York: Doubleday, 1995).

Calendar of the State Papers relating to Ireland…1625–30, ed. R.P. Mahaffy (London, 1900).

Callan, Maeve Brigid, *The Templars, the witch, and the wild Irish: Vengeance and heresy in medieval Ireland* (New York: Cornell University Press, 2015).

Campbell, Ian W.S., 'Truth and calumny in Baroque Rome: Richard O'Ferrall and the *Commentarius Rinuccinianus*, 1648–1667', *Irish Historical Studies* 38:150 (2012), pp. 211–229.

Campbell, Ian W.S., *Renaissance humanism and ethnicity before race: The Irish and the English in the seventeenth century* (Manchester: Manchester University Press, 2013).

Campbell, Ian W.S., 'Calvinist absolutism: Archbishop James Ussher and royal power', *Journal of British Studies* 53:3 (2014), pp. 588–610.

Canny, Nicholas, 'Why the reformation failed in Ireland: *Une question mal posée*', *Journal of Ecclesiastical History* 30 (1979), pp. 423–450.

Canny, Nicholas, *Making Ireland British, 1580–1650* (Oxford: Oxford University Press, 2001).

Carew, Mairead, *The quest for the Irish Celt: The Harvard Archaeological Mission to Ireland, 1932–1936* (Newbridge: Irish Academic Press, 2018).

Carey, John, 'Saint Patrick, the druids, and the end of the world', *History of Religions* 36:1 (1996), pp. 42–53.

Carey, John, 'The Old Gods of Ireland in the later middle ages', in Katja Ritari and Alexandra Bergholm (eds), *Understanding religion: Revisiting the pagan past* (Cardiff: University of Wales Press, 2015), pp. 51–68.

Carey, John, 'Learning, imagination and belief', in Brendan Smith (ed.), *The Cambridge history of Ireland*, vol. 1: *600–1550* (Cambridge: Cambridge University Press, 2018), pp. 47–75.

Carey, Vincent, ' "Neither good English nor good Irish": Bi-lingualism and identity formation in sixteenth-century Ireland', in Hiram Morgan (ed.), *Political ideology in Ireland, 1541–1641* (Dublin: Four Courts, 1999), pp. 45–61.

Carroll, Michael P., *Irish pilgrimage: Holy wells and popular Catholic devotion* (Baltimore, MD: Johns Hopkins University Press, 1999).

Cassidy, L.M., Rui Martiniano, Eileen Murphy, Matthew D. Teasdale, James Mallory, Barrie Hartwell, and Daniel G. Bradley, 'Neolithic and Bronze Age migration to Ireland and establishment of the insular Atlantic genome', *Proceedings of the National Academy of Sciences of the United States of America* 113 (2016), pp. 368–373.

Cassidy, Lara M., Ros Ó Maoldúin, Thomas Kador, Ann Lynch, Carleton Jones, Peter C. Woodman, et al., 'A dynastic elite in monumental Neolithic society', *Nature* 582 (2020), pp. 384–388.

' "Catholic majority possible" in NI by 2021', *BBC News* 19 April 2018, available at https://www.bbc.co.uk/news/uk-northern-ireland-43823506, accessed 20 June 2020.

Census of Ireland, 1871: Part III: General report (Dublin: Alexander Thom, 1876).

Census of Ireland, 1911: Province of Ulster: Area, houses, and population; also the ages, civil or conjugal condition, occupations, birthplaces, religion, and education of the people (London: HMSO, 1912).

Chadwick, Henry, *The early Church* (London: Penguin, 1993).

Charles-Edwards, T.M., *Early Christian Ireland* (Cambridge: Cambridge University Press, 2000).

Charles-Edwards, T.M., 'Prehistoric and early Ireland', in Dáibhí Ó Cróinín (ed.), *A new history of Ireland*, vol. 1: *Prehistoric and early Ireland* (Oxford: Oxford University Press, 2005), pp. lvii–lxxx.

Childs, John, 'The laws of war in seventeenth-century Europe and their application during the Jacobite War in Ireland, 1688–91', in David Edwards et al. (eds), *Age of atrocity: Violence and political conflict in early modern Ireland* (Dublin: Four Courts, 2007), pp. 283–300.

Clark, Gemma, *Everyday violence in the Irish civil war* (Cambridge: Cambridge University Press, 2014).

Clarke, Aidan, *Prelude to Restoration in Ireland: The end of the Commonwealth, 1659–1660* (Cambridge: Cambridge University Press, 1999).

Clarke, Howard B., '*Quo vadis*? Mapping the Irish "monastic town"', in Seán Duffy (ed.), *Princes, prelates and poets in medieval Ireland: Essays in honour of Katherine Simms* (Dublin: Four Courts, 2013), pp. 261–278.

Clarke, Howard B., Ruth Johnston, and Sheila Dooley, *Dublin and the Viking world* (Dublin: O'Brien Press, 2018).

Clarkson, L.A., *A university in troubled times: Queen's Belfast, 1945–2000* (Dublin: Four Courts, 2004).

Clarkson, Tim, *Columba* (Edinburgh: John Donald, 2011).

Cleary, Joe, 'The Catholic twilight?' in Eamon Maher and Eugene O'Brien (eds), *Tracing the cultural legacy of Irish Catholicism: From Galway to Cloyne and beyond* (Manchester: Manchester University Press, 2017), pp. 209–225.

Coad, Roy, *A history of the Brethren movement* (Carlisle: Paternoster, 1976).

Coffey, Donal, *Drafting the Irish constitution, 1935–1937* (Basingstoke: Palgrave Macmillan, 2018).

Coffey, John, 'Puritanism and liberty revisited: The case for toleration in the English revolution', *Historical Journal* 41:4 (1998), pp. 961–985.

Coffey, John, *Persecution and toleration in protestant England, 1558–1689* (London: Pearson, 2000).

Coleman, Marie, *The Irish revolution, 1916–1923* (London: Routledge, 2013).

Coll, Niall, and Paschal Scallon (eds), *A church with a future? Challenges to Irish Catholicism today* (Dublin: Columba Press, 2005).

Collins, Liam, 'Brendan Smyth's evil deeds can never be forgotten', *Irish Independent* 23 July 2017, available at https://www.independent.ie/irish-news/brendan-smyths-evil-deeds-can-never-be-forgotten-35958053.html, accessed 20 June 2020.

Connolly, Hugh, *The Irish penitentials and their significance for the sacrament of penance today* (Dublin: Four Courts, 1995).

Connolly, S.J., 'The moving statue and the turtle dove: Approaches to the history of Irish religion', *Irish Economic and Social History* 31 (2004), pp. 1–22.

Connolly, S.J., *Contested island: Ireland, 1460–1630* (Oxford: Oxford University Press, 2007).

Connolly, S.J., *Divided kingdom: Ireland, 1630–1800* (Oxford: Oxford University Press, 2008).

Connolly, S.J., 'Religion and society, 1600–1914', in Liam Kennedy and Philip Ollerenshaw (eds), *Ulster since 1600: Politics, economics and society* (Oxford: Oxford University Press, 2012), pp. 74–89.

Cooke, Colm, 'The modern Irish missionary movement', *Archivium Hibernicum* 35 (1980), pp. 234–246.

Cooney, John, *John Charles McQuaid: Ruler of Catholic Ireland* (Dublin: O'Brien, 1999).

Corkery, Daniel, *The hidden Ireland: A study of Gaelic Munster in the eighteenth century* (1925; rpr. Dublin: Gill and Macmillan, 1975).

Corish, P.J., *The Irish Catholic experience* (Dublin: Gill and Macmillan, 1985).

Corish, P.J. (ed.), *A history of Irish Catholicism*, 6 vols (Dublin: Gill, 1968).

Cornils, Ingo, '"The struggle continues": Rudi Dutschke's long march', in Gerard J. DeGroot (ed.), *Student protest: The sixties and after* (London: Addison Wesley Longman, 1998), pp. 100–114.

Corning, Caitlin, 'Columbanus and the Easter controversy: Theological, social and political contexts', in Roy Flechner and Sven Meeder (eds), *The Irish in early medieval Europe* (New York: Palgrave Macmillan, 2016), pp. 101–115.

Cowdrey, H.E.J., *The epistolae vagantes of Pope Gregory VII* (Oxford: Clarendon Press, 1972).

Crawford, John, and Raymond Gillespie (eds), *St Patrick's cathedral, Dublin: A history* (Dublin: Four Courts, 2009).

Cromwell, Oliver, *Declaration of the Lord Lieutenant of Ireland for the undeceiving of deluded and seduced people* (1650).

Cronin, Michael, *The Blueshirts and Irish politics* (Dublin: Four Courts, 1997).

Crowe, Catriona, 'The Ferns Report', *Éire-Ireland* 43 (2008), pp. 50–73.

Crowley, John, and William J. Smyth (eds), *Atlas of the Great Irish Famine* (Cork: Cork University Press, 2012).

Cullen, Olive M., 'A question of time or a question of theology: A study of the Easter controversy in the insular church' (unpublished PhD thesis, Pontifical University, St Patrick's College, Maynooth, 2007), available at http://mural.maynoothuniversity.ie/1331/1/PHD_Thesis_corrected_copy_1st_July_08.pdf, accessed 20 June 2020.

Cunningham, Bernadette, '"Zeal for God and for souls": Counter-reformation preaching in early seventeenth-century Ireland', in Alan J. Fletcher and Raymond Gillespie (eds), *Irish preaching, 700–1700* (Dublin: Four Courts, 2001), pp. 108–126.

Cunningham, Bernadette, *The annals of the four masters: Irish history, kingship and society in the early seventeenth century* (Dublin: Four Courts, 2010).

Cunningham, John, 'Oliver Cromwell and the "Cromwellian" settlement of Ireland', *Historical Journal* 53:4 (2010), pp. 919–937.

Cunningham, N., and I. Gregory, 'Religious change in twentieth-century Ireland: A spatial history', *Irish Geography* 45:3 (2012), pp. 209–233.

Curtin, Nancy J., *The United Irishmen: Popular politics in Ulster and Dublin, 1791–1798* (Oxford: Oxford University Press, 1998).

Curtis, Edmund, 'The English and Ostmen in Ireland', *English Historical Review* 23 (1908), pp. 209–219.

Curtis, Maurice, *A challenge to democracy: Militant Catholicism in modern Ireland* (Dublin: The History Press, 2010).

d'Alton, Ian, '"A vestigial population": Perspectives on southern Irish protestants in the twentieth century', *Éire-Ireland* 44 (2009), pp. 9–42.

d'Alton, Ian, and Ida Milne (eds), *Protestant and Irish: The minority's search for place in independent Ireland* (Cork: Cork University Press, 2019).

Darby, J.N., *Letters of J.N.D.*, 3 vols, second edition (London: Morrish, n.d.).

Darby, J.N., *Letters of J.N. Darby, Supplement from French*, 2 vols (Chessington, UK: Bible and Gospel Trust, 2016).

Darcy, Eamon, *The Irish rebellion of 1641 and the wars of the three kingdoms* (Woodbridge, UK: Boydell, 2013).

Davies, Norman, *Vanished kingdoms: The history of half-forgotten Europe* (London: Penguin, 2012).

Dawson, Elizabeth, 'Brigit and Patrick in *Vita Prima Sanctae Brigitae*: Veneration and jurisdiction', *Peritia* 28 (2017), pp. 35–50.

Dawson, Elizabeth, 'Paganism, Celtic', in *The Oxford dictionary of late antiquity*, s.v.

Dawson, Jane, 'Calvinism and the Gaidhealtachd in Scotland', in Andrew Pettegree et al. (eds), *Calvinism in Europe, 1540–1620* (Cambridge: Cambridge University Press, 1996), pp. 231–253.

de Cléir, Síle, *Popular Catholicism in twentieth-century Ireland: Locality, identity and culture* (London: Bloomsbury, 2017).

de Paor, Liam, *St Patrick's world: The Christian culture of Ireland's apostolic age* (Notre Dame, IN: University of Notre Dame Press, 1993).

de Valera, Éamon, *Speeches and statements, 1917–83*, ed. Maurice Moynihan (Dublin: Gill and Macmillan, 1980).

Delaney, Enda, *Demography, state and society: Irish migration to Britain, 1921–1971* (Liverpool: Liverpool University Press, 2000).

Delaney, Enda, 'Political Catholicism in post-war Ireland: The Revd Denis Fahey and Maria Duce, 1945–54', *Journal of Ecclesiastical History* 52:3 (2001), pp. 487–511.

Delay, Cara, 'Confidantes or competitors: Women, priests and conflict in post-famine Ireland', *Éire-Ireland* 40 (2005), pp. 107–125.

Delay, Cara, *Irish women and the creation of modern Catholicism, 1850–1950* (Manchester: Manchester University Press, 2019).

Dickson, David, *New foundations: Ireland, 1660–1800*, second edition (Dublin: Irish Academic Press, 2000).

Dickson, David, 'Jacobitism in eighteenth-century Ireland: A Munster perspective', *Éire-Ireland* 39 (2004), pp. 38–99.

Dictionary of Irish biography, ed. James McGuire and James Quinn (Cambridge: Cambridge University Press, 2009).

Dillon, Martin, *God and the gun: The church and Irish terrorism* (London: Routledge, 1999).

Dixon, C. Scott, *The church in the early modern age* (London: I.B. Taurus, 2016).

Doherty, Gillian, *The Irish Ordnance Survey: History, culture and memory* (Dublin: Four Courts, 2006).

Donachie, T.C., *Irish Covenanters: Politics and society in the nineteenth century* (privately published, 2016).

Douglas, R.M., *Architects of the resurrection: Ailtirí na hAiséirghe and the fascist 'new order' in Ireland* (Manchester: Manchester University Press, 2009).

Downey, Declan, 'Purity of blood and purity of faith in early modern Ireland', in Alan Ford and James McCafferty (eds), *The origins of sectarianism in early modern Ireland* (Cambridge: Cambridge University Press, 2005), pp. 217–227.

Downham, Clare, *Medieval Ireland* (Cambridge: Cambridge University Press, 2017).

Doyle, Aidan, *A history of the Irish language: From the Norman invasion to independence* (Oxford: Oxford University Press, 2015).

Doyle, Simon, 'Review into why protestant boys do worse at school will be "meaningless" unless followed up by action', *Irish News* 20 January 2020, available at https://www.irishnews.com/news/northernirelandnews/2020/01/20/news/new-review-into-why-protestant-boys-do-worse-at-school-will-be-meaningless-unless-followed-up-by-action-1818408/, accessed 20 June 2020.

Duffy, Patrick J., et al., 'Introduction: Recovering Gaelic Ireland, c. 1250–c. 1650', in Patrick J. Duffy, David Edwards, and Elizabeth Fitzpatrick (eds), *Gaelic Ireland, c. 1250–c. 1650: Land, lordship and settlement* (Dublin: Four Courts, 2004), pp. 21–75.

Duffy, Seán, 'Ireland and the Irish Sea region, 1014–1318' (unpublished PhD thesis, Trinity College Dublin, 1993).

Duffy, Seán, 'The Welsh conquest of Ireland', in Emer Purcell, Paul MacCotter, Julianne Nyhan, and John Sheehan (eds), *Clerics, kings and Vikings: Essays on medieval Ireland in honour of Donnchadh Ó Corráin* (Dublin: Four Courts, 2015), pp. 103–114.

Duggan, Anne J., 'The power of documents: The curious case of *Laudabiliter*', in Brenda Bolton and Christine Meek (eds), *Aspects of power and authority in the middle ages* (Turnhout, Belgium: Brepols, 2007), pp. 251–275.

Dumville, D.N., 'Some British aspects of the earliest Irish Christianity', in P.Ní Chatháin and M. Richter (eds), *Irland und Europa/Ireland and Europe: Die Kirche im Frühmittelalter/The early church* (Stuttgart: Klett-Cotta, 1984), pp. 16–24.

Dunleavy, Janet Egleson, and Gareth W. Dunleavy, *Douglas Hyde: A maker of modern Ireland* (Berkeley, CA: University of California Press, 1991).

Dunlop, Robert, 'Alexander Carson of Tobermore: An Ulster giant', *Irish Baptist Historical Society Journal* 9 (1976–1977), pp. 14–28.

Dunn, James D.G., *The partings of the ways between Christianity and Judaism and their significance for the character of Christianity*, second edition (London: SCM, 2006).

Dunne, Eamonn, 'Action and reaction: Catholic lay organisations in Dublin in the 1920s and the 1930s', *Archivium Hibernicum* xlviii (1994), pp. 107–118.

Edwards, David, 'A haven of popery: English Catholic migration to Ireland in the age of plantations', in Alan Ford and James McCafferty (eds), *The origins of sectarianism in early modern Ireland* (Cambridge: Cambridge University Press, 2005), pp. 95–125.

Edwards, David, 'Out of the blue? Provincial unrest in Ireland before 1641', in Jane Ohlmeyer and Micheál Ó Siochrú (eds), *Ireland 1641: Contexts and reactions* (Manchester: Manchester University Press, 2013), pp. 99–114.

Edwards, Nancy, *The archaeology of early medieval Ireland* (London: Routledge, 1996).

Eipper, Chris, 'Moving statues and moving images: Religious artefacts and the spiritualisation of materiality', *The Australian Journal of Anthropology* 18:3 (2007), pp. 253–263.

Elliot, Marianne, *The Catholics of Ulster: A history* (London: Allen Lane, 2000).

Elliot, Marianne, 'Religious polarization and sectarianism in the Ulster rebellion', in Thomas Bartlett et al. (eds), *1798: A bicentenary perspective* (Dublin: Four Courts, 2003), pp. 279–297.

Elliot, Marianne, *When God took sides: Religion and identity in Ireland* (Oxford: Oxford University Press, 2009).

Ellis, Steven G., *Tudor Ireland: Crown, community and the conflict of cultures, 1470–1603* (London: Longman, 1985).

Ellis, Steven G., 'Nationalist historiography and the English and Gaelic worlds in the late middle ages', *Irish Historical Studies* 25:97 (1986), pp. 1–18.

Ellis, Steven G., *Tudor frontiers and noble power: The making of the British state* (Oxford: Oxford University Press, 1995).

Ellul, Jacques, *The subversion of Christianity*, trans. Geoffrey W. Bromiley (Grand Rapids, MI: Eerdmans, 1986).

'Enda Kenny speech on Cloyne Report', *RTÉ News* 20 July 2011, available at https://www.rte.ie/news/2011/0720/303965-cloyne1/, accessed 20 June 2020.

Etchingham, Colmán, 'Bishops in the early Irish church: A reassessment', *Studia Hibernica* 28 (1994), pp. 35–62.

Etchingham, Colmán, *Church organisation in Ireland, AD. 650 to 1000* (Maynooth: Laigin Publications, 1999).

Etchingham, Colmán, 'The organization and function of an early Irish church settlement: What was Glendalough?' in Charles Doherty et al. (eds), *Glendalough: City of God* (Dublin: Four Courts, 2011), pp. 22–53.

Etchingham, Colmán, 'Conversion in Ireland', in Roy Flechner and Máire Ní Mhaonaigh (eds), *The introduction of Christianity into the early medieval insular world* (Turnhout, Belgium: Brepols, 2016), pp. 181–204.

Evans, Bryce, *Ireland during the Second World War: Farewell to Plato's Cave* (Manchester: Manchester University Press, 2014).

Evans, Estyn, *Prehistoric and early Christian Ireland: A guide* (London: Batsford, 1966).

Farrell, Gerard, *The 'mere' Irish and the colonisation of Ulster, 1570–1641* (London: Palgrave, 2017).

Farrell, Mel, *Party politics in a new democracy: The Irish Free State, 1922–37* (London: Palgrave Macmillan, 2017).

Farren, Sean, *The politics of Irish education, 1920–65* (Belfast: Institute of Irish Studies, 1995).

Father, son and the housekeeper (dir. Alison Millar, 2008).

Faughnan, Seán, 'The Jesuits and the drafting of the Irish constitution of 1937', *Irish Historical Studies* 26:101 (1988), pp. 79–102.

Ferriter, Diarmaid, *The transformation of Ireland* (London: Profile, 2004).

Finkelstein, David, and Alistair McCleery, *An introduction to book history* (London: Routledge, 2005).

Fitzmaurice, E.B., and A.G. Little (eds), *Materials for the history of the Franciscan province of Ireland, 1230–1450* (Manchester: Manchester University Press, 1920).

Fitzpatrick, David, 'Protestant depopulation and the Irish revolution', *Irish Historical Studies* 38:152 (2013), pp. 643–670.

Fitzpatrick, David, *Descendancy: Irish protestant histories since 1795* (Cambridge: Cambridge University Press, 2014).

Fitzpatrick, David, 'Irish consequences of the Great War', *Irish Historical Studies* 39:165 (2015), pp. 643–658.

Fitzpatrick, Elizabeth, 'Assembly and inauguration places of the Burkes in late medieval Connacht', in Patrick J. Duffy, David Edwards, and Elizabeth Fitzpatrick (eds), *Gaelic Ireland, c.1250–c.1650: Land, lordship and settlement* (Dublin: Four Courts, 2004), pp. 357–374.

Fitzpatrick, Maurice, *John Hume in America: From Derry to DC* (Dublin: Irish Academic Press, 2017).

Flanagan, Marie Therese, *The transformation of the Irish church in the twelfth century* (Woodbridge, UK: Boydell and Brewer, 2010).

Flechner, Roy, 'Conversion in Ireland: Reflections on the state of the art', in Roy Flechner and Máire Ní Mhaonaigh (eds), *The introduction of Christianity into the early medieval insular world* (Turnhout, Belgium: Brepols, 2016), pp. 41–55.

Flechner, Roy, *Saint Patrick retold* (Princeton, NJ: Princeton University Press, 2019).

Follett, Westley, *Céli Dé in Ireland: Monastic writing and identity in the early middle ages* (Woodbridge, UK: Boydell and Brewer, 2006).

Ford, Alan, 'The Church of Ireland, 1558–1641: A puritan church?' in Alan Ford et al. (eds), *As by law established: The Church of Ireland since the reformation* (Dublin: Lilliput Press, 1995), pp. 52–68.

Ford, Alan, 'Dependent or independent? The Church of Ireland and its colonial context, 1536–1649', *The Seventeenth Century* 9 (1995), pp. 163–187.

Ford, Alan, 'The origins of Irish dissent', in Kevin Herlihy (ed.), *The religion of Irish dissent, 1650–1800* (Dublin, 1996), pp. 9–30.

Ford, Alan, *The protestant reformation in Ireland, 1590–1641* (Dublin: Four Courts, 1997).

Ford, Alan, 'Martyrdom, history and memory in early modern Ireland', in Ian McBride (ed.), *History and memory in modern Ireland* (Cambridge: Cambridge University Press, 2001), pp. 43–66.

Ford, Alan, *James Ussher: Theology, history and politics in early modern Ireland and England* (Oxford: Oxford University Press, 2007).

Ford, Alan, 'Scottish protestant clergy and the origins of dissent in Ireland', in David Edwards and Simon Egan (eds), *The Scots in early Stuart Ireland: Union and separation in two kingdoms* (Manchester: Manchester University Press, 2015), pp. 116–140.

Forrest, G. Andrew, 'Religious controversy within the French protestant community in Dublin, 1692-1716: An historiographical critique', in Kevin Herlihy (ed.), *The Irish dissenting tradition, 1650–1750* (Dublin: Four Courts, 1995), pp. 96–110.

Forrestal, Alison, *Catholic synods in Ireland, 1600–1690* (Dublin: Four Courts, 1998).

Foster, R.F., *Modern Ireland, 1600–1972* (London: Allen Lane, 1988).

Foster, R.F., *W. B. Yeats: A life*, vol. 1: *The apprentice mage, 1865–1914* (Oxford: Oxford University Press, 1997).

Foster, R.F., *Luck and the Irish: A brief history of change, c. 1970–2000* (London: Allen Lane, 2007).

Frame, Robin, '"Les Engleys nées en Irlande": The English political identity in medieval Ireland', *Transactions of the Royal Historical Society* 3 (1993), pp. 83–103.

Frame, Robin, *Ireland and the classical world* (Austin, TX: University of Texas Press, 2001).

Freeman, Philip, *St Patrick of Ireland: A biography* (New York: Simon & Schuster, 2004).

A full confutation of the Covenant, lately sworne and subscribed by many in Scotland (1639).

Fuller, Louise, *Irish Catholicism since 1950: The undoing of a culture* (Dublin: Gill and Macmillan, 2002).

Furholt, M. 'Massive migrations? The impact of recent aDNA studies on our view of third millennium Europe', *European Journal of Archaeology* 21 (2018), pp. 159–191.

'Further details of Brú na Bóinne aerial survey released', available at https://www.archaeology.ie/news/bru-na-boinne-aerial-survey, accessed 20 June 2020.

Gailey, Alan, 'The Scots element in North Irish popular culture', *Ethnologica Europeae* 11:1 (1975), pp. 2–22.

Ganiel, Gladys, *Evangelicalism and conflict in Northern Ireland* (Basingstoke: Palgrave Macmillan, 2008).

Ganiel, Gladys, *Transforming post-Catholic Ireland: Religious practice in late modernity* (Oxford: Oxford University Press, 2016).

Gefreh, Tasha, 'Sun of understanding: The iconographic programme of Iona's free-standing crosses', in Conor Newman et al. (eds), *Islands in a global context: Proceedings of the seventh international conference on Insular art, held at the National University of Ireland, Galway, 16–20 July 2014* (Dublin: Four Courts, 2017), pp. 75–83.

Gerald of Wales, *The history and topography of Ireland*, trans. John O'Meara (London: Penguin, 1982).

Gibney, John, *The shadow of a year: The 1641 rebellion in Irish history and memory* (Madison, WI: University of Wisconsin Press, 2013).

Gibney, John, *A short history of Ireland, 1500–2000* (New Haven, CT: Yale University Press, 2018).

Gibson, William, *Year of grace: A history of the Ulster revival of 1859* (Edinburgh: Andrew Elliot, 1860).

Gilbert, E., Seamus O'Reilly, Michael Merrigan, Darren McGettigan, Anne M. Molloy, Lawrence C. Brody, et al., 'The Irish DNA Atlas: Revealing fine-scale population structure and history within Ireland', *Nature Scientific Reports* 7 (2017), article 17199.

Gillen, Ultán, 'The Enlightenment and Irish political culture in the age of revolutions', in Richard Butterwick et al. (eds), *Peripheries of the Enlightenment* (Oxford: Voltaire Foundation, 2008), pp. 163–182.

Gillespie, Raymond, 'Dissenters and nonconformists, 1661–1700', in Kevin Herlihy (ed.), *The Irish dissenting tradition, 1650–1750* (Dublin: Four Courts, 1995), pp. 11–28.

Gillespie, Raymond, *Devoted people: Belief and religion in early modern Ireland* (Manchester: Manchester University Press, 1997).

Gillespie, Raymond, 'Traditional religion in sixteenth-century Gaelic Ireland', in Tadhg Ó hAnnracháin and Robert Armstrong (eds), *Christianities in the early modern Celtic world* (London: Palgrave Macmillan, 2014), pp. 29–41.

Gilmore, Peter, *Irish Presbyterians and the shaping of western Pennsylvania* (Pittsburgh: University of Pittsburgh Press, 2018).

Girvin, Brian, 'Church, state and society in Ireland since 1960', *Éire-Ireland* 43 (2008), pp. 74–98.

Gostelo, Walter, *Charls Stuart and Oliver Cromwel united* (1655).

Gray, Peter, *The Irish famine* (London: Thames & Hudson, 1995).

Greaves, Richard L., *God's other children: Protestant nonconformists and the emergence of denominational churches in Ireland, 1660–1700* (Stanford, CA: Stanford University Press, 1997).

Greaves, Richard L., *Dublin's merchant Quaker: Anthony Sharp and the community of Friends, 1643–1707* (Stanford, CA: Stanford University Press, 1998).

Gregory, Brad S., *The unintended reformation: How a religious revolution secularised society* (Cambridge, MA: Belknap Press of Harvard University Press, 2015).

Gregory, Lady Augusta, *Gods and fighting men: The story of the Tuatha De Danaan and of the Fianna of Ireland* (London: John Murray, 1905).

Gribben, Crawford, ' "The worst sect a Christian man can meet": Opposition to the Plymouth Brethren in Ireland and Scotland, 1859–1900', *Scottish Studies Review* 3:2 (2002), pp. 34–53.

Gribben, Crawford, 'Introduction', in Crawford Gribben and Andrew R. Holmes (eds), *Protestant millennialism, evangelicalism and Irish society, 1790–2005* (Basingstoke: Palgrave Macmillan, 2006), pp. 1–30.

Gribben, Crawford, *God's Irishmen: Theological debates in Cromwellian Ireland* (New York: Oxford University Press, 2007).

Gribben, Crawford, 'Protestant millennialism, political violence and the Ulster conflict', *Irish Studies Review* 15:1 (2007), pp. 51–63.

Gribben, Crawford, *Evangelical millennialism in the trans-Atlantic world, 1500–2000* (New York: Palgrave Macmillan, 2011).

Gribben, Crawford, 'Angels and demons in Cromwellian and Restoration Ireland: Heresy and the supernatural', *Huntington Library Quarterly* 76:3 (2013), pp. 377–392.

Gribben, Crawford, *John Owen and English puritanism: Experiences of defeat* (Oxford: Oxford University Press, 2016).

Gribben, Crawford, 'The future of Northern Ireland: What is going wrong?' Foreign Policy Research Institute blog 23 August 2017, available at https://www.fpri.org/article/2017/08/future-northern-ireland-going-wrong/, accessed 20 June 2020.

Gribben, Crawford, *The revival of Particular Baptist life in Ireland, 1780–1840* (Louisville, KY: The Andrew Fuller Center for Baptist Studies, 2018).

Griffiths, David, *Vikings of the Irish Sea: Conflict and assimilation, AD 790–1050* (London: History Press, 2010).

Gurrin, Brian, Kerby A. Miller, and Liam Kennedy, *Catholics and protestants in eighteenth-century Ireland: The Irish religious censuses of the 1760s* (Dublin: Irish Manuscript Commission, 2016).

Hadfield, Andrew, *Edmund Spenser: A life* (Oxford: Oxford University Press, 2021).

Hagan, J. 'Miscellanea Vaticano-Hibernia, 1580–1631', *Archivium Hibernicum* 3 (1914), pp. 300–301.

Hall, Diane, *Women and the church in medieval Ireland, c. 1140–1540* (Dublin: Four Courts, 2003).

Hanley, Brian, *The IRA, 1926–1936* (Dublin: Four Courts, 2002).

Hanley, Brian, and Scott Millar, *The lost revolution: The story of the Official IRA and the Workers' Party* (London: Penguin, 2010).

Hannon, Patrick, 'Religion, the constitution, and the new Ireland', *Irish Theological Quarterly* 74:3 (2009), pp. 258–271.

Hanson, R.P.C., *Saint Patrick: His origins and career* (Oxford: Clarendon Press, 1968).

Harrington, Christina, *Women in a Celtic church: Ireland, 450–1150* (Oxford: Oxford University Press, 2002).

Harrison, Richard S., ' "As a garden enclosed": The emergence of Irish Quakers, 1650–1750', in Kevin Herlihy (ed.), *The Irish dissenting tradition, 1650-1750* (Dublin: Four Courts, 1995), pp. 81–95.

Hart, Peter, *The I.R.A. and its enemies: Violence and community in Cork, 1916–1923* (Oxford: Oxford University Press, 1999).

Hauerwas, Stanley, *After Christendom: How the church is to behave if freedom, justice and a Christian nation are bad ideas* (Nashville, TN: Abingdon Press, 1991).

Hauerwas, Stanley, and William H. Willimon, *Resident aliens: Life in the Christian colony* (Nashville, TN: Abingdon Press, 1989).

Hawkes, Jane, 'Art and society', in Brendan Smith (ed.), *The Cambridge history of Ireland*, vol. 1: *600–1550* (Cambridge: Cambridge University Press, 2018), pp. 76–106.

Hayes-Healy, Stephanie, '"Irish pilgrimage': A romantic misconception"', in Seán Duffy (ed.), *Princes, prelates and poets in medieval Ireland: Essays in honour of Katherine Simms* (Dublin: Four Courts, 2013), pp. 241–260.

Haywood, John, *The historical atlas of the Celtic world* (London: Thames & Hudson, 2009).

Hayton, D.W., 'Anglo-Irish attitudes: Shifting perceptions of national identity', in D.W. Hayton, *The Anglo-Irish experience, 1680–1730: Religion, identity and patriotism* (Woodbridge, UK: Boydell, 2012), pp. 25–48.

Healy, John, *Insula sanctorum et doctorum, or Ireland's ancient schools and scholars*, sixth edition (Dublin: Sealy, Bryers and Walker, 1912).

Heaney, Seamus, *New selected poems, 1966–1987* (London: Faber, 1990).

Hempton, David, and Myrtle Hill, *Evangelical protestantism in Ulster society, 1740–1890* (London: Routledge, 1992).

Hepburn, A.C., *Catholic Belfast and nationalist Ireland in the era of Joe Devlin, 1871–1934* (Oxford: Oxford University Press, 2008).

Herbert, Máire, *Iona, Kells, and Derry: The history and hagiography of the monastic familia of Columba* (Oxford: Clarendon Press, 1988).

Herlihy, Kevin, '"The faithful remnant": Irish Baptists, 1650–1750', in Kevin Herlihy (ed.), *The Irish dissenting tradition, 1650–1750* (Dublin: Four Courts, 1995), pp. 65–79.

Herlihy, Kevin, '"A gay and flattering world": Irish Baptist piety and perspective, 1650–1780', in Kevin Herlihy (ed.), *The religion of Irish dissent, 1650–1800* (Dublin: Four Courts, 1996), pp. 48–67.

Herren, Michael, 'The "Papal letters to the Irish" cited by Bede: How did he get them?' in Emer Purcell, Paul MacCotter, Julianne Nyhan, and John Sheehan (eds), *Clerics, kings and Vikings: Essays on medieval Ireland in honour of Donnchadh Ó Corráin* (Dublin: Four Courts, 2015), pp. 3–10.

Hesketh, Tom, *The second partitioning of Ireland: The abortion referendum of 1983* (Dun Laoghaire: Brandsma Books, 1990).

The Hibernensis: A study and edition, ed. Roy Flechner (Washington, DC: The Catholic University of America Press, 2019).

Hick, Vivien, '"As nearly related as possible": Solidarity amongst the Irish Palatines', in Kevin Herlihy (ed.), *The Irish dissenting tradition, 1650–1750* (Dublin: Four Courts, 1995), pp. 111–125.

Hill, Jacqueline R., 'National festivals, the state, and "Protestant Ascendency" in Ireland', *Irish Historical Studies* 24:93 (1984), pp. 31–51.

Hill, Jacqueline R., 'Dublin Corporation, protestant dissent, and politics, 1660–1800', in Kevin Herlihy (ed.), *The politics of Irish dissent, 1650–1800* (Dublin: Four Courts, 1997), pp. 28–39.

Hill, Myrtle, 'Gender, culture and "the spiritual empire": The Irish protestant female missionary experience', *Women's History Review* 16 (2007), pp. 203–226.

Holm, Poul, 'The naval power of Norse Dublin', in Emer Purcell, Paul MacCotter, Julianne Nyhan, and John Sheehan (eds), *Clerics, kings and Vikings: Essays on medieval Ireland in honour of Donnchadh Ó Corráin* (Dublin: Four Courts, 2015), pp. 67–78.

Holmes, Andrew R., 'The shaping of Irish Presbyterian attitudes to mission, 1790–1840', *Journal of Ecclesiastical History* 57 (2006), pp. 711–737.

Holmes, Andrew R., *The shaping of Ulster Presbyterian belief and practice, 1770–1840* (Oxford: Oxford University Press, 2006).

Holmes, Andrew R., 'Presbyterian religion, historiography, and Ulster Scots identity, c. 1800 to 1914', *Historical Journal* 52 (2009), pp. 615–640.

Holmes, Andrew R., 'Covenanter politics: Evangelicalism, political liberalism and Ulster Prebsyterians, 1798–1914', *English Historical Review* 125 (2010), pp. 340–369.

Holmes, Andrew R., 'The Ulster revival of 1859: Causes, controversies and consequences', *Journal of Ecclesiastical History* 63 (2012), pp. 488–515.

Holmes, Andrew R., 'Personal conversion, revival, and the Holy Spirit: Presbyterian evangelicalism in early nineteenth-century Ulster', in John Coffey (ed.), *Heart religion: Evangelical piety in England and Ireland, 1690–1850* (Oxford: Oxford University Press, 2016), pp. 191–200.

Holmes, Andrew R., 'Protestants and "greater Ireland": Mission, migration and identity in the nineteenth century', *Irish Historical Studies* 41:160 (2017), pp. 275–285.

Holmes, Andrew R., *The Irish Presbyterian mind: Conservative theology, evangelical experience, and modern criticism, 1839–1930* (Oxford: Oxford University Press, 2018).

Holmes, Andrew R., 'Protestant dissent in Ireland', in Andrew Thompson (ed.), *The Oxford history of protestant dissenting traditions*, vol. 2: *1689 to the repeal of the Test and Corporation Acts* (Oxford: Oxford University Press, 2018), pp. 119–138.

Holmes, Andrew R., 'Protestantism in nineteenth-century Ireland: Revival and crisis', in James Kelly (ed.), *The Cambridge history of Ireland*, 4 vols (Cambridge: Cambridge University Press, 2018), 2, pp. 331–349.

Holmes, Janice, *Religious revivals in Britain and Ireland 1859–1905* (Dublin: Irish Academic Press, 2000).

Holmes, Janice, 'The role of open-air preaching in the Belfast riots of 1857', *Proceedings of the Royal Irish Academy* 102 C (2002), pp. 47–66.

Holmes, R.T.G., 'United Irishmen and unionists: Irish Presbyterians, 1791–1886', in W.J. Sheils and Diana Wood (eds), *The churches, Ireland and the Irish*, Studies in Church History (Oxford: Blackwell, 1989), pp. 171–189.

Holohan, Carole, 'Challenges to social order and Irish identity? Youth culture in the 1960s', *Irish Historical Studies* 38:151 (2013), pp. 389–405.

Holohan, Carole, *Reframing Irish youth in the sixties* (Liverpool: Liverpool University Press, 2018).

Houston, Matthew, 'Presbyterianism, unionism, and the Second World War in Northern Ireland: The career of James Little, 1939–46', *Irish Historical Studies* 43:164 (2019), pp. 252–268.

Howard, John Eliot, 'The Island of the Saints'; or Ireland in 1855 (London: Seeleys, 1855).

Howlin, Gerard, 'Abortion is the final nail in our old identity's coffin: Who are we now?' The Irish Examiner 2 January 2019, available at https://www.irishexaminer.com/breakingnews/views/abortion-is-the-final-nail-in-our-old-identitys-coffin-who-are-we-now-895034.html#.Xu3i9iFg6cw.gmail, accessed 20 June 2020.

Hughes, Kathleen, and Ann Hamlin, The modern traveller to the early Irish church (1977; rpr. Dublin: Four Courts, 1997).

Hunter, R.J., Ulster transformed: Essays on plantation and print culture, c. 1590–1641 (Belfast: Ulster Historical Foundation, 2012).

Hutton, Ronald, Blood and mistletoe: The history of the druids in Britain (New Haven, CT: Yale University Press, 2011).

Hylton, Raymond Pierre, 'The less-favoured refuge: Ireland's nonconformist Huguenots at the turn of the eighteenth century', in Kevin Herlihy (ed.), The religion of Irish dissent, 1650–1800 (Dublin: Four Courts, 1996), pp. 83–99.

Hynes, Eugene, Knock: The Virgin's apparition in nineteenth-century Ireland (Cork: Cork University Press, 2009).

Hynes, Sandra, 'Becoming convinced: The use of Quaker testimonies in late seventeenth-century Ireland', in Michael Brown et al. (eds), Converts and conversions in Ireland, 1650–1850 (Dublin: Four Courts, 2005), pp. 107–127.

'Irish census (2016)', Faith Survey, available at https://faithsurvey.co.uk/irish-census.html, accessed 20 June 2020.

Irish Inter Church Meeting, 'Removal of blasphemy from the Constitution of Ireland', 31 October 2013, available at https://www.irishchurches.org/news-blog/919/removal-of-blasphemy-from-the, accessed 20 June 2020.

Irish historical documents, 1172–1922, ed. E. Curtis and R.B. McDowell (London, 1943).

'Iron Age "bog man" used imported hair gel', National Geographic 17 January 2006.

Irvine, Maurice, Northern Ireland: Faith and faction (London: Routledge, 1991).

Ischebeck, Gustav, John Nelson Darby: Son temps et son oeuvre (Yverdon/Lausanne, [1937]).

Jameson, David, 'The religious upbringing of children in "mixed marriages": The evolution of Irish law', New Hibernia Review 18:2 (2014), pp. 65–83.

Jefferies, Henry A., The Irish church and the Tudor reformations (Dublin: Four Courts, 2010).

Jefferies, Henry A., 'Elizabeth's reformation in the Irish Pale', Journal of Ecclesiastical History 66:3 (2015), pp. 524–542.

Jefferies, Henry A., 'Why the reformation failed in Ireland', Irish Historical Studies 40 (2016), pp. 151–170.

Jeffery, Keith, Ireland and the great war (Cambridge: Cambridge University Press, 2000).

Jeffery, Keith, 1916: A global history (London: Bloomsbury, 2015).

Johnston, Elva, 'Ireland in late antiquity: A forgotten frontier?' Studies in Late Antiquity 1:2 (2017), pp. 107–123.

Jones, Frederick M., 'Canonical faculties on the Irish mission in the reign of Queen Elizabeth, 1558–1603', Irish Theological Quarterly 30 (1953), pp. 152–171.

Jones, Valeria, *Rebel Prods: The forgotten story of protestant radical nationalists and the 1916 Rising* (Dublin: Ashfield, 2014).

Jordan, Jane, 'The English Delilah: Katharine O'Shea and Irish politics, 1880–1891', in Roger Swift and Christine Kinealy (eds), *Politics and power in Victorian Ireland* (Dublin: Four Courts, 2006), pp. 69–83.

Joyce, James, *A portrait of the artist as a young man*, ed. Seamus Deane (London: Penguin, 1992).

Justin Martyr, 'First apology', in *Ante-Nicene Fathers*, ed. Alexander Roberts and James Donaldson, 10 vols (Buffalo, NY: Christian Literature Publishing Company, 1885), I, pp. 163–187.

Kelly, Joseph, 'Pelagius, Pelagianism and the early Christian Irish', *Mediaevalia* 4 (1978), pp. 99–124.

Kelly, Laura, 'Irishwomen United, the Contraception Action Programme and the feminist campaign for free, safe and legal contraception in Ireland, c. 1975–81', *Irish Historical Studies* 43:164 (2019), pp. 269–297.

Kelly, Michael, 'End of era as Rome's Irish College shuts as seminary after nearly 400 years...for now', *The Irish Catholic* 18 June 2020, available at https://www.irishcatholic.com/end-of-era-as-romes-irish-college-shuts-as-seminary-after-nearly-400-yearsfor-now/, accessed 20 June 2020.

Kelly, Stephen Austin, 'Anglo-Irish drama? Writing for the stage in Restoration Dublin', in Kathleen Miller and Crawford Gribben (eds), *Dublin: Renaissance city of literature* (Manchester: Manchester University Press, 2017), pp. 206–227.

Kelly, William, *An exposition of the epistle to the Hebrews* (London: T. Weston, 1905).

Kennedy, Finola, *Frank Duff: A life story* (Dublin: Burns and Oates, 2007).

Kierkegaard, Søren, *The moment and late writings*, ed. and trans. Howard V. Hong and Edna H. Hong (Princeton, NJ: Princeton University Press, 1998).

Killen, W.D., *The ecclesiastical history of Ireland*, 2 vols (London: Macmillan, 1875).

Kilroy, Phil, *Protestant dissent and controversy in Ireland, 1660–1714* (Cork: Cork University Press, 1994).

King, Heather, 'Late medieval Irish crosses and their European background', in Colum Hourihane (ed.), *From Ireland coming: Irish art from the early Christian to the late Gothic period and its European context* (Princeton, NJ: Princeton University Press, 2001), pp. 333–350.

Kingston, Simon, 'Delusions of Dál Riada: The co-ordinates of Mac Domnaill power, 1461–1550', in Patrick J. Duffy, David Edwards, and Elizabeth Fitzpatrick (eds), *Gaelic Ireland, c.1250–c.1650: Land, lordship and settlement* (Dublin: Four Courts, 2004), pp. 98–113.

Kinsella, Eoin, *Catholic survival in protestant Ireland, 1660–1711: Colonel John Browne, landownership and the Articles of Limerick* (Woodbridge, UK: Boydell and Brewer, 2018).

Kissane, Noel, *Saint Brigid of Kildare: Life, legend and cult* (Dublin: Four Courts, 2017).

Kruger, Michael J., *Christianity at the crossroads: How the second century shaped the future of the church* (London: SPCK, 2017).

Lafaye, Annejulie, 'The Dominicans in Ireland: A comparative study of the east Munster and Leinster settlements', *Journal of Medieval Monastic Studies* 4 (2015), pp. 79–108.

Lalor, Brian, *The Irish round tower: Origins and architecture explored* (Dublin: Collins Press, 1999).

Larcom, Captain, 'Observations on the census of the population of Ireland in 1841', *Journal of the Statistical Society of London* 6:4 (1843), pp. 323–351.

Larkin, Emmet, *The pastoral role of the Roman Catholic Church in pre-famine Ireland, 1750–1850* (Dublin: Four Courts, 2006).

Leerssen, Joep, *Mere Irish and Fior-Ghael: Studies in the idea of Irish nationality, its development and literary expression prior to the nineteenth century* (Cork: Cork University Press, 1996).

Leeson, D.M., *The Black and Tans: British police and auxiliaries in the Irish war of independence, 1920–21* (Oxford: Oxford University Press, 2011).

Leighton, C.D.A., *Catholicism in a protestant kingdom: A study of the Irish ancien régime* (London: Palgrave Macmillan, 1994).

Lenihan, Pádraig, 'War and population, 1649–52', *Irish Economic and Social History* 24 (1997), pp. 1–21.

Lenihan, Pádraig, *Confederate Catholics at war, 1642–49* (Cork: Cork University Press, 2001).

Lennon, Colm, 'Mass in the manor house: The counter-reformation in Dublin, 1560–1630', in James Kelly and Daire Keogh (eds), *History of the Catholic diocese of Dublin* (Dublin: Four Courts, 2000), pp. 112–126.

Lennon, Colm, 'Taking sides: The emergence of Irish Catholic ideology', in Vincent P. Carey and Ute Lotz-Heumann (eds), *Taking sides? Colonial and confessional mentalities in early modern Ireland* (Dublin: Four Courts, 2003), pp. 78–93.

The letters of Lafranc, archbishop of Canterbury, trans. H. Clover and M. Gibson (Oxford: Clarendon Press, 1979).

The letters of Saint Oliver Plunkett, 1625–81, ed. J. Hanly (Dublin: Colin Smythe, 1979).

Linehan, Thomas, 'History and development of Irish population censuses', *Journal of the Statistical and Social Inquiry Society of Ireland* 16:4 (1991–1992), pp. 91–132.

Livingstone, John, *A brief historical relation of the life of Mr. John Livingstone*, ed. Thomas Houston (Edinburgh: John Johnstone, 1848).

Longford, The earl of, and Thomas P. O'Neill, *Éamon de Valera* (Boston, MA: Houghton Mifflin, 1971).

Lotz-Heumann, Ute, 'Confessionalisation in Ireland: Periodisation and character, 1534–1649', in Alan Ford and James McCafferty (eds), *The origins of sectarianism in early modern Ireland* (Cambridge: Cambridge University Press, 2005), pp. 24–53.

Loughery, John, *Dagger John: Archbishop John Hughes and the making of Irish America* (New York: Cornell University Press, 2018).

Lucan, *Pharsalia (The civil war)*, trans. J.D. Duff, The Loeb Classical Library (Cambridge, MA: Harvard University Press, 1962).

Luddy, Maria, and Mary O'Dowd, *Marriage in Ireland, 1660–1925* (Cambridge: Cambridge University Press, 2020).

Lyons, F.S.L., *Charles Stewart Parnell* (Dublin: Gill and Macmillan, 2005).

Maas, John, 'The Viking events of AD 902–19 and the Lough Ennell hoards', in Emer Purcell, Paul MacCotter, Julianne Nyhan, and John Sheehan (eds), *Clerics, kings and Vikings: Essays on medieval Ireland in honour of Donnchadh Ó Corráin* (Dublin: Four Courts, 2015), pp. 251–262.

Macauley, Ambrose, *Patrick McAlister: Bishop of Down and Connor, 1886–95* (Dublin: Four Courts, 2006).

Mac Cana, Proinsias, *The cult of the sacred centre: Essays on Celtic ideology* (Dublin: Dublin Institute for Advanced Studies, 2011).

Mac Craith, Micheál, ' "Do chum glóire Dé agus an mhaitheasa phuiblidhe so / For the glory of God and the public good ": The reformation and the Irish language', *Studies* 106:424 (2017–2018), pp. 476–483.

Mac Cuarta, Brian, 'Religious violence against settlers in south Ulster, 1641–2', in David Edwards et al. (eds), *Age of atrocity: Violence and political conflict in early modern Ireland* (Dublin: Four Courts, 2007), pp. 154–175.

Mac Cuarta, Brian, 'The Catholic Church in Ulster under the plantation', in Éamonn Ó Ciardha and Micheál Ó Siochrú (eds), *The plantation of Ulster: Ideology and practice* (Manchester: Manchester University Press, 2012), pp. 119–142.

MacIntyre, Alasdair, *After virtue*, third edition (London: Bloomsbury, 2007).

MacKenzie, Caitriona, and Eileen Murphy, *Life and death in medieval Gaelic Ireland: The skeletons from Ballyhana, co. Donegal* (Dublin: Four Courts, 2018).

MacKenzie, Kirsteen M., *The Solemn League and Covenant of the three kingdoms and the Cromwellian Union, 1643–1663* (London: Routledge, 2018).

Mac Mathúna, Séamus, 'The relationship of the chthonic world in early Ireland to chaos and cosmos', in Jacqueline Borsje et al. (eds), *Celtic cosmology: Perspectives from Ireland and Scotland*, Papers in Mediaeval Studies 26 (Toronto: Pontifical Institute of Mediaeval Studies, 2014), pp. 53–76.

MacShane, Bronagh A., 'Negotiating religious change and conflict: Female religious communities in early modern Ireland, c. 1530–c. 1641', *British Catholic History* 33:3 (2017), pp. 357–382.

Mallory, J.P., *In search of the Irish dreamtime: Archaeology and early Irish literature* (London: Thames & Hudson, 2016).

Mallory, J.P., *The origins of the Irish*, second edition (London: Thames & Hudson, 2017).

Mapping death: Peoples, boundaries and territories in Ireland, available at http://www.mappingdeathdb.ie/idlocs, accessed 20 June 2020.

Mark-Fitzgerald, Emily, *Commemorating the Irish famine: Memory and the monument* (Liverpool: Liverpool University Press, 2013).

Márkus, Gilbert, 'Pelagianism and the "Common Celtic Church"', *Innes Review* 56 (2005), pp. 165–213.

Martin, Peter, ' "Why have a Catholic hospital at all?" The Mater Infirmorum Hospital Belfast and the state, 1883–1972', in Donnacha Seán Lucey and Virginia Crossman (eds), *Healthcare in Ireland and Britain from 1850: Voluntary, regional and comparative perspectives* (London: Institute for Historical Research, 2014), pp. 101–116.

McBride, I.R., *Scripture politics: Ulster Presbyterians and Irish radicalism in the late eighteenth century* (Oxford: Clarendon Press, 1998).

McCafferty, John, *The reconstruction of the Church of Ireland: Bishop Bramhall and the Laudian reforms, 1633–1641* (Cambridge: Cambridge University Press, 2007).

McCafferty, John, 'A mundo valde alieni: Irish Franciscan responses to the dissolution of the monasteries, 1540–1640', *Reformation and Renaissance Review* 19:1 (2017), pp. 50–63.

McCarthy, R.B., 'The Church of Ireland in south Tipperary in the twentieth century', *Tipperary Historical Journal* (2007), pp. 145–152.

McCormack, Anthony, 'The social and economic consequences of the Desmond Rebellion of 1579-1583', *Irish Historical Studies* 34:113 (2004), pp. 1–15.

McCosh, James, *The Ulster revival and its physiological accidents: A paper read before the Evangelical Alliance, September 22, 1859* (Belfast: C. Aitchison, 1859).

McEnroe, Juno, '"We did not just hide away the dead bodies of tiny human beings, we dug deep and deeper still to bury our compassion, our mercy"', *Irish Examiner* 8 March 2017, available at https://www.irishexaminer.com/ireland/we-did-not-just-hide-away-the-dead-bodies-of-tiny-human-beings-we-dug-deep-and-deeper-still-to-bury-our-compassion-our-mercy-444626.html, accessed 20 June 2020.

McGarry, Fearghal, *Eoin O'Duffy: A self-made hero* (Oxford: Oxford University Press, 2005).

McGarry, Fearghal, *The rising: Ireland, Easter 1916* (Oxford: Oxford University Press, 2010).

McGarry, Patsy, 'Further drop in seminarians entering St Patrick's College, Maynooth', *Irish Times* 5 October 2018, available at https://www.irishtimes.com/news/social-affairs/religion-and-beliefs/further-drop-in-seminarians-entering-st-patrick-s-college-maynooth-1.3653247, accessed 20 June 2020.

McGarry, Patsy, 'Religious congregations yet to fully honour compensation deals', *Irish Times* 11 May 2019, available at https://www.irishtimes.com/news/social-affairs/religion-and-beliefs/religious-congregations-yet-to-fully-honour-compensation-deals-1.3887870, accessed 20 June 2020.

McGettigan, Darren, *The kings of Aileach and the Vikings, AD 800–1060* (Dublin: Four Courts, 2020).

McGrath, Charles Ivar, 'The provisions for conversion in the penal laws, 1695–1750', in Michael Brown et al. (eds), *Converts and conversions in Ireland, 1650–1850* (Dublin: Four Courts, 2005), pp. 35–59.

McGuire, James, 'Ormond and Presbyterian nonconformity, 1660–63', in Kevin Herlihy (ed.), *The politics of Irish dissent, 1650–1800* (Dublin: Four Courts, 1997), pp. 40–51.

McKenny, Kevin, 'The Restoration land settlement in Ireland: A statistical interpretation', in Coleman A. Dennehy (ed.), *Restoration Ireland: Always settling and never settled* (Aldershot, UK: Ashgate, 2007), pp. 35–52.

McKitterick, David, et al., *Lost lives: The stories of the men, women and children who died as a result of the Northern Ireland troubles* (Edinburgh: Mainstream, 2000).

McNamara, Martin, *The Bible and the apocrypha in the early Irish church (AD 600–1200): Collected essays*, Instrumenta Patristica et Medievalia (Turnhout, Belgium: Brepols, 2015).

Meehan, Neil, 'Uncovering Peter Hart', *Field Day Review* 10 (2014), pp. 102–147.

Meens, Rob, *Penance in medieval Europe, 600–1200* (Cambridge: Cambridge University Press, 2014).

Megahey, Alan, *The Irish protestant churches in the twentieth century* (Basingstoke: Macmillan, 2000).

Megahey, Alan, '"God will defend the right": The protestant churches and opposition to Home Rule', in D.G. Boyce and Alan O'Day (eds), *Defenders of the union: A survey of British and Irish unionism since 1801* (London: Routledge, 2001), pp. 159–175.

Meigs, Samantha, *The reformation in Ireland: Tradition and confessionalism, 1400–1690* (Dublin: Gill and Macmillan, 1997).

Miller, D.W., 'Presbyterianism and "modernization" in Ulster', *Past and Present* 80 (1978), pp. 66–90.

Miller, D.W., 'Irish Presbyterians and the great famine', in Jacqueline Hill and Colm Lennon (eds), *Luxury and austerity*, Historical Studies 21 (Dublin: UCD Press, 1999), pp. 165–181.

Miller, D.W., 'Landscape and religious practice: A study of mass attendance in pre-famine Ireland', *Éire-Ireland* 40 (2005), pp. 90–106.

Miller, John, 'The earl of Tyrconnell and James II's Irish policy', *Historical Journal* 20:4 (1997), pp. 803–823.

Milne, Kenneth (ed.), *Christ Church Cathedral Dublin: A history* (Dublin: Four Courts, 2010).

The minutes of the Antrim ministers' meeting, 1654–8, ed. Mark S. Sweetnam (Dublin: Four Courts, 2012).

Mitchel, Patrick, *Evangelicalism and national identity in Ulster 1921–1998* (Oxford: Oxford University Press, 2003).

Moran, D.P., 'The battle of two civilizations', in Lady Gregory (ed.), *Ideas in Ireland* (London: Unicorn, 1901), pp. 25–44.

Morgan, Hiram, *Tyrone's rebellion: The origins of the Nine Years War in Tudor Ireland* (Woodbridge, UK: Boydell, 1992).

Moriarty, Gerry, 'Cardinal Brady part of process which "silenced" abuse victim', *Irish Times* 20 January 2017, available at https://www.irishtimes.com/news/ireland/irish-news/cardinal-brady-part-of-process-which-silenced-abuse-victim-1. 2945594, accessed 20 June 2020.

Morley, Vincent, *Irish opinion and the American revolution, 1760–1783* (Cambridge: Cambridge University Press, 2009).

Morrill, John, 'The Drogheda massacre in Cromwellian context', in David Edwards et al. (eds), *Age of atrocity: Violence and political conflict in early modern Ireland* (Dublin: Four Courts, 2007), pp. 242–265.

Morris, Nicola K., 'Traitors to their faith? Protestant clergy and the Ulster Covenant of 1912', *New Hibernian Review*, 15:3 (2011), pp. 16–35.

Morrissey, Thomas J., *The Ireland of Edward Cahill, SJ: A secular or a Christian state?* (Dublin: Messenger Publications, 2016).

Moss, Rachel, 'Continuity and change: The material setting of public worship in the sixteenth century', in Thomas Herron and Michael Potterton (eds), *Dublin and the Pale in the Renaissance, 1494–1660* (Dublin: Four Courts, 2011), pp. 182–206.

Moss, Rachel, et al. (eds), *Art and devotion in late medieval Ireland* (Dublin: Four Courts, 2006).

Movius, Hallam L., *The Irish Stone Age: Its chronology, development and relationships* (Cambridge: Cambridge University Press, 1942).

Mullowney, Peter, 'The expansion and decline of the O'Donel estate, Newport, county Mayo, 1785-1852' (unpublished PhD thesis, NUI Maynooth, 2002).

Murray, Griffin, 'Viking influence in Insular art: Considering identity in early medieval Ireland', in Cynthia Thickpenny et al. (eds), *Peopling Insular art: Practice, performance, perception* (Havertown, PA: Oxbow, 2020), pp. 51–57.

Murray, James, *Enforcing the English reformation in Ireland: Clerical resistance and political conflict in the diocese of Dublin, 1534–1590* (Cambridge: Cambridge University Press, 2009).

Murray, Raymond, 'A new Ireland in a new Europe', *Irish Theological Quarterly* 69:2 (2004), pp. 189–201.

'The martyrdom of the holy fathers', in *Ante-Nicene Fathers*, ed. Alexander Roberts and James Donaldson, 10 vols (Buffalo, NY: Christian Literature Publishing Company, 1885), 1: 305–306.

The National Board for Safeguarding Children in the Catholic Church, *Annual Report 2009*, available at https://www.safeguarding.ie/images/Article_Images/ NBSCCC_Report_2009.pdf, accessed 20 June 2020.

The need for rural organisation (Muintir na Tíre Publication, 1932).

The new Oxford book of Irish verse, ed. and trans. Thomas Kinsella (Oxford: Oxford University Press, 1986).

'The "Nicene" creed', in Henry Bettenson and Chris Maunder (eds), *Documents of the Christian Church*, fourth edition (Oxford: Oxford University Press, 2011), pp. 27–28.

Nicholls, K.W., *Gaelic and Gaelicised Ireland in the middle ages*, second edition (Dublin: Lilliput, 2003).

Nicholls, K.W., 'The other massacre: English killings of Irish, 1641–3', in David Edwards et al. (eds), *Age of atrocity: Violence and political conflict in early modern Ireland* (Dublin: Four Courts, 2007), pp. 176–191.

Nicholson, Helen, 'The Hospitallers' and Templars' involvement in warfare on the frontiers of the British Isles in the late thirteenth and early fourteenth centuries', *Ordines Militares Colloquia Torunensia Historica: Yearbook for the Study of the Military Orders* 17 (2012), pp. 105–119.

Nicholson, Helen, 'A long way from Jerusalem: The Templars and Hospitallers in Ireland, c. 1172–1348', in Martin Browne and Colmán Ó Clabaigh (eds), *Soldiers of Christ: The Knights Templar and the Knights Hospitaller in medieval Ireland* (Dublin: Four Courts, 2016), pp. 1–22.

Northern Ireland House of Commons Official Report, vol. 34, col. 1095, 24 April 1934.

Nugent, Louise, *Journeys of faith: Stories of pilgrimage from medieval Ireland* (Dublin: Columba Press, 2020).

O'Brien, Elizabeth, *Mapping death: Burial in late Iron Age and early medieval Ireland* (Dublin: Four Courts, 2020).

O'Brien, Harvey, *The real Ireland: The evolution of Ireland in documentary film* (Manchester: Manchester University Press, 2004).

Ó Buachalla, Breandán, '"James our true king": The ideology of Irish royalism in the seventeenth century', in D.G. Boyce et al. (eds), *Political thought in Ireland since the seventeenth century* (London: Routledge, 1993), pp. 9–14.

Ó Buachalla, Breandán, 'From Jacobite to Jacobin', in Thomas Bartlett et al. (eds), *1798: A bi-cententary perspective* (Dublin: Four Courts, 2003), pp. 75–96.

O'Byrne, Theresa, 'Centre or periphery? The role of Dublin in James Yonge's *Memoriale* (1412)', in Kathleen Miller and Crawford Gribben (eds), *Dublin: Renaissance city of literature* (Manchester: Manchester University Press, 2017), pp. 16–37.

O'Callaghan, Margaret, and Catherine O'Donnell, 'The Northern Ireland government, the "Paisleyite movement" and Ulster Unionism in 1966', *Irish Political Studies*, 21 (2006), pp. 203–222.

Ó Carragáin, Tomás, 'The architectural setting of the cult of relics in early medieval Ireland', *Journal of the Royal Society of Antiquaries of Ireland* 133 (2003), pp. 130–176.

Ó Carragáin, Tomás, *Churches in early medieval Ireland: Architecture, ritual and memory* (New Haven, CT: Yale University Press, 2010).

Ó Catháin, Diarmiad, 'When a priest is accused of a crime', *Irish Theological Quarterly* 70:4 (2005), pp. 367–374.

Ó Ciardha, Éamonn, *Ireland and the Jacobite cause, 1685–1766: A fatal attachment* (Dublin: Four Courts, 2002).

Ó Clabaigh, Colmán, *The Friars in Ireland, 1224–1540* (Dublin: Four Courts, 2011).

O'Connor, Catherine, 'Mixed marriage, "a grave injury to our church": An account of the 1957 Fethard-on-sea boycott', *History of the Family* 13 (2008), pp. 395–401.

O'Connor, T.P., *The life of Charles Stewart Parnell* (London: Ward, Lock, Bowden and Co., [1891]).

O'Connor, Thomas, *An Irish theologian in Enlightenment France: Luke Joseph Hooke, 1714–96* (Dublin: Four Courts, 1995).

O'Connor, Thomas, 'Towards the invention of the Irish Catholic *natio*: Thomas Messingham's *Florilegium*', *Irish Theological Quarterly* 64:2 (1999), pp. 157–177.

O'Connor, Thomas, 'Custom, authority and tolerance in Irish political thought: David Rothe's *Analecta sacra et mira* (1616)', *Irish Theological Quarterly* 65:2 (2000), pp. 133–156.

O'Connor, Thomas, 'Religious change, 1550–1800', in *The Oxford history of the Irish book*, vol 3: *The Irish book in English, 1550–1800*, ed. Raymond Gillespie and Andrew Hadfield (Oxford: Oxford University Press, 2006), pp. 169–193.

O'Connor, Wayne, 'Simon Harris under fire for backing Amnesty despite abortion donation dispute', *Irish Times* 11 April 2018, available at https://www.independent.ie/irish-news/abortion-referendum/simon-harris-under-fire-for-backing-amnesty-despite-abortion-donation-dispute-36796015.html, accessed 20 June 2020.

O'Conor, Keiran D., 'The morphology of Gaelic lordly sites in North Connacht', in Patrick J. Duffy, David Edwards, and Elizabeth Fitzpatrick (eds), *Gaelic Ireland, c.1250–c.1650: Land, lordship and settlement* (Dublin: Four Courts, 2004), pp. 329–345.

Ó Corráin, Donnchadh, 'Prehistoric and early Christian Ireland', in R.F. Foster (ed.), *The Oxford history of Ireland* (Oxford: Oxford University Press, 1989), pp. 1–43.

Ó Corráin, Donnchadh, 'Viking Ireland: Afterthoughts', in H. Clarke et al. (eds), *Ireland and Scandinavia in the early Viking age* (Dublin: Four Courts, 1998), pp. 485–498.

Ó Corráin, Donnchadh, 'St Patrick and the kings', in Seán Duffy (ed.), *Princes, prelates and poets in medieval Ireland: Essays in honour of Katherine Simms* (Dublin: Four Courts, 2013), pp. 211–220.

Ó Corráin, Donnchadh, *The Irish church, its reform and the English invasion* (Dublin: Four Courts, 2017).

Ó Cróinín, Dáibhí, ' "New heresy for old": Pelagianism in Ireland and the papal letter of 640', *Speculum* 60 (1985), pp. 505–516.

Ó Cróinín, Dáibhí, *Early medieval Ireland, 400–1200* (London: Longman, 1995).

O'Dowd, Mary, *A history of women in Ireland* (London: Routledge, 2004).

O'Dwyer, Peter, *Mary: A history of devotion in Ireland* (Dublin: Four Courts, 1988).

Ó Faoleán, Gearóid, *A broad church: The Provisional IRA in the Republic of Ireland, 1969–1980* (Dublin: Merrion Press, 2019).

Ó Gráda, Cormac, *Black '47 and beyond: The Great Irish Famine in history, economy, and memory* (Princeton, NJ: Princeton University Press, 1999).

Ó hAnnracháin, Tadhg, *Catholic reformation in Ireland: The mission of Rinuccini, 1645–1649* (Oxford: Oxford University Press, 2002).

Ó hAnnracháin, Tadhg, *Catholic Europe, 1592–1648: Centres and peripheries* (Oxford: Oxford University Press, 2015).

O'Hara, Alexander, 'Introduction: Columbanus and Europe', in Alexander O'Hara (ed.), *Columbanus and the peoples of post-Roman Europe* (Oxford: Oxford University Press, 2018), pp. 3–18.

O'Hara, Alexander, *Jonas of Bobbio and the legacy of Columbanus: Sanctity and community in the seventh century* (Oxford: Oxford University Press, 2018).

O'Hara, David A., *English newsbooks and Irish rebellion, 1641–1649* (Dublin: Four Courts, 2006).

O'Kelly, Michael J., *Newgrange: Archaeology, art and legend* (London: Thomas & Hudson, 1985).

O'Kelly, Michael J., 'Ireland before 3000 B.C.', in Dáibhí Ó Cróinín (ed.), *A new history of Ireland*, vol 1: *Prehistoric and early Ireland* (Oxford: Oxford University Press, 2005), pp. 49–68.

O'Leary, Daniel J., *Lost soul? The Catholic Church today* (Dublin: Columba Press, 1999).

O'Leary, Eleanor, *Youth and popular culture in 1950s Ireland* (London: Bloomsbury, 2018).

O'Loughlin, Thomas, *Celtic theology: Humanity, world, and God in early Irish writings* (London: Continuum, 2000).

O'Loughlin, Thomas, ' "Celtic spirituality", ecumenism, and the contemporary religious landscape', *Irish Theological Quarterly* 67 (2002), pp. 153–168.

O'Loughlin, Thomas, *Adomnán and the holy places* (London: T&T Clark, 2007).

Ó Muraíle, Nollaig, 'Settlement and place-names', in Patrick J. Duffy, David Edwards, and Elizabeth Fitzpatrick (eds), *Gaelic Ireland, c.1250–c.1650: Land, lordship and settlement* (Dublin: Four Courts, 2004), pp. 223–245.

O'Reilly, Jennifer, 'The art of authority', in Thomas Charles-Edwards (ed.), *After Rome* (Oxford: Oxford University Press, 2003), pp. 141–190.

O'Reilly, Jennifer, *Early medieval text and image*, vol. 1: *The insular Gospel books* (London: Routledge, 2019).

O'Reilly, Jennifer, *Early medieval text and image*, vol. 2: *The Codex Amiatinus, the Book of Kells and Anglo-Saxon art* (London: Routledge, 2019).

Ó Riain-Raedel, Dagmar, and Pádraig Ó Riain, 'Irish saints in a Regensburg litany', in Emer Purcell, Paul MacCotter, Julianne Nyhan, and John Sheehan (eds), *Clerics, kings and Vikings: Essays on medieval Ireland in honour of Donnchadh Ó Corráin* (Dublin: Four Courts, 2015), pp. 55–66.

Ó Siochrú, Micheál, *Confederate Ireland, 1642–1649: A constitutional and political analysis* (Dublin: Four Courts, 1999).

Ó Siochrú, Micheál, *God's executioner: Oliver Cromwell and the conquest of Ireland* (London: Faber and Faber, 2008).

O'Sullivan, Aidan, et al., *Early medieval Ireland, AD 400–1100: The evidence from archaeological excavations* (Dublin: Royal Irish Academy, 2014).

O'Sullivan, Eoin, and Ian O'Donnell (eds), *Coercive confinements in post-independence Ireland: Patients, prisoners and penitents* (Manchester: Manchester University Press, 2012).

Ordnance Survey memoirs of Ireland, vol. 19: *Parishes of county Antrim VI, 1830, 1833, 1835–38*, ed. Angélique Day and Patrick McWilliams (Belfast: Institute of Irish Studies, 1993).

Owen, John, *Works*, 16 vols, ed. William H. Goold (Edinburgh: Johnstone & Hunter, 1850–1855).

Palmer, Patricia, ' "An headlesse lady" and "a horses loades of heads": Writing the beheading', *Renaissance Quarterly* 60:1 (2007), pp. 25–57.

Parkinson, Alan F., *Belfast's unholy war: The troubles of the 1920s* (Dublin: Four Courts, 2004).

Pearse, Pádraic H., *Songs of the Irish rebels*, Collected Works of Pádraic H. Pearse (Dublin: The Phoenix Publishing Company, n.d.).

Penn, William, *The new witnesses proved old heretics* (1672).

Pepperdene, M., 'Baptism in the early British and Irish churches', *Irish Theological Quarterly* 22 (1955), pp. 110–123.

Petts, David, *Christianity in Roman Britain* (Dublin: History Press, 2003).

Petty, William, 'The political anatomy of Ireland', in *The economic writings of Sir William Petty*, ed. C.H. Hull, 2 vols (London, 1899).

Pike, Clement, *The story of religion in Ireland* (London: The Sunday School Association, 1895).

Pliny, *Natural history*, vol. 4, trans. H. Rackham, The Loeb Classical Library (Cambridge, MA: Harvard University Press, 1960).

Poblacht na hÉireann, The Provisional Government of the Irish Republic to the people of Ireland (1916).

Pollak, Sorcha, 'Organiser "guesstimates" turnout of 200,000 for papal Mass', *Irish Times* 27 August 2018, available at https://www.irishtimes.com/news/social-affairs/religion-and-beliefs/papal-visit/organiser-guesstimates-turnout-of-200-000-for-papal-mass-1.3609073, accessed 20 June 2020.

Potter, David, *Constantine, the emperor* (Oxford: Oxford University Press, 2013).

Power, Thomas P., ' "A weighty, serious business": The conversion of Catholic clergy to Anglicanism', in Michael Brown et al. (eds), *Converts and conversions in Ireland, 1650–1850* (Dublin: Four Courts, 2005), pp. 183–213.

Powerscourt, *Letters and papers of the late Theodosia A. Viscountess Powerscourt*, ed. Robert Daly (London, 1838).

Preston-Matto, Lahney, 'Saints and fosterage in medieval Ireland: A sanctified social practice', *Eolas: The Journal of the American Society of Irish Medieval Studies* 5 (2011), pp. 62–78.

Pullin, Naomi, *Female Friends and the making of trans-Atlantic Quakerism, 1650–1750* (Cambridge: Cambridge University Press, 2018).

Raftery, Barry, 'Iron-Age Ireland', in Dáibhí Ó Cróinín (ed.), *A new history of Ireland*, vol. 1: *Prehistoric and early Ireland* (Oxford: Oxford University Press, 2005), pp. 134–181.

Raftery, Deirdre, 'The "mission" of nuns in female education in Ireland, c. 1850–1950', *Pedagogica Historica* 48:2 (2012), pp. 299–313.

Raftery, Deirdre, ' "Je suis d'aucune nation": The recruitment and identity of Irish women religious in the international mission field, c. 1840–1940', *Pedagogica Historica* 49:4 (2013), pp. 513–530.

Raughter, Rosemary, 'Pious occupations: Female activism and the Catholic revival in eighteenth-century Ireland', in Rosemary Raughter (ed.), *Religious women and their history: Breaking the silence* (Dublin: Irish Academic Press, 2005), pp. 25–49.

Regan, John, 'The "Bandon valley massacre" as a historical problem', *History* 97:325 (2012), pp. 70–98.

Regan, John, *Myth and the Irish state* (Dublin: Irish Academic Press, 2014).

Review of George Petrie, 'The ecclesiastical architecture of Ireland, anterior to the Anglo-Norman invasion', *The Quarterly Review* 76 (1845), pp. 354–387.

Richardson, John, *A proposal for the conversion of the popish natives of Ireland to the establish'd religion* (London, 1712).

Roddie, Robin, 'John Wesley's political sensibilities in Ireland, 1747–89', in Kevin Herlihy (ed.), *The politics of Irish dissent, 1650–1800* (Dublin: Four Courts, 1997), pp. 93–103.

Roddy, Sarah, *Population, providence and empire: The churches and emigration from nineteenth-century Ireland* (Manchester: Manchester University Press, 2014).

Rogers, John, *Ohel or Bethshemesh* (London, 1653).

Ryan, Salvador, 'From late medieval piety to Tridentine pietism? The case of 17th century Ireland', in Fred Van Lieburg (ed.), *Confessionalism and pietism: Religious reform in the early modern period* (Göttingen: Vandenhoeck and Ruprecht, 2006), pp. 51–69.

Ryan, Salvador, ' "New wine in old bottles": Implementing Trent in early modern Ireland', in Thomas Herron and Michael Potterton (eds), *Ireland in the Renaissance, c.1540–1660* (Dublin: Four Courts Press, 2007), pp. 122–137.

Ryan, Salvador, 'The devotional landscape of medieval Irish cultural Catholicism *inter hibernicos et inter anglicos, c.*1200–c.1550', in Oliver Rafferty (ed.), *Irish Catholic identities* (Manchester: Manchester University Press, 2013), pp. 62–74.

Ryan, Salvador, 'Holding up a lamp to the sun: Hiberno-papal relations and the construction of Irish orthodoxy in John Lynch's *Cambrensis Eversus* (1662)', in Charlotte Methuen and John Dolan (eds), *The Church on its past*, Studies in Church History 49 (Abingdon, UK: Boydell Press, 2013), pp. 168–180.

Ryan, Salvador, 'The arma Christi in medieval and early modern Ireland', in Lisa Cooper and Andrea Denny-Brown (eds), *The Arma Christi in medieval and early modern material culture* (Farnham, UK: Ashgate, 2014), pp. 243–272.

Ryan, Salvador, ' "Scarce anyone survives a heart wound": The wounded Christ in Irish bardic religious poetry', in Larissa Tracy and Kelly de Vries (eds), *Wounds and wound repair in medieval culture* (Leiden: Brill, 2015), pp. 291–312.

Ryan, Salvador, 'Christ the wounded lover and affective piety in late medieval Ireland and beyond', in Henning Laugerud et al. (eds), *The materiality of devotion in late medieval northern Europe: Images, objects and practices* (Dublin: Four Courts, 2016), pp. 70–89.

Ryan, Salvador (ed.), *Treasures of Irish Christianity*, vol. 3: *To the ends of the earth* (Dublin: Veritas Publications, 2015).

Ryan, Salvador, and Anthony Shanahan, 'How to communicate Lateran IV in 13th century Ireland: Lessons from the *Liber Exemplorum* (c. 1275)', *Religions* 9:3 (2018), pp. 1–14.

Ryan, Tim, and Jurek Kirakowski, *Ballinspittle: Moving statues and faith* (Dublin: Mercier, 1985).

'Saint Patrick's *Confessio*', available at https://confessio.ie/etexts/confessio_english#, accessed 12 August 2020.

Sánchez-Quinto, Federico, et al., 'Megalithic tombs in western and northern Neolithic Europe were linked to a kindred society', *Proceedings of the National Academy of Science of the United States of America* 116 (2019), pp. 9469–9474.

Sawyer, Kathryn Rose, 'A "disorderly tumultuous way of serving God": Prayer and order in Ireland's church and state, 1660–89', *Irish Historical Studies* 42:162 (2018), pp. 207–224.

Scholes, Andrew, *The Church of Ireland and the third Home Rule bill* (Dublin: Irish Academic Press, 2009).

Schryver, James G., 'Converting the land of the Irish: Saint Patrick, the Church, and the Irish landscape', in James Lyttleton and Matthew Stout (eds), *Church and settlement in Ireland* (Dublin: Four Courts, 2018), pp. 1–16.

Scott, Brendan, *Religion and reformation in the Tudor diocese of Meath* (Dublin: Four Courts, 2006).

Searle, Joshua, *The scarlet woman and the red hand: Evangelical apocalyptic belief in the Northern Ireland troubles* (Eugene, OR: Pickwick, 2014).

Severin, Tim, *The Brendan voyage* (London: Arrow Books, 1979).

Sharpe, Richard, *Medieval Irish saints' lives: An introduction to Vitae Sanctorum Hiberniae* (Oxford: Clarendon Press, 1991).

Shaw, Jane, *Miracles in Enlightenment England* (New Haven, CT: Yale University Press, 2006).

Sheldon, Gwendolyn, 'The conversion of the Vikings of Dublin', in Seán Duffy (ed.), *Medieval Dublin XIV* (Dublin: Four Courts, 2014), pp. 51-97.

Smith, James M., *Ireland's Magdalene Laundries and the nation's architecture of containment* (South Bend, IN: University of Notre Dame Press, 2007).

Smith, Paul, *The countrywoman* (1961; rpr. London: Penguin, 1989).

Snyder, Harlow Gregory, '"Above the bath of Myrtinus": Justin Martyr's "school" in the city of Rome', *Harvard Theological Review* 100:3 (2007), pp. 335–362.

Soderberg, J., 'Anthropological *civitas* and the possibility of monastic towns', *Journal of the Royal Society of Antiquaries of Ireland* 144–5 (2014–2015), pp. 45–59.

Spenser, Edmund, *A view of the state of Ireland*, ed. Andrew Hadfield and Willy Maley (Oxford: Blackwell, 1997).

Spurlock, R. Scott, 'Cromwell and Catholics: Towards a reassessment of lay Catholic experience in Interregnum Ireland', in Mark Williams and Stephen. P. Forrest (eds), *Constructing the past: Writing Irish history, 1600–1800* (Woodbridge, UK: Boydell, 2010), pp. 157–179.

St Bernard of Clairvaux's life of St Malachy of Armagh, trans. H.J. Lawlor (London: SPCK, 1920).

Stalley, Roger, *The Cistercian monasteries of Ireland: An account of the history, art and architecture of the White Monks in Ireland from 1142 to 1540* (New Haven, CT: Yale University Press, 1987).

Stancliffe, Clare, 'Christianity amongst the Britons, Dalriadan Irish and Picts', in Paul Fouracre (ed.), *The New Cambridge medieval history* (Cambridge: Cambridge University Press, 2005), 1:426–461.

'Statement by the Catholic bishops in Northern Ireland in advance of the Assembly election on 2 March 2017', Diocese of Down & Connor 22 February 2017, available at http://www.downandconnor.org/press_office/press-releases/statement-catholic-bishops-northern-ireland-advance-assembly-election-2-march-2017, accessed 20 June 2020.

Staunton, Michael, *The illustrated story of Christian Ireland: From St Patrick to the peace process* (Dublin: Emerald Press, 2001).

Stewart, A.T.Q., *The Ulster crisis: Resistance to Home Rule, 1912–1914* (London: Faber, 1969).

Stewart, A.T.Q., *The shape of Irish history* (Belfast: Blackstaff Press, 2001).

Stewart, Andrew, 'History of the Church of Ireland', in Patrick Adair, *A true narrative of the rise and progress of the Presbyterian Church in Ireland* (Belfast: Aitchison, 1870).

Stewart, David, *The Seceders in Ireland, with annals of their congregations* (Belfast: Presbyterian Historical Society, 1950).

Stooke, P.J., 'Neolithic lunar maps at Knowth and Baltinglass, Ireland', *Journal for the History of Astronomy* 25 (1994), pp. 39–55.

Stout, Geraldine, and Matthew Stout, 'Early landscape: From prehistory to plantation', in F.H.A. Aalen et al. (eds), *Atlas of the Irish rural landscape* (Cork: Cork University Press, 1997), pp. 31–63.

Strabo, *Geography*, trans. Horace Leonard Jones, The Loeb Classical Library (Cambridge, MA: Harvard University Press, 1923).

'Summary of clerical sex abuse scandals in Ireland', *Belfast Telegraph* 24 August 2018, available at https://www.belfasttelegraph.co.uk/news/republic-of-ireland/summary-of-clerical-sex-abuse-scandals-in-ireland-37248116.html, accessed 20 June 2020.

Tacitus, *Agricola*, trans. Maurice Hutton, The Loeb Classical Library (Cambridge, MA: Harvard University Press, n.d.).

Tertullian, *Against the Jews*, 7, in *Ante-Nicene Fathers*, ed. Alexander Roberts and James Donaldson, 10 vols (Buffalo, NY: Christian Literature Publishing Company, 1885), III: 151–173.

Thom, Catherine, *Early Irish monasticism: An understanding of its cultural roots* (London: T&T Clark, 2006).

Thomas, Charles, *Christianity in Roman Britain to AD 500* (Berkeley, CA: University of California Press, 1981).

Thomson, E.A., *Who was Saint Patrick?* (Woodbridge, UK: Boydell, 1985).

Tobin, Robert, *The minority voice: Hubert Butler and southern Irish protestantism, 1900–1991* (Oxford: Oxford University Press, 2012).

Tutino, Stefanio, *Thomas White and the Blackloists: Between politics and theology during the English Civil War* (Aldershot, UK: Ashgate, 2008).

Twomey, Vincent, *The end of Irish Catholicism?* (Dublin: Veritas, 2002).

Usher, Robin, *Protestant Dublin, 1660–1760: Architecture and iconography* (Basingstoke: Palgrave Macmillan, 2012).

Vitae Sanctorum Hiberniae, ed. Charles Plummer, 2 vols (Oxford: Clarendon Press, 1910).

Walker, Graham, *A history of the Ulster Unionist Party: Protest, pragmatism and pessimism* (Manchester: Manchester University Press, 2004).

Watt, Eva Stuart, *Ireland awakening* (Chicago: Moody Press, 1952).

Watt, J.A., *The Church and the two nations in medieval Ireland* (Cambridge: Cambridge University Press, 1970).

Watt, J.A., *The Church in medieval Ireland* (Dublin: University College Dublin Press, 1998).

Weir, John, *The Ulster awakening: Its origin, progress, and fruit* (London: Arthur Hall, Virtue and Co., 1860).

Wesley, John, *The journal of the Rev John Wesley*, 4 vols (London, 1895).

Whan, Robert, *The Presbyterians of Ulster, 1680–1730* (Woodbridge, UK: Boydell, 2013).

Wheeler, James Scott, *Cromwell in Ireland* (Dublin: Gill and Macmillan, 1999).

Whelan, Irene, *The Bible war in Ireland: The 'second reformation' and the polarization of protestant–Catholic relations, 1800–1840* (Dublin: Lilliput, 2005).

Whelan, Kevin, 'An underground gentry: Catholic middlemen in eighteenth-century Ireland', in Kevin Whelan (ed.), *The tree of liberty: Radicalism, Catholicism and the construction of Irish identity* (Cork: Cork University Press, 1996), pp. 3–56.

Whelan, Kevin, *Religion, landscape and settlement in Ireland: From Patrick to present* (Dublin: Four Courts, 2018).

Whelan, Ruth, 'Sanctified by the word: The Huguenots and Anglican liturgy', in Kevin Herlihy (ed.), *Propagating the word of Irish dissent* (Dublin: Four Courts, 1998), pp. 74–94.

Whitefield, Andrew, 'Neolithic "Celtic" fields? A reinterpretation of the chronological evidence from Céide Fields in north-western Ireland', *European Journal of Archaeology* 20:2 (2017), pp. 257–279.

Whyte, J.H., *Church and state in modern Ireland, 1923–1970* (Dublin: Gill and Macmillan, 1971).

Whyte, J.H., 'How much discrimination was there under the unionist regime, 1921–68?' in Tom Gallagher and James O'Connell (eds), *Contemporary Irish Studies* (Manchester: Manchester University Press, 1983), pp. 1-35.

Wilkinson, Alexander S., 'Peripheral print cultures in Renaissance Europe', in Kathleen Miller and Crawford Gribben (eds), *Dublin: Renaissance city of literature* (Manchester: Manchester University Press, 2017), pp. 228–249.

Williams, Bernadette, 'Heresy in Ireland in the thirteenth and fourteenth centuries', in Seán Duffy (ed.), *Princes, prelates and poets in medieval Ireland: Essays in honour of Katharine Simms* (Dublin: Four Courts, 2013), pp. 345–346.

Williams, Mark, *Fiery shapes: Celestial portents and astrology in Ireland and Wales, 700–1700* (Oxford: Oxford University Press, 2010).

Wills, Clair, *That neutral island: A cultural history of Ireland during the Second World War* (London: Faber, 2007).

Wilson, David A., *United Irishmen, United States: Immigrant radicals in the early republic* (Dublin: Four Courts, 1998).

Wilson, James, 'Orangeism in 1798', in Thomas Bartlett, David Dickson, Daire Keogh, and Kevin Whelan (eds), *1798: A bicentenary perspective* (Dublin: Four Courts, 2003), pp. 345–362.

Wolf, Nicholas M., *An Irish-speaking island: State, religion, community, and the linguistic landscape in Ireland, 1770-1870* (Madison, WS: University of Wisconsin Press, 2014).

Wood, I.N., 'The Irish in England and on the continent in the seventh century: Part I', *Peritia* 26 (2015), pp. 171–198.

Wood, I.N., 'The Irish in England and on the continent in the seventh century: Part II', *Peritia* 27 (2016), pp. 189–214.

Wooding, Jonathan M., '*Peregrini* in the ocean: Spirituality and reality', in Emer Purcell, Paul MacCotter, Julianne Nyhan, and John Sheehan (eds), *Clerics, kings and Vikings: Essays on medieval Ireland in honour of Donnchadh Ó Corráin* (Dublin: Four Courts, 2015), pp. 411–417.

Woods, David, 'Under the abbot's cloak: The symbolism of Columba's clothing in Adomnán's *Vita Columbae*' in Emer Purcell, Paul MacCotter, Julianne Nyhan, and John Sheehan(eds), *Clerics, kings and Vikings: Essays on medieval Ireland in honour of Donnchadh Ó Corráin* (Dublin: Four Courts, 2015), pp. 341–351.

Woolf, Alex, 'On the nature of the Picts', *Scottish Historical Review* 96:2 (2017), pp. 214–217.

Woolf, Alex, 'Columbanus's Ulster education', in Alexander O'Hara (ed.), *Columbanus and the peoples of post-Roman Europe* (Oxford: Oxford University Press, 2018), pp. 91–101.

Woolf, Alex, 'The Scandinavian intervention', Brendan Smith (ed.), *The Cambridge history of Ireland*, vol. 1: *600–1550* (Cambridge: Cambridge University Press, 2018), pp. 107–130.

Worden, Blair, 'Toleration and the Cromwellian Protectorate', in W.J. Sheils (ed.), *Persecution and Toleration*, Studies in Church History 21 (Oxford: Blackwell, 1984), pp. 199–233.

Wycherley, Niamh, *The cult of relics in early medieval Ireland*, Studies in the Early Middle Ages 43 (Turnhout, Belgium: Brepols, 2015).

Yates, Nigel, *The religious condition of Ireland, 1770–1850* (Oxford: Oxford University Press, 2006).

Yeats, W.B., 'The literary movement in Ireland', in Lady Gregory (ed.), *Ideas in Ireland* (London: Unicorn, 1901), pp. 87–104.

Yeats, W.B., *The Senate speeches of W. B. Yeats*, ed. Donald Pearce (London: Faber, 1961).

Yorke, Barbara, *The conversion of Britain: Religion, politics and society in Britain, 600–800* (London: Routledge, 2006).

Figure acknowledgements

Index